ELMALI-KARATAŞ I

The Neolithic and Chalcolithic Periods: Bağbaşı and Other Sites

Christine Eslick

BRYN MAWR COLLEGE

ARCHAEOLOGICAL MONOGRAPHS

BRYN MAWR, PA.

1992

Printed in the United States of America
by the Science Press
Published and distributed by
Bryn Mawr Commentaries
Thomas Library
Bryn Mawr College
Bryn Mawr, PA 19010-2899

ISBN 0-929524-73-X

PREFACE

Excavations at Elmalı-Karataş started in 1963 and continued annually as a graduate field seminar of the Department of Classical and Near Eastern Archaeology of Bryn Mawr College through 1975. The purpose of the enterprise was to investigate the prehistory and Bronze Age history of Lycia in southwestern Anatolia, where citadels and rockcut monuments of the classical period had attracted archaeological attention from the nineteenth century on. The physical remains of prehistoric sites remained elusive. Geophysical changes in the coast line and river valleys have buried and drowned them, and the perishable timber architecture of prehistoric Lycia left no residue for mound formation.

The plain of Elmalı is the first agricultural and prehistoric oasis on the road up from the east Lycian coast through the Taurus mountains via the Arykandos valley. In the yeşil yayla (green upland plain), ca 60 km from the coast, prehistoric residents built their houses of timber combined with clay and mud, thus leaving mounds as landmarks and stratified cultural records. From the Elmalı region modern and ancient connections can be traced northward via natural roads and passes to the plains of Korkuteli and Burdur and the southern plateau around Afyon.

The excavations concentrated on the Early Bronze Age mound and cemetery area of Karataş, 2 km west of the village of Semayük (now Bozüyük) in the northeast part of the Elmalı plain. The prehistoric mound of Semayük, larger and higher than that of Karataş, has a sizeable classical and Byzantine overlay and now is covered by the cemetery of the modern village. At Karataş, the small central mound turned out to contain a fortified mansion rebuilt in several stages during the Early Bronze period. A village of freestanding rectangular houses developed around the central establishment, and the jar burials of this community were found in one large and several smaller cemeteries on the edges of the habitation zones.

Exploratory trenches were made over an area of 350 × 400 m around the mound of Karataş, with an extension to higher ground at Bağbaşı some 600 m to the northwest on the edge of the vineyards of the villagers. The range of settlement in the explored areas turned out to be from Late Chalcolithic (at Bağbaşı) to a floruit in the Early Bronze Age, continuing unmistakably but frugally in the Middle Bronze and Iron Ages. The site had a light scatter of late Roman pottery.

The Bryn Mawr College expedition also dedicated much time and effort to the rescue excavation and preservation of two painted tomb chambers in tumuli near Elmalı in the years 1969–1986.

Preliminary reports have appeared in the *American Journal of Archaeology* in the years 1964–1976, in *Türk Arkeoloji Dergisi* 1964–1980 and in the annual *Kazı Sonuçları Toplantısı* of the Turkish Ministry of Culture from 1980 on.

Dissertations by graduate student-excavators have presented detailed studies of Early Bronze Age materials from Karataş: Burial Customs by Tamara Stech (1973), Metal Artifacts by Louise

A. Bordaz (1973), Domestic Architecture by Jayne L. Warner (1976) and a study of Late Chalcolithic pottery from Bağbaşı by Christine Eslick (1978).

The final reports of the excavations will now appear in the ELMALI-KARATAŞ series to make the complete results of the digging and analysis available for comparative study. Volume I, presented herewith, opens the series with the earliest material. The next volumes planned are the following:

II. The Early Bronze Age Village of Karataş (J.L. Warner)
III. The Central Complex at Karataş (M.J. Mellink and J.L. Warner)
IV. The Cemeteries of Karataş (T. Stech) and the Anthropological Evidence (based on the records of J.L. Angel)
V. The Early Bronze Age Pottery of Karataş (C. Eslick)
VI. Small Artifacts from Karataş (M.H. Gates)

The excavations at Karataş have been supported through the years by the Hetty Goldman Fund of Bryn Mawr College, by the Ford Foundation's program for the training of graduate students in field archaeology in 1968–1972, and by a generous anonymous benefactor in 1968–1974. Our sincere thanks go to these donors whose support made the field work in the Elmalı region possible and to the Turkish and American graduate students who worked hard and intelligently for many long campaigns at Karataş.

Our thanks to the Directors of the Department of Antiquities in Turkey and to the Museum Directors in Ankara and Antalya have been recorded annually and are part of our lasting gratitude for liberal assistance and hospitality. We are indebted especially to the representatives of the Department of Antiquities who came to guide and help the expedition efficiently in the framework of official relations as well as in creative archaeological collaboration. In the years of the work at Bağbaşı reported on in volume I, the representatives were Mehmet Yılmaz, then of the Burdur Museum, in 1967 and 1968, and Orhan Gürman of the Alanya Museum in 1969.

Machteld J. Mellink

ACKNOWLEDGMENTS

In preparing this report I have received help from many sources. First, I am most grateful to Machteld J. Mellink, director of the Bryn Mawr College Expedition to Lycia, who made this material available to me, supervised its study and organized its publication. Her advice and encouragement have been invaluable.

My indebtedness to the members of the expedition who excavated or collected the material is obvious. They include Dian Duryea at Bağbaşı and Kızılbel, Janet Spencer and Michael Karp at Bağbaşı, Sevim Buluç at Boztepe and Karaburun, Jayne Warner and Phyllis della Croce at Karaburun. In 1977 İlhan Ünlüsoy, archaeological representative from the Antalya Museum, accompanied me on a survey of the Bağbaşı-Karaburun area.

I am most grateful also to M.S.F. Hood for showing me the notebooks from his 1949 survey of the plain, and allowing me to use the relevant material. He also showed me drawings and photographs of the material from Emporio.

The following persons allowed me to see material in their care, for which I thank them—Kenan Erim and Martha Joukowsky for the Aphrodisias pottery; Manfred Korfmann for the pottery from Demirci Hüyük; Mehmet Özsait for survey material from Kuruçay Höyük and Refik Duru for excavation material from the same site; the staff of the Antalya Museum, especially the former director, Tanju Özoral, and the former assistant director, Selahattin Erdemgil, for the prehistoric material in the Antalya and Karain Museums; Chr. Doumas and E. Zervoudaki of Rhodes Museum for the Aspripetra Cave material; and D.H. French who allowed me access to the pottery collection in the British Institute of Archaeology in Ankara.

The study of the pottery thin sections was devised and supervised by Maria Luisa Crawford; Jacques Bordaz read and commented on the parts of the manuscript dealing with chipped stone; David S. Reese provided identification and information on the shell; Jayne L. Warner commented on the architecture. To all I am grateful. Finally, my thanks to Nancy Leinwand for her work preparing the manuscript and plates for publication.

Financial support for the study came from a scholarship from the British Institute of Archaeology in Ankara (1976), and a Whiting Fellowship in the Humanities at Bryn Mawr College (1977–1978).

CONTENTS

APPENDICES

CHARTS

PLATES

PLATES continued

PLATES continued

PLATES continued

PLATES continued

BIBLIOGRAPHICAL ABBREVIATIONS

The abbreviations used are those given in *AJA* 82 (1978) 3–8 and 84 (1980) 3–4. In addition, the following are used:

Aphrodisias I	Martha Joukowsky, *Aphrodisias au sud-ouest de la Turquie durant les périodes du néolithique et du chalcolithique final* (Doctorat d'État thesis, University of Paris I, Panthéon-Sorbonne 1982)
Aphrodisias II	Martha Sharp Joukowsky, *Prehistoric Aphrodisias. An Account of the Excavations and Artifact Studies* (Providence and Louvain 1986)
Beycesultan I	Seton Lloyd and James Mellaart, *Beycesultan I. The Chalcolithic and Early Bronze Age Levels* (London 1962)
BIAL	*Bulletin of the Institute of Archaeology,* London
Emporio	Sinclair Hood, *Excavations in Chios 1938–1955. Prehistoric Emporio and Ayio Gala* (British School of Archaeology at Athens 1981)
Hacılar	James Mellaart, *Excavations at Hacılar* (Edinburgh 1970)
Kuruçay I	Mehmet Özsait, "Pisidya Bölgesinde Yeni Prehistorik İskân Yerleri (I)," *Anadolu Araştırmaları* 4–5 (1976–1977)
Kuruçay II	Refik Duru, "Kuruçay Höyüğü Kazıları. 1978–1979 Çalışma Raporu," *Anadolu Araştırmaları, EK Yayın* 2 (1980)
Kuruçay III	Refik Duru, "Excavations at Kuruçay Höyük 1980," *Anadolu Araştırmaları* 8 (1980) 18–38
Kuruçay IV	Refik Duru, "Excavations at Kuruçay Höyük 1981," *Anadolu Araştırmaları* 9 (1983) 41–50
Kuruçay V	Refik Duru, "Kuruçay Höyüğü kazıları 1982 çalışma raporu," *Anadolu Araştırmaları* 9 (1983) 81–9
Kuruçay VI	Refik Duru, "Kuruçay Höyüğü kazıları 1983 çalışma raporu," *Belleten* 49 (1985) 595–606
Saliagos	John D. Evans and Colin Renfrew, *Excavations at Saliagos near Antiparos* (Oxford 1968)
Tigani	Robert Heidenreich, "Vorgeschichtliches in der Stadt Samos. Die Funde," *AthMitt* 60–61 (1935–1936) 125–183

OTHER ABBREVIATIONS

EN	Early Neolithic
LN	Late Neolithic
EC	Early Chalcolithic
MC	Middle Chalcolithic
LC	Late Chalcolithic
EB	Early Bronze
MB	Middle Bronze
IA	Iron Age
L	left
R	right
L.	length
W.	width
D.	diameter
Th.	thickness
fr.	fragment
frr.	fragments
ca	about
pres.	preserved

INTRODUCTION

In the Elmalı Plain, pottery of the Neolithic and Chalcolithic periods was first collected in 1949 by M.S.F. Hood; two painted sherds from this survey were published by James Mellaart in 1954.[1] Further research into the prehistory of the area did not take place until the surveys conducted by Machteld J. Mellink in 1954, 1962, 1963, and the subsequent excavations and investigations by the expedition from Bryn Mawr College.[2] The material in this monograph comes primarily from the Bryn Mawr College expedition, but also includes relevant material from the Hood survey.

The pattern of prehistoric research including sporadic surface exploration and few and scattered excavations prevails in the other areas of southwestern Anatolia. Excavations at Karain from 1946 produced Neolithic and Chalcolithic remains, but in contexts that made their exact relationships uncertain.[3] Mellaart's surveys in 1951–1954 added considerably to our knowledge of the prehistoric southwest,[4] but it was only later in the 1950s that excavations that were to form the basis of a sequence for the area were undertaken, at Beycesultan in 1954–1959, and at Hacılar in 1957–1960.[5] More recent surveys in the 1960s have added to our knowledge of the distributions of the various pottery styles,[6] while the deposits at Aphrodisias, where excavation of prehistoric deposits took place in 1967–1972, provide a check on the universality of the Hacılar-Beycesultan sequence.[7] Excavations undertaken at Kuruçay Höyük from 1978–1988 have also yielded evidence from these periods.[8]

Our knowledge of the Neolithic and Chalcolithic periods of southwestern Anatolia is, therefore, derived from only a few, widely scattered sites and is still incomplete. It is based mainly on pottery, as there is little other evidence yet available. We do have a basic sequence for the southwest and, in general terms, it is no doubt correct, although its validity for any one part of the area has yet to be shown. Not one complete local sequence, verified by stratigraphy, has been produced, nor is the information available to construct one.

In southwestern Anatolia four pottery traditions assignable to the Neolithic and Chalcolithic periods have so far been recognized—the Early Neolithic tradition which is represented in level B

[1] James Mellaart, "Preliminary report on a survey of pre-Classical Remains in southern Turkey," *AnatSt* 4 (1954) 188–89.

[2] Machteld J. Mellink, in *Yearbook of the American Philosophical Society* (1954) 326–37; and "Excavations at Karataş-Semayük in Lycia, 1963," *AJA* 68 (1964) 269–71.

[3] İ. Kılıç Kökten, "Antalya'da Karain Mağarasında Yapılan Prehistorya Araştırmalarına Toplu Bir Bakış," *Belleten* 19 (1955) 271–83; and "Die Stellung von Karain Innerhalb der Türkischen Vorgeschichte," *Anatolia* 7 (1963) 59–86. This material is now divided between the Archaeology Museum, Antalya and the Karain Museum.

[4] James Mellaart, *AnatSt* 4 (1954) 179–239.

[5] *Beycesultan* I; *Hacılar.*

[6] See e.g. *Hacılar* I 146.

[7] Barbara Kadish, "Excavations of Prehistoric Remains at Aphrodisias, 1967," *AJA* 73 (1969) 49–65; and "Excavations of Prehistoric Remains at Aphrodisias, 1968 and 1969," *AJA* 75 (1971) 121–40; *Aphrodisias* I and II.

[8] *Kuruçay* I–VI. See also now Refik Duru, "Kuruçay Höyüğü Kazıları 1984 Çalışma Raporu," *Belleten* 50 (1986) 247–59; "Kuruçay Höyüğü Kazıları 1985 Çalışma Raporu," *Belleten* 51 (1987) 305–313; "Kuruçay Höyüğü Kazıları 1986–1987 Çalışmaları," *Belleten* 52 (1988) 653–66.

at the Beldibi cave but has not been identified in the Elmalı Plain, the Late Neolithic/Early Chalcolithic or Hacılar tradition, the Late Chalcolithic tradition exemplified at Beycesultan, and the Elmalı Kızılbel/Lower Bağbaşı tradition for which a Middle Chalcolithic date has been proposed.[9]

The conventional terms, Early and Late Neolithic or Chalcolithic, used to designate the various cultures of southwestern Anatolia are far from satisfactory, for they do not reflect the basic divisions in the cultural sequence but have resulted from comparison of individual parts of the sequence with culture sequences in different parts of Anatolia.[10] In particular, the equation of the beginning of the Chalcolithic with the use of painted designs on pottery takes no account of the basic continuity of culture at this point. The main change in the culture sequence of southwestern Anatolia falls not at the end of the Neolithic or at the end of the Chalcolithic, but between Early and Late Chalcolithic. However, the association of these terms with particular assemblages is now so well established that to invent new terms or reshuffle the material would only lead to confusion.

In this monograph I have collected all the evidence of Neolithic and Chalcolithic date from the Elmalı Plain, one of the more extensively explored plains in the region, and have attempted to construct a local sequence. Chapter 1 presents the evidence from the Late Chalcolithic settlement at Bağbaşı. It contains descriptions of the architectural remains by trench; the pottery under the headings of fabric, shape and decoration, with a catalogue of sherds chosen to show the range of shape and decoration; and the other artifacts. Chapter 2 discusses this material from the point of view of the functioning of the settlement. In Chapter 3 the material, mainly pottery, from the earlier occupation at Bağbaşı and from the other sites in the plain is described, and in Chapter 4 the relationships of the various Elmalı assemblages with areas outside the plain are explored, and a sequence of the Elmalı area suggested.

Illustrations are provided for almost every catalogue entry.[11] For the pottery they are usually in the form of profile drawings, as this method of illustration was best suited to its fragmentary and largely undecorated nature. The drawings are arranged, as far as possible, in catalogue order. The external rim diameter (in centimeters) is placed on the profile just above the rim line.

Most of the pottery and other artifacts are now stored in Elmalı. However, the twenty Bağbaşı objects catalogued in 1967–1969 (see Appendix 3) and the sherds from the survey of M.S.F. Hood and from the surveys of M.J. Mellink are in the Archaeology Museum, Antalya.

This report was completed in 1982, and although attempts have been made to include comparative material published since that date, it remains essentially unchanged.

[9] Christine Eslick, "Middle Chalcolithic Pottery from Southwestern Anatolia," *AJA* 84 (1980) 5–14.

[10] Seton Lloyd and James Mellaart, "Beycesultan Excavations," *AnatSt* 8 (1958) 102 and 125; James Mellaart, "Excavations at Hacılar," *AnatSt* 8 (1958) 152–53.

[11] Except the undecorated body sherd, Tekke **2**.

Chapter 1 BAĞBAŞI—THE MAIN SETTLEMENT

SITE AND EXCAVATIONS

The site of Bağbaşı is 7 kilometers northeast of Elmalı and about 1.5 kilometers to the east of the Korkuteli-Elmalı road (pls 1b and 2).[1] It is on a low, natural rise, 1158 meters above sea level, and overlooks the lower part of the plain to the east, although it is not much higher than the surrounding area to the west (pl. 83a). Slight rises lie to the north and south of the site, but Bağbaşı is distinguished by a poplar-lined stream, which runs down from the western hills and around the northern side of the rise. This provides an excellent water supply, and the area is now covered with vineyards and orchards. It has about 0.50 to 1.00 meter of soil cover, consistently disturbed by ploughing in the upper 0.30 meter.

In 1967 trenches 102 to 105 were opened on the top of the rise to explore the possibility of second millennium remains in the area.[2] Some EB, MB and IA sherds were found, but the principal deposits were of the LC period. Because of the shallowness of the deposit and its often disturbed nature, deposits uncontaminated by later remains were rare. However, the importance of the LC remains was recognized, and further excavations were carried out in 1968 and 1969 in trenches 105 and 107–120. These trenches yielded architecture of the LC and IA, and a few burials of MB and IA date.

In this chapter the remains attributed to the LC settlement are described. Those objects recognized as belonging to later periods were excluded from the study. The identification of intrusive pieces was usually obvious, but some of the non-pottery objects posed problems. If the material and form were not known from the LC period and if the object was from a badly disturbed context, it was regarded as intrusive.

In all an area of 1035 square meters was opened on the summit and eastern slope of the rise (pl. 3). Five or six houses of the LC settlement were revealed, but in only two trenches were superimposed LC remains found. In trench 105 pottery, burnt animal bones and ashes were found at a lower level than the walls of the house, which itself had two building phases. In trench 116 were excavated three superimposed house levels. Stratigraphic connections were not made between the two trenches and it is not known whether the levels in trench 105 correspond to those in 116. No difference could be discerned in the finds from the three phases (see Chart 1, p. 96 below), and it seems that the LC settlement was sufficiently short-lived that no real development took place, even in the pottery repertoire. A small group of MC sherds from the lowest level of 116, but not associated with the house in that level, is discussed in Chapter 3 (p. 51).

[1] For preliminary reports see Machteld J. Mellink, "Excavations at Karataş-Semayük in Lycia, 1967," *AJA* 72 (1968) 254–55; "Excavations at Karataş-Semayük in Lycia, 1968," *AJA* 73 (1969) 328–30; "Excavations at Karataş-Semayük in Lycia, 1969," *AJA* 74 (1970) 246.

[2] The east corner of trench 105 is 652 m to the northwest of the west corner of the main house at Karataş. All level marks on the plans refer to the arbitrary zero level at Karataş which equals 1128 m above sea level.

Trenches 102–105 were opened on the highest part of the Bağbaşı rise in 1967. All were 3.00 × 10.00 m. With the exception of inventoried objects, the finds from the 1967 excavations were merged as one lot. Chart 1 (p. 000) shows the number of sherds kept for study. The pots and sherds catalogued from this group include **2, 5, 7, 9, 40, 44, 45, 47, 55, 58, 74, 78, 79, 127, 147, 158, 159, 163, 164, 168, 199, 204, 208, 211, 216, 239, 243, 247.** A mortar (**315**) and a grinding stone (**318**) also belong to this lot.

Trench 102 contained fragments of burnt mud walling. At the northwestern end of the trench, the fragments lay 0.50 to 0.60 m below the surface. They sloped down gradually towards the southeastern end. The finds included a basin (**42**), a jug (**93**), spit supports, a stamp seal (**273**), an obsidian blade (**277**), a copper tool (**322**) and an antler.

Trench 103 yielded no mud walling, but considerable quantities of pottery.

Trench 104 produced burnt mud walling over the whole area of the trench. Wet conditions did not allow further investigation.

Trench 105 was originally 3.00 × 10.00 m; in 1968 it was widened 6.00 m to the northwest to cover an area of 9.00 × 10.00 m, with a further 2.00 × 5.00 m extension at the western corner. The pottery described as being from 105 is from the 1968 excavations. Three levels of LC occupation were identified in this trench. About 0.20 m below the surface (level I) was found burnt mud walling debris. The lower part of a large jar was found above the debris but was not saved (see pl. 83a).

In level II, two mud slab and timber walls (walls 1 and 2) and a substantial partition of mud-coated timber divided the trench into four areas, as shown on pl. 5. In the main eastern area (unit A) evidence of occupation came from a strip about 5.00 m wide and running parallel with wall 1. It did not extend to the eastern corner of the trench. Near the northeastern edge of this strip was found part of a mud-plastered hearth, with jar **114** nearby. A number of objects was found *in situ* including three jugs (**88, 91, 92**). Just to the east of wall 1 was a group of four open jars (**63, 71, 82,** and **87**), of which the largest (**82**) had been sunk into the floor, and the neck from a jar or jug (**122**). A rim sherd from an everted neck (**129**), fragments of flat and disk bases, a loomweight (**258**) and a bead (**270**) were also found in this area.

The northern corner of the trench contained sherds, including a fragment of a basin (**39**), the rim of a small open pot with handle from the rim (**54**), a rim fragment of a large open pot, a rim sherd with a wide strap handle, a body sherd of a small jug with a knob (**150**), three disk base fragments (including **217**) and two flat base fragments. There were also two feet, possibly from a cooking pan (**233–234**) and two spindle whorls (**264** and **267**).

A second occupied area (unit B) lay in the western part of the trench. It was bounded by walls 1 and 2 and by the remains of the partition, that lay 1.90 m from wall 1 and parallel to it. Within the area were found a copper needle (**324**) and the tip of a bone pin (**325**). Beyond the partition, in unit C, were an antler and some animal bones. There were no finds from unit D, the area to the south of wall 2.

In level III there were no architectural remains. Under wall 1 were found a few bones, twelve body sherds, the base and lower part of a pot (**196**), a rim sherd from a pot with a short inverted neck (**145**) and three fragments of a vertical neck (**121**). Both **196** and **121** had been refired. Ashes were found below wall 2 and jug **95** at a corresponding level (30.58 m) to the southwest.

Other finds from 105 included loomweights (**256** and **257**), spindle whorls (**259, 260, 265**), a bead (**271**), two flints (**288** and **289**) and animal bones. Most of the pottery from 105 was from general fill and included **8, 11, 12, 13, 14, 16, 18, 23, 27, 29, 30, 31, 33, 35, 37, 41, 46, 48, 49, 50, 62, 70, 73, 75, 89, 90, 96, 98, 104, 105, 109, 111, 117, 118, 128, 134, 137, 138, 140, 144, 146, 151, 156, 160, 161, 165, 166, 167, 177, 178, 179, 184, 185, 186, 187, 188, 190, 192, 193, 194, 197, 198, 200, 201, 202, 203, 205, 206, 207, 209, 210, 212, 213, 214, 215, 218, 220, 222, 224, 236, 238, 240, 242, 246.**

Trench 107 was opened to the north of 105 and measured 3.00 × 10.00 m. In the west end were a number of small stones, including a grinding stone found at a level ca. 0.20 m below the surface. In the fill were fragments of mud walling and objects including a flaring bowl (**6**), and a flat pan fragment (**241**), a flint (**291**), and animal bones. Of the pottery, only distinctive pieces were kept. A MB pithos burial had disturbed the LC stratum.

Trench 108 was another 3.00 × 10.00 m trench parallel to and to the northeast of trench 107. A level of stones was found 0.10 to 0.20 m below the surface. The only other finds were potsherds which were discarded after examination.

Trench 109 lay to the east and was originally 3.00 × 10.00 m, but was extended to the southeast to cover an additional area of 7.50 × 4.00 m. It produced stones in the northeastern part; mud walling and mud plaster fragments in the extension at a level ca. 0.20 m below the surface. Among the latter were some fragments possibly from a hearth, and a spit support was found in the fill. Other finds included potsherds **19, 61, 100** and **142,** a spindle whorl (**266**), sickle blades (**281, 284, 287**), a flint (**300**), a bone spatula (**326**) and an antler hammer (**328**). The LC level in this trench was disturbed by an IA jar burial.

Trench 110 was a large trench, measuring 15.00 × 6.00 m with a 16.00 × 3.00 m extension to the southeast. It was located down the slope (southeast) of trench 109 (pl. 8). At the southeast end of the main part of the trench were found stone foundations from the corner of a rectangular unit. Within this area was a stone-paved area, about 1.00 m wide, which contained some potsherds, and on its north edge was a long grinding stone. The northwestern end of the trench was covered by a stone scatter. Southeast of the built corner, an ashy dump deposit extended for 11.00 m. This contained a broken grinding stone, two broken spindle whorls (**262** and **263**) and a mass of pottery including a flaring bowl rim, a base of an open pot (**66**), necked pots (**120, 125, 141**), a lug with thumb impression (**173**) and three other plain lugs, three spouts from bowls, both disk and flat bases, a small double pot with impressed decoration (**228**), a foot (**235**), flat pans and a pan with raised side (**248**), stands (**250** and **254**), spit supports (**251** and **252**) and a scoop (**255**). Finds from the general fill of the trench included **32, 34, 38, 52, 72, 81, 83, 103, 131, 152, 169, 171, 175, 181, 182, 219, 221** and two flints (**293** and **303**). Bedrock was reached at 0.45 to 0.80 m below the surface.

Trench 111, like trenches 112–114, was placed further down the slope and measured 3.00 × 10.00 m. It yielded only a few sherds which were discarded.

Trench 112 produced a scatter of sherds in an ashy fill. Only a few were kept, including the miniature basin, **227.** Other finds were a bead (**272**) and a flint (**302**). Virgin soil was reached at a depth of 0.30 to 0.65 m.

Trench 113 produced one small piece of burnt mud plaster or walling and some sherds, none of which was kept, in an ashy fill. A spindle whorl (**268**) and a whetstone (**314**) came from this trench.

Trench 114 yielded a little pottery in the same ashy fill. It was also discarded. Virgin soil was reached at a depth of 0.20 to 0.50 m.

MB pottery was found in trenches 112, 113 and 114.

Trench 115 was opened just to the east of trench 109, near the top of the rise. It was extended a number of times, eventually measuring approximately 8.00 × 9.50 m with a 3.00 × 5.00 m extension at the northwest and a 4.50 × 3.00 m extension at the southeast (pls 3 and 9). The remains of three walls of a mud-plastered log house with an earth floor were found in the southeastern part of the trench; stone foundations in the northwest were probably Iron Age. On the floor of the log house a two-handled pot with decoration of impressed circles (**229**) was found beside wall 1, near a two-handled jar and the remains of an open pot, unrestorable but with a base diameter of ca. 0.30 m. Among the floor fragments in this area was a copper awl (**323**). A spit support (**253**) with a circular base and one side cavity stood in the western corner of the house. Immediately outside wall 1 lay a jug (**94**). A cache of four unused flint blades (**304–307**) was found among stones in the northwest scarp, and the counter (**274**) was found in the south corner of the trench. Other finds from this trench included a fragment of a vertical neck with ribbed handle (**130**), a solid foot (**237**), a flint (**280**) and the shell (**329**).

Trench 116 was laid out 8.00 m southwest of 105 and its final dimensions were 8.00 × 10.00 m. It had three levels of LC occupation (pls 10, 13–15). All the pottery from this trench was kept for study.

Between 0.20 and 0.40 m below the surface, in the east part of the trench, were found large patches of burnt mud walling, the remains of a house (pls 10 and 94a). Below this tumble, the floor was partially preserved and in the middle of the area was a fixed mud hearth (not yet visible on pl. 94a, but dotted in on pl. 10). Among the wall fragments were found the objects that had apparently been on the floor. These included a large storage jar (**135**) beside the hearth, a smaller jar (**123**) and a jar with combination handles (**116**). A small bowl (**225**) and a quern were also found here. To the west of the house a pit contained fragments of a large open pot with thumb impressed lugs (**76**). Other finds from level I include an open pot (**85**), a vertical neck (**113**), a pattern burnished sherd (**148**), painted sherds (**153** and **154**), a pierced lug (**157**), a lug (**170**), a pan (**245**) and flints (**278, 279, 294**).

Since this floor was preserved only in patches, some of the finds attributed to level II would have belonged with it although others came from below the floor level and thus do belong to the intermediate level II. Catalogued objects from level II are pottery fragments **20, 21, 22, 28, 36, 51, 56, 59, 97, 101, 107, 108, 110, 112, 126, 132, 172, 180, 183, 189, 191, 195, 226, 231,** a spindle whorl (**261**), flints (**282, 286, 296, 297, 298, 308, 309**), and a bone fragment (**327**).

Only two features of level II were preserved (pl. 13). In the north corner was a fragment of a mud hearth, with a finished concave stretch along its southeast edge. Below the hearth the soil was burnt red to a depth of 0.10–0.20 m. To the southeast of it was a circle of stones, possibly a pot emplacement. It contained parts of three necked jars (**115, 124, 136**). Fragments of an open pot (**77**) were found above the hearth. Such features are usually found inside buildings, but no remains of walls survived at this level.

Below chunks of a tough, creamy material, probably unburnt mud walling, the lower level (III) was better preserved (pls 14 and 97a). In the north corner was a shallow pit, 1.50 m in diameter and 0.45 m deep, filled with fine clean soil and sherds. They consisted mainly of burnished bowl fragments (nine rim sherds including **3, 4, 10, 15, 17** and two bases), with an open pot rim fragment, two disk and one flat bases, a miniature bowl (**223**), an elongated lug (**162**), a body sherd with ridge at the neck, a pan with raised side (**249**) and a flat pan. Large areas of white ashy floor were intact to the south of the pit. To the east of the pit were the remains of stone wall foundations and a large jar (**65**) lay in line with it, at the level of the floor. There may have been a doorway there, or the jar may have been pushed into this position during the collapse of the building. To the south lay a large open jar (**67**) and a smaller one (**68**), as well as a deep bowl (**25**). Patches of floor were preserved in the south part of the trench. Small areas of stone paving occur in four places in this level, on the southwest edge of the pit, near the center of the trench, to the southeast of the wall, and near the southeast scarp, but in no case could the function of the structure be established. A clay animal figurine (**275**) was found in the west corner of the trench.

Associated with this level were the finds from the "channel cuts," the 1.50 m wide test trenches dug along the southwest and northwest sides of the square, from the upper level. They include pottery fragments **24, 43, 53, 57, 60, 80, 86, 99, 139, 174, 176, 232, 244,** a spindle whorl (**269**) and flints (**292** and **312**).

Six flints (**283, 285, 299, 301, 310, 311**) were found on top of virgin soil, below the lower floor level. Two mortars (**316** and **317**), two grinding stones (**319** and **320**) and a circular stone with pock-marked surface (**321**) were also found in trench 116.

Trenches 117–120 were placed low on the slope, to the southeast of trenches 112–114, and produced only fragmentary remains of LC habitation. Trench 117 had dimensions of 10.00 × 3.00 m, and the pottery from it included **1, 26, 84, 102, 133, 143,** and **155.** Trench 119, which measured 20.00 × 10.00 m, extended to trench 117, and produced pottery fragments **64, 106** and **230.** The animal figurine **276** came from trench 117 or 119.

Trench 118 measured 3.00 × 10.00 m with a 3.00 × 7.00 m extension. Fragments of mud walling with timber impressions were found here, and a stone axe (**313**) came to light just above bedrock. Other finds included pottery fragment **69** and **119.** Trench 120, 3.00 × 12.50 m with a 1.40 m extension, produced nothing noteworthy attributable to the period.

MB occupation was attested in the area of trenches 117–120.

ARCHITECTURE

Architectural remains were found in most of the Bağbaşı trenches, but they were usually very fragmentary. This was in part due to the disturbed nature of the deposits, and in part to the character of the buildings. Walls were made of timber and chaff-tempered mud (which served as walling, mortar, packing and plaster). When such houses caught fire, the timbers burnt out completely, leaving their impression in the fire-hardened mud packing which tumbled down once deprived of its supports. Unburnt houses left few traces as the timber decayed and the mud collapsed and was levelled off.

TRENCH 102

Fragments of burnt walling were found all over the area of this trench at a depth of 0.50 to 0.60 m below the surface. Four well-preserved pieces are illustrated on pl. 4, left column.

1. Max pres. L. 0.26.[3] Pl. 4, upper left. Fragment of roughly triangular section with five timber impressions: (1) a flat timber, W. at least 0.06, running along the piece for two-thirds of its length;

[3] L. = measurement at right angles to section drawn. Calculations of diameters of impressions are approximate only.

(2) a smaller, partly rounded timber, squared in one place; (3) a flattish piece with bark, W. 0.06; (4) a flat piece, W. 0.03, placed at an angle to (1) and set at a lower level; (5), on the short side of the fragment, and parallel to (1) and (3), the end of a stick, D. 0.025. This fragment is a long piece of mud packing that was enclosed within vertical timbers (1)–(4) and supported at one end by the shorter sapling (5). The unlabelled right side of the section is worn and without impressions; it was probably wall surface.

2. Max. pres. L. 0.23, max. pres. W. 0.14. Pl. 4, left row. Section of fragment with seven impressions: (1)–(4) parallel saplings with diameters of 0.01–0.03; (5) a smooth impression with rounded end D. 0.04, running at a 45° angle beside (4); (6), not visible in this section, is a rounded smooth timber, with a round end, D. 0.04, set at right angles to (1)–(4); (7) poorly preserved, cuts across the end of (6). Saplings (1)–(4) stood vertically while (6) is one of the horizontal ties. Impression (7) suggests incidental wattling and (5) is an internal diagonal timber supported on (6). The worn side of the broken walling fragment must have been the wall surface.

3. Max. pres. L. 0.085. Pl. 4, left row, (section only). Small fragment with two smooth, rounded, parallel impressions, D. at least 0.08 and 0.06. Flat wall face on opposite side.

4. Max. pres. L. 0.12. Pl. 4, lower left, (section only). Fragment with two parallel impressions: (1) rounded and ridged, D. ca. 0.07; (2) smooth and rounded, D. ca. 0.08. They are set at uneven distances from a smoothed wall surface.

All fragments are pieces of smooth wall surface behind which saplings stood vertically but irregularly in the mud packing. Horizontal ties and wattling are evident in fragment 2.

TRENCH 105

In trench 105 (pl. 5) were found burnt remains of two mud slab and timber walls meeting at right angles. The longer wall (wall 1), oriented N/S, was about 0.45 m wide and was preserved to a length of about 4.00 m. The cross wall (wall 2), oriented E/W, was about 0.40 m wide and preserved for a length of about 2.00 m to the west of wall 1. The walls were not well preserved because the many timbers used in their construction had burnt out; considerable settling resulted and rodents inhabited the cavities. The tops and faces of the wall stumps were badly weathered and had evidence of later interference, which removed the upper parts of walls 1 and 2 near their junction (pls 83a, b; 84a). A N/S partition, also burnt, was preserved for 1.20 m length, and ran parallel to wall 1 at a distance of 1.90 m to the west. It had lost its core of horizontal parallel timbers and had collapsed to the east (pls 87b; 88a, b).

Materials

Walls 1 and 2 were of large, flat, chaff-tempered mud slabs, each the width of the wall but of no standard length. The dimensions of measurable slabs are given on the following page. They were laid before they were dry, for the slabs in wall 1 bear impressions from the timbers that were above and below them. The impressions in wall 2 were on the mud mortar laid between courses of slabs. The lack of standardization in length and thickness of the slabs (the width being determined by the width of the wall) suggests some method of forming the slabs as they were laid in the wall, perhaps using wooden boards to pat the walling into shape.

Wall	*Course*	*Length (m)*	*Width (m)*	*Thickness (m)*
1	7S	0.75	0.44	0.05
	6S	1.18	0.44	0.07
	6N	1.18	0.48	0.12
	4N	0.75	0.45	0.12
	3	?	0.38	0.06
2	4	ca 0.75	0.40	0.75 and thicker
	4	ca 0.80	0.40	0.11 and thinner
	3	0.52	0.40	0.075
	3	0.43	0.40	0.075
	3	0.73+	0.40	0.075
	2	0.54	0.39	0.07
	2	0.45	0.39	0.07
	2	0.45	0.39	0.07

Extensive use was made of timbers laid horizontally either lengthwise or crosswise in the wall. There was no standard method of including the timbers, the disposition of which varied from one section of the wall to another. At one point in wall 1, a timber was placed vertically, but it did not continue for more than a few courses. Although the impressions were often poorly preserved, some were flat, suggesting that some of the larger timbers, such as the beams in wall 1, courses 8S and 4S, were split or trimmed.

Chaff-tempered mud was used as mortar between some of the courses of the walls, probably principally as a levelling agent. It was also used as plaster to coat the faces of the walls, traces being found on both faces of wall 1 and on the south face of wall 2. These plaster coats were about 0.02 m thick and showed finger grooves on the west face of wall 1 and the fallen north face of wall 2.

Construction

The remaining stumps of walls 1 and 2 were investigated layer by layer. Eight or nine layers (courses) could be identified, numbered here from the bottom up. The two walls were bonded together in the lower courses by means of the mud-slab course 2 and the mud-mortar layer above course 3. In courses 1–3, wall 1 was built as a continuous wall, but in the upper courses (4–9), the two parts of the wall north and south of the south face of the crosswall were constructed independently (pl. 7a).

Wall 1 (pls 83b–84)

The lowest course of mud slabs was laid directly on the ground, perhaps with some timber for levelling at the north end. Course 2 was bonded into the crosswall by means of a "tongue" 0.15 m long that projected into the crosswall. These lowest courses were soft and unburnt. On top of course 3 was a level of mud plaster, which was continuous over both the northern part of wall 1 and the crosswall. Above it, the two parts of wall 1 were built separately.

In the north part of the wall a course of mud slabs (4) lies directly on the mortar above course 3. Horizontal timbers were then placed lengthwise in the wall (course 5), and above them three courses of mud slabs (6–8) were preserved only at the north end of the wall. The top course was

0.12 to 0.18 m thick. A 0.02 m thick layer of plaster was preserved on the west face of these upper courses.

A vertical timber, about 0.20 m in diameter, was placed in the northern part of the wall, near the east face and 0.85 m from the north face of wall 2. It was embedded in mud plaster and rose through courses 1–4, but it did not continue any higher. It may have helped to support the horizontal timbers of course 5.

The southern part of the wall contained more timbers. Above course 3, two lengthwise beams, each at least 0.12 m wide, were placed along the faces of the wall with mud packing between them (course 4). The beam on the east face continued to the bond with wall 2; that on the west face ended 0.20 m before the bond. Course 5 was made of a 0.12 m thick mud slab made in one with the packing between the beams of course 4. Course 6 is a plain mud slab, 0.07 m thick, with a join on the north side along which mud mortar oozed in from above, apparently along a straight dried edge. Course 7 had cross-timbers about 0.05 m in diameter, placed at the joins between 0.75 m long mud slabs. Course 8 consisted of lengthwise beams, with a preserved combined width of 0.23 m. On the top surface of mud slab course 9 were further impressions of timbers, placed both along and across the wall. One of the lengthwise impressions was about 0.25 m long and about 0.04 m wide; a crosspiece was about 0.20 m wide.

Wall 2 (pls 85a–87a)

Two cross-timbers were preserved, placed about 0.25 m apart, and the lowest course of mud slabs (1) was laid on them. It was 0.08–0.09 m thick and was covered by a 0.03 m thick layer of mud mortar. On this mortar, and on the lower side of the mud slabs of course 2, were impressions of two or more cross-timbers, one 0.06 m in diameter and 0.59 m from the west end of the wall, and the other 0.05 m in diameter and 0.48 m further east (see pl. 85a, showing timber holes and mouse holes). Course 2 itself consisted of three well-preserved mud slabs. It was at this level that the bonding with wall 1 occurred, the "tongue" of brick from wall 1 extending into wall 2 (pl. 85b, left). Course 2 was covered by a layer of mud plaster, 0.02 m thick, bonding with the plaster of wall 1.

Course 3 consisted of four mud slabs 0.075 m thick (pl. 86a). Again they were covered by a layer of plaster 0.02 m thick, which continued across the width of wall 1 and over its northern part (pl. 86b). The top of this plaster layer bore clear finger impressions, indicating that the plaster layers were smoothed by hand.

The two slabs of course 4 had a thickness varying from 0.11 m at the west end to 0.075 m at the east end (pl. 87a). On top of course 4 was a layer of plaster bearing numerous wood impressions of small cross-timbers, and on the west end of the wall was an impression of a beam laid lengthwise on the wall, apparently on top of the cross-timbers. This long beam was 0.18 m wide and at least 0.80 m long. At the east end of this lengthwise impression, a lump of mud was covered with the same mortar as the top of course 4. It bore impressions of cross-timbers on its east and west edges where such timbers overlay the mortar on top of course 4, and also at a higher level on the east side. Course 5 then consisted of two layers of timber laid crosswise and lengthwise.

Above course 5 was a course of mud slabs (course 6) which varied from 0.10 to 0.15 or 0.05 m in thickness because of the deep impressions on its underside from the logs of course 5. Two more thin courses of mud slabs (course 7, 0.06 m thick, and course 8) were placed over this, but were poorly preserved. A layer of mud plaster, about 0.02 m thick, was preserved on the south face of these courses. On it was an impression from a timber placed horizontally along its face.

Above the remnants of courses 7 and 8 were fragments of upper courses that had fallen from the wall (pls 83a, b, and 84a). Large slabs had slid off their timber underpinnings and were lying against and in front of the north face of wall 2. They showed finger marks on the mortar of their upper faces. These slabs overlay the tumble of the partition discussed below, which had not been excavated when the photograph in plate 84a was taken.

Fragments of Walling W of Wall 1

Two fragments of walling were found near the preserved northwest end of wall 1 (pls 5 and 84b). These pieces had fallen with their lowest edges at level 30.66 m. Because of the slope of the deposits downward from the partition to wall 1, these pieces were well above the level of the partition debris (discussed below, p. 10).

1. Max. pres. H. 0.32, W. 0.40, Th. 0.18. Pl. 4, upper right; pl. 84b, left foreground. Fragment broken into two pieces. One smooth face formed the wall surface. On the opposite face, six parallel impressions of contiguous timbers: (1) a flat, ridged timber, W. 0.06; (2) a small smooth, rounded sapling, D. 0.025; (3)–(5) smooth, rounded saplings D. 0.07, 0.025, 0.05; (6) the edge of another flat timber, W. at least 0.025. The fragment had fallen with the impressions facing wall 1.

2. Max. pres. H. 0.35, W. 0.41, Th. 0.20 m. Pl. 4, right side, middle and below; pl. 84b, leaning against west face of wall 1, impressions on side away from wall 1. One smooth face forming wall surface. On opposite face, three parallel impressions: (1) a smooth and rounded timber, D. 0.045; (2) a ridged timber, D. 0.06; (3) a ridged flattish timber set at an angle to the others and more deeply, W. 0.10; (4), a rounded sapling, D. 0.06, set at one end of (1) and (2), and in the same plane but at right angles. Sapling (4) did not extend as far as timber (3).

Given their thickness of 0.18–0.20 m, these two fragments were part of a substantial wall. Structurally they differ from the technique in which the preserved parts of walls 1 and 2 were built. If we set the parallel timbers vertically we have a wall resembling those attested by the fragments from trenches 102 and 116. Stratigraphically, fragments 1 and 2 could belong to a rebuilding of wall 1 on top of the stump left after the initial destruction of the house by fire. Fragments 1 and 2 had also burnt and turned reddish-yellow.

Fragments of Walling E of Wall 1

At a general level of about 31.10 m lay many fallen wall fragments extending over an area about 2.50 m E/W and 4.50 m N/S (pls 5, 83a). Most of the fragments were badly weathered after burning. Their average thickness was 0.15–0.20 m. The upper surfaces were wall face and the lower sides had parallel timber impressions, resembling the pieces found to the (north)west of wall 1.

One large fragment lay face down, broken in two, about 0.50 m east of wall 1, south of the junction with wall 2, "niche" on plate 5.

Niche

Max. pres. L. 0.66, max. pres. W. 0.55, max. pres. Th. 0.20. Pls. 6 and 89a. On the finished side, a flat rectangular area of 0.50 × 0.29 m is framed by raised edges along three sides. One long edge has the impression of a rounded timber, L. 0.54, D. 0.06, with remnants of its mud plaster coating. The opposite long edge is mostly broken away, but a fragmentary ridge remains. Attached to one short side, 0.035 m from the damaged corner, is a rectangular projection measuring ca. 0.05 × 0.05 m with a preserved height of 0.03 m. This may be a piece of mud packing between framing timbers. A faint impression remains along this short edge. The opposite short edge has a straight break. The external surfaces of this fragment are worn and broken and have no readable timber impressions. The substance of the piece was built up in layers of chaff-tempered mud, at least two of which can be seen in section.

The dimensions of the fragment as a whole are too bulky for it to have fitted in wall 1, which was only 0.45 m wide, in any position except with the finished surface upright and placed along the line of the wall. The piece could have formed the back of a niche. As the fragment was originally at least 0.21 m thick, the niche would not have been more than 0.23 or 0.24 m deep. The best preserved timber impression is only as long as the finished framed surface, serving probably as the complete frame along that side. Alternatively the piece could have formed the side of a window if it was placed at a corner so that the bulk of the mud was in the crosswall.

Partition

Parallel to the northern part of wall 1, and 1.90 m to the west of it, was another wall or partition. Preserved *in situ* was the bottom part of the mud plaster which covered the west face. It had a thickness of 0.03–0.06 m and was weathered on the outside (west). It was preserved to a length of ca 1.00 m and a height of 0.20–0.25 m. The partition was supported and partly buttressed by a brown clay layer which extended to the west for some 0.50 m (pl. 88 a, b).

The partition had collapsed to the east. Fallen fragments of its outer mud coating, 0.06–0.12 m thick, were found smooth face up in a coherent area measuring ca 1.60 m E/W and 2.00 m N/S, and following the slope of the underlying floor downward to the east (pl. 5). The plaster had toppled as its timbers burnt out. As N/S impressions on the lower faces showed, the inner face of this partition consisted of parallel saplings of various sizes, 0.025 to 0.07 m in diameter, stacked horizontally. One timber had a diameter of 0.13 m. No traces of vertical supports were identified. This construction is similar to but flimsier than that of the log house in trench 115 (see pp. 11–12).

Hearth

In the northeastern part of the trench, ca 4 m east of wall 1, was found a large smooth area of chaff-tempered mud plaster at level 30.91. It was 0.05 m thick and had dimensions of approximately 0.60 × 0.90 m. No edges were preserved. The plaster was hard and crumbly and layers of burnt earth below it showed that it had been subjected to intense heat *in situ*.

Reconstruction

There were three levels of occupation in this trench. The earliest (level III) produced no architectural remains and is represented only by the finds below walls 1 and 2 and the jug **95** found at level 30.58 m in unit C. Level II is the best preserved. It consists of walls 1 and 2 and the partition. The plan of the house is not clear but it must have consisted of at least two rooms. No remains of a wall east of wall 1 were identified and the distribution of finds suggests unit A extended from wall 1 to beyond the hearth (top level 30.91 m). The jar **114** and the three jugs (**88, 91, 92**) were all found at level 30.81 m and the group of storage pots (**63, 71, 82, 87**) found just east of wall 1 also belonged to this floor. Unit A would thus have been at least 8 m long and at least 5 m wide, a span made possible by the solid wall construction.

Unit B was a second room (width 1.9 m) of this house, although it is not clear whether there was a door connecting it to unit A. An opening beyond the preserved north end of wall 1 is possible. The top of the partition tumble was at level 30.73–30.62 m and the floor below it sloped down from west to east. The plaster on the western face of the partition was weathered and it was, therefore, probably an exterior wall. Unit C, which produced only bones and an antler at this level, would then have been an outside area, as would unit D, which produced no finds at all.

Level I was very poorly preserved but traces of floor were found at a level of 31.08–31.12 m. At this level was the base of a large jar, found to the northeast of wall 1, the highest preserved debris of walls 1 and 2, and the unconnected burnt wall tumble east of wall 1. There is no evidence that unit B was reused at this time. The partition was not apparently rebuilt and wall 2 was probably left to collapse. The south part of wall 1 appears to have been in good enough condition to reuse (the niche fragment must have come from a wall of solid mud-slab construction) but the northern part of the wall was apparently rebuilt using the vertical sapling and mud packing technique on a foundation formed by the stump of the mud-slab wall.

TRENCH 109

No indisputable remains of walls were found *in situ* in this trench, although a line of stones, some set on edge, at the southeast end of the extension is possibly a foundation. A fragment of a mud plaster hearth with smooth upper surface was found. It had two layers, the upper one 0.01–0.02 m thick and the lower about 0.03–0.04 m.

TRENCH 110

In the southeastern part of the original trench were the stone foundations from one end of a rectangular building (pls 8, 89b, 90a). At its east corner the southeast wall was preserved for a length of 1.60 m. It was 0.70 m wide and consisted of a triple or quadruple row of stones. Large boulders were used to reinforce the foundations at the corner. The northeast wall can be traced over the whole side of the structure (3.90 m internal measurement). Only one row of stones is preserved, and one section of the wall is off-set, perhaps indicating that there was a niche at that point. A 1.70 m long section of the northwest wall again consists of a triple row of stones, about 0.50 m wide. This wall, on the uphill side of the building, does not contain the large boulders used in the southeast wall. The length of the building could not be determined, but it apparently included the circular stone pavement. Remains of the superstructure have not survived.

The stone scatter in the northwest part of the trench could indicate further construction in that area, but its nature, beyond a possible extension of the northeast wall, could not be determined (pl. 89b).

TRENCH 115

Trench 115 contained the remains of two buildings (pls 9, 90b). In the central part of the trench were stone foundations from the Iron Age (not shown on pl. 9), and in the east part were LC remains. They were from a rectangular, apparently unpartitioned, structure, which measured 3.75

m NW/SE and at least 3.85 m SW/NE. It had a 0.10 m thick chaffless earth floor laid over bedrock, which consisted here of rough stones. The structure was destroyed by fire.

Parts of the footings of the walls were preserved *in situ* (pls 91a, b and 92a, b). The northwest wall footing, wall 1, was preserved in two places, one of which was at a corner of the structure. The footing fragments consisted of pieces of mud mortar with impressions of three parallel timbers on the upper as well as lower surfaces. The footing therefore had been made of two layers of three small logs each, laid in the direction of the wall. The logs had a combined width of about 0.25 m; in the upper layer the central log was larger than the flanking ones. The wood base was set on the floor level which directly supported the lower three logs. These logs were then covered with a layer of mud mortar in which the upper three were embedded. The footing of walls 2 and 3 showed the same method of construction. The wall 2 fragment (pl. 92b) had the lower layer of logs laid directly on bedrock.

Large fallen sections of mud plaster were found in this house, as well as outside. Wall 2 had fallen outwards and its fragments were not well-preserved. Better evidence came from wall 1, which had fallen inwards at the time of the fire (pl. 91a). Parts of its mud plaster lay flush against the wall footing, the smooth outer face up. As the impressions on the lower face of the mud plaster showed (pl. 93a and b), the wall had been constructed of stacked logs, each 0.12 to 0.15 m in diameter, the interstices occasionally filled with stone chinking (pl. 7b). The total height of the wall was at least 2.85 m. The straw-tempered mud plaster, 0.04 to 0.06 m thick, covered the outer face of the wall only. The impressions show that the logs were not trimmed in any way; many still had their bark (perhaps of pine).

No evidence was found for the position of the doorway or the roofing method or material.

Reconstruction

This structure consisted of a single rectangular unit 3.75 m by at least 3.85 m, with walls of horizontal logs plastered on the outer face. The walls were at least 2.85 m high. They rested on footings that consisted of two wood courses, each of three parallel logs and packed with mud mortar. An earth floor had been deliberately laid over the uneven stone surface. Although this structure was comparatively well-preserved, no trace of a hearth was found.

TRENCH 116 UPPER LEVEL I

Fragments of burnt mud walling were found in the upper level of trench 116 about 0.20 to 0.40 m below the surface (pls 10, 94a). They occurred over a roughly rectangular area with unworked stones scattered along the northern and eastern edges. The mud walling was not found in a coherent mass. It lay in a disorderly fashion in two or three layers, as if the walls of the structure had crumbled rather than fallen whole. All wall fragments had been burnt, and many of the fallen pieces preserved clues to the method of construction. Among these were sections with parallel timber impressions facing up, including fragments with five log impressions lying near the northwest edge of the tumble area (pl. 10). The logs were up to 0.15 m in diameter. Fifteen fragments are illustrated on plates 11 and 12 in drawings or sections; photographic illustrations appear on plate 98a–f.

1. Max. pres. L. 0.18, W. 0.20. Pl. 11:1 and pl. 98a. Wall packing with two parallel log impressions, one showing striations of bark, with a thick ridge of mud between them. A smooth, shaped edge projects on the side near A′. On the lower side, a diagonal rounded impression (not shown) in an otherwise smooth surface.

2. Max. pres. L. 0.145. Pl. 11:2 and pl. 98 b and c. Mud packing within four vertical timbers (1)–(4) and on top of one cross-log (5). Plate 98b shows the 0.13 wide impression of log (5), with bark; plate 98c gives a good sample of the mud pressed in the interstices between two timbers, (1), D. 0.10, and the sapling (2), D 0.03. Two sticks, (3) and (4), both D 0.015, lie against the other side of (1).

3. Max. pres. L. 0.25. Pl. 11:3. Mud packing against three vertical timbers, with wall face partly preserved. Timbers D. ca 0.08, 0.10 and 0.04.

4. Max. pres. L. 0.115. Pl. 11:4 and pl. 98d. Fragment comparable to 3. Two smooth, probably vertical timbers, D. 0.045 and 0.07; flat surface probably wall face.

5. Max. pres. L. 0.165. Pl. 11:5 and pl. 98e. Mud packing from wall interior. Three parallel saplings: (1) and (2) (D. 0.025, 0.045) set in the core of the wall; (3) (D. ca 0.035) perhaps near the face.

6. Max. pres. L. 0.22. Pl. 11:6. Fragment of packing against four non-aligned saplings, D. ca 0.02, 0.035, 0.035, and 0.025. The curved worn surface at the other side of the packing may be the impression of another parallel log of much larger diameter.

7. Max. pres. L. 0.20. Pl. 11:7. Fragment of mud packing within four saplings (1)–(4), D. ca 0.04, 0.035, 0.03, and 0.025. A flat timber (5) crosses at right angles to sapling (4).

8. Max. pres. L. 0.175. Pl. 12:8. One smooth rounded timber, D. ca 0.07, set in the interior of mud walling with two finished surfaces meeting at an obtuse angle.

9. Max. pres. L. 0.115. Pl. 12:9. Similar to 8, with timber of ca 0.09 diameter, and outer surfaces meeting at a blunt angle.

10. Max. pres. L. 0.13. Pl. 12:10. Fragment of walling with finished outer surfaces meeting at a blunt angle. The outer side near A has grooves made by finger smearing. The lower side has a worn, curved surface, with a smooth rounded impression (1), D. ca 0.10, across one end.

11. Max. pres. L. 0.155. Pl. 12:11 and pl. 98f. Upper surface has four impressions of rounded timber: (1), D. ca 0.03, along left edge; smaller timbers (3)–(5) at right angles to (1), D. ca 0.015 each. Below (1), an irregular timber (2) is set at a slightly different angle (see face B-B′ and section A-A′). The other side of this piece is the finger-smeared, roughly finished wall surface.

12. Max. pres. L. 0.17. Pl. 12:12. Mud packing with two parallel impressions (2) and (3) of D. 0.055 and 0.05. Not shown in the section is impression (1), D. 0.025, which runs at right angles to (2) and (3) along the wall surface and curves into it; it is a horizontal tie for the uprights (2) and (3).

13. Max. pres. L. 0.13. Pl. 12:13. Mud packing with impressions of a flat timber (1), W. at least 0.05, cut diagonally by a rounded impression (2), D. 0.018.

14. Max. pres. L. 0.18. Pl. 12:14. Mud packing formed by parallel timbers, impressions (1)–(4), D. 0.025, 0.035, 0.025 and 0.03. Impression 4 is curved and at a slight angle to (1)–(3).

15. Max. pres. L. 0.155. Pl. 12:15. Two small flat impressions, W. ca 0.02 and 0.015, cross diagonally. Timber (1) ran the length of the mud fragment, (2) crosses (1) at the top.

The fragments from trench 116 upper level suggest that the fallen and crumbled walls originally consisted of mud mortar packed against and around vertical timbers which varied in diameter from 0.15 to 0.025 m. These saplings were set vertically but were neither aligned nor contiguous (see fragments 2–7 and 14). Although most saplings were smooth, some left impressions of bark in the mud. Verticals were tied together by horizontal timbers as in fragments 7 (impression 5), 11 (impressions 3–5), 12 and perhaps 13. The presence of heavier timber (logs) in horizontal position in fragment 2 (impression 5) and 10 (near a corner) may indicate that longitudinal or cross-timbers served as a base for some of the vertical timbers.

Mud was packed to a thickness of 0.05 m against the outermost vertical timber to make a smooth wall face, in which finger impressions are sometimes visible (fragments 3 and 4). Corners are shaped in the mud mortar (fragments 8 and 9). Large stones were placed against the base of the walls. Fragment 1 has a smooth rear surface with diagonal timber impression and a smooth, shaped vertical edge near A′ (pl. 10.1; pl. 98a). The piece may be from an aperture in the wall, whether a door, window or niche.

Hearth

Beneath the fallen wall fragments, near the center of the trench, were found the remains of a hearth formed of two or three layers of mud plaster (pl. 15, section). The total thickness varied from 0.05 m at the edge of the hearth to 0.01–0.03 m at the center. About half the perimeter was well preserved, and its original diameter was about 1.20 m. A rectangular section, 0.18 m deep and 0.38 m wide, projected from the northwestern edge (pls 94b, 95a). On the south side of the projection and extending to its edge lay a piece of walling which had damaged the hearth rim in falling.

Reconstruction

The walling debris lay in an ashy brown fill and covered a rectangular area suggesting a house size of approximately 6.00 × 4.00 m. The stones scattered along the north and east edges of the burnt debris may have been placed against the walls of the house along the outside.

The floor was of beaten earth and the well-preserved hearth would have been situated about two-thirds of the way along the long axis. The position of the doorway is unknown. Some of the mud fragments with reed impressions may have belonged to roofing.

The construction technique is somewhat irregular but the system of vertical saplings packed in and daubed with chaff-tempered mud is found in a number of trenches at Bağbaşı. Postholes were not found, and the exact placing of horizontal and diagonal ties was not observable in the crumbled state of the fallen walling.

TRENCH 116 LOWER LEVEL III

Little remains of the building from the lower level of this trench, for it had not been burnt (pls 14, 15, 95b, 96a, b). A foundation, 1.00 m long, 0.50 m wide and 0.35 m high, of undressed stones extended approximately southwestwards from the northeast scarp (pl. 96b). It was covered by a creamy walling debris which was also found over much of the area of the trench above the ashy white floor. This floor was found in fragments on both sides of the wall, especially in the southwest part of the trench. In the southwest part of the northwest scarp this walling debris appeared to form four rather neat layers of irregular slabs. Two layers of slabs could also be seen at the northeast end of the southeast scarp, on the other side of the stone foundation. Although no other walls could be defined, the long east/west scatter of stones across the trench south of the wall may indicate the existence of a crosswall in this area. The number of pots just beyond it supports this idea.

Reconstruction

The architectural remains in this level were badly preserved, but the building would seem to have been of mud slabs on stone foundations. No evidence was found for the use of timbers, but this is probably because the house was not burnt. The distribution of the walling debris all over the trench, and the traces of preserved floor on both sides of the wall, suggest that here, as in trench 105, the house had more than one room.

TRENCH 118

From this trench came fragments of burnt walling or roofing, smooth on one side and indented on the other where it had been applied over logs and reeds (pl. 97b). Both LC and EB pottery fragments were found scattered in this area and the house could have belonged to either period.

ARCHITECTURE: BUILDING TECHNIQUES

In all of the Bağbaşı structures we found the same basic building materials: chaff-tempered mud and timbers of varying sizes (D. 0.015 to 0.15 m) and finish (with bark, smoothed or split). Stones were occasionally used.

WALLS

Walls were made using three main techniques: mud slabs, horizontal timbers stacked, and vertical timbers packed in mud plaster. In level II of trench 105, the walls were built of mud slabs made *in situ,* shaped as the walls were being erected. Layers of transverse and longitudinal timbers formed intermediate courses and short timbers were used as cross-pieces between the mud slabs as they were formed. Some short vertical timbers were also employed. The lower level of trench 116, level III, apparently had walls built of light clay slabs over a single course of stone foundations. This house was not burnt and no traces of wood remained.

In the house in trench 105 (level II), a partition or outer wall of one room was made of saplings stacked horizontally and presumably held together by vertical props, not preserved in the fallen remains. This timber wall was coated on the outside with mud plaster, 0.06–0.12 m thick. A sturdier structure of this type was the "log cabin" in trench 115. The fallen wall consisted of logs ca 0.12–0.15 m in diameter, stacked horizontally and coated on the outside with 0.04–0.06 m of mud plaster. The base of the wall was made of two layers of three logs, each embedded in mud packing (pl. 7b).

The third technique, found in trenches 102 and the top levels of 105 and 116, is the use of vertical saplings, irregularly placed in one or two rows with chaff-tempered mud packed around them. The mud is smoothed on the outer face of the wall. Horizontal ties and occasionally wattling occur in this technique. Post holes were not found.

Most walls do not seem to have had special foundations, although in two cases (the houses in trench 110 and trench 116, level III) a course of stones was used. Stones were occasionally used to support the base of walls.

All building techniques were found in at least two trenches and as our knowledge of the site is incomplete (even within the excavated area the building techniques of some houses, such as that in trench 116, level II, are unknown), it would be unwise to comment on the relative popularity of the techniques. Likewise, in the absence of stratigraphic links between the trenches, we cannot determine the relative chronological positions of the houses and thus any change over time in the methods used. In the top levels of trenches 105 and 116, the technique using vertical saplings was the main one used but we do not know if slab construction or horizontal timbering was still in use elsewhere in the settlement.

ROOFS

It is not clear how the roofs were made. Some of the fallen debris, especially the burnt fragments with reed impressions, may have belonged to roofing (pl. 97b).

FLOORS

The floors consisted of compacted earth and were poorly preserved because of fire damage and collapse. Later building activities and rodents added to the ruination.

HEARTHS

Fixed hearths existed in the best preserved houses. Trench 116, level I, gave an example of a raised disk of ca 1.20 m in diameter, which was set centrally towards the back of the house (pl. 95a). These inside hearths were undoubtedly the cause of the fires that destroyed many of the houses.

THE HOUSES

The poor state of preservation and lack of recognizable entrances makes reconstruction of the house plans difficult. The houses were each freestanding and the orientation varied. In some cases the house consisted of a single rectangular unit—that in trench 116 level I measured about 4 by 6 m and that in trench 115, 3.75 by at least 3.85 m. The house in trench 105 consisted, at least in its earlier phase, of at least two rooms, possibly a large rectangular room (about 8 by 5 m) with a better-preserved small room (1.90 by at least 2.10 m) to one side. The house in trench 116 level III also consisted of several rooms.

The highest part of the site, the area from trench 116 to trench 115 (pl. 3), was densely settled. Habitation extended down the slope to the area of trench 110, suggesting an area of some 60 by 100 m for the area of the LC village. If the house remains in trench 118 are LC, the settlement would have extended another 100 m down the SE slope.

POTTERY

This study is based on a selection of the total pottery found. From most trenches only a small amount was retained (see Chart 1), and this material is not necessarily representative. However, the pottery from trench 116, all of which was kept for study, served as a control.

FABRICS AND MANUFACTURING TECHNIQUES[4]

The Bağbaşı pottery was handmade, and the clay appears to have had little preparation. It was not much refined and large pieces of grit were left in the body. The grits could be quite large—commonly 0.50 cm in diameter and some pieces up to 1.00 cm. Fiber inclusions also occur in every pot, and although the proportion of fiber to grit varies from pot to pot, the amount is usually so great that it was surely added intentionally. Indentations from burnt-out fiber pockmark the surfaces of all pots.

The walls of the pots were built with coils pressed together so that the upper coil overlapped the lower on the outside. Additional coils for the necks of necked pots were added in the same way; the tendency for these to separate from the body suggests that the pot body was allowed to dry a little before they were added. The pot rim was usually smoothed with the fingers. The flat rims on some open pots seem to have been formed by holding the wall of the pot between the thumb and second finger and pressing the first finger down onto the top.

The coils were added around a base usually formed from a single disk of clay, although some disk bases may have been made from coils. If the base was a plain flat base, of narrower diameter than that of the lower walls, the first coil was added to the edge of the base and smoothed into place, as on **135** and **114.** However, most of the open pots and basins have disk bases. They have approximately the same diameter as the lower wall of the pot, and the clay from the wall is pushed downwards around the edge of the disk and not later smoothed (e.g., **47–49** and **71**). On **220** (pls. 53 and 104c), it is clear that the first coil was placed around the top of the disk, near the edge, and smoothed right down the outside to the base of the disk. Pl. 105d shows base fragments with the wall broken away.

The bottoms of the disk bases sometimes bear impressions, in a few cases apparently from mats (e.g. **44** and **27**), but other impressions are very irregular. During manufacture the pots do not seem to have been placed on any particular material. The flat bases are usually smoothed underneath in the same way as the walls of the pots.

The various types of handles were almost all added to the pot by means of a hole pierced through the wall and a plug on the end of the handle. The walls were then smoothed around the plug. The process appears to have been carried out when the pot was partly dry, as is customary because the handle dries faster than the pot and so shrinks faster, and the bonding is often not thorough. Sherds with holes in the wall, as **2, 13** and **14,** and handles with the plugs clearly preserved, as **161, 167** and the examples on pl. 105e, are therefore quite common. Where handles are connected to the rim of the pot, they may be attached either by plugs or by folding the handle over the rim as can be seen on **44. 114** is exceptional in that its pierced lugs were applied flat against the wall of the pot.

The lug handles were made by holding a lump of clay in one hand and shaping it with the other. In most cases it was not possible to determine in which hand it was held, but in thirty-eight cases the lug was asymmetrically shaped with one side curving away more sharply, where the potter's fingers would have curved around it. In twenty-one of these cases it could be determined that the lug was held in the right hand, and in seventeen that it was held in the left, and the lugs were,

[4] Many aspects of this section have benefited from reading H.J. Franken, *In Search of the Jericho Potters* (Oxford 1974) and H.J. Franken and J. Karlsbeek, *Potters of a Medieval Village in the Jordan Valley* (Oxford 1975).

therefore, probably shaped when they were already attached to the pot. Impressions were sometimes added to the top of the lug, perhaps with the thumb, either by simply pressing the thumb on the lug or by digging it into the lug and swivelling.

The loop and strap handles were made in various ways. The large handles were made by using one hand to squeeze out the shape from a lump of clay. The irregular shape thus achieved could be smoothed down one side with the other hand, giving an asymmetrical effect that can be observed on **133.** Again, either the right or left hand could be used to hold the clay. The thin strap handles were probably made by smoothing a loop handle made in this way, but the small handles used on the bowls and jugs seem to have been made from a coil of clay.

The ribbed handles from trenches 115 and 116 (**130, 136;** pls. 101d and 102a) each had three ridges made by pulling two fingers down the handle. As the two depressions were of equal depth, the two index fingers or two thumbs were possibly used, rather than two fingers of the same hand. The example from trench 105 (**62;** pl. 100c) has much shallower and more uneven ridges, probably made by pulling three fingers of one hand down the handle.

The surface of the Bağbaşı pottery received little treatment. On most vessels the surface was only roughly smoothed, although occasionally a more compact finish was achieved. Ten per cent of the sherds were burnished (the same proportion from trench 116 and overall) and, as it was the bowls and jugs that were so treated, the percentage of burnished pots would have been higher. The burnish varies from a rough irregular burnish to a fine, high, even gloss. Both the interior and exterior of the bowls were burnished, including beneath the base; only the exterior of the vessel and interior of the neck were burnished on the jugs. The bowls were usually burnished with vertical strokes on the exterior and horizontal ones on the interior, although sometimes both exterior and interior would have either horizontal or criss-cross burnishing. The jug fragments were too few to make generalizations possible, but many of the bodies seem to have been criss-cross burnished; the necks were often vertically burnished. The shapes of the burnished pots tend to be more regular than the unburnished ones, but this is perhaps because they were the smaller pots. The evenness of the bowl rims was doubtless due to their being turned upside down to burnish the exterior. The burnished pots are usually dark in color—black, brown, gray—but again this may not be a deliberate differentiation between burnished and unburnished pots. It may simply be due to the darkening effect of the burnishing process.[5]

The pottery was poorly fired so that black cores, due to incomplete burning out of the carbon, were usual. In only one percent of the sherds (not including obviously refired pieces) had the carbon been completely burnt out. The firing atmosphere was apparently uncontrolled, for there was considerable mottling of the surfaces. The colors on a pot could range from gray to yellow, brown and red, and black mottling from smoke and ash staining were common.[6] The firing atmosphere was not high as the uncracked surfaces of the burnished pots show.[7]

A small number of sherds from trench 105, including **29–30, 89** and **146,** seem to be fine and dense in texture, more powdery and duller in color than the other pottery. The surface is usually orangey brown with black mottling. The difference between these pieces and the sherds of normal

[5] Christine Eslick, The Early Pottery from Mersin (unpublished MA thesis, University of Sydney 1972) vol. 2, pp. 69–75.

[6] See Appendix 1 for a correlation of the terms used to describe pottery colors with the *Munsell Soil Color Chart* (Baltimore 1975).

[7] The burnished surface will be destroyed as soon as the clay begins to shrink when the water of crystallization begins to evaporate at about 800°C.

fabric could be due to the use of a different firing technique or to effects of the soil. There was no apparent difference in the composition of the body.

The pans are of the normal fabric but have been fired thoroughly so that the carbon has often been completely removed. Black cores and black mottling of the surfaces are, therefore, rare.

SHAPES

A detailed system of shape classification was not used at Bağbaşı, because of the lack of standardization in the assemblage. The pots are divided only into general categories, within some of which there is considerable variation of attributes. This is particularly obvious in the jar and jug categories, in which no two examples are precisely the same. The shapes of the individual pots are also irregular; the drawings show the profile at only one point. The smaller vessels, including the bowls and jugs, are more regular than the large ones. Handles could be applied crookedly and were not always at the same level on opposite sides of the pot. Irregularities caused when the handle was applied were sometimes not smoothed away, as the example on pl. 106b shows.

Bowls

The bowls at Bağbaşı are simple open shapes with flaring or curved walls. They display more standardization than do some of the other shapes (sixty-two of the ninety-three bowl rims are from plain flaring bowls), and are more regularly made. Most are dark (gray to black) and burnished. The bases are always flat, and vertical loop handles beginning at the rim or just below it are common. Four handles were placed on one bowl; other pots could have had no more than two. Two bowls had lug handles (**23** and **30**) and perforations, possibly string-holes, occurred on two of the flaring bowls (e.g. **9**).

The depth of the bowls varied from one-half to one-third of the rim diameter, with most of the bowls falling toward the deeper end of the scale. The diameters of these bowls varied from 18 to 36 cm with the shallower bowls tending to also be smaller in diameter, although no absolute progression was observable.

On the flaring bowls the shapes of the rims varied from flat everted to simple rounded, and the precise rim form could vary from one part of a bowl to another. There are three types of everted rims—**1, 2** and **3** respectively. **1** with flat, wide everted rim is the most common with eight examples, six of which were definitely burnished; the other two may have been so originally. They had loop handles and the diameters were large (38 to ca 44 cm). **2** with its thin, everted rim was the only example of the second type. It, too, had a loop handle and was burnished. **3** and an example from trench 112 also have a bent-over rim, but it is thickened instead of thinned. Both examples of this third type were burnished.

The rim variations for the main type of flaring bowl are shown by **13–17.** They vary from slightly everted to straight, but usually are flattened. Others, especially those on the shallower bowls, can be more rounded as are **6** and **8.** In four cases, including **11–12,** the bowl sides are concave, and **12** has an unusual outward angled rim. Only five of the deeper bowls are not burnished (e.g. **20** and **22**), and it was clearly usual for flaring bowls to be burnished. The flaring bowls comprised eighty per cent of the bowl occurrences.

From the lower level of trench 116 came three deep bowls (**24** and **25**), two of which are burnished, with diameters of 21 and 35 cm. **24** had two vertical loop handles from the rim. Of seven bowls with curved sides (**26–28**), six are unburnished. **27** may have been imported as its fabric is not otherwise known at the site.

A wide bowl shape, always unburnished, is represented by four fragments from trench 105 (**29–30**). They are possibly from two bowls. On **30** is the root of a lug handle. Lugs are rare on bowls, the only other occurrence being on **23,** a unique bowl with flaring rim. The bowl with outcurved rim (**31**) is also unique, and it is also of unusual fabric. This fabric contains large white inclusions, which were otherwise found only in a body sherd from trench 116. Another unusual vessel is **50,** which, despite its everted rim, is midway between a deep bowl and an open pot.

Two types of spouted vessel occur in the assemblage. There are ten examples, all unburnished, of flat rimmed bowls with spouts of regular shape at the rim. They include **32** and **33.** Two spouts of the usual burnished fabric, **34** and **35,** are more irregular in shape. They were not well preserved, and it is not certain that they are from the rims of bowls. They may have been from the walls of closed pots, for the interior of neither is burnished.

Two other fragments of uncertain shape are **36** and **37,** with slightly carinated bodies and handles from the rim. **37** is unusual both in the fineness of its fabric and the circular section of its handle, but has been included here with **36** which is of similar shape and is clearly made in the LC tradition. The term "tankard" has been used for them as their small rim diameter separates them from both the bowls and the basins.

Basins

The basins are distinguished from the bowls by their upright sides and disk bases. They are wide and shallow, usually having a proportion of height to diameter of about 1:2. Two examples with flaring rims, including **48,** are related to the bowl shapes, but are unburnished and have disk bases. Of the other basins a group of four small ones (**38–40**) with diameters ranging from 13 to 14 cm are well smoothed or lightly burnished. They can have a loop handle from the rim. The main group, **41–47,** is unburnished and often only very roughly smoothed. They are larger, with diameters of 20 to 30 cm, and have either a loop handle from the rim or a lug handle low on the body. None of the basins was sufficiently well preserved to indicate whether basins could have more than one handle.

The basins were made in the same way as the open pots and one, **49,** could be considered either as a deep basin or a shallow open pot.

Open Pots

Most of the pottery fragments at Bağbaşı were from open pots. Up to about twenty sherds could constitute one open pot rim but, even so, these pots were still the most numerous shape (see Chart 1). These vessels, usually quite deep, have upright walls and, except for the largest examples, disk bases. They are usually roughly cylindrical in shape, but a few of the larger pots have their mouths compressed into an oval shape, probably because of the difficulty of moving them before they were fired. This feature was probably not intentional on the part of the potter. The open pots are often irregular in shape and height, and are usually only roughly smoothed. There is a considerable size range, from about 15 to 80 cm in mouth diameter, and the proportion of height to diameter also varies. **70** had similar proportions to **49** but is a larger pot; **82** is much deeper. The rim could be flat or rounded.

The first type of open pot is small and has one or more vertical handles from the rim. **51–59** belong to this class. Loop handles with roughly rounded section and strap handles with wide thin section occur on this shape. Only fragments of the pots were found, and the base form is not known. All the examples are catalogued. Three of these handles have a series of holes pierced at the junction of the handle and rim (**51–53**), and **58** has a thin band of red paint around the base of the wide strap handle. The fabric of some, such as **52** and **58,** is fine and well smoothed, but others are less refined.

Related to this type are **60–62** which are larger open jars with handles from the rim. **62** has rudimentary ribs on the handle. Again, only fragments of the type were found.

Another type of open pot has vertical strap handles attached to the wall of the pot. On **63** and **64** they are on the upper part of the pot; on **65** half-way up it. **63** has a disk base; **65** a slightly concave one. **66** is a disk base that probably had a vertical strap handle added at base level. Horizontal loop handles were also used with both flat and disk bases, as shown by **67–69.** Again one example, **69,** seems to have had the handle placed low on the wall of the pot. Three of these large pots with loop handles—**65, 67** and **68**—have a single perforation about one-quarter of the way up the pot. On **67** and **68** it was pierced before firing and is of regular shape, 0.08 cm in diameter. On **65** the hole was made from the outside of the pot after it had been fired.

The largest category of open pots, however, is that with lug handles. **70–79** and **82** belong here. The lug handles usually occurred in combination with disk bases, but some are found on pots with flat bases. Where over half the pot diameter is preserved, there are always two lugs, one on either side of the pot, on the upper part of the wall. The shape of the lugs varies from rounded to angular; some are almost knobs, others flat ledges. The only decoration on these pots was an occasional impression on the lug. **80** and **81** and most of the indeterminate rims from open pots probably belong to this category.

Related shapes are the open jar with thickened rim (**83**) and the rectilinear vessel (**87**). The latter is made in the same way as the pots with disk bases, and clearly belongs with them although its exact shape is uncertain.

The flat, thickened rims, **84–86,** may be from open pots, but they would also have been suitable as the bases of circular stands. However, the large diameters (that of **86** is ca 42 cm and another example from trench 116 level II is ca 40 cm) argue against their being from stands.

Jugs and Jars

Pots with restricted necks have been termed jugs or jars. Except in the most general way, there is no standardization in these shape categories, possibly because they presented more points at which the shape could be varied than did the more simple shapes discussed above.

The term "jug" will be used to designate a small vessel with fairly narrow neck and normally one handle. It would be suitable for carrying or transferring liquids or grains. "Jars" are necked vessels of any size that seem suitable for use as storage vessels. Working with the complete jugs and jars, I found there was no correlation between form of neck and type of pot, although most of the jugs had some form of everted rim and none of them had straight vertical necks. However, some jars also had flaring necks and everted rims. The proportions of the necks were also examined, but again without positive results. Of the identified jugs and jars the height:diameter ratio of jug necks ranged from 1:3 to 2:3 and that of the jars from 1:3 to 1:2. The height:diameter ratios of all the neck sherds for which diameters could be estimated were also calculated. There was no significant correlation between this ratio and the type of neck, although the ratio for vertical necks is wider (1:4 to 5:4) than that for the other necks (1:3 to 2:3).

Seven complete or reconstructible jugs were found at Bağbaşı—all of different shapes. The jugs are **88** with short outcurved neck and elongated body; **89** with similar neck but shorter body; **91** with flaring neck and short, squat body; **92** with everted rim on a vertical neck and sharply marked-off body; **93** with high vertical neck and everted rim; **94** with neck varying from everted to vertical and flattened body; **95,** a juglet with short flaring neck and slightly pointed base. All have one handle from the rim to the shoulder or maximum body diameter, and almost all (except **92** and **94**) are burnished on the exterior of the vessel and interior of the neck. The rim diameter is not large, varying from 4.8 to 12.5 cm, and the line of the rim is flat. The only decoration on this shape is two small knobs on the body opposite the handle of **92.**

On this basis, burnished necks of small diameter and with outcurved or everted neck or rim were added to the jug category. **90** and **96–105** all fit this description, as does the pattern burnished neck, **148.** Not all the jugs were burnished and it is possible that some of the unburnished necks were also from jugs, but it is not possible to separate them from the necks of small jars. **106** and **107** could be from jugs because flaring necks, with the exception of **123,** are associated with jugs. **108–110** with thinned rims and **111** with its everted rim are also likely to belong here. The bases **181–183** are burnished and of small diameter, and were probably from jugs.

90 and **92** both have two small knobs placed on the body close together and, in the case of **92,** opposite the handle. Jugs are the only shape on which these knobs definitely appear, but there were also seven body sherds, including **150,** with a single knob. These knobs were of two types, the small flat type of **90, 92** and **150,** and a more prominent conical variety.

The jars, with the possible exception of **113** and **119,** are unburnished. **113** is one of two examples of small jars with vertical or everted neck and apparently no handles. **112** is the other. The only features associated with them are a ridge, on **113,** and a moulding, on **112,** at the base of the neck.

The second jar category consists of **114** and **115.** They both bear evidence of secondary firing. The neck was vertical or slightly everted, the base flat, and the only evidence for handles is the pierced lugs on **114.** The rim diameters were not large. The base and lower part of another jar, **196,** probably also belongs here, along with **116,** a well-fired jar with two combination strap/lug handles. **147, 155, 157, 158** and **165** with strap and lug handles may also belong with these small jars, although they have no evidence of secondary firing.

123, despite its flaring neck and handles from rim to shoulder, is unburnished and it seems too heavy in the body to have been a jug. **124** would be from a similar vessel with everted rim, and **125–127** could be from such jars or from large coarse jugs. Vertical or everted rims of this size are **117–122** and **128–130.**

There are a number of large jars with necks. A variety without handles did exist (**131–132**), but most seem to have had a handle, probably originally two, from the rim to the shoulder (**133–135**). **136** shows that the handles could also be placed low on the neck. **156** must also be from a large jar, while **137–139** could have been from any type of jar or jug.

The final category of jars consists of those pots with short necks, or closed shapes without necks.

140–141 have short, roughly vertical necks; **145** and **146** have short inverted necks. Both types are from fairly small pots. **142–144** are apparently from hole-mouth pots with everted rim, although they may have been from wide-mouthed jugs. **143** is burnished.

One feature that occurs on both jars and jugs is a slight ridge at the base of the neck. It is found on jugs (**92**), small jars (**113**), larger jars (**131**) and on five other necks, including **125, 138, 147** and **149.** Moldings are found on only two pots, the small jar **112** and the neck **139.** The molding on **112** is so slight as to be almost imperceptible; that on **139** is more prominent.

Handles

The most characteristic handle form at Bağbaşı is the lug. It occurs only on unburnished pots. The lugs are usually large, flat and ledge-like, and are added perpendicular to the wall of the pot. All were applied with plugs, in the vast majority of cases to open jars, but occasionally to small round-bodied jars (**165**) or bowls (**23** and **30**). They fall into various categories according to their shape. Sixty examples have an angular shape, such as **166,** while sixty-two examples have a rounded shape, such as **161.** Two of the latter, including **171,** are concave in shape. The largest lugs are angular, for example that on **77.**

Sixteen lugs have a single thumb impression on the top and, with two exceptions, they were on angular lugs. The impressions fall into two groups—ten lugs had a simple impression like that on **71** and that shown on pl. 105f; six lugs had deep impressions like those on **76** and **172–173** (pl. 103d,e). The impression was usually placed near the center of the top surface, but three simple impressions and a deep one were placed at the back of the lug, against the wall of the pot (pl. 106a). Another angular lug, **169,** had three simple impressions on the top and one on the end.

Rarer types of lug include the eight narrow elongated lugs, the widest of which is 4.50 cm wide. They have rounded ends, but are narrower than the normal lugs and tend to be less flattened. They are usually upturned, like **159** and **160,** and in the case of **162** bore distinct smoothing marks. There were also two lugs with an impressed end, one of which, **176,** is shown on pl. 104b. One knob-like lug, **163,** two examples of thickened lugs (**72** and **164**) and the small upturned lug on **23** complete the range.

Only four pierced lugs were found at Bağbaşı. **114** and **157** are two of three lugs with a single hole, while **158** has two holes.

Plain lugs, both rounded and angular, also occur in combination with vertical loop handles. They are placed either at the lower junction of the handle and pot, or just below this junction. Nine examples of combination handles were found, including **116, 128** and **147.**

Most of the remaining handles from Bağbaşı were unburnished, irregular loop handles. They were used on open pots, in both vertical and horizontal positions, and on large-necked jars where they were usually attached from the rim to the shoulder. Forty-six examples were found in the sample, including **124, 130, 133** and **134.** Two handles with a more regular, square section were also found (e.g. **129**).

Less common types included thirty-four strap handles, including **155–156.** They have wider, flatter sections than the loop handles. There were also twenty-seven small, irregular loops from bowls, basins and jugs, for example those on **6, 51** and **107.** Many of these were burnished. The ring handle on the tankard, **37,** is unparalleled at the site.

The only decoration on the large loop handles was rudimentary ribs on three examples (**62, 130** and **136**). The strap handles could be decorated either with a knob (**156**), or in six cases with a series of holes pierced at the junction of handle and rim. There could be three (two examples), four (two examples), five or six holes. Five examples have large holes, often completely piercing the handle as on **51–53.** They are from open pots and necks. The sixth example, **101,** has six small shallow holes on what is apparently the neck of a jug.

Bases

The disk bases consist of a large flat disk with the wall rising approximately vertically, and often inset slightly from the edge of the disk. The base of the wall is smoothed down to cover the joint, and give a sharp edge to the base. **202–221** are disk bases, and they show the range of finish achieved. It varies from one part of the base to another, as well as from pot to pot. These bases are found on open pots and basins.

The remaining bases, **177–201,** are also flat, but the base is smaller than the lower diameter of the walls and the edge of the base is smoothed. These bases were used for burnished jugs (**180–183**), for unburnished jugs or small jars (**177–178** and **184–187**), for burnished bowls (**199**) and wide bowls (**200**), and for large jars and pots (**82, 196** and **201**).

Miniature and Unusual Pots

221 with its disk base and tall cylindrical shape is unique at Bağbaşı. It was perhaps some sort of beaker. Another unusual pot is **229,** the lower part of a small jar with disk base and two small vertical loop handles on the body. It was covered with circular impressions, probably made with a reed.

Miniature vessels are not common at Bağbaşı, but there are some miniature bowls and basins. The miniature flaring bowls, **225** and **226,** and basin, **227,** are clearly copies of full-size pots, but the small vessels with outcurved rim, **222–224,** have no exact parallels in the main repertoire.

The double vessel with impressed pointillé decoration, **228,** is unique at Bağbaşı, as is the solid pedestal base or lid knob, **230.** Two fragments of small pedestal bases with outcurved feet, **231** and **232,** were also found, but there is no indication of the type of pot to which they belonged.

Pans and Feet

These are objects probably associated with the hearth, for all the examples are well baked and they are usually without black cores. **233–237** are solid feet of various sizes. There is no indication of the type of vessel from which they came.

No complete pans were found, but there were many fragments from large circular, oval or rectilinear pans with smooth upper surface. Four varieties were produced—flat circular or oval pans (**238–240**); flat rectilinear pans (**241**); circular or oval pans with a raised rim (**242–245**) that was sometimes triangular in section and, in one case, had diagonal impressions across it; and circular or oval pans with deep sides and disk bases (**246–249**). **249** and another example from trenches 102–105 had a wavy rim curving down toward the base.

Two flat fragments of well-baked pan fabric with burnished upper surface came from trench 116. No edge was preserved, and the type of pan from which they came could not be determined.

DECORATION

Most of the decorative features used on the Bağbaşı pottery have already been mentioned as they are related to the shape of the vessels. There are the pairs of knobs on jug bodies, the knob on the strap handle, thumb impressions on lugs, ribbing of loop handles, holes pierced at the top of strap handles, and the use of a ridge or moulding at the base of the neck of jugs and jars.

Other instances of decoration are rare. There was one case of shallow incised patterning on a body sherd from a large jar (**152;** pl. 102f), but it may not have been intentional. Impressed decoration occurs on two pots. The jar, **229,** had its exterior covered with impressed circles probably made with the end of a reed, and the double pot, **228,** was covered with clusters of fine deep pointillé impressions. There was one sherd with pattern burnishing. The jug neck, **148,** had vertical stripes produced by this method.

Six sherds bore traces of red paint. In no case did the traces form a design, and the painting seems to have consisted of either areas of paint or rough stripes. **58** had a line of paint around the base of the handle; **147** the edge of a stripe or area of paint; **153** an indeterminate smudge and **128** and **154** and another example from trench 105 seem to have been covered with areas of paint, although it was not well preserved. The color of the paint varied from crimson to pinkish red. It was applied directly to the ground of the pot, without a slip. **154** had a somewhat finer fabric than usual and was well burnished after it was painted.

CATALOGUE

Bowls

1. Flaring bowl with flat everted rim. Rim fr. with vertical loop handle from below rim. Burnished gray exterior; pale brown and gray interior. Trench 117. pl. 16.

2. Flaring bowl with thin everted rim. Rim fr. with hole for attachment of handle below rim (fr. is broken diagonally so that the area of the lower attachment is not preserved). Gray exterior with black mottling, burnished with heavy horizontal strokes; black interior with burnish preserved in places. Trenches 102–105. pl. 16.

3. Flaring bowl with thick everted rim. Rim fr. Slightly burnished gray exterior with black mottling; burnished gray interior with black at rim. Wall thickness varies considerably. Trench 116, pit of lower level III. pl. 16.

4. Flaring bowl with slightly everted rim. Rim fr. with vertical loop handle from rim. Black exterior, heavily but not evenly burnished in criss-cross fashion; black interior with heavy, uneven vertical burnish (horizontal at rim). Trench 116, pit of lower level III. pl. 16.

5. Flaring bowl with flattened rim. Rim fr. Burnished brown and gray mottled exterior; burnished black interior. Trenches 102–105. pl. 16.

6. Flaring bowl with flattened base and four vertical loop handles from below rim. Approx. ¼ preserved with one handle set on crookedly and attachment holes for a second. Diagonally burnished gray exterior with black mottling; burnished gray interior. Trench 107. pl. 16.

7. Flaring bowl. Fr. with flattened base and vertical loop handle from below rim. Burnished pale brown and gray exterior with black mottling; burnished gray interior with black mottling. Trenches 102–105. pl. 16.

8. Flaring bowl. Rim fr. Burnished black exterior and interior with light brown at rim. Trench 105. pl. 17.

9. Flaring bowl with flat rim. Rim fr. with string-hole (?) made by piercing from both sides. Burnished gray with light brown patches on both exterior and interior. Trenches 102–105. pl. 17.

10. Flaring bowl. Rim fr. with stump of vertical loop handle from rim. Burnished black exterior and interior. Trench 116, pit of lower level III. pl. 17.

11. Flaring bowl with slightly concave walls. Rim fr. Slightly burnished orange and brown mottled exterior; burnished brown-black interior. Trench 105. pl. 17.

12. Flaring bowl with concave walls. Rim fr. Burnished gray and black mottled exterior and interior. Trench 105. pl. 17.

13. Deep flaring bowl with everted rim. Rim fr. with two holes for attachment of vertical loop handle below rim. Burnished gray exterior; burnished gray-brown interior. Trench 105. pl. 17.

14. Deep flaring bowl with flat rim. Rim fr. with stump of vertical loop handle from below rim and hole for lower attachment. Burnished brown and gray mottled exterior; burnished black interior. Trench 105. pl. 17.

15. Deep flaring bowl with slightly everted rim. Rim fr. Slightly burnished black exterior and interior with patches of brown on rim. Trench 116, pit of lower level III. pl. 17.

16. Deep flaring bowl with flat rim. Rim fr. Roughly burnished gray exterior; gray interior. Trench 105. pl. 17.

17. Deep flaring bowl with flat rim and flattened base. Approx. ⅛ of pot preserved. Crisscross burnished exterior, dark gray above and yellow-brown with black mottling below; unburnished interior ranges from black at rim to orange at base with brown and black mottling. Trench 116, pit of lower level III. pl. 17.

18. Deep flaring bowl with flat rim. Rim fr. Burnished gray exterior with some orange and black mottling; unburnished orange interior. Trench 105. pl. 17.

19. Deep flaring bowl with flat rim. Rim fr. Burnished gray exterior with black mottling; burnished black interior. Trench 109. pl. 17.

20. Deep flaring bowl with flat rim. Rim fr. Well-smoothed pale brown exterior with black mottling; black interior. Trench 116, level II. pl. 17.

21. Deep flaring bowl with flat rim. Rim fr. Burnished gray and black mottled exterior and interior. Trench 116, level II. pl. 17.

22. Deep flaring bowl. Rim fr. Orange exterior with black mottling; gray interior. Trench 116, level II. pl. 17.

23. Flaring bowl with slightly everted rim. Rim fr. with small upcurved lug (half preserved). Brown exterior; orange interior. Trench 105. pl. 18.

24. Deep bowl. Approx. ½ preserved with one vertical loop handle from rim. Burnished gray with light brown and black mottled patches on exterior; burnished gray-brown interior. Trench 116, level III. pl. 18.

25. Deep bowl. Approx. ¼ of pot preserved and the height of the rim varies considerably, from 2 cm below to 8 cm above the point drawn. Exterior mottled gray, pale brown and black with the lower wall blackened; interior light brown. Trench 116, lower level III. pl. 18.

26. Bowl with flat rim and curved sides. Rim fr. with the stumps of a vertical loop handle from rim. Roughly finished brown exterior with black area at rim; black interior. Trench 117. pl. 18.

27. Bowl with curved sides. Approx. ¼ of pot preserved with mat (?) marks on base. Exterior brown with black mottling; interior orange with brown near rim. The fabric is unique at Bağbaşı and contains platey stone inclusions. Trench 105. pl. 18.

28. Bowl with incurved sides. Rim fr. Burnished brown exterior with gray mottling; dark gray interior. Trench 116, level II. pl. 19.

29. Wide bowl. Rim fr. Pale orange exterior with small black patches; pale brown interior. Fabric is finer than usual and more powdery. Trench 105. pl. 19.

30. Wide bowl. Rim fr. with stump of lug handle low on wall. Orange and pale brown mottled exterior; orange and black mottled interior. Fabric as last. Trench 105. pl. 19.

31. Bowl with outcurved rim. Rim fr. with rim mostly crumbled away. Brown exterior, possibly originally burnished; orange-brown interior. Coarse fabric with large white grits. Trench 105. pl. 19.

32. Bowl with flat rim and spout. Rim fr. Well-smoothed orange and gray mottled exterior; orange and brown mottled interior. Trench 110, upper fill. pl. 19.

33. Bowl with flat rim and spout. Rim fr. Burnished gray exterior and interior. Trench 105. pl. 19.

34. Fr. with spout of irregular shape. Burnished brown exterior with black patch; brown interior. Trench 110, upper fill. pl. 19.

35. Fr. with spout. Burnished black exterior; black interior. Trench 105. pl. 19.

"Tankards"

36. Tankard. Rim fr. with vertical loop handle from rim. Exterior and interior brown with black mottling and only roughly smoothed. Trench 116, level II. pl. 20.

37. Tankard. Rim fr. with ring handle from rim. Well-smoothed red exterior with black mottling; brown-black interior. Fabric is finer than usual. Trench 105. pl. 20.

Basins

38. Basin with flat rim and flat base. Fr. Very well-smoothed brown and orange mottled exterior; orange interior. Regular shape. Trench 110. pl. 20.

39. Basin with flat base. Fr. Orange exterior with gray mottling on base; interior black with gray at rim. Trench 105, level II, N corner. pl. 20.

40. Basin. Fr. with loop handle from rim. Burnished brown exterior with orange and black mottling; burnished pale brown interior. Trenches 102–105. pl. 20.

41. Basin with disk base and rim thickened on interior. Fr. with square-sectioned loop handle from rim to near base. Pale orange-brown exterior with black mottling; orange interior. Trench 105. pl. 20.

42. Basin with disk base and flat rim. Approx. ⅓ preserved with loop handle from rim to near base. Irregular shape with walls varying from straight to concave. Patched in plaster. Creamy gray exterior with black and orange mottling; creamy gray interior with black mottling. Trench 102, burnt debris. KA 621. pls. 20 and 99f.

43. Basin with disk base and uneven rim. Approx. ⅓ preserved with irregular loop handle from rim to near base. Very irregular in shape. Completed, including a small part of the handle and all the interior of the base, in plaster. Muted red-orange exterior with black mottling on base; muted red-orange interior with some black mottling on rim. Trench 116, level III channel cuts. KA 767. pl. 21.

44. Basin with disk base. Fr. with loop handle from inside rim to near base. Pale brown exterior; black interior with some pale brown near rim. Mat (?) marks on base. Trenches 102–105. pl. 21.

45. Basin with disk base (very irregular edge) and flat thickened rim. Fr. is refired which may account for incurved shape. Pale brown and gray mottled exterior; gray interior. Trenches 102–105. pl. 21.

46. Basin. Rim fr. with hole for attachment of lug. Pale brown exterior with black mottling; pale orange interior. Trench 105. pl. 21.

47. Basin with disk base. Fr. with hole for attachment of lug. Exterior and interior red-orange with black mottling. Trenches 102–105. pl. 21.

48. Basin with outcurved sides and disk base. Fr. with hole for attachment of lug or handle (area above hole is missing). Exterior and interior brown with black mottling. Trench 105. pl. 21.

Open Pots

49. Open jar with flat rim and disk base. Fr. Brown-gray exterior with black mottling; black interior. Trench 105. pl. 21.

50. Large flaring bowl with everted rim. Rim fr. Cream and gray exterior and interior. Coarse and poorly fired. Trench 105. pl. 21.

51. Open pot. Rim fr. with strap handle from rim. Four shallow holes at junction of handle and rim. Orange exterior and interior. Trench 116, level II. pl. 22.

52. Open pot. Rim fr. with strap handle from rim. Three large holes and one small one pierced at junction of handle and rim. Pale brown exterior and interior. Trench 110. pl. 22.

53. Open pot. Rim fr. with strap handle from rim. Three shallow holes in rim at handle junction. Exterior and interior orange with black mottling. Trench 116, level III channel cuts. pl. 22.

54. Open pot. Rim fr. (angle uncertain) with strap handle from rim. Creamy orange exterior; orange interior. Rather coarse fabric. Trench 105, level II, N corner. pl. 22.

55. Open pot. Rim fr. with thick strap handle from rim. Red-orange exterior and interior with small creamy brown patches on exterior. Trenches 102–105. pl. 22.

56. Open pot. Rim fr. with incompleted strap handle from rim. Stump is slightly twisted near its end. Brown exterior and interior with darker patches on exterior. Trench 116, level II. pl. 22.

57. Open pot (?). Rim fr. with loop handle from rim. Gray exterior; brown interior with black mottling. Trench 116, level III. pl. 22.

58. Open pot (?). Rim fr. with broad strap handle from rim. Well-smoothed gray exterior with black patches on handle; black interior. A thin band of red paint, very faint, around base of handle. Trenches 102–105. pl. 22.

59. Open pot (?). Rim fr. with stump of loop handle from rim and hole for lower attachment. Orange exterior and interior. Trench 116, level II. pl. 23.

60. Large open pot. Rim fr. with square-sectioned handle from rim. Exterior and interior orange with black mottling on exterior. Rather coarse fabric. Trench 116, level III, channel cuts. pl. 23.

61. Large open pot. Rim fr. with large loop handle from rim. Exterior and interior brown with dark mottling. Trench 109, upper fill. pl. 23.

62. Large open pot with flat rim. Rim fr. (angle uncertain, possibly upright) with roughly square-sectioned loop handle from rim. On upper side of handle are irregular ribs. Orange exterior with black mottling; pale orange interior. Trench 105. pls. 23 and 100c.

63. Open jar with flat rim and disk base. Approx. ½ preserved with vertical strap handle below rim. Exterior gray and black mottled; interior black with large yellow patches on lower wall. Trench 105, level II, E of wall 1. pl. 24.

64. Open jar with flat rim. Rim fr. with stump of vertical (?) strap handle. Brown and black mottled exterior with orange and gray patch; orange interior. Trench 119. pl. 24.

65. Open jar with slightly concave base and two vertical loop handles on upper body. Irregular oval shape (rim ca 48 × 41 cm) with the handles on the narrow ends. A small hole (D. 2.00 cm) was added 12 cm up from the base after firing. About ⅓ of the upper part of the pot and most of the rim have been restored in plaster. Exterior mottled orange, pale brown, brown and black; interior mottled pale brown, brown, gray and black. Trench 116, lower level III. KA 972. pls. 25 and 99a–c.

66. Open jar (?). Disk base fr. with handle stump at base level, possibly for vertical strap handle. Pale brown exterior and interior. Trench 110, ashy fill. pl. 24.

67. Open jar with flat rim, flat base and two horizontal loop handles. The height varies from 38 to 38.50 cm and there is some irregularity in shape. A small hole (D. 0.80 cm) was pierced 11.50 cm from the bottom on one side. Over ½ preserved including both handles. Orange and light brown exterior with black mottling; orange interior. Trench 116, lower level III. pl. 26.

68. Open jar with flat rim and disk base. Approx. ¾ preserved with a stump of one handle (the angle of attachment suggests horizontal loop handles). Somewhat oval in shape with the handles at the narrow ends; rim height is very irregular, varying from 40 to 43 cm. A small hole (D. 0.80 cm) was pierced 7.50 cm from the bottom. Part of the base has been restored in plaster. Brown exterior with black mottling; brown interior. Trench 116, lower level III. KA 970. pl. 27.

69. Open jar (?). Disk base fr. with horizontal loop handle. D. base ca 45 cm. Orange exterior with brown and black mottling and black base; orange to brown interior. Trench 118. pl. 28.

70. Squat open jar with rounded rim and disk base. Frr. with stump of lug handle and very irregular rim. Exterior brown with black mottling; interior orange with black areas on base. Trench 105. pl. 28.

71. Open jar with flat rim, disk base and two angular lug handles (only one is preserved) with a thumb impression on top. Exterior gray and pale brown mottled with black around base; black interior. Trench 105, level II, E of wall 1. KA 953. *AJA* 79 (1975) pl. 59, fig. 8. pls. 29 and 99d–e.

72. Open jar with flat rim. Frr. of rim and body, including fr. with angular lug. Orange with black mottling on exterior and interior. Trench 110. pl. 30 shows fr. with lug.

73. Open jar with flat rim. Rim fr. with angular lug. Well-smoothed brown mottled exterior; orange interior. Trench 105. pl. 30.

74. Open jar with flat rim. Rim fr. with angular lug. Red-orange exterior with small areas of brown mottling; black interior. Trenches 102–105. pl. 30.

75. Open jar with flat rim. Frr. with lug. Well-smoothed red-orange and gray mottled exterior; pale brown and gray mottled interior. Trench 105. pl. 31.

76. Open jar with flat rim. Frr. of large part of one side with angular lug with thumb impression on top. Orange exterior with some black mottling; red-orange interior. Trench 116, pit of upper level I. pl. 31.

77. Open jar. Frr. of rim, body and one angular lug. D. rim unknown. Orange, gray and black mottled exterior; pale orange interior. Refired. Trench 116, N corner, level II. pl. 32 shows fr. with lug.

78. Open jar. Rim fr. with slightly upturned lug. Creamy brown exterior with black at rim; black interior. Trenches 102–105. pl. 32.

79. Open jar. Rim fr. with slightly upturned lug. Orange exterior and interior. Trenches 102–105. pl. 32.

80. Open jar with flat rim and disk base. Fr. Brown exterior with black mottling; orange interior with black at base. Trench 116, level III, channel cuts. pl. 32.

81. Open jar with disk base. Fr. Gray exterior; pale brown interior. Trench 110, upper fill. pl. 33.

82. Open jar with flat rim and flat base. Approx. ½ preserved including one angular lug. Exterior mottled orange, brown, yellow, gray and black; interior brown and creamy brown with darker patches. Trench 105, level II, E of wall 1. pl. 34.

83. Open jar with flat rim thickened on both exterior and interior. D. rim over 44 cm. Orange exterior with black mottling; orange interior. Trench 110. pl. 33.

84. Open pot. Rim fr. Brown exterior; orange and gray mottled interior. Trench 117. pl. 33.

85. Open pot. Rim fr. Brown exterior; creamy brown interior. Trench 116, level I. pl. 33.

86. Open pot. Rim fr. Brown exterior and interior. Trench 116, level III, channel cuts. pl. 33.

87. Rectilinear vessel. Frr. of rim and of base with holes for attachment of handles in both sections. A horizontal loop handle on at least one side is probable but other handle forms cannot be eliminated. A deeper vessel than that drawn, with one or more vertical handles, is also possible. Gray exterior with black mottling; interior black at top, yellow below. Trench 105, level II, E of wall 1. pl. 35a and d (horizontal and vertical sections of rim frr.); b and c (outline and vertical section of base frr.); e (possible reconstruction). Also pl. 100 a–b.

Jugs

88. Jug with ovoid body, flattened base and curving neck with everted rim. Strap handle from rim to shoulder. Unbroken with crack in rim near handle. Burnished exterior, light brown in part but mostly blackened including base and handle; black interior with inside of rim burnished. Trench 105, level II, KA 685, *AJA* 73 (1969) pl. 77, fig. 37. pls. 36 and 100d.

89. Pot with short outcurved neck and loop handle from rim to shoulder. Approx. ½ preserved. Inside base very irregular. Burnished gray-brown exterior with orange at rim; gray-brown interior. Powdery fabric. Trench 105. pl. 36.

90. Small pot with outcurved neck and two very slight knobs 4.80 cm apart at level of maximum body diameter. Approx. ⅓ preserved. Lightly burnished yellow exterior; yellow interior and core. Trench 105. pl. 36.

91. Jug with flaring neck, squat baggy body and loop handle from rim to body. The base is rounded and unsteady. Patched with plaster including most of rim. Burnished yellow exterior with gray mottling; yellow interior. Trench 105, level II, E area. KA 714. pl. 37.

92. Jug with cylindrical body, flattened base and tall neck with everted rim. The neck is marked off from the body by a distinct offset and there is a stump for a strap handle on the upper body. On the opposite shoulder of the pot are two flattened knobs, 4.50 cm apart (one is directly opposite the handle stump, the other is to the left of it). Rim and neck above handle stump and handle restored in plaster. Well-smoothed gray exterior with black mottling; gray interior. Trench 105, level II, E of center. KA 712, *AJA* 74 (1970), pl. 55, fig. 4. pls. 37 and 101a.

93. Jug with rounded body, flat base and tall neck with everted rim. A wide strap handle from rim to maximum body diameter. Broken, and part of base, neck and most of rim restored in plaster. Orange and brown mottled exterior, heavily burnished vertically on the neck and horizontally on the body; brown interior with inside of neck burnished. Trench 102, burnt debris. KA 620, *AJA* 72 (1968), pl. 85, fig. 37. pls. 37 and 100 e–f.

94. Jug with squat body, somewhat flattened on handle side, flat base and neck that varies from vertical to everted and is irregular in height. A loop handle is applied from the rim to the shoulder. Unbroken except for chips from the rim. Creamy brown exterior with some small orange patches; creamy brown interior. Trench 115, N of wall 1. KA 710. pls. 38 and 101b.

95. Juglet with short flaring neck, ovoid body, pointed base and loop handle from rim to body. Unbroken. Burnished brown, gray and black mottled exterior (surface partly worn away); gray to black interior with inside of neck burnished. Trench 105, W of partition (at lower level III). KA 709. pls. 38 and 101c.

96. Rim fr. of flaring neck. Approx. ½ neck diameter preserved. Burnished gray-brown with black mottling on exterior and interior. Trench 105. pl. 38.

97. Rim fr. of flaring neck. Approx. ⅓ neck diameter preserved. Lightly burnished gray-brown exterior; lightly burnished brown interior with black mottling. Trench 116, level II. pl. 38.

98. Rim fr. of small pot with outcurved neck. Roughly burnished brown and gray mottled exterior; smoothed light brown interior with black mottling. Trench 105. pl. 38.

99. Rim fr. of everted neck. Burnished black exterior and interior. Trench 116, level III, channel cuts. pl. 38.

100. Rim fr. of everted neck. Gray to black exterior, originally burnished; brown interior. Trench 109, upper fill. pl. 38.

101. Inverted neck fr. with stump of thin strap handle from rim. At junction of handle and rim are at least six fine holes. Burnished dark brown exterior and interior. Trench 116, level II. pl. 38.

102. Neck fr. D. lower neck 9 cm. Burnished brown exterior with black mottling; orange-brown interior with black mottling. Trench 117. pl. 38.

103. Neck fr. D. top ca 10 cm. Roughly burnished gray exterior; orange interior. Trench 110. pl. 38.

104. Rim fr. of neck with everted rim. Burnished orange exterior; burnished light brown and black mottled interior. Trench 105. pl. 39.

105. Neck and shoulder fr. of vertical neck with loop handle from rim to shoulder. Lightly burnished gray exterior with black mottling; black interior. Trench 105. pl. 39.

106. Rim fr. of flaring neck. Brown exterior and interior. Only roughly finished. Trench 119. pl. 39.

107. Rim fr. of flaring neck with stump of loop handle from rim. Brown exterior with black mottling; gray and black interior. Trench 116, level II. pl. 39.

108. Rim fr. of everted neck. Orange exterior and interior. Trench 116, level II. pl. 39.

109. Rim fr. of everted neck. Black exterior and interior. Trench 105. pl. 39.

110. Rim fr. of everted neck. Orange exterior; light brown and orange mottled interior. Trench 116, level II. pl. 39.

111. Rim fr. of neck with everted rim. Gray-brown exterior; gray interior with brown at rim. Trench 105. pl. 39.

Jars

112. Small pot with everted neck and very fine molding around base of neck. Approx. ¼ preserved. Orange exterior and interior. Rather coarse fabric. Trench 116, level II. pl. 39.

113. Rim fr. of vertical neck with ridge at base of neck. Burnished gray exterior; gray interior. Trench 116, level I. pl. 39.

114. Jar with everted neck, flat base and two lug handles on shoulder. Approx. ⅔ preserved with part of lower side and most of base restored in plaster; rim, most of neck and one lug (its position is clear) missing. The remaining lug is pierced vertically. The pot is very lopsided and the lugs are at different heights and are not exactly opposite one another. Exterior yellow to green with large blackened area on one side; orange interior. Trench 105. pl. 40.

115. Body of pot with straight (?) neck and flat base. Approx. ½ pot preserved but most of upper part missing. A slight thickening of the broken edge on the shoulder suggests a lug or loop handle was attached there. Orange exterior with lots of black mottling especially on the lower walls (but not on base) where surface is roughened; smooth black interior. Hard fired. Trench 116, in circle of stones of level II. pl. 39.

116. Jar with vertical neck, loop handles to shoulder and a lug placed a short distance below each handle. Approx. ½ preserved with one lower handle stump and two lugs. Not restorable. Very irregular shape. Orange, light brown and yellow exterior; orange interior. Rather gritty fabric. Trench 116, upper level I. pl. 41.

117. Rim fr. with vertical neck. Orange exterior and interior. Trench 105. pl. 42.

118. Rim fr. with vertical neck. Well-smoothed orange exterior; light brown interior. Trench 105. pl. 42.

119. Rim fr. with curving neck. Burnished dark brown exterior and interior. Trench 118. pl. 42.

120. Rim fr. with straight neck, irregular in height. Yellow throughout. Trench 110, ashy fill. pl. 42.

121. Neck frr. with everted neck. Approx. ½ neck diameter preserved. Pale brown to gray exterior; brown-gray interior. Trench 105, level III, below wall 1. pl. 42.

122. Neck fr. with everted neck. Orange exterior and interior. Trench 105, level II, E of wall 1. pl. 42.

123. Jar with flaring neck and elongated body. Approx. ½ preserved, including one loop handle from rim to shoulder. D. rim irregular. Well-smoothed yellow-brown exterior with orange and brown toward base; brown and gray interior. Trench 116, upper level I. pl. 43.

124. Neck and shoulder fr. with sharply everted rim and loop handle from rim to shoulder. Approx. ½ neck diameter preserved. Brown exterior with rim and handle orange and with black mottling; yellow-brown interior with orange at rim. Trench 116, in circle of stones of level II. pl. 42.

125. Neck fr. with everted rim and slight ridge at junction with shoulder. Orange exterior and interior. Trench 110, ashy fill. pl. 42.

126. Neck fr. with everted rim. Gray and brown mottled exterior and interior. Trench 116, level II. pl. 42.

127. Neck and shoulder fr. with everted rim and strap handle from rim to shoulder. Exterior mottled gray, black and brown; interior brown. Trenches 102–105. pl. 42.

128. Neck and shoulder fr. with everted neck and combination strap/lug handle from rim to shoulder. Creamy yellow exterior with small patches of red-orange paint preserved on handle and lug and a vertical drip down inside of neck; creamy yellow interior. Trench 105. pl. 44.

129. Neck and shoulder frr. with everted neck and rectangular sectioned strap handle from rim to shoulder. Approx. ½ neck diameter preserved. Cream exterior; orange interior; pink core. Refired. Trench 105, level II. pl. 44.

130. Rim fr. with vertical neck and strap handle from rim to shoulder. Upper side of handle has prominent central rib. Brown exterior with orange at shoulder; light brown interior with orange on lower part. Trench 115, pls. 44 and 101d.

131. Neck and shoulder frr. with inverted neck and ridge around base of neck. ½ neck diameter preserved. Light brown exterior with black mottling; creamy brown interior with gray mottling. Trench 110, upper fill. pl. 44.

132. Rim and shoulder fr. with straight neck and sharply outcurved shoulder. Red-orange exterior; orange interior. Trench 116, level II. pl. 44.

133. Neck and shoulder fr. with vertical neck and loop handle from rim to shoulder. Handle set on diagonally; line of neck junction partly marked with a fine ridge. Well-smoothed orange exterior and interior. Trench 117. pl. 45.

134. Neck and shoulder fr. with everted neck and large loop handle from below rim to shoulder. Handle is irregular in shape. Orange and brown exterior with small area of black mottling; orange to brown interior. Trench 105. pl. 45.

135. Jar with vertical neck, everted rim and two loop handles from below rim to shoulder. Body is irregular but roughly rounded; base is flat. Broken and large parts, especially of base and lower part, restored in plaster. Exterior pale brown with orange and, on one side, a large area of black mottling; interior orange and brown. Trench 116, upper level I. KA 967. pls. 46 and 101e–f.

136. Jar with vertical neck and two loop handles from neck junction to body. Neck and shoulder frr. with one handle and body fr. with stump of second handle. Both handles have three fairly regular and pronounced ribs on the upper side. Red smoothed exterior; gray-brown interior. Trench 116, in circle of stones of level II. pls. 47 (main frr.) and 102a.

137. Rim fr. of neck with everted rim. Orange exterior; black interior. Trench 105. pl. 47.

138. Neck and shoulder fr. with ridge at base of neck. D. base of neck ca 20 cm. Gray exterior; black interior. Trench 105. pl. 47.

139. Frr. of neck and shoulder of pot with molding at base of neck. Approx. ¼ of diameter (at lower neck 26 cm) preserved. Orange exterior and interior. Trench 116, level III. pl. 47.

140. Frr. of upper part of pot with short vertical neck. Approx. ½ diameter preserved. Green-gray throughout. Refired. Trench 105. pl. 47.

141. Fr. of upper part of pot with short vertical neck. Gray exterior; light brown interior. Trench 110, ashy fill. pl. 47.

142. Rim fr. of pot with everted rim. Gray exterior; black interior. Trench 109, upper fill. pl. 47.

143. Rim fr. of pot with everted rim. Burnished dark brown exterior and interior; chocolate brown core. Trench 117. pl. 47.

144. Rim fr. of pot with incurved sides and everted rim. Brown exterior and interior. Trench 105. pl. 47.

145. Rim fr. of pot with short inverted neck. Gray exterior; brown interior. Trench 105, level III, below wall 1. pl. 47.

146. Rim fr. of pot with short inverted neck. Brown exterior with black mottling; pale brown interior. Powdery fabric. Trench 105. pl. 47.

147. Body fr. with ridge at base of neck and lower stump of combination strap/lug handle on shoulder. D. base of neck ca 21 cm. Cream exterior with black smudge beside handle and bright orange paint along bottom break; cream interior. Trenches 102–105. pls. 48 and 102b.

148. Neck fr. D. lower neck 6 cm. Exterior gray with pattern burnishing forming vertical stripes; interior black. Trench 116, level I. pls. 48 and 102c.

149. Neck and shoulder fr. with ridge at base of neck. Gray exterior; black interior. Trench 116, pit of lower level III. pl. 102d.

Handles

150. Body fr. with knob. Burnished orange and light brown mottled exterior; dark gray interior. Trench 105, level II, N corner. pl. 48.

151. Body fr. with projection. Black exterior; yellow-brown interior with black mottling. Trench 105. pl. 102e.

152. Body fr. of large pot with shallow incised decoration. Striated effect obtained with soft material, perhaps dried grasses. Orange-brown and black mottled exterior; orange interior. Trench 110, upper fill. pl. 102f.

153. Body fr. Exterior cream to gray-green with a smear of crimson paint; orange interior. Coarse, poorly fired fabric. Trench 116, upper fill, level I. pl. 48.

154. Body fr. Orange exterior and interior. Exterior surface, where preserved, is covered with pink-red paint, now partly worn off, and burnished. Trench 116, level I. pl. 103a.

155. Body fr. with strap handle, possibly vertical. D. base of fr. ca 20 cm. Orange exterior; brown interior. Trench 117. pl. 48.

156. Body fr. with strap handle. Knob at center bottom of handle. Orange exterior; brown interior. Trench 105. pl. 48.

157. Body fr. with small lug with one vertically pierced hole. Dark brown exterior and interior. Trench 116, upper fill, level I. pl. 49.

158. Body fr. with small lug with two vertically pierced holes. D. bottom of fr. ca 10 cm. Exterior and interior brown. Fabric rather coarse. Trenches 102–105. pl. 49.

159. Body fr. with ovoid lug handle, either upturned or downturned. Brown exterior; interior of pot gray and brown. Trenches 102–105. pl. 49.

160. Lug handle of ovoid shape, probably upturned. Orange exterior. Trench 105. pl. 49.

161. Lug handle of ovoid shape with plug for attachment to body. Orange exterior with black mottling. Trench 105. pl. 49.

162. Lug handle of elongated ovoid shape with smoothing marks on the side. Orange exterior with black mottling. Trench 116, pit of lower level III. pls. 49 and 103b.

163. Body fr. with knob-like lug which has diagonal smoothing marks on the top (?) and one side. Orange exterior. Trenches 102–105. pl. 49.

164. Body fr. with thickened angular lug, attached at sharp downward angle. Exterior brown with black mottling; interior brown. Trenches 102–105. pl. 49.

165. Body fr. with angular lug handle. D. top ca 24 cm. Orange exterior and interior. Trench 105. pl. 50.

166. Lug handle of angular shape. Orange exterior with gray mottling. Trench 105. pl. 50.

167. Lug handle of angular shape with plug attachment. Orange upper surface; gray lower surface. Trench 105. pl. 50.

168. Body fr. with angular lug handle. Pale orange exterior. Trenches 102–105. pl. 50.

169. Lug handle of angular shape with three shallow thumb impressions on top and one placed off-center on end. On corner nearest end impression is a fine deep hole. Light brown exterior. Trench 110, upper fill. pls. 50 and 103c.

170. Body fr. with rounded lug. Exterior and interior orange; brown to gray core. Trench 116, upper fill I.pl. 50.

171. Body fr. with ovoid, concave lug. Orange exterior. Trench 110, upper fill. pl. 50.

172. Body fr. with angular lug handle with deep thumb impression on top. Orange exterior and interior. Trench 116, level II. pl. 103d.

173. Body fr. with angular lug handle with deep thumb impression on top. Orange exterior and interior. Trench 110, ashy fill. pl. 103e.

174. Body fr. with lug handle with thumb impression on top. Orange exterior and interior. Trench 116, lower level III. pl. 103f.

175. Angular lug handle with thumb impression on top. Brown, gray and black mottled exterior. Trench 110, upper fill. pl. 104a.

176. Lug handle with impressed end. Gray exterior. Trench 116, lower level III. pl. 104b.

Bases

177. Flattened base fr. D. unknown. Gray exterior; black interior. Trench 105. pl. 51.

178. Flattened base fr. D. 4 cm. Orange exterior; light brown interior. Trench 105. pl. 51.

179. Flattened base fr. D. 14 cm. Orange exterior and interior. Trench 105. pl. 51.

180. Flattened base fr. D. 7 cm. Diagonally burnished dark brown exterior; black interior. Trench 116, level II. pl. 51.

181. Flattened base and lower wall of small pot. Approx. ⅓ of diameter preserved. Well-smoothed brown exterior with some black mottling; black interior. Trench 110. pl. 51.

182. Flattened base and lower wall of small pot. Approx. ⅓ of diameter preserved. Burnished gray and black mottled exterior; black interior. Trench 110. pl. 51.

183. Flattened base and lower wall fr. with handle stump. Approx. ½ diameter preserved. Well-burnished (including under base) light brown, gray and black mottled exterior; black interior. Trench 116, level II. pl. 51.

184. Flat base fr. D. 8 cm. Black exterior and interior. Trench 105. pl. 51.

185. Flat base fr. D. 7 cm. Orange exterior with black mottling; black interior. Trench 105. pl. 51.

186. Flat base fr. D. 3 cm. Orange exterior and interior. Trench 105. pl. 51.

187. Flat base fr. D. 7 cm. Red-orange exterior; black interior. Trench 105. pl. 51.

188. Flat base fr. D. 8 cm. Orange exterior with black area in center of base; brown-black interior. Trench 105. pl. 51.

189. Flat base fr. D. 12 cm. Brown-black exterior; black interior. Trench 116, level II. pl. 51.

190. Flat base fr. D. 6 cm. Brown exterior with black on bottom; black interior. Trench 105. pl. 51.

191. Flat base fr. D. 9 cm. Well-smoothed gray and black mottled exterior; black interior. Trench 116, level II. pl. 51.

192. Flat base fr. D. 28 cm. Light brown exterior with black mottling on side and base; black interior. Trench 105. pl. 51.

193. Flat base fr. D. 28 cm. Orange exterior; interior surface destroyed. Trench 105. pl. 51.

194. Flat base fr. D. 7 cm. Burnished dark brown exterior; burnished black interior. Trench 105. pl. 51.

195. Flat base fr. D. 6.5 cm. Burnished orange and gray exterior; burnished black interior. Trench 116, level II. pl. 51.

196. Flat base and lower part of pot. Most of

circumference preserved. D. 13 cm. Lower ½ black throughout with external surface damaged; upper part yellow throughout. Trench 105, level III, below wall 1. pl. 52.

197. Flat base fr. D. 15 cm. Probably belongs with **30.** Orange exterior with black mottling on base; orange interior. Trench 105. pl. 52.

198. Flat base fr. D. 18 cm. Orange and gray exterior; orange interior. Trench 105. pl. 52.

199. Flat base fr. D. 8 cm. Black exterior with orange patches, burnished including under base with heavy, slightly uneven and mostly vertical strokes; gray interior burnished with heavy criss-cross strokes. Trenches 102–105. pl. 52.

200. Flat base fr. D. 18 cm. Orange exterior with small black patch; orange interior. Trench 105. pl. 52.

201. Flat base fr. D. ca 36 cm. Orange exterior; interior surface destroyed. Trench 105. pl. 52.

202. Disk base fr. D. 24 cm. Brown-gray exterior; light brown interior. Trench 105. pl. 52.

203. Disk base fr. D. 24 cm. Gray-brown exterior with black mottling; black interior. Trench 105. pl. 52.

204. Disk base fr. D. ca 40 cm. Two concentric ridges below base. Orange and brown mottled exterior; gray-brown interior. Trenches 102–105. pl. 52.

205. Disk base fr. D. 18 cm. Orange exterior and interior. Trench 105. pl. 52.

206. Disk base fr. D. 36 cm. Brown exterior; orange-brown interior with black on base. Trench 105. pl. 52.

207. Disk base fr. D. ca 30 cm. Orange exterior with black mottling; brown-black interior. Trench 105. pl. 52.

208. Disk base fr. D. 20 cm. Orange exterior with black mottling; pale orange interior. Trenches 102–105. pl. 52.

209. Disk base fr. D. 26 cm. Gray and black mottled exterior and interior. Trench 105. pl. 52.

210. Disk base fr. D. 32 cm. Gray-brown exterior with black mottling; interior surface destroyed. Trench 105. pl. 52.

211. Disk base fr. D. 28 cm. Well-smoothed red exterior with black mottling; red interior. Trenches 102–105. pl. 52.

212. Disk base fr. D. 44 cm. Bottom uneven. Red exterior with black mottling; gray interior with black mottling. Trench 105. pl. 53.

213. Disk base fr. D. 26 cm. Orange exterior; interior surface destroyed. Trench 105. pl. 53.

214. Disk base fr. D. 30 cm. Orange exterior with black mottling; orange interior. Trench 105. pl. 53.

215. Disk base fr. D. 42 cm. Brown exterior with dark mottling; orange interior. Trench 105. pl. 53.

216. Disk base fr. D. ca 30 cm. Profile of base varies from that drawn to a profile like the last. Brown exterior; orange interior. Trenches 102–105. pl. 53.

217. Disk base fr. D. 22 cm. Approx. ¼ of base preserved. Well-smoothed orange exterior; orange interior. Trench 105, level II, N corner. pl. 53.

218. Disk base fr. D. 12 cm. Light brown exterior with black mottling; black interior. Trench 105. pl. 53.

219. Disk base fr. D. ca 25 cm. Profile varies considerably; in part it is straighter than that drawn. Black exterior; orange-brown interior. Trench 110. pl. 53.

220. Disk base fr. showing method of manufacture with coils. D. 30 cm. Brown exterior with dark mottling; orange interior. Trench 105. pls. 53 and 104c.

Miscellaneous and Miniature Pots

221. Cylindrical vessel with disk base. Approx. ¾ of base preserved but edges broken off. Interior bottom is rough except for one finger smoothing in center (base too deep to reach?). Orange-brown exterior and interior. Trench 110. pl. 53.

222. Bowl with outcurved rim. Rim fr. Burnished gray exterior with black mottling; burnished gray interior with brown rim. Trench 105. pl. 54.

223. Miniature deep bowl with outcurved rim and carinated body. Approx. ¼ upper part of pot preserved. Orange exterior and interior. Trench 116, pit in lower level III. pl. 54.

224. Miniature deep bowl with outcurved rim. Approx. ¼ of pot with a loop handle from rim to lower body. Light brown exterior with extensive black mottling; brown interior. Trench 105. pl. 54.

225. Miniature flaring bowl with flat base and everted rim. Approx. ⅓ preserved with two string-holes (?) pierced from interior 0.50 cm below rim and 1 cm apart. Completed in plaster. Exterior light brown and gray with black mottling; interior well-smoothed light brown and gray. Fairly coarse fabric. Trench 116, level I. KA 746, *AJA* 74 (1970), pl. 55, fig. 3. pls. 54 and 104d.

226. Miniature bowl with flat base and flaring sides. Approx. ¼ preserved. Brown exterior and interior. Trench 116, level II. pl. 54.

227. Miniature basin with flat rim and flat base. Fr. Orange exterior with brown mottling on base and lower side; orange interior with brown mottling. Trench 112. pl. 54.

228. Twin vessels, each with ovoid body and slightly everted rim. Bodies connected by a solid cylindrical bar and perhaps also joined by a high loop handle (rims of both pots broken away at relevant point). Bodies irregular in shape, flattened on connecting sides, and one is smaller than the other. Bar and larger pot patched with plaster. Slightly burnished yellow-brown exteriors with one side of composite vessel blackened; yellow-brown interiors. Exterior of both pots, except for rims and bases, and bar covered with clusters of fine, deep impressions (16 to 32 in each cluster), executed after burnishing with the end of a fine cylindrical tool (straw or small bone?). Trench 110, SE extension. KA 690, *AJA* 73 (1969), pl. 77, fig. 35. pls. 54 and 104e.

229. Lower part of pot with disk base, slightly bulging sides and two small vertical strap handles. Refired. Cream exterior with some black mottling on base; orange interior; pink core with white grits. Outer surface smoothed and then impressed while still fairly damp with a tubular implement (reed?). Impressions are deep and clear, of fairly uniform size (1.7 to 1.9 cm outer diameter) and irregularly spaced over pot. Trench 115, in "log cabin," against wall 1. KA 711, *AJA* 74 (1970), pl. 55, fig. 2. pls. 55 and 104f.

230. Miniature cylindrical pedestal base or knob of lid. Solid, with slightly concave base and stumps of applied struts in four places. Two stumps (alternate ones) are double. Orange exterior with some light brown patches. Trench 119. pl. 55.

Pans and Feet

231. Pedestal foot or stand. Base fr. with exterior edge of base thickened. D. ca 12 cm. Brown exterior and interior. Trench 116, level II. pl. 55.

232. Pedestal foot or stand. Base fr. with exterior edge thickened. Irregular in shape. D. ca 8 cm. Gray exterior and interior. Trench 116, level III. pl. 55.

233. Foot. Solid, with diameter increasing from bottom to top. Broken off at top. Creamy brown exterior; pink core. Trench 105, level II, N corner. pl. 55.

234. Foot. Solid, with diameter decreasing from top to bottom. Broken off at top. Creamy brown exterior; pink core. Trench 105, level II, N corner. pl. 55.

235. Foot. Solid, of semi-circular section. Tapers slightly from top where it is broken off. Creamy brown throughout. Trench 110, ashy fill. pl. 55.

236. Foot. Solid, with diameter decreasing from top to bottom. Both top and bottom missing. Creamy brown exterior; pink core. Trench 105. pl. 55.

237. Foot. Solid, with top broken off. Exterior green, cream, brown and orange mottled, brown core. Trench 115. pl. 105a.

238. Flat pan. Edge fr. Pink-orange throughout with upper surface well smoothed. Trench 105. pl. 56.

239. Flat pan. Edge fr. Brown throughout with black mottling on smoothed upper surface. Trenches 102–105. pl. 56.

240. Flat pan. Edge fr. Creamy brown throughout. Trench 105. pl. 56.

241. Flat rectangular pan. Corner fr. Light brown surfaces; pink-orange core. Trench 107, upper fill. pl. 56.

242. Pan with raised edge, possibly rectangular. Edge fr. Yellow-brown throughout. Includes large grits to 1.5 cm diameter. Trench 105. pl. 56.

243. Pan with raised edge. Edge fr. Irregularly made. Exterior surface brown with black mottling; interior surface smoothed black. Trenches 102–105. pl. 56.

244. Pan with short sides. Edge fr. with rim irregular in height. Orange-brown exterior; smoothed orange-brown interior; brown core. Trench 116, level III. pl. 56.

245. Pan with short sides. Edge fr. On top of rim a series of diagonal impressions; mat impressions on base. Exterior orange; interior smoothed dark brown; core orange. Trench 116, upper fill, level I. pl. 56.

246. Pan with deep sides, possibly rectangular. Edge fr. Exterior smoothed orange; interior and core orange. Trench 105. pl. 56.

247. Pan with disk base and deep sides, possibly rectangular. Edge fr. Orange throughout. Finger marks on exterior not smoothed away; mat marks on base. Trenches 102–105. pls. 56 and 105b.

248. Pan with disk base and deep sides. Edge fr. with uneven rim. Orange exterior; light brown interior; orange core. Trench 110, ashy fill. pl. 56.

249. Pan with disk base and deep sides. Edge fr. Rim uneven, sloping up to its highest point and then curving down abruptly. Red-orange exterior and interior with dark mottling on interior. Surfaces only roughly smoothed. Trench 116, pit of lower level III. pls. 56 and 105c.

OTHER ARTIFACTS

CLAY OBJECTS

These objects are all of much the same composition as the pottery. The clay is only roughly prepared and contains grits and fiber fragments, although the latter are not nearly as numerous in the smaller objects—the spindle whorls, beads, seal and figurines. All have been fired to the same low temperature, but most of the objects do not have black cores. In the case of the spit supports and stands this was probably due to their use in close proximity to the hearths; in the other objects to their small size which ensured more thorough firing.

Spit Supports and Stands

Ten objects identified as spit supports were found. They were usually solid, roughly conical in shape, with a circular or oval base and sides tapering upward. In no case was the top of the support preserved, and it is possible that some (especially those without side cavities?) had grooved tops. The sides of the supports could be either concave or convex. Most of the spit supports were without cavities, and similar to **250.** Two of these—**253** and an example from trench 116, level III—had square bases. Two of the supports had side cavities. **251,** an example with concave sides, has a diagonal cavity on one side; **252** has two, at different angles and heights, that meet in the center of the support.

Other objects probably associated with the hearth, as all the examples are well baked and often lack a black core, are stand fragments. **254** is perhaps an end fragment from a horse-shoe stand. Four similar fragments were also found.

250. Spit support or pedestal. Tapering upward from a roughly circular base. Top not preserved. Cream exterior; pink core. Pres. H. 8.55, D. base 10.30 cm. Trench 110, ashy fill. pl. 57.

251. Spit support. Fr. with one conical cavity leading diagonally into it. Profile varies. Base apparently circular, but top appears to have been oval in shape. Creamy brown exterior; pink core. Pres. H. 8.10, D. base 13.50 cm. Trench 110, ashy fill. pl. 57.

252. Spit support. Frr. with two cavities, one from a higher level than the other, which join toward the center of the support. Profile varies, but base roughly circular. Creamy brown exterior; pink core. Pres. H. 10.00, D. base 12.70 cm. Trench 110, ashy fill. pl. 57.

253. Spit support. Solid with square base. Fr. with top and part of base missing. Orange with black mottling; pink-orange core. Pres. H. 11.20 cm. Trench 115. pl. 106c.

254. Horseshoe (?) stand. Fr. with rounded end, one straight side and one side with batter on lower part. Creamy brown and orange exterior; pink core. H. 10.80 cm. Trench 110, ashy fill. pl. 58.

Scoop

Only one example of this category was found.

255. Scoop with sharply curved cup. Front edge and handle broken off. Creamy brown exterior with black mottling; creamy brown interior of cup. Pres. L. 5.75, pres. H. 2.45 cm. Trench 110, ashy fill. pl. 58.

Loomweights

They are all of the same rounded, conical shape with a perforation near the narrow end. **258** is smaller than the other two which are of approximately the same size and were found together with spindle whorl **260.** All the loomweights have more wear on one side of the perforation than the other. The hole is straight and regular.

256. Rounded conical shape with oval base and one perforation. Brown burnished, though surface now mostly destroyed; brown-black core. H. 8.20 cm. Trench 105, level II, debris around walls 1 and 2. pl. 58.

257. Rounded conical shape with oval base and one perforation. Brown burnished, though surface now mostly destroyed; gray-black core. H. 8.50 cm. Trench 105, level II, debris around walls 1 and 2. pl. 58.

258. Rounded conical shape with oval base and one perforation. Pink-brown; pink core. H. 7.20 cm. Trench 105, level II, area E of wall 1. pl. 58.

Spindle Whorls and Beads

Fourteen small objects of fired clay with a hole through the center were found. The shapes of the objects ranged from conical to spherical; their diameters from ca 4.20 to 1.70 cm, and the diameter of the hole from 0.80 to 0.075 cm. The hole in each is regular and even, as if the object had been shaped around a smooth stick. Eight were burnished, and another bore very faint incised lines. Most were battered, but marks that could be related to function were not observed.

259. Truncated biconical whorl, partly concave in both upper and lower halves. Approx. ½ preserved. Brown and black mottled; brown core. Irregular shape. D. ca 4.20, pres. H. 2.60 cm. Trench 105. pl. 59.

260. Truncated biconical whorl with rounded carination. Complete though worn in places. Pale brown. D. 3.50, H. 2.50 cm. Trench 105, level II, area of walls. pl. 59.

261. Biconical whorl, flattened at top and bottom and with slightly rounded carination. Complete; carefully formed. Brown and black mottled. D. 3.30, H. 2.20 cm. Trench 116, level II. pl. 59.

262. Truncated biconical whorl with rounded carination. Approx. ½ preserved. Gray-brown; gray core. D. 3.00, H. 2.10 cm. Trench 110, SE extension, upper fill. pl. 59.

263. Truncated biconical whorl. Carefully formed. Complete except one chip from top. Lightly burnished brown, with black and orange mottling; black core. D. 2.50–2.60, H. 1.70 cm. Trench 110, SE extension, upper fill in area of stone circle. pl. 59.

264. Spherical whorl. Approx. ½ preserved. Brown burnished; black core. D. 2.90, H. 2.60 cm. Trench 105, level II, N area. pl. 59.

265. Conical whorl on flat base. Complete; regularly made. Lightly burnished brown and black mottled. D. 2.70, H. 1.20 cm. Trench 105, upper fill. pl. 59.

266. Roughly globular whorl with one flattened end at the center of which is a concave depression. Complete; chipped. Light brown; gray core. D. 2.60, H. 1.90 cm. Trench 109, SE extension, upper fill. pl. 59.

267. Roughly globular whorl with one flattened end at the center of which is a concave depression. Complete; very hard baked. Burnished light brown. D. 2.10, H. 1.70 cm. Trench 105, level II. N area. pl. 59.

268. Truncated biconical whorl with sharp carination. Approx. ½ preserved; well formed. Burnished brown; brown core. D. 2.30, H. 1.90 cm. Trench 113, upper fill. pl. 59.

269. Truncated biconical whorl. Approx. ½ preserved; well formed. Burnished brown and black; black core. D. 2.10, H. 1.60 cm. Trench 116, level III, "channel cuts." pl. 59.

270. Truncated biconical whorl with rounded carination. Complete. Decorated with rough, faint incised lines. Light brown. D. 1.70–1.80, H. 1.50 cm. Trench 105, level II. pls. 59 and 106d.

271. Biconical whorl; upper half slightly concave, lower slightly convex. Complete. Burnished brown-gray. D. 2.30, H. 1.70 cm. Trench 105, level II, area around walls. pl. 59.

272. Cylindrical whorl. Complete; chipped. Burnished brown and gray mottled. D. 1.80–1.90, H. 2.30 cm. Trench 112, ashy fill. pl. 59.

Stamp

Only one example of this category was found.

273. Stamp with irregular, slightly convex disk face and uneven lumpy stalk handle. Complete except for chip from disk edge. Face has deep incised decoration. It is divided by a line into two roughly equal parts. One half is again divided by a line, on one side of which is a chevron and a stroke, on the other a lop-sided chevron. The other half of the face is filled by lines forming irregular angles. Light brown; pink-brown core. Pres. H. 3.30, D. 3.60–3.70 cm. Trench 102, near burnt walling. KA 582. pls. 59 and 106 e–f.

Counter

Again, only one example was found.

274. Counter. Conical with rounded apex and concave sides; flat circular base. Complete, though worn and cracked. Undecorated. Pink-brown. H. 3.30, D. 2.60–2.80 cm. Trench 115, upper fill in S corner. KA 733. pls. 59 and 107a.

Animal Figurines

Two stylized animal figurines were found. They both represent quadrupeds, but possibly not the same species.

275. Bovine (?) figure on four stump legs. Body is short and thick with raised high and wide hind-quarters, narrow middle. Neck rises to clearly defined horns set sideways; face is a plain convex surface without features. Rear end is smoothed down and suggests a tail. Intact except for tips of horns. Precisely modelled and surfaces well smoothed. Orange with gray mottling; black core. L. 3.30, max. H. rump 1.90, D. waist 1.50–1.60 cm. Trench 116, W corner, in fill on lower floor, level III. KA 722, *AJA* 74 (1970), pl. 58, fig. 24,b. pls. 59 and 107b.

276. Quadruped (lion?) on four stump legs. Lumpy body with large tail raised in curve above line of back. Neck rises to "aureole" above face. Muzzle pierced with a slit and a hole in the front. Complete except for tip of tail, tip of snout and abrasion on back of head. Brown mottled. L. 4.00, max. H. head 3.20, D. waist 1.50–1.90 cm. Found in dump from trenches 117 and 119. KA 737, *AJA* 74 (1970), pl. 58, fig. 24,c. pls. 59 and 107c–d.

STONE OBJECTS

Chipped Stone

All the chipped stone found at Bağbaşı is presented in this section, including six pieces found on top of virgin soil in trench 116. It is possible that some of these belong with the Lower Bağbaşı pottery described in Chapter 3. However, they could belong to the main occupation, and cannot be differentiated from the rest of the chipped stone assemblage.

The chipped stone industry at Bağbaşı was primarily a blade industry, twenty-seven of the thirty-six pieces being blades. Seven flakes and two small core fragments complete the assemblage. Most of the pieces were cutting tools (including sickles) with some scrapers and one denticulate tool. The striking platforms of both blades and flakes were approximately perpendicular, and the longitudinal axis of the blades is usually perpendicular to the striking platform. The blades are regular in shape. Although a number of examples have been deliberately retouched, most bear evidence only of wear (irregular chipping of the edges).

Coarse brown flint was the most common material in the Bağbaşı chipped stone assemblage. Nine blades were made from it, and they were used primarily for cutting tools. The other flints used, a pale gray-brown with white flecks, a purple-brown streaked, and a dark gray with white specks, were used for both cutting and scraping tools. All the chipped stone was of flint with the exception of one small blade of obsidian, **277.**

Sickles

Ten blade fragments were used as sickles (**278–287**). Five had sheen on both edges and five on only one. The sheen was evenly distributed along the edge and occurred on both dorsal and bulbar faces, often in a wider band on the dorsal face. All the edges with sheen, and some without, bore irregular use retouch, often quite heavy and varying in size and angle. The length of the blades varied from 7.74 to 3.10 cm, the width from 1.89 to 1.34 cm and the thickness from 0.04 to 0.31 cm. Only one of the blades, **287,** bore deliberate retouch, possibly to facilitate hafting.

Cutting Tools

The second group of cutting tools (**288–291**) consists of flakes retouched on one edge. The retouch is fine and achieves an angle of 35–40° at the edge. Two, **288** and **290,** also have signs of wear on other edges. **292–296** and **277** would also have been suitable for cutting. **297** is a blade retouched at one end to form a small cutting edge.

Notched Tools

Two possible examples of notched tools, **298** and **299,** were found.

Denticulate Tool

The most unusual flint tool at Bağbaşı, in terms of the total collection, is the flake **300.** It has large irregular and discontinuous bifacial denticulate retouch.

Scrapers

Three blades and flakes were used as scrapers. **301** and **302** were retouched as side scrapers and have heavy mashing on the retouched edge. **303** had been retouched to form a double-sided scraper.

Other

The remaining nine fragments, all blades or fragments thereof, bore no retouch or visible traces of use. Four of them, **304–307,** were of similar coarse brown flint and were found together.

Catalogue

277. Blade fr. broken both ends. Wear and regular diagonal striations along both edges (angle approx. 60°). Obsidian—clear with dark parallel streaks diagonally across the blade. L. 2.75, W. 0.82, Th. 0.15 cm. Trench 102, in walling debris. pl. 60.

278. Sickle blade. Fr. broken both ends. Wear and sheen along R edge on both dorsal and bulbar faces. Flint—dark gray with white specks. L. 7.74, W. 1.70, Th. 0.35 cm. Trench 116, walling debris of upper level I. pl. 60.

279. Sickle blade. Fr. broken both ends. Wear and sheen along both edges on both dorsal and bulbar faces. Flint—pale gray-brown with white specks. L. 4.30, W. 1.50, Th. 0.60 cm. Trench 116, surface. pl. 60.

280. Sickle blade. Fr. broken both ends. Wear and sheen on both edges on both dorsal and bulbar faces; especially deep retouch in places on one edge on bulbar face. Flint—dense brown speckled. L. 3.95, W. 1.36, Th. 0.45 cm. Trench 115, upper fill. pl. 60.

281. Sickle blade. Fr. broken both ends. Wear and sheen on L edge on both dorsal and bulbar faces. Flint—coarse brown speckled. L. 4.54, W. 1.82, Th. 0.31 cm. Trench 109. pl. 60.

282. Sickle blade. Fr. broken both ends. Wear and sheen on both edges on both dorsal and bulbar faces. On bulbar face both edges have additional chipping, post sickle-use. Flint—pale brown. L. 3.41, W. 1.68, Th. 0.48 cm. Trench 116, level II. pl. 60.

283. Sickle blade. Fr. broken both ends. Wear and sheen on R edge on both dorsal and bulbar faces. Flint—white. L. 3.31, W. 1.55, Th. 0.45 cm. Trench 116, level III, on top of virgin soil. pl. 60.

284. Sickle blade. Fr. broken both ends. Wear and sheen on L edge; chipping on R edge. Flint—translucent gray-brown. L. 3.10, W. 1.34, Th. 0.31 cm. Trench 109. pl. 60.

285. Sickle blade. Fr. with striking platform and bulb of percussion, broken. Wear and sheen on both edges on both dorsal and bulbar faces. Flint—coarse brown speckled. L. 6.08, W. 1.89, Th. 0.59 cm. Trench 116, level III, on top of virgin soil. pl. 60.

286. Sickle blade. Fr. broken both ends. Wear and sheen on both edges on both dorsal and bulbar faces. Flint—coarse brown speckled. L. 5.18, W. 1.89, Th. 0.50 cm. Trench 116, level II. pl. 60.

287. Sickle blade. Fr. with striking platform and bulb of percussion, broken. Wear and sheen on L edge on both dorsal and bulbar faces and retouch at bulb end of same edge (L. 0.20, W. 0.15 cm; 45°). Flint—coarse brown speckled. L. 4.88, W. 1.83, Th. 0.64 cm. Trench 109. pl. 60.

288. Cutting tool. Flake/blade with regular wear on R edge on dorsal face (L. 0.10, W. 0.05 cm; 40°); upper R edge has irregular wear on both dorsal and bulbar faces. Flint—dark gray with white streaks. L. 7.47, W. 4.01, Th. 0.81 cm. Trench 105. pl. 60.

289. Cutting tool. Flake fr. with bulb of percussion. Broken on two sides with retouch on either side of bulb where original edge preserved (retouch—L. 0.10, W. 0.05 cm; 35–40°). Flint—pale gray-brown with white specks. L. 4.08, W. 3.40, Th. 0.68 cm. Trench 105. pl. 60.

290. Cutting tool. Flake fr. broken on two sides. Retouch along L edge (L. 0.15, W. 0.10 cm; 35°), wear on other two. Flint—translucent yellow. L. 2.31, W. 2.55, Th. 0.48 cm. Trench 116. pl. 60.

291. Cutting tool. Flake with striking platform and bulb of percussion; tip broken. Wear along both edges. Flint—translucent yellow. L. 3.38, W. 1.64, Th. 0.31 cm. Trench 107. pl. 60.

292. Cutting (?) tool. Flake with striking platform and bulb of percussion. Wear on L edge on both dorsal and bulbar faces. Flint—purple-brown with white streaks. L. 4.33, W. 1.98, Th. 1.21 cm. Trench 116, level III. pl. 60.

293. Core fr. with wear on top edge (L. 0.05, W. 0.05 cm; 60°). Flint—dense gray-brown. L. 2.47, W. 3.22, Th. 1.60 cm. Trench 110, upper fill. pl. 60.

294. Flake with striking platform and bulb of percussion. Regular wear (L. 0.10–0.05, W. 0.05 cm; 85°) on R edge and irregular wear on top and L edge. Flint—light brown. L. 3.96, W. 4.15, Th. 0.90 cm. Trench 116, level I. pl. 60.

295. Blade fr. broken both ends. Wear on both edges. Flint—coarse gray with white specks. L. 3.15, W. 3.72, Th. 0.78 cm. Trench 116. pl. 60.

296. Blade fr. Broken. Slight wear on dorsal face of R edge. Flint—purple-brown with black and orange streaks. L. 3.87, W. 2.85, Th. 0.64 cm. Trench 116, level II. pl. 60.

297. Cutting (?) tool. Blade fr. broken one end and the other end had dorsal retouch on R side (L. 0.10, W. 0.075 cm; 55°). Wear along R edge. Flint—dense dark gray. L. 2.57, W. 1.52, Th. 0.29 cm. Trench 116, level II. pl. 60.

298. Notched tool. Core fr. broken at both ends. Wear on R edge with dorsal retouch at end (L. 0.10–0.15, W. 0.10 cm; 30°) to form notch; some later chipping. Flint—coarse brown speckled. L. 5.24, W. 2.46, Th. 0.77 cm. Trench 116, level II. pl. 61.

299. Notched tool. Flake with striking platform and bulb of percussion. Retouch (L. 0.20–0.025, W. 0.5 cm; 65°) on part of R side forms concave edge. Flint—pale gray-brown with white flecks. L. 3.06, W. 2.04, Th. 0.68 cm. Trench 116, level III, on top of virgin soil. pl. 61.

300. Denticulate tool. Flake with striking platform and bulb of percussion, partly removed. Bifacial retouch (L. 0.70–0.25, W. 0.40–0.30 cm; 50–70°) on all sides forms irregular, discontinuous denticulation. Flint—opaque yellow. L. 3.79, W. 2.85, Th. 1.23 cm. Trench 109. pl. 61.

301. Side scraper. Blade with bulb of percussion and striking platform removed. Retouch along L edge and around to bulb end (L. 0.30–0.60, W. 0.60 cm; 65°). Heavy mashing on lower edge and some on upper edge too. Flint—dense dark gray with white specks. L. 7.28, W. 3.03, Th. 0.76 cm. Trench 116, level III, on top of virgin soil. pl. 61.

302. Side scraper. Flake with striking platform and bulb of percussion, roughly trimmed away in part. Retouch along one edge (L. 0.15–0.25, W. 0.10–0.20 cm; 70°) and heavy mashing at edge, bulbar face. Flint—pale gray-brown with white flecks. L. 2.87, W. 3.08, Th. 1.28 cm. Trench 112. pl. 61.

303. Double sided scraper. Blade with striking platform and bulb of percussion. Dorsal retouch along L edge and on top half of R edge (L. 0.20, W. 0.10 cm; 50°). End chipped and worn on both dorsal and bulbar faces. Flint—purple-brown. L. 6.02, W. 2.91, Th. 0.90 cm. Trench 110. pl. 61.

304. Blade with striking platform and bulb of percussion. Unused. Flint—coarse brown speckled. L. 9.46, W. 2.06, Th. 0.39 cm. Trench 115, cache beside NW scarp. pl. 61.

305. Blade with striking platform and bulb of percussion. Unused. Flint—gray-brown with white specks. L. 9.05, W. 2.32, Th. 0.41 cm. Trench 115, cache beside NW scarp. pl. 61.

306. Blade with striking platform and bulb of percussion. Unused. Flint—coarse brown speckled. L. 9.11, W. 1.83, Th. 0.50 cm. Trench 115, cache beside NW scarp. pl. 61.

307. Blade fr. broken both ends. Unused. Flint—coarse brown speckled. L. 5.83, W. 1.94, Th. 0.52 cm. Trench 115, cache beside NW scarp. pl. 61.

308. Blade fr. with striking platform and bulb of percussion, broken. Unused. Flint—coarse brown speckled. L. 5.47, W. 1.73, Th. 0.55 cm. Trench 116, level II. pl. 61.

309. Blade fr. broken both ends. Chipping on one edge but probably unused. Flint—pale brown. L. 2.16, W. 1.36, Th. 0.30 cm. Trench 116, level II. pl. 61.

310. Blade fr. broken both ends. Flint—pale gray-brown with white specks. L. 4.82, W. 1.33, Th. 0.58 cm. Trench 116, level III, on top of virgin soil. pl. 61.

311. Blade fr. broken both ends. Flint—translucent gray-brown. L. 3.02, W. 2.49, Th. 0.57 cm. Trench 116, level III, on top of virgin soil. pl. 61.

312. Blade fr. with bulb end broken off. Flint—dark gray with white specks. L. 5.25, W. 2.11, Th. 0.67 cm. Trench 116, level III. pl. 61.

Other Stone

Various other stone objects were also assignable to the LC period.

313. Axe. Intact. Ground to regular shape with rounded butt and one face flatter than the other. Rounded convex sides flare to the slightly convex cutting edge which is symmetrically bevelled, smooth and has a sheen. Hard, dense green stone. Max. L. 5.10, max. W. 3.70, max. Th. 1.50 cm. Trench 118. KA 717. pl. 62.

314. Whetstone. Cylindrical with one flat end; broken other end. Smooth and carefully made. Schist. Pres. L. 11.80, max. D. 1.35, D. end 0.80 cm. Trench 113, ashy fill. pl. 62.

315. Mortar with smooth, deep curved depression. Fr. Top and bottom rough but flat; sides roughly curved. Depression: D. approx. 11.00, depth 4.30 cm. Coarse sandy gray stone. Pres. L. 10.80, pres. W. 9.80, Th. 4.55 cm. Trenches 102–105. pl. 107e.

316. Mortar with smooth, deep curved depression. Complete. Set in roughly shaped rectangular block. Depression: D. 11.80–13.00, depth 4.30 cm. Coarse sandy stone varies from gray to brown to red. Max. L. 19.40, max. W. 16.90, max. Th. 10.30 cm. Trench 116. pl. 108a–b.

317. Mortar with smooth, deep curved depression. Fr. set in roughly shaped trapezoidal stone. Depression: D. 12.60, depth 5.30 cm. Light green stone with red discoloration. Pres. L. 15.80, max. W. 19.20, max. Th. 8.80 cm. Trench 116. pl. 108c.

318. Grinding stone. Corner fr. of flat trapezoidal (?) stone. Much of top surface, except along side where the stone sloped away, worn smooth. Coarse blue-gray stone. Pres. L. 19.30, pres. W. 13.40, Th. 3.30 cm. Trenches 102–105. pl. 108d.

319. Grinding stone. Very rough trapezoidal shape with irregular, unstable base. Top surface slightly rises in smooth even curve (H. curve in center 2.50 cm). Coarse gray-brown stone. Max. L. 34.00, max. W. 23.50, max. Th. 7.40 cm. Trench 116. pl. 108e.

320. Grinding stone. Worn away so that top surface curves deeply from one end to the other (depth curve in center 5.80 cm). Base rounded and follows same curve as upper surface. Green to black stone. Max. L. 34.00, max. W. 14.50, max. Th. 7.30 cm. Trench 116. pl. 108f.

321. Fr. of flat circular (?) stone. On one flat surface numerous irregular pockmarks; on other a small depression near center of fr. (D. 3.70, depth ca 0.50 cm). Very coarse sandy red-brown stone. Max. pres. D. 17.00, Th. 4.70 cm. Trench 116. pl. 107f.

METAL OBJECTS

Three copper objects of LC date were found at Bağbaşı.[8] Two had a rounded working point for use as an awl, and one of these had a chisel edge on the opposite end; the third was a needle with loop head.

[8] Only one (**322**) has been analyzed. Hugh McKerrell subjected it to non-dispersive X-ray fluorescence at the Museum of Anatolian Civilizations in Ankara in 1972. The tool was almost pure copper, with a trace of silver. These objects were included in the study by Louise Alpers Bordaz, *The Metal Artifacts from the Bronze Age Excavations at Karataş-Semayük, Turkey and Their Significance in Anatolia, the Near East, and the Aegean* (Ann Arbor Michigan 1978).

322. Composite tool with awl on one end and chisel edge on the other. Intact, well preserved. Short, heavy square shaft tapers into rounded point at one end and flattens into curved bevelled edge at the other end. L. 5.26, max. W. 0.53, W. chisel end 0.44, D. point 0.13–0.10 cm. Trench 102, in burnt floor fill. B 32. pl. 109a.

323. Long awl with short tang. Tang end broken. Shaft square in section, tapers to rounded point and at opposite end begins to taper. Preserved point shows possible traces of wear. Pres. L. 3.90, max. W. 0.25, W. broken end 0.12, D. point 0.10 cm. Trench 115. B 120. pl. 109b.

324. Needle with looped head. One end of rounded shaft was bent back on itself to form the eye and the edges of this end hammered around the shaft; the other end tapered to a point. Complete but shaft now bent. Shaft: pres. L. 7.10 (original L. ca 7.50), D. 0.16 cm. Head: L. 0.50, W. 0.20 cm. Eye: L. 0.10, W. 0.13 cm. Point: D. 0.05 cm. Trench 105, level II, between wall 1 and partition. B 119. pl. 109c.

BONE AND ANTLER ARTIFACTS

Bone Tools

Three objects of worked bone were recovered. They are examples of what would have been a varied bone assemblage.

325. Point. Fr. broken both ends. Rounded section, polished. Pres. L. 2.70, D. tip 0.125, D. end 0.30 cm. Trench 105, level II, between wall 1 and partition. pl. 62.

326. Polisher on rib (?) bone. Fr. broken at unused end. Irregular curved and twisted bone, polished. Very worn on lower side near tip and around edges of tip. Pres. L. 9.40 cm. Trench 109, E extension. pl. 62.

327. Tube (?). Fr. with exterior and one end polished. Jagged teeth at other end. Pres. L. 6.60, pres. W. 3.30 cm. Trench 116, Level II. pl. 62.

Antler

Among the deer antlers found at Bağbaşı was one that had been fashioned into a hammer.

328. Antler hammer with rounded end, made from the base of a large antler. Concave undercutting at right angles to wide shaft hole. End opposite rounded end slants. Damaged below rounded end; strengthened with PVA. Pres. L. 12.40, pres. H. 7.90, D. perforation 2.80–3.50 cm. Trench 109, SE extension. KA 727. pls. 62 and 109e–f.

SHELL ARTIFACT

One shell from Bağbaşı had been fashioned into a pendant. It is a common Mediterranean type.

329. Bivalve shell. *Donax trunculus.* Distal end worn. Pierced from the outer side and decorated on exterior with red and black painted horizontal lines. L. 2.72 cm. Trench 115. pl. 109d.

Chapter 2 BAĞBAŞI—THE MAIN SETTLEMENT (continued)

FUNCTIONS AND ACTIVITIES

In this section the finds from the main LC settlement at Bağbaşı will be described in terms of their contexts: their relationships to the buildings of the settlement. Because of the incomplete nature of the sample, accurate patterning of the material is not possible, but some insight into the relationships of the various objects and their users can be gained.

FUNCTIONS OF THE POTS

In the examination of the various pot shapes at Bağbaşı, a number of points were taken into consideration, including the position in which the pot was found, its overall shape, handles, capacity and stability, whether it is burnished or shows evidence of secondary firing. The results are given below. In every case they are far from conclusive, but they give some indication of the sorts of uses to which the various pots may have been put. It is possible that the categories were not rigid, and that pots of the same shape had different functions and pots of different shapes had the same function.

Bowls

At Bağbaşı few of the bowls were found *in situ* on floors. The miniature bowl (**225**) was found on the upper (level I) floor of trench 116, and a deep bowl (**25**) was found on the lower floor (level III) of the same trench. The latter, however, is a large unburnished pot, and it may have had a function closer to that of the open pots.

Fragments of a number of burnished flaring bowls came from the pit in the lower floor of 116 (**3, 4, 10, 15, 17**). None of the typical flaring bowls was found on the preserved areas of floor, and no whole examples of the shape were found. In view of the proportion of burnished bowls in the assemblage, this is surprising and may indicate that the bowls, unlike the jugs, jars and open pots, were not in the buildings when they were abandoned. However, it is unlikely that broken examples would have been placed in the pit unless they sometimes were used inside the building. At Beycesultan bowls were found in the houses near the hearths. In level XXXIa a bowl and a jug were found in a pit behind the hearth, and in level XXV a flaring bowl and two juglets were amongst the pottery found *in situ* around the hearth.[1] Thus not only were the bowls found near hearths, they were found in association with jugs.

Burnishing, a surface treatment that makes pots more attractive and less porous, was used only

[1] *Beycesultan* I 23, 25 and fig. 6.

on bowls and jugs at Bağbaşı.[2] It is, therefore, possible that they were used as containers for a liquid or porridge-like substance that would have soaked into the untreated fabric. The large diameters of the bowls makes their use as drinking vessels unlikely.

A few bowl sherds have two holes pierced close together and just below the rim. If a corresponding pair is hypothesized on the opposite side, they could have been used to suspend the pots. However, the holes do occur only in the smaller bowls, and it is possible that these small bowls were used as lids and that the holes facilitated their attachment to the handles of jugs or jars.

Basins

This category contains pots of various sizes and with different surface finishes, and they may not all have had the same function. The small burnished examples may have been close to the burnished bowls in function, while the larger examples have shapes close to those of the pans, although the fabric is less thoroughly fired and the diameter smaller. No whole examples of the shape were found.

Open Pots

Several of the open pots were found *in situ.* In trench 105 a group of four open pots was found in unit A. It included a large example (**82**) sunk into the floor, and the rectilinear pot (**87**). The other two (**63** and **71**) completed a quartet of graduated sizes. In trench 116 a large open pot (**76**) was found sunk into a pit in the level I floor, and on the level III floor two open pots (**67** and **68**) lay south of the hearth, and a third (**65**) apparently stood beside the wall.

The most obvious use to which these pots could have been put was storage. Despite their deep shape, the customary wide flat bases made them stable. Neither the lugs nor the loop handles would have been strong enough to use for lifting the larger pots, but they could have served to help tip or steady them. The lug handles were, surprisingly, often applied so that they sloped up, but the impressions on some would have helped to provide a firm grip. Pottery lids for these vessels were not found, and the extreme unevenness of the rims would have made such covers impractical. It would also rule out the efficient use of wooden covers, but cloth or other soft coverings may have been tied on.

The extreme porosity of the fabric would have restricted the usefulness of these pots and made them unsuitable for most liquid storage. They would, however, have served adequately for storing grain or other solids. Their somewhat cumbrous open shape may have been derived from the open bins used for storage at other LC sites.[3] This is reinforced by the fact that some of the larger examples were sunk into the floor.

Three open pots from the level III floor of 116 (**65, 67** and **68**) had a single hole pierced one-third of the way up one side. In **67** and **68** the holes were made before firing; in **65** it was pierced from the outside after firing. These holes were not mending holes. They may have been designed to allow some air to reach the contents in the bottom of the jar but, in that case, would have been more effectively placed at an even lower position in the wall. If some of the pots were

[2] Burnishing has a number of effects on a pot. It deepens and intensifies the color, makes the surface glossy, and usually increases the attractiveness of the vessel. It also reduces the porosity of the pot fabric, but only to a small degree (Christine Eslick, The Early Pottery from Mersin (unpublished MA thesis, University of Sydney 1972) vol. 2, pp 57–75).

[3] E.g. at Beycesultan in levels XXXI and XXVIII (*Beycesultan* I figs. 5 and 6).

used for liquid storage, the holes could have served as "taps" to drain the liquid, perhaps after allowing inclusions to settle. Similar holes are found in some EB jars, but they are never common.[4]

Jugs

Three jugs were found *in situ* in trench 105, and one in trench 115. The three in 105 (**88, 91** and **92**) were found scattered over the floor close to the hearth in unit A. In 115 the jug (**94**) was found on the floor.[5]

The jugs with their restricted neck, everted rim and one handle from the rim to the shoulder are well suited to pouring either liquids or solids such as grain. The burnished surface increases their suitability for use with liquids. Flat bases are usual, but a number of the pots have unstable bases, notably the juglet (**95**) and the squat jug (**91**). They were thus better adapted for transporting or transferring, rather than for storing.

Jars

There is no indication of the function of the smallest jars (**112** and **113**), but there are some hints as to the use of the medium sized jars. In trench 105 one (**114**) was found near the hearth. It is very irregular in shape, has an everted neck and two pierced lug handles on the shoulder, and the lower part shows evidence of secondary firing. The shape is well suited to cooking: it is not so open that it would boil dry too quickly, and yet it has a wide enough neck to allow escape of the steam and stirring of the contents.[6] If its identification as a cooking pot is correct, and its findplace and the evidence of secondary burning makes this likely, some of the other jars could also have been used in this way. **115** and **196** bear evidence of secondary burning on the lower body, and **116** has an extremely gritty fabric which would allow it to be constantly reheated.

Of the other jars, **123** with its elongated body and small neck poses a problem. The base is not preserved, but the long body must have made it unstable, and it is unlikely that it could have stood without support. It was found lying on the level I floor of trench 116. It does not seem to be a cooking pot and was probably used for storage.

Many of the necked jars must have been used for storage, and the larger ones, for example **135**, would have been difficult to move. The small necks would have made them more suitable than the open jars for liquid storage, but the fabric was not noticeably less porous.

Pans

No pans were found *in situ* on the floors at Bağbaşı, nor were they associated with the hearths, although fragments were found in the pits in the level I and III floors of trench 116 and in the fill of most trenches. The thoroughly fired fabric suggests that they would have been used close to a fire, and as the large flat bases would have required a flat surface to stand on, the pans were probably used on the flat mud hearths.[7]

[4] E.g. at Karataş (Machteld J. Mellink, "Excavations at Karataş-Semayük in Lycia, 1965," *AJA* 70 (1966) 245 and note 2 for examples at Tarsus and Troy. Similar holes were found in the storage bins at Çatal Hüyük, just above floor level—James Mellaart, *Çatal Hüyük. A Neolithic Town in Anatolia* (London 1967) 62–63—but not at Beycesultan or Hacılar.

[5] At Beycesultan jugs were found in similar situations—in level XXXIa a jug filled with lentils was found in a hole behind the hearth, and in XXV two juglets were found near the hearth. *Beycesultan* I 23 and 25, fig. 6.

[6] Ralph Linton, "North American Cooking Pots," *American Antiquity* 9 (1944) 370. Also compare the Greek chytra used for heating water or making soup—Brian A. Sparkes and Lucy Talcott, *The Athenian Agora XII. Black and Plain Pottery of the 6th, 5th and 4th centuries B.C.* (Princeton 1970) 224.

[7] At Beycesultan in level XIIIc a pan was found *in situ* in an oven (*Beycesultan* I 90). Pans at that site occurred in great numbers from

The variety of pan shapes suggests that they were used for a number of different, if related, functions. The flat pans could not have been used for anything that would spill, but would be suitable for cooking some form of bread or dough. The pans with sides could have held contents more likely to roll or spill, and been used to roast beans or parch grain.

FREQUENCIES OF POTTERY SHAPES

Much of the Bağbaşı material is in sherd form, and in considering the frequencies of the various shapes shown on Chart 1, allowance must be made for the differing numbers of sherds into which each pot would have broken. For example, a bowl rim sherd usually forms one-quarter to one-eighth of the total rim diameter; a jar or jug neck sherd about one-quarter and an open pot rim sherd about one-tenth.

The most common shape is quite clearly the open pot with three hundred twenty-five pots and rim sherds, including ten whole or almost whole pots. There were only one hundred three rim sherds of bowls in the sample, and one hundred ten rim sherds from necked jars and jugs. Trench 116, the control trench, produced similar proportions—two hundred fourteen open pots and rim sherds including five considerable parts of pots, forty-five bowl rim sherds and thirty-two neck sherds.

The pots found *in situ* in the various houses are in similar proportions. Although the figures are likely to be affected by a greater tendency to abandon large unportable pots, the emphasis on open jars is again apparent. The available information can be summarized as:

House	*105*	*115*	*116 level III*	*116 level I*
cooking pot	1	—	—	—
open jar	5	1	3	1
closed jar	2	1	—	2
small jar	—	1	—	—
jug	3	1	—	—
bowl	—	—	1	1
total	11	4	4	4

In trench 105, at least, the distribution of the finds suggests that the house was abandoned very hurriedly, and yet only eleven pots were left *in situ.* All the houses contained fewer pots than might have been expected, and the absence of bowls, usually the most numerous category, is especially noteworthy;[8] the possibility of the extensive use of perishable vessels cannot be excluded. The small number of cooking pots is also worthy of mention.

The preponderance of open pots suggests that the potters at Bağbaşı were oriented toward the production of storage vessels. This surely would have affected the attitude of the potter, if the pots were to be primarily placed in dark corners, and could be one reason for the lack of decoration on the pottery. It also explains the lack of other storage arrangements, such as bins.

level XXXI on, and many of the published LC ones were from level XXII, where an oven was found (*Beycesultan* I 26 and fig. P13: 13–17).

[8] E.g. *Hacılar* I 132 ff.

FUNCTIONS OF THE OTHER ARTIFACTS

The functions of the artifacts other than pottery cannot always be determined with any precision, although there are indications of the ways in which some of them were used.

One or two spit supports were found in the fill of each of the Bağbaşı houses, and one was found *in situ* on the floor of the house in trench 115. With their thoroughly fired fabric, a hearth-associated function seems probable, although none was found on a hearth. The piercings in some were designed to hold a diagonal rod, perhaps for spitting meat, as the angle is too low for suspending pots. The various "feet" and stand fragments also appear, from their well-baked fabric, to have been used on hearths, possibly as supports for cooking pots.

Prominent among the minor artifacts were loomweights and clay whorls. The loomweights were all found in the vicinity of wall 1 in trench 105; they attest to the use of a warp-weighted loom in that area. The three examples were in two sizes, a customary arrangement for the warp-weighted loom.[9] Of the clay whorls, some were probably spindle whorls and some beads. They cannot be divided into distinct classes, but the large, heavy and roughly made **259–262** would have been suitable as spindle whorls. **270–272**, which are small and light with decorated surface or a small hole suitable only for thread or a very fine shaft, could have had a more decorative function. They may have been used on necklaces or attached to metal pins.[10] The shell, too, was used as a bead or pendant.

273 has been called a stamp seal, for although impressions from such objects have not been found at Bağbaşı or other LC sites, they do occur on EB pots.[11] The slightly convex face of the Bağbaşı example would be suitable for use on a yielding material such as clay. "Stamp seals" are also known from the Neolithic and EC periods, but impressions were not preserved. It has been suggested that they may have been used for patterning skin or fabric.[12] **274** was clearly designed to stand on its flat, undecorated face. Its purpose is still unclear.

Most common in the chipped stone assemblage were blade fragments with sickle sheen on one or both edges. They would have been set into a handle of wood or antler to form a sickle, and those with sheen on both edges had presumably been reversed at some stage.[13] Also in the stone assemblage were blades with sharp, thin edges that could have served as knives, and a few thick pieces with edges heavily mashed from scraping skins. None of the pieces found would have been suitable for use as a point on arrow or spear. Nor were there any awls, a function apparently performed with metal tools.

Stone was also used for the axe and the whetstone. Two types of grinding stone were found. The saddle querns were probably used for grain; the mortars would have been suitable for crushing small amounts of foods.

[9] Loomweights in three sizes were found *in situ* in room 206, level IIg at Troy (Carl W. Blegen et al., *Troy* I:1 350, 353). In EB levels at Tarsus three large groups of loomweights were found, two in living rooms and one in a storage room (Hetty Goldman, *Excavations at Gözlü Kule, Tarsus* II (Princeton 1956) 15, 17, 28; at Mersin a loom emplacement was found in level XIIB (John Garstang, *Prehistoric Mersin* (Oxford, 1953) 173). For their use see e.g. R.J. Forbes, *Studies in Ancient Technology* IV (Leiden 1964) 203–205.

[10] Machteld J. Mellink, *AJA* 73 (1969) 323 and pl. 74:fig. 23 for examples from the EB cemetery at Karataş.

[11] E.g. at Karataş-Semayük—Machteld J. Mellink, "Excavations at Karataş-Semayük in Lycia, 1963," *AJA* 68 (1964) 275 and pl. 82: fig. 26.

[12] *Hacılar* I 164.

[13] See *Hacılar* II pl. CXX:a–d.

Metal seems to have been used primarily for tools for piercing—awls and needles. As copper is a relatively soft metal, they were probably used on materials such as textiles and bone.[14] The few fragmentary bone implements found allow little interpretation of their function, although the wear on **326** suggests it could have served as a polisher for dressing skins.[15]

ACTIVITIES

The LC settlement at Bağbaşı consisted of a number of free-standing houses, concentrated near the top of the rise. There was no standard orientation, but if all or most of the buildings excavated were contemporary, the occupation must have been quite dense.

There is little evidence for areas of specialist activity—such as pot making or flint knapping—within the settlement; these tasks must have taken place outside the area of the settlement, or more probably were normal household chores. Each building seems to have housed a range of domestic activities.[16]

The house in trench 115 is most completely defined. It consisted of a single rectangular room with a laid mud floor. The hearth was not discovered, but the spit support found in one corner suggests that it did contain a hearth. In both this house and the houses in trenches 105 and levels I and III of 116, the most prominent finds were large jars suitable for storage.

Food preparation also seems to have taken place within the houses. The only hearths discovered were the flat mud hearths inside the houses. The pans are suitably shaped for use with them, and the cooking pots also have flat bases. Grinding stones were found in several trenches. One lay on the level I floor in trench 116, and one on the floor of the house in trench 110.[17]

The building in trench 105 differs from the others in a number of respects. Although unit A contained a hearth, cooking pot and storage pots, it also contained some finds not paralleled in any of the other buildings. Most noteworthy were the loomweights and seven of the fourteen clay whorls found at the site. The loomweights, one spindle whorl (**260**) and one bead (**271**) were all discovered in the area around walls 1 and 2. Two other whorls (**264** and **267**) came from the northern part of the trench. Trench 105 also yielded an unusually large number of jugs, and an equally unusual scarcity of stone tools (see Charts 1 and 5).

If units B and C also belonged to this house, it would have been the largest on the site. It was the most solidly built, and contained two unique features—the partition between units B and C, and the large niche in the west wall of unit A. The greater effort and attention put into this building, and the additional activities that seem to have taken place there, distinguish it from the other buildings at the site. However, like the other buildings, it was essentially domestic in character.

Pits were associated with two of the houses in trench 116. One was found to the west of the level I house, and another was apparently inside the level III house. They were both wide and shallow, and it is unlikely that they were designed for storage. When found they had been filled with broken pottery, but they may originally have been dug to obtain mud for building. A large rubbish

[14] Keith Branigan, *Aegean Metalwork of the Early and Middle Bronze Age* (Oxford 1974) 135.

[15] S.A. Semenov, *Prehistoric Technology* (Bradford-on-Avon 1964) fig. 93.

[16] See Chapter 1 pp. 2–5 for a full description of the finds from each trench.

[17] These grinding stones could not be identified with any of the preserved examples, though that from trench 116 was presumably **319** or **320**.

dump extended down the slope for 11.00 m from the southeast wall of the house in trench 110. It contained ash, broken pottery and other domestic objects.

No burials were found at Bağbaşı, and burial outside the settlement was clearly the rule.[18]

SUBSISTENCE

The situation of Bağbaşı conforms to the pattern of LC settlement in the Elmalı Plain. Unlike the LN/EC sites which are in the flat plain, the LC sites are situated on high ground on the 1150–1200 m contour level.[19] The LC pottery from each site is homogeneous and shows no sign of development, so that all seem to have been occupied for only a short time. On the basis of the evidence from Bağbaşı, it may be estimated that each settlement lasted only one or two generations. This factor may be responsible for the large number of sites known for this period—eleven compared with four LN/EC sites. No evidence of LC habitation has been found at any of the large mounds in the plain, such as Semayük or Hacımusalar, although the possibility that it existed cannot be excluded. Most LC settlements known from other areas of western Anatolia have long sequences at the base of large mounds.[20]

The economic basis of the settlement at Bağbaşı is only partly known. Plant remains were not recoverable, although it is probable that cultivation of grains and vegetables was an important part of the economy. The flint blades with sickle sheen probably attest to the harvesting of grains,[21] the grinding stones to their preparation, and the deep cooking pots would have been most suited to the boiling of soups or porridges.

Animal bones were recovered, but those from the LC settlement could not be separated from those of the later occupations on the site. The presence of equid bones clearly indicates some later contamination of the collection, although most of the bones were probably from the LC occupation. The following summary, based on the preliminary study of Hesse and Perkins,[22] should, therefore, be treated with caution.

The bones from Bağbaşı included domesticated cattle, sheep/goats, pigs and a medium-sized dog. The cattle represented 43–47 percent of the sample, the sheep/goats 27–33 percent and the pigs 24–26 percent. The cattle tended to be slaughtered at a later stage than the other animals (85.7 percent apparently passed the age of 3½–4 years), and may have been kept for milk or traction rather than meat. They would have dominated the animal herds. Seven antlers of red deer show that hunting had a place in the economy at Bağbaşı, although it was not apparently an

[18] This is the usual practice in the LC period in western Anatolia. The cemetery at Kusura begins in this period; at Beycesultan only infant burials were found within the settlement—J.R. Stewart, "Excavations at Kusura near Afyon Karahisar. The Cemetery" *Archaeologia* 86 (1937) 57–58 and 63–64 and *Beycesultan* I 23, 26. The burials at Kumtepe were not necessarily associated with contemporary buildings—Jerome W. Sperling, "Kumtepe in the Troad: Trial Excavation, 1934," *Hesperia* 45 (1976) 311 and 326.

[19] See Chapter 3 and pl. 2.

[20] *Beycesultan* I 17. Also see D.H. French, "Late Chalcolithic Pottery in North-west Turkey and the Aegean," *AnatSt* 11 (1961) 99; "Prehistoric Sites in Northwest Anatolia I. The Iznik Area," *AnatSt* 17 (1967) 53 (an exception is Pazaryeri I, a site on a ridge); and James Mellaart, "Early Cultures of the South Anatolian Plateau, II," *AnatSt* 13 (1963) 199–200, 203, fig. 1.

[21] M.-C. Cauvin, "Les faucilles préhistoriques du proche-orient: données morphologiques et fonctionelles," *Paléorient* 9 (1983) 63–79 points out that the sheen can also result from cutting reeds and grasses used for building, baskets or fuel.

[22] Brian Hesse and Dexter Perkins, Jr., "Faunal Remains from Karataş-Semayük in Southwest Anatolia. An Interim Report," *JFA* 1 (1974) 149–60.

Distribution of Specimens[24]			
Ovis	6	*Sus*	24
Capra	2	*Cervus*	7
Ovis/Capra	49	*Equus*	4
Bos	92	*Canis*	5

important one. No other deer bones were found, and the antlers were probably brought to the site to be used as tools.[23]

Bağbaşı appears to have been an essentially self-sufficient village, but some objects and materials with especially desirable characteristics were introduced from outside the Elmalı Plain.[25] Most obvious were the obsidian blade (**277**), the greenstone axe (**313**), the objects of copper (**322–324**) and the pierced and painted shell (**329**). The shell is from the Mediterranean, and the worn condition of the distal end suggests that it was collected from the beach for ornament, not as food.[26] It is, therefore, not surprising that it was the only example found. The other obvious imports were desirable for their special qualities for particular tools. The sharpness of the obsidian and the hardness of the greenstone—and the small size of the axe suggests that it was valued and had been in use for some time—had obvious advantages that had long been recognized. New in this period is the widespread use of copper, which must have considerably altered the local economy, whether it was imported as raw material or as finished objects. Finally, the hemispherical bowl (**27**) may have been imported. The temper used in this pot is not found in any other pot so far known from the plain, and the shape is also unique.[27]

[23] See Chapter 1, p.41.

[24] From Brian Hesse and Dexter Perkins, Jr., *JFA* 1 (1974) 150, Table 1.

[25] These are, of course, only those objects that have survived in the archaeological record. Exchanges of perishable goods were probably considerable. See George Dalton, in *Exchange Systems in Prehistory,* eds. Timothy K. Earle and Jonathon E. Ericson (New York 1977) 204.

[26] Pers. comm. from David S. Reese (13 January 1981).

[27] See Appendix 2 for analysis of the temper.

Chapter 3 OTHER MATERIAL FROM THE ELMALI PLAIN

LOWER BAĞBAŞI

The pottery described in this chapter was found during the excavations at Bağbaşı, but it is distinguished from the main LC assemblage by its fabric, shapes and the methods with which it was made. It came primarily from the lower level III of trench 116, with a few pieces from trench 105. It was not found in any of the other trenches, or in the upper levels of trench 116. Nor was it directly associated with the lower floor of trench 116. Although the telescoped and disturbed nature of the deposits made precise stratigraphic correlations difficult, the evidence suggests that this pottery was not associated with the main Bağbaşı settlement. It probably belonged to an earlier occupation on the highest part of the site, and the very fragmentary nature of the pottery supports this view. No other finds were definitely associated with it, but some of the chipped stone discussed in Chapter 1 may have come from the earlier period.

FABRIC

The fabric is dense and grit tempered with only a little fiber inclusion. The pots were poorly fired and have black cores. The surface color varies from orange to black, but is usually light brown, and the surface is lightly burnished to give a smooth compact surface without achieving a high lustre. The pots were coil-built around flat, thick bases. Handles were attached flat to the pot with both ends of the handle and the pot deeply scored, as shown on **10.** There was a continuous range from fine to coarse fabrics with the bowls and necked jars tending to be at the finer end of the range, and the hole-mouth pots at the coarser.

15 and **16** are possibly from one pot. It was made in the same tradition as the rest of the pottery assigned to this phase and the shape of the handle also connects it to this material. It has been refired, at least in part; this explains the hardness and the orange color of the fabric. It may have had a cream slip.

SHAPES

The range of shapes is limited. There are jars with high and low vertical necks, hole-mouth pots and bowls with curved sides. Bases are flat, heavy and of small diameter. They are thickened toward the center. With the exception of the ledge-lug, the handles were strap handles, two of which had a pinched up ridge at the top. They were probably all placed vertically on the pots. The illustrated handles are all from large closed pots, blackened on the interior.

DECORATION

This pottery was normally undecorated, but a knob occurred on one body sherd, **12,** and the refired pot, **15–16,** had red painted designs.

CATALOGUE

1. Jar with high neck. Rim frr. Burnished orange exterior (one fr. has black mottling that occurred after breaking); pale brown to orange interior. Trench 116, level III. pl. 63.

2. Jar with short neck. Rim and body frr. Burnished light brown exterior; light brown interior. Trench 116, level III. pl. 63.

3. Lower neck and shoulder of jar. Fr. Burnished orange exterior; brown interior. Trench 116, level III. pl. 63.

3. Bowl with curved sides. Rim and body frr. with stump of loop handle. Burnished orange-brown exterior with dark mottling; light brown interior. Trench 116, level III. pl. 63.

5. Bowl with curved sides. Rim fr. Burnished light brown exterior; orange interior. Trench 116, level III. pl. 63.

6. Hole-mouth pot with perforation below rim. Rim fr. Brown exterior; orange interior. Trench 116, level III. pl. 63.

7. Hole-mouth pot. Rim fr. Gray exterior and interior. Trench 116, level III. pl. 63.

8. Body fr. with ledge handle. Burnished light brown exterior; black interior. Trench 116, level III. pl. 63.

9. Body fr. (D. top ca 20 cm) with vertical strap handle which has pinched up ridge at top. Burnished (?) black exterior with light brown patch to one side of handle; black interior. Trench 116, level III. pl. 64.

10. Body frr. and joining handle stump, showing method of attachment by scoring both areas. Coarse brown exterior; black interior. Trench 116, level III. pl. 110a.

11. Body fr. with vertical strap handle. Burnished gray-black exterior with orange handle; black interior. Trench 116, level III. pl. 64.

12. Body fr. with knob. Brown exterior; black interior. Trench 116, level III. pl. 110b.

13. Rounded base fr. with clay from base pushed out toward edge. D. unknown. Brown exterior; orange interior. Trench 116, level III. pl. 64.

14. Rounded base fr. D. ca 16 cm. Exterior and interior orange with dark mottling. Trench 105. pl. 64.

15. Body fr. with vertical strap handle which has slight pinched up ridge at top. Orange throughout. Area around handle and handle covered with thin red-orange paint and burnished. Trench 116, level III. pl. 64.

16. Body frr., possibly from same pot as last, including one with handle stump. Some are orange throughout, others from lower wall have black core and greenish-black mottled exterior. Exterior of some shows possible traces of cream slip. Decorated with red paint and burnished. Diagonal, irregular but roughly parallel lines below solid painted areas. Trench 116, level III. pls. 65 and 110c (best frr.).

BOZTEPE

The site is on a projecting rise, 1170 meters above sea level, known as Çeçtepe. The eastern end is cut by the Korkuteli-Elmalı road. It is 1.5 kilometers south of Karaburun, about 8 kilometers northeast of Elmalı, and is just to the north of Bağbaşı. The rise runs parallel to the main Karaburun ridge, where the nearest stream is to be found (pl. 66a).

Sherds were picked up in this area in 1967, and in 1972 a fifth century B.C. tumulus on the highest point of the ridge was excavated.[1] In the course of this investigation, evidence of LC occupation came to light. This consisted of a thin habitation stratum, about 0.10 m deep, found in pockets of the bedrock. Pottery and small lumps of burnt mud walling had also been scraped up

[1] Machteld J. Mellink, "Excavations at Karataş-Semayük in Lycia, 1972," *AJA* 77 (1973) 296.

and incorporated in the tumulus fill. Surface investigation in 1976 and 1977 revealed sherds of LC type extending from the tumulus to the eastern side of the road and back twice as far to the west. However, they were concentrated near the end of the rise, in the area of the tumulus.

FABRIC

In fabric the pottery is similar to that of the main Bağbaşı assemblage. It is handmade with fiber temper, but is slightly more dense and gritty than the Bağbaşı ware. It is poorly fired and has black cores. Most of the bowl fragments are burnished (fifteen of the seventeen examples), but the jars were not. Less than ten percent of the sherds were burnished.

SHAPES

The bowl shapes fall into two categories. The first, which includes **1–4,** has a broad everted rim. The second is that represented by **5–9;** it has a shallow curved body and an internally thickened rim. These are the rolled rim bowls.

The other sherds are mostly from necked vessels. Large jars predominate, although four small burnished necks (**17–18**) are probably from jugs. The same range of lug shapes as occurs at Bağbaşı is found here. This is especially noteworthy as open pots do not seem to have been popular, and the lugs may have been used on large necked jars. They are too large to have been used on bowls and are unburnished. The handles are all applied with plug attachments, but there were no disk bases at Boztepe.

The two pan fragments, **21** and the example shown on pl. 110d–e, are from flat pans with numerous perforations in the base. The perforations have all, with the exception of those around the edge, been blocked by smoothing the inside surface.

DECORATION

The only decoration found was a row of applied knobs on **20.**

CATALOGUE

1. Bowl with wide, flat everted rim. Rim fr. Gray throughout and originally burnished, at least on interior. 1967, surface. pl. 67.

2. Bowl with flat everted rim. Rim fr. Burnished black exterior with brown coloring at edge of rim; burnished black interior. 1972. pl. 67.

3. Bowl with everted rim. Rim fr. Burnished black exterior with light brown rim; burnished gray interior. 1972. pl. 67.

4. Bowl with flaring everted rim. Rim fr. Brown and black mottled exterior with orange at rim edge; gray and brown interior. 1972. pl. 67.

5. Bowl with rolled rim. Rim fr. Burnished black and brown exterior with orange patch; burnished black interior. 1972. pl. 67.

6. Bowl with rolled rim. Rim fr. Burnished brown exterior with light brown at top and on rim edge; burnished black interior. 1972. pl. 67.

7. Bowl with rolled rim and curved body. Rim and wall fr. Burnished light brown exterior with black mottling especially on rim; burnished gray-brown interior. 1972. pl. 67.

8. Bowl with rolled rim. Rim fr. Burnished gray exterior with rim light brown and black mottled; burnished gray interior. 1972. pl. 67.

9. Bowl with rolled rim. Rim fr. Burnished black exterior; burnished gray interior. 1972. pl. 67.

10. Bowl with folded over rim. Rim fr. Orange and brown mottled exterior; orange interior. Walls of irregular thickness. 1976, surface. pl. 67.

11. Miniature hemispherical bowl. Approx. ⅓ preserved. Burnished brown exterior and interior with orange on upper walls. 1972. pl. 67.

12. Pot with short vertical neck. Rim fr. Light brown to orange exterior; orange interior. 1972. pl. 68.

13. Large jar with vertical neck. Rim fr. Light brown and gray mottled exterior; black interior. 1972. pl. 68.

14. Pot with everted neck and flat rim. Rim fr. Orange exterior; orange interior. 1972. pl. 68.

15. Pot with curving neck. Rim fr. Brown exterior; black interior with brown at rim. 1972. pl. 68.

16. Pot with curving neck and everted rim. Rim fr. Rim is folded over in irregular fashion. Orange exterior; orange interior. 1972. pl. 68.

17. Pot with curving neck. Rim fr. Burnished gray-brown exterior; burnished black interior. 1972. pl. 68.

18. Jug with curving neck. Rim fr. Approx. ⅓ of neck diameter preserved. Burnished brown and black mottled exterior; light brown and black interior. 1972. pl. 68.

19. Open jar. Rim fr. Burnished orange and brown mottled exterior; orange and black interior. 1972. pl. 68.

20. Body fr. with a row of three and possibly four bosses. Black exterior; gray interior. 1972. pl. 68.

21. Flat pan with perforated base. Rim fr. with a row of four holes below the rim. A number of small perforations elsewhere on the sherd were blocked by the burnishing of the upper surface. All were originally made from the upper surface. Burnished gray, brown and orange upper surface; orange lower surface. 1972. pl. 68.

22. Lug handle, upturned, with plug attachment. Orange and brown exterior. 1972. pl. 69.

23. Lug handle, slightly upturned. Orange, brown and gray mottled exterior. 1972. pl. 69.

24. Lug handle. Orange and brown mottled exterior. 1972. pl. 69.

25. Lug handle. Orange exterior. 1967, surface. pl. 69.

26. Small pot. Body fr. Burnished black exterior; burnished black interior. 1972. pl. 69.

KARABURUN

The site is on the end of a high ridge, 1220 meters above sea level, projecting into the plain to the west of the Korkuteli-Elmalı road, about 10 kilometers northeast of Elmalı (pl. 66a). In the early fifth century B.C. tumulus tombs were built on the ridge. The LC pottery was found in the course of their excavation. Pockets of early habitation were found on bedrock beneath tumulus I, and beneath tumulus II in the area in front of the tomb, although the deposit was very eroded and disturbed.[2] The best deposit was beneath the eastern part of tumulus I where bedrock sloped away. A very soft, dark soil, mixed with pockets of yellow pebbles and soft yellow soil, contained quantities of pottery. At the base of this deposit fragments of the large jar, **9,** were crushed *in situ,* and to the north of it was a pit filled with dark soil, some pebbles and two sherds. The pit was lined with medium-sized stones on its north and west sides, and a few large pebbles were found on its bottom. Fragments of the same large jar were also found throughout the tumulus fill. Most of the pottery came from the fill of the two tumuli, but it was also found on the surface all over the area to the south of tumulus II.

FABRIC

This pottery is made in the same tradition as that from Bağbaşı, but it is denser and more closely resembles that from Boztepe. It is handmade, poorly fired with black cores almost universal, and the surface color varies from dirty cream to orange with considerable black mottling. Less than five percent of the sherds were burnished and they were all from bowls, except for one sherd from the neck of a small jug with everted rim.

[2] Machteld J. Mellink, "Excavations at Karataş-Semayük in Lycia, 1970," *AJA* 75 (1971) 250–55 and "Excavations at Karataş-Semayük in Lycia, 1974," *AJA* 79 (1975) 355 and especially "Excavations at Karataş-Semayük in Lycia, 1971," *AJA* 76 (1972) 262 for contour map and section.

SHAPES

The bowls at Karaburun are of two types—shallow bowls with flat, everted rim (**1–2**) and flaring bowls with rounded rim (**3–6**). Three of the latter were left unburnished, and all the examples of this second category were very large in diameter (ca 34, 38, 40, 40 and ca 46 cm).

The jars show more variety than do those from Boztepe. Vertical necks, usually short, are most common (**9–13**), but inverted necks (**14**), everted necks (**15–16**), and necks with everted rim (**17–18**) are also found. The occurrence of small flaring necks such as **19–20** and open pots (albeit with restricted mouths) such as **21** and **22** connect this pottery to that of Bağbaşı. Lug handles are the most common handle form, although horizontal tubular handles are also characteristic of this site. Both plug and flat application of handles were used here. There were no disk bases.

26 is a pan with a row of perforations below the rim, and there is a fragment of a pierced pan with burnished surface, similar to Boztepe **20.**

DECORATION

Only two sherds were decorated. The bowl rim, **1,** bears a row of applied bosses, and a body sherd, **27,** has an applied moulding.

CATALOGUE

1. Bowl with flat everted rim. Rim fr. with a row of five bosses on the rim. Light brown exterior; interior and rim burnished brown-black. Karaburun I, tumulus fill, 1970. pl. 70.

2. Bowl with flat everted rim. Rim fr. Black exterior; black interior, probably originally burnished. Karaburun I, trench 4 east of tumulus, 1974. pl. 70.

3. Flaring bowl with rounded rim. Rim fr. Brown exterior; brown and black mottled interior, probably unburnished. Karaburun I, tumulus fill, 1970. pl. 70.

4. Flaring bowl with rounded rim. Rim fr. Brown and black mottled exterior; burnished light brown interior with black mottling. Large air bubble in core. Karaburun I, tumulus fill, 1970. pl. 70.

5. Flaring bowl with rounded rim. Rim fr. Light brown exterior; light brown interior. Karaburun I, tumulus fill, 1970. pl. 70.

6. Flaring bowl with slightly everted rim. Rim fr. Burnished brown and black mottled exterior; interior black with carbon deposit. Karaburun I, cleaning below eastern part of tumulus, 1974. pl. 70.

7. Bowl with flat rim and shallow curved sides. Rim fr. Light brown and black mottled exterior; black interior. Karaburun II, area east of base, 1975. pl. 70.

8. Bowl with flat rim thickened on interior and curved sides. Rim fr. Red slipped and burnished exterior; red slipped and burnished interior with black mottling. Karaburun, 1974. pl. 70.

9. Jar with vertical neck. Frr. of rim, shoulder and body. No evidence of handles. Rim and shoulder creamy brown exterior and interior; lower body orange; black mottling on all surface. Karaburun I, deposit beneath eastern part of tumulus and throughout tumulus fill, 1970 and 1974. pl. 71 and pl. 110f show the neck junction.

10. Rim fr. of short vertical neck. Orange exterior; orange and brown mottled interior. Karaburun I, tumulus fill, 1970. pl. 70.

11. Rim fr. of short vertical neck. Light brown, orange and black mottled exterior; orange interior. Karaburun II, tumulus fill, 1976. pl. 70.

12. Rim fr. of short vertical neck. Orange throughout. Karaburun II, tumulus fill, 1976. pl. 70.

13. Rim fr. of short vertical neck. Brown and orange mottled exterior; brown and orange mottled interior. Karaburun I, cleaning, 1974. pl. 70.

14. Rim fr. of inverted neck. Orange exterior with gray and black mottling; black mottled interior. Karaburun II, tumulus fill, 1976. pl. 70.

15. Rim fr. of everted neck. Orange exterior with light brown and gray mottling; orange interior. Karaburun II, tumulus fill, 1976. pl. 70.

16. Rim fr. of everted neck. Orange exterior and interior with black mottling on rim. Karaburun surface, 1977. pl. 72.

17. Rim fr. of neck with everted rim. Light brown exterior; light brown interior. Karaburun I, tumulus fill, 1970. pl. 72.

18. Rim fr. of neck with everted rim. Brown-black exterior; brown interior. Rather coarse fabric. Karaburun II, tumulus fill, 1976. pl. 72.

19. Rim fr. of small flaring neck. Light brown exterior; light brown and black mottled interior. Karaburun II, tumulus fill, 1976. pl. 72.

20. Rim fr. of small flaring neck. Pale brown exterior and interior. Karaburun I, cleaning, 1974. pl. 72.

21. Open jar with slightly constricted vertical neck and rounded base. Frr. including one that shows thickening at the edge for beginning of a handle or lug. Both exterior and interior orange at top and brown-black at bottom. Coarse and lower body hard fired. Karaburun II, area in front of tomb, 1976. pl. 72.

22. Open jar with slightly constricted vertical neck. Rim and upper body frr. Well-smoothed orange exterior with small black patches; orange interior. Karaburun II, area in front of tomb, 1976. pl. 72.

23. Open jar with slightly constricted vertical neck. Rim fr. with loop handle from rim. Brown exterior with dark mottling on handle; brown interior with dark mottling. Karaburun I, tumulus fill, 1970. pl. 73.

24. Horizontal tubular handle. Orange exterior. Karaburun I, tumulus fill, 1970. pl. 73.

25. Lug handle, angular and with plug attachment. Orange exterior. Karaburun II, tumulus fill, 1976. pl. 73.

26. Flat pan. Rim fr. with row of perforations below rim. Brown exterior; brown interior; red-orange core. Very gritty fabric. Karaburun I, tumulus fill, 1970. pl. 73.

27. Body fr. with applied moulding of triangular section. Light brown exterior; black interior. Karaburun I, cleaning under eastern part of tumulus, 1974. pl. 111a.

28. Body fr. with slightly carinated shape. Lightly burnished orange and light brown mottled exterior; red interior. D. carination ca 15.00 cm. Karaburun II, tumulus fill, 1976. pl. 73.

29. Neck and shoulder fr. of small pot. Brown and black mottled exterior and interior. Exterior now worn but perhaps originally burnished. D. neck ca 12 cm. Karaburun I, cleaning, 1974. pl. 73.

KIZILBEL

The site is on the end of the high ridge of Uzunburun, 1080 meters above sea level, which projects southwards into the plain, 5.5 kilometers southwest of Elmalı (pl. 66b). It overlooked the Karagöl, a marshy lake that was drained only recently. Prehistoric pottery was found in the fill of the tumulus over a late sixth century B.C. tomb. It also lay scattered on the surface towards the end of the ridge.[3]

FABRICS

The prehistoric pottery forms an almost homogeneous group and is apparently from an early occupation of the ridge. It is similar in fabric to the Lower Bağbaşı pottery—handmade and poorly fired with black cores. Red, black and white grit inclusions occur with a little fiber. The surface color is usually red to deep orange, although some dark sherds occur, notably the fine incurved bowls. One body sherd had a high burnish, but this was not customary. Most of the pots had been well smoothed to give a compact, smooth surface without achieving a high lustre. The handles were scored and applied flat to the wall of the pot, except for one large handle that was attached with a plug.

22 and three related fragments are heavily stone tempered with large quartz-like particles and no fiber. They are similar to Neolithic sherds from Akçay and, like them, have a red slip or paint.

[3] Machteld J. Mellink, "Excavations at Karataş-Semayük in Lycia, 1969," *AJA* 74 (1970) 251 and *AJA* 79 (1975) 355.

SHAPES

Hole-mouth and incurved shapes form the bulk of the repertoire, but **1** and **2** may be from open bowls. Pots with distinct necks also occur. Fourteen handles or fragments were found. Ten were flat strap handles, three were loop handles and one was a small, upturned lug. The handles on closed pots seem, from the angles of attachment and their asymmetrical shapes, to have been horizontal. The three base fragments were from flattened bases, varying from ca 6 to 24 cm in diameter. The other sherds, **13–15,** were from two different types of pans and from a stand.

DECORATION

Incised lines or dashes occurred on three sherds (**18–20**), but otherwise single knobs on three handles, including **2** and **11,** and the impressions on **1** were the only decoration.

CATALOGUE

1. Flat rim fr. with impressions across rim. Exterior black and possibly burnished; interior black. pls 74 and 111b.

2. Bowl with straight side (angle?). Rim fr. with strap handle rising above rim and round knob on top of handle. Red-orange exterior; red-orange interior. pls 74 and 111c.

3. Incurved bowl. Rim fr. Black exterior; black interior. pl. 74.

4. Hole-mouth pot. Rim fr. Mottled brown exterior; black interior. pl. 74.

5. Hole-mouth pot. Rim fr. Mottled orange, brown and gray exterior; orange interior. pl. 74.

6. Hole-mouth pot. Rim fr. Orange exterior; orange interior. pl. 74.

7. Hole-mouth pot. Rim fr. Brown mottled exterior; black interior. Fabric is coarse with large inclusions. pl. 74.

8. Rim fr. of neck with everted rim. Red and brown mottled exterior; brown interior. pl. 74.

9. Rim fr. of short vertical neck. Red exterior with black at rim; red interior. pl. 74.

10. Rim fr. of everted neck. Red exterior; red and black mottled interior. pl. 74.

11. Body fr. from open vessel with strap handle with round knob at center bottom (?). Red-orange exterior; brown burnished interior. pl. 74.

12. Upturned lug fr. Orange exterior. pl. 74.

13. Pan with row of perforations. Body fr. Red-orange exterior; dark red to black interior; red-orange core. pl. 111d.

14. Pan with wavy rim. Rim fr. with hole pierced below rim and beginning of second hole on break. Brown-red exterior; light brown interior. pl. 75.

15. Stand (?) fr. Orange exterior with black mottling. pl. 75.

16. Rim fr. with broad ledge (?) on interior. Orange exterior; orange interior. pl. 75.

17. Miniature pot with inverted neck. Rim fr. Unburnished black exterior; black interior. pl. 75.

18. Hole-mouth pot. Rim fr. Orange exterior with two incised lines; orange interior with traces of crimson paint/slip; orange-brown core. pl. 75.

19. Body fr. of closed pot with handle stump. Roughly smoothed brown-orange exterior with series of short incised dashes below handle stump; pale brown interior. pl. 75.

20. Body fr. Black exterior with incised lines; black interior. pl. 75.

21. Flat base fr. D. ca 24 cm. Brown exterior; brown interior. pl. 75.

22. Body fr. of small rounded vessel with loop handle. Light brown exterior covered with streaky crimson paint; light brown interior. Fabric includes quantities of quartz-like inclusions. pl. 75.

OTHER SITES

Various other sites in the Elmalı plain have also produced pottery of the Neolithic and Chalcolithic periods. They remain unexcavated and are known from surface surveys conducted by M.S.F. Hood in 1949[4] and by Machteld J. Mellink in 1954 and since 1961.

[4] Two sherds from this survey were published by James Mellaart, *AnatSt* 4 (1954) 188 and figs. 51 and 59.

AKÇAY I HÜYÜK

The site is just to the east of the road, about 1 kilometer southeast of the town of Akçay, which is about 25 kilometers southwest of Elmalı. The mound is large, about 125 m in diameter, but artificially flattened by ploughing. A stream runs around the east and north sides. Surface material was collected here in 1949 by M.S.F. Hood, and in 1961 and 1962 by Machteld J. Mellink. More recent visits, including one in 1977, have also been made.

Three general periods of occupation have been identified—Byzantine, EB/LC and Neolithic. Pottery from the later two occupations was found all over the surface of the mound, while in 1977 most of the Neolithic sherds came from one area on the western edge of the mound, near the road. From this same area came two obsidian and ten flint blades.

Neolithic Pottery (**1–35**)

Fabric

The Neolithic pottery is handmade and coil-built, but is fine and dense in texture. The temper is exclusively grit, varying from white to black in color, and often consisting of schist fragments. The firing has left black cores; the surface color is predominantly light brown. The pots were usually burnished, sometimes over a slip, which varies from crimson to pink-red and from dark to light brown. All the sherds, whether slipped or not, form a homogeneous group, with the possible exception of **13.**

Shapes

The small size of many of the sherds often made identification of the shapes difficult, especially as bowls of this period could have deep vertical or everted rims. The following discussion and the catalogue entries resulted from consideration of both the diameter of the rim and the treatment of the inside surface.

The sherds obviously from open vessels—deep and flaring bowls—tend either to have slip applied over the whole interior as well as the exterior, or to have the slip on the exterior continued to form a band on the inside of the rim. Some of these pots, however, are unslipped (**18, 25, 27, 30**) on both exterior and interior. The sherds clearly from jars either have the interior left unslipped, as do **4–5** and **13,** or have a band of slip around the interior of the rim, as do **1** and **14.**

The everted rim fragments were from two types of pots. **6–8** have small diameters and are unslipped on the interior. They were probably from jars with everted rims. **9–12,** with a band on the interior or a completely slipped interior, had large diameters and were probably from bowls. The vertical neck fragment, **16,** is slipped and burnished on the inside as well as the outside and the large diameter of the fragment suggests that it is from a bowl.

Of the deep bowls one, **18,** was completely unslipped, and the others were either slipped on the interior and the exterior (four examples), or were slipped on the exterior and had a band on the interior at the rim (two examples). **17** had had paint daubed on the interior before it was burnished.

The proportions of different shapes in the repertoire are:

	Everted Rim	*Inverted Rim*	*Vertical Rim*	*Hole-mouth*	*Deep Bowl*	*Flat Rim Bowl*	*Flaring Bowl*
bowl	4	1	1	—	8	3	4
jar	3	1	2	2	—	—	—

Both tubular lugs and loop handles were used. Three examples of the latter were found, at least one of which was placed horizontally on the pot. The two base sherds were from plain flattened bases, 8 and 11 cm in diameter.

Decoration

Two forms of decoration were used on this pottery. Three sherds had painted decoration (**31–33**), which was either applied directly to the smoothed ground or to a white slip. The color of the paint varied from pink-red to light-brown, depending on the firing conditions, and the designs were simple linear ones. The painting occurs on the exterior of the pots.

14 and **15** bear incised patterns executed deeply after burnishing. The completed designs may have been more complex than the painted ones.

Catalogue

1. Inverted rim jar. Rim fr. Exterior covered with crimson paint and burnished; interior is burnished and has a deep band of crimson paint (4.5 cm deep) on the rim; black core. Survey of M.J.M., 1961–1962. pl. 76.

2. Inverted rim bowl. Rim fr. Burnished exterior has streaky brown paint; interior is burnished only on the 1.2 cm deep band of paint at the rim. Pale brown fabric; gray core. Survey of M.S.F.H. pl. 76.

3. Inverted or straight-rimmed pot. Rim fr. (angle uncertain). Burnished brown exterior with black mottling at rim; burnished yellow-brown interior; black core. On right-hand edge of sherd is beginning of handle stump. pl. 76.

4. Hole-mouth pot. Rim fr. Brown burnished slip on exterior; gray burnished interior; black core. Survey of M.S.F.H. pl. 76.

5. Hole-mouth pot. Rim fr. Lightly burnished pale brown exterior; pale brown interior; gray core. pl. 76.

6. Jar with everted neck. Rim fr. Light brown slipped and burnished exterior; gray burnished interior; gray core. pl. 76.

7. Jar with everted neck. Rim fr. Red slipped and burnished exterior; orange to gray burnished interior; gray core. pl. 76.

8. Jar with everted neck. Rim fr. Pale brown and gray burnished exterior; light brown interior; gray core. pl. 76.

9. Bowl with everted rim. Rim fr. Brown slipped and burnished exterior; gray interior with 1.2 cm deep brown painted and burnished band at rim; gray core. pl. 76.

10. Bowl with everted rim. Rim fr. Red slipped and burnished exterior and interior. Fabric has orange exterior; gray interior; black core. pl. 76.

11. Bowl with everted rim. Rim fr. Brown burnished slip on exterior and interior; brown to gray core. pl. 76.

12. Bowl with everted rim. Rim fr. Brown burnished slip on exterior and interior; black core. pl. 76.

13. Vertical neck. Rim fr. Well-burnished brown and black mottled exterior; black interior, burnished just inside rim (0.9 cm) and smoothed below; black core. pl. 76.

14. Vertical neck. Rim fr. Deep brown burnished slip on exterior; interior burnished light brown with a red-brown painted band, 3 cm deep, at rim; black core. Exterior bears incised decoration, executed after burnishing and before firing. A vertical line runs up almost to the rim with, approaching from the left, two diagonally opposed lines and a horizontal line above them. At the lower right-hand corner is a diagonal line. pls 76 and 111e.

15. Body fr., probably from same pot as last. Deep brown burnished slip on exterior with incised festoon; light brown burnished interior; black core. pls 76 and 111e.

16. Bowl with vertical neck. Rim fr. Burnished red and brown mottled slip on exterior and interior; black core. pl. 76.

17. Deep bowl. Rim fr. Dark brown slipped and burnished exterior; interior daubed with red paint and burnished. Fabric is orange; black core. pl. 77.

18. Deep bowl. Rim fr. with very uneven rim. Brown burnished exterior; brown burnished interior; black core. pl. 77.

19. Deep bowl. Rim fr. Dark brown slipped and burnished exterior; dark brown slipped interior, burnished at top. Pale brown fabric; gray core. Survey of M.S.F.H. pl. 77.

20. Deep bowl. Rim fr. Red slipped and burnished exterior and interior. Fabric orange; black core. pl. 77.

21. Deep bowl. Rim fr. Burnished red slipped exterior; burnished light brown interior with red painted band, 1.2 cm deep, at rim; gray core. pl. 77.

22. Deep bowl. Rim fr. Red slipped and burnished exterior and interior. Orange fabric; black core. pl. 77.

23. Deep bowl. Rim fr. Heavily burnished mid-brown slip on exterior and interior. Brown fabric; black core. Survey of M.J.M., 1961–1962. pl. 77.

24. Deep bowl with flat rim. Rim fr. Streaky brown burnished slip on exterior; burnished pale brown interior with streaky brown painted band, 1.3 cm deep, at rim; gray core. Survey of M.S.F.H. pl. 77.

25. Bowl with flat rim. Rim fr. Burnished orange-brown exterior; burnished brown interior; black core. Coarser than usual. pl. 77.

26. Small bowl with flat rim. Yellow-brown burnished slip on exterior; red-yellow burnished slip on interior; brown core. pl. 77.

27. Small bowl with flat rim. Rim fr. Pale orange burnished exterior; lightly burnished interior, pale orange at top and gray below; black core. pl. 77.

28. Flaring bowl. Rim fr. Red-brown burnished slip on exterior and interior; gray core. Survey of M.S.F.H. pl. 77.

29. Flaring bowl. Rim fr. Red-brown burnished slip on exterior and interior; gray core. Survey of M.S.F.H. pl. 77.

30. Flaring bowl. Rim fr. Mottled brown and gray exterior, roughly smoothed; brown burnished interior; black core. pl. 77.

31. Flaring bowl. Rim fr. Burnished pale brown exterior with matt red painted decoration; pale brown interior with red painted band at top and on rim; black core. Survey of M.S.F.H. James Mellaart, *AnatSt* 4 (1954) fig. 59 and p. 188.

32. Body fr. Exterior burnished orange with pink-red painted stripes; light brown burnished interior; gray core. pls 77 and 111f.

33. Body fr. D. 22 cm. Exterior is very worn but originally was burnished on a cream slip and decorated with a painted zig-zag design in brown paint shading to crimson on right hand edge; light brown interior; black core. pls 77 and 112a.

34. Body fr. of small pot with stump of small tubular lug on edge of sherd. Red slipped and burnished exterior except for what would have been inside handle piercing; light brown burnished interior; brown core. pl. 77.

35. Large strap handle or leg. Fr. Burnished orange and brown mottled exterior; black core. pl. 77.

Chalcolithic/Early Bronze Pottery (**36–38**)

The fabric of this pottery is of the usual grit and fiber tempered LC variety, but could be finer than usual. Light brown was the dominant color, and the burnish was high and even. The shapes included a disk base of Bağbaşı type and a fragment of a burnished bowl, possibly with a slight carination. Two rim fragments of burnished open pots were also found.

36. Small jar with everted neck and pierced lug handles. Approx. ¼ preserved with one lug. Well-burnished gray-brown exterior with some black mottling; gray-brown interior; black core. pl. 78.

37. Body fr. of bowl. Well-burnished gray-brown exterior; well-burnished brown interior; black core. pl. 78.

38. Disk base fr. D. unknown. Brown and black mottled exterior; orange interior; black core. pl. 78.

Chipped Stone (**39–50**)

Twelve chipped stone tools were found at Akçay, all in the same area as the Neolithic pottery. One was a flake, and the rest were fragments of blades. Two blades were of obsidian; the remainder of the assemblage was flint.

Most of the pieces were small, and most were cutting tools, including one denticulate blade. Only the flake had a striking platform (L. 1.44, W. 0.35 cm) and bulb of percussion (L. 0.82, W. 1.05 cm) preserved.

39. Cutting tool. Blade fr. broken both ends. Dorsal retouch along both edges (L. 0.10, W. 0.05 cm, 40°) with mashing along R edge above notch and on upper L edge. Obsidian—opaque gray. L. 1.81, W. 0.86, Th. 0.34 cm. pl. 78.

40. Cutting (?) tool. Blade fr. broken off at bulb end and partly so at other end. Irregular wear on both edges. Obsidian—clear gray-black. L. 1.73, W. 1.35, Th. 0.29 cm. pl. 78.

41. Cutting tool. Blade fr. broken at butt end. Retouch along both edges (L. 0.05, W. 0.05 cm, R edge 30°, L edge 10–25°). Most of the striking platform broken away. Flint—yellow with white specks. L. 2.95, W. 1.23, Th. 0.30 cm. pl. 78.

42. Cutting tool. Flake with striking platform and bulb of percussion. Retouched along R edge (L. 0.04, W. 0.04 cm, 45°). Flint—purple speckled. L. 1.91, W. 1.53, Th. 0.31 cm. pl. 78.

43. Cutting tool (?). Blade fr. with bulb end broken off. Wear along both edges. Bulbar retouch along part of end (L. 0.15, W. 0.05 cm, 80°). Flint—purple speckled. L. 1.34, W. 1.83, Th. 0.43 cm. pl. 78.

44. Cutting tool (?). Blade fr. broken both ends. Irregular wear along both edges. Flint—white. L. 1.60, W. 1.36, Th. 0.33 cm. pl. 78.

45. Denticulate tool. Blade fr. broken both ends. Retouched on upper part of R edge from both faces, to form denticulation (L. 0.30, W. 0.025 cm, 70°). Flint—brown speckled. L. 3.72, W. 2.40, Th. 0.54 cm. pl. 78.

46. Borer (?). Blade fr. broken at one end. Irregular wear along both edges on dorsal face. Cortex trimmed off with one strike to form point. Flint—yellow with white specks. L. 3.60, W. 1.90, Th. 0.42 cm. pl. 78.

47. Blade fr. with bulb end broken off. Irregular wear and mashing along both edges. Flint—dark brown. L. 2.25, W. 2.00, Th. 0.50 cm. pl. 78.

48. Blade with bulb end broken off. Wear along both edges and around butt end. Flint—clear red-brown. L. 1.72, W. 1.60, Th. 0.34 cm. pl. 78.

49. Blade fr. with bulb end broken off. Irregular wear around edges. Flint—purple speckled. L. 3.22, W. 3.62, Th. 1.15 cm. pl. 78.

50. Blade fr. with bulb end broken off. Irregular wear around edges. Flint—coarse brown speckled. L. 3.18, W. 3.85, Th. 1.06 cm. pl. 78.

BAYINDIRKÖY

A site on a hill spur west of the village of Bayındır, which is 6 kilometers northeast of Elmalı. The pottery found included sherds of Kızılbel type.

Catalogue

1. Pan with wavy rim. Rim fr. with a row of perforations below rim. Holes pierced from inside. One side of fragment is curved up, and may be a corner of the vessel. Orange exterior; orange interior; black core. pls 78 and 112b.

BURALIA

An acropolis on natural rock and a level site, north of Avlan Gölü and about 15 kilometers south of Elmalı. Probably ancient Podalia.[5] Most of the material was of later date than that covered by this survey, but some LC sherds were found.

Catalogue

1. Disk base fr. D. unknown. Light brown exterior; gray and black interior; black core. pl. 78.

[5] For discussion see George E. Bean, *Lycian Turkey* (London/New York 1978) 153–56. He places Podalia in the northern part of the plain, near the modern village of Söğle.

DINSIZ

The area of Dinsiz consists of a series of ridges just to the west of the Elmalı-Korkuteli road and to the south of its junction with the road to Gölova. Only the southernmost of the ridges has evidence of occupation—an Iron Age tomb on the summit and, about half-way down the slope, a scatter of sherds on the surface. A stream skirts the southern edge of the ridge.

The pottery is similar to that from the LC sites of Bağbaşı, Boztepe and Karaburun, but contains a larger proportion of pebble temper, and the surface color is more red and brown. Gray and black wares were not found. A red slip occurs on a few of the sherds. The handles were applied with plug attachments.

Catalogue

1. Flaring bowl. Rim fr. Red-brown, originally burnished exterior; red slipped and burnished interior; black core. pl. 79.

2. Rim fr. Red-orange exterior; red-orange interior; black core. pl. 79.

3. Open pot. Rim fr. Orange exterior; orange interior; black core. pl. 79.

4. Lug handle of rounded shape. Red-brown exterior; black core. pl. 79.

5. Lug handle of angular shape. Frr. showing width of lug (7 cm) and plug attachment. Orange exterior; black core. pl. 112c.

6. Horizontal tubular handle with upturned shape. Fr. showing irregularity of application and plug attachment. Brown exterior; black core. pl. 112d.

GÖKPINAR

The village of Gökpınar lies in the plain on the main Korkuteli-Elmalı road, about 5 kilometers east of Elmalı. A spring within the village provides water. In 1964 one of the villagers, Mehmet Kırcan, dug a well in the eastern part of the village and encountered evidence of early occupation. He preserved four LN sherds (**1–4**) and a fragment of a ground stone axe with shaft hole (probably Bronze Age).

In July 1977 Kırcan's well had been extended and the new part had not yet been walled. The well was then about 4–5 m in diameter with the occupation level visible in the north, south and east sides at a depth of 1.70–2.70 m. In the south section the remains of a plastered floor were visible and large stones, suitable for wall foundations, occurred in both north and south sections. Sketches were made of the exposed sections (pl. 81:a–b).

By 1977 other wells had also been dug in the village and they were examined to determine the extent and depth of the Neolithic deposit. A sketch plan (pl. 81:c) shows the approximate location of the wells in the village, and the position of the two wells that produced prehistoric material. The second well, that of Ali Riza Göcer, was just to the west of Mehmet Kırcan's well. The Neolithic occupation thus seems to have been restricted to an area northeast of the present spring. The well of Ali Riza Göcer had been walled before the investigation, but occupation debris—burnt bone and mud brick fragments, an epiphysial bone awl, small flints and some pottery—was found in the earth dump (**5–8**).

The Gökpınar LN pottery is tempered with small grits and, although most sherds have black cores, they are hard fired. The walls of the pots were thin and of even thickness. They were coil-built and the handles were applied flat against the wall of the pot. It is worth noting that **3** and **4** may have formed a twin lug. They have the same asymmetrical shape and are from the same vessel shape. In general the shapes belong to the same categories as the Akçay LN sherds. The surface has a high, even burnish, often over a red slip; no decorated sherds were found.

Catalogue

1. Pot with inverted sides. Rim fr. with horizontal loop handle. Burnished brown exterior; burnished black-brown interior. pl. 79.

2. Body fr. with horizontal loop handle. D. body ca 27 cm. Burnished brown exterior; burnished black-brown interior. pl. 79.

3. Body fr. with vertical tubular lug. D. body ca 40 cm. Burnished red slipped exterior with black mottling; lightly burnished gray interior. pl. 79.

4. Body fr. with vertical tubular lug. D. body ca 40 cm. Burnished red slipped exterior with black mottling; lightly burnished gray interior. Possibly from same pot as last. pl. 79.

5. Deep bowl. Rim fr. Angle of fr. is uncertain as rim height is very irregular. Exterior and interior red slipped and burnished. Fabric orange with red-brown core. pl. 79.

6. Flaring bowl. Rim fr. Exterior and interior pale brown and well smoothed; gray core. pl. 79.

7. Vertical neck. Rim fr. Exterior well-burnished yellow-brown; interior well-burnished dark gray; brown core. pl. 79.

8. Inverted pot. Rim fr. Red-orange, well-smoothed exterior and interior; brown-gray core. pl. 79.

GÖKPINAR WEST

A site in the fields to the north of the main Korkuteli-Elmalı road. The pottery includes body sherds possibly of Kızılbel-Lower Bağbaşı type, and LC sherds.

Catalogue

1. Disk base fr. D. unknown. Red-brown exterior; gray interior; black core. pl. 80.

2. Loop handle fr. Red-brown exterior; black core. pl. 80.

3. Open pot. Rim fr. Exterior red-brown; interior red-brown; black core. pl. 80.

HACIMUSALAR

This is the largest mound in the Elmalı Plain, about 10 m high and 250 × 350 m in area. It is 15 kilometers southwest of Elmalı, to the east of the road, between the villages of Beyler and Hacımusalar. It is also known as Beyler Hüyük, and by its classical name of Choma.[6]

It has been sherded a number of times (collections in Elmalı and those of M.S.F. Hood and Machteld J. Mellink in Antalya), but has produced no Neolithic or Chalcolithic pottery, with the exception of one Neolithic sherd from the Hood survey.

Catalogue

1. Hole-mouth pot. Rim fr. Exterior lightly burnished gray-brown with brown at rim; interior lightly burnished gray-brown with brown at rim; black core with white grits. Survey of M.S.F.H. pl. 80.

KARABAYIR

The site is on a spur in the hills to the north of the Elmalı Plain, about 30 kilometers to the northeast of Elmalı.[7] Among the LC sherds from this site were both burnished and unburnished wares.

[6] G.E. Bean and R.M. Harrison, "Choma in Lycia," *JRS* 57 (1967) 40–44.

[7] The site has been known for some time. See B. Pace, "Escursioni in Licia," *Annuario* 3 (1916–1920) 63.

Catalogue

1. Flaring bowl with flat rim. Rim fr. Gray and black mottled exterior; burnished brown interior with orange mottling; black core. pl. 80.

SEMAYÜK BEKLEME

The site is about 7 kilometers northeast of Elmalı, on a rise at the junction of the main Korkuteli-Elmalı road and the road to Semayük. Pottery was found over the whole area intersected by the roads, but the prehistoric pottery seems to have been confined to the quadrant southeast of the main road and northeast of the Semayük road, closest to the stream that runs around the north side of the rise.

The early pottery, including LC sherds, was found on the higher ground immediately east of the road junction, and on the slope further to the east. In July 1977 the farmer had cut a trench in the orchard to the north of this lower slope. In the section, 1.50–2.00 m below the surface, was an occupation level with round stones suitable for wall foundations and large pieces of pottery. Pottery was also collected from the earth dumped beside the trench.

The pottery was of the normal LC fabric found at Bağbaşı, Boztepe and Karaburun. The surface was usually orange with some brown, black and yellow mottling; the cores were black. Handles were applied with a plug, such as that on **3.**

The shapes also fit into the LC repertoire. The pan, **5,** has parallels at Boztepe and Karaburun, the lug handle at both these sites and at Bağbaşı too, while the bowl and neck rims would not be out of place at those sites. Most of the body sherds are from large closed pots.

The only decoration was the applied knob on the body sherd, **4.** It has parallels at Bağbaşı.

Catalogue

1. Flaring neck. Rim fr. Black exterior; black interior; black core. Trench. pl. 80.

2. Open pot or flaring bowl. Rim fr. with indented rim. Angle uncertain. Orange exterior; light brown interior; black core. Trench. pl. 80.

3. Lug handle of regular shape with plug attachment. Orange exterior with yellow-green and black mottling on upper side; black core. Trench. pl. 80.

4. Body fr. with applied knob. Exterior orange; interior orange; black core. Trench. pl. 112e.

5. Pan with perforations made from the top surface and later blocked by burnishing. Body fr. Dark brown burnished top surface; red-brown bottom surface; red-brown core. Surface, east of main road. pl. 112f.

TEKKE

A large low mound, about 100 × 140 m in area and 3 m high, in the fields south of Tekkeköy, 6 or 7 kilometers west of Avlan Gölü. Also known as Koca Hüyük, it has been sherded by M.S.F. Hood and Machteld J. Mellink. The pottery included a body sherd of LN fabric and possible Chalcolithic fragments.

Catalogue

1. Neck. Rim fr. Exterior brown; interior brown; black core. pl. 80.

2. Body fr. Exterior burnished red-brown slip; interior light brown; core light brown with white grits.

3. Rim fr. Exterior burnished orange-yellow with red-brown painted decoration of swags; interior burnished orange-yellow with cross-hatching on interior. Survey of M.S.F.H. J. Mellaart, *AnatSt* 4 (1954) 188 and fig. 51.

YAKA ÇIFTLIĞI

A low mound on a hill spur on the west edge of the plain, about 12 kilometers south of Elmalı. The pottery included LC sherds.

Catalogue

1. Lug handle of angular shape. Fr. Orange exterior; black core. pl. 80.

2. Disk base fr. D. unknown. Brown exterior; brown interior; black core. pl. 80.

OTHER

There are also other sites, with less characteristic pottery types, that have produced pottery that appears from its fabric to be early in date. They are *Arapkuyusu,* about 10 kilometers west of Elmalı on the north side of Balıklar Dağı, from which came a handle fragment possibly of Kızılbel type (pl. 80), and *Maltepe,* a rise just north of Karaburun, which produced a possible LC fragment (pl. 80).

Chapter 4 GEOGRAPHICAL AND CHRONOLOGICAL RELATIONSHIPS

COMPARATIVE MATERIAL

An excavated sequence of the Neolithic and Chalcolithic periods is not yet available for the Elmalı Plain, for the excavated sites were all small settlements of short duration. This section is an attempt to determine the relative chronological positions of the different groups of material from the plain, by comparison with stratified sites in other parts of southwestern Anatolia. Assemblages have been considered as a whole and only those with sufficient parallels to offer a firm impression of their relationship to the Elmalı material are discussed. The small amount of material available from many of the Elmalı sites and their distance from the comparative sites should be borne in mind.

GÖKPINAR AND AKÇAY

Gökpınar (pl. 79)

The pottery from Gökpınar is possibly the earliest yet discovered in the Elmalı Plain. Its most characteristic features are tubular lugs (**3–4**). They have a wide distribution on the early pottery of western Anatolia, where they are found from the Akhisar area to Çatal Hüyük.[1] The closest parallels for the fabric and shape of the Gökpınar lugs are from Karain and from Hacılar levels IX to VII.[2] The horizontal loop handles (**1–2**), the jar with inverted sides (**8**) and the flat rimmed jar (**7**) can also be paralleled at Hacılar,[3] and although the flaring bowl has no precise parallels there, the general type does occur.[4]

Kızılkaya, geographically closer to Elmalı, has also produced a range of pottery shapes similar to those from Gökpınar.[5] Tubular lugs, flaring bowls and inverted jars are found at both sites.[6] However, the fabric of the Kızılkaya pottery, with large flat fragments of stone temper, is unlike that of Gökpınar.

[1] D.H. French, "Early Pottery Sites from Western Anatolia," *BIAL* 5 (1965) 24, fig. 5:1–3; Jacques Bordaz, "A preliminary report of the 1969 excavations at Erbaba, a Neolithic site near Beyşehir, Turkey," *TürkArkDerg* 18:2 (1969) 61 and Jacques Bordaz and Louise Bordaz, "Erbaba Excavations, 1974," *TürkArkDerg* 23:2 (1976) 42; James Mellaart, "Early Cultures of the South Anatolian Plateau I," *AnatSt* 11 (1961) 165, fig. 3.

[2] For Karain see examples in Antalya Museum; for Hacılar see *Hacılar* I 103–104 and II fig. 46:15.

[3] *Hacılar* II figs. 46:6, 15 and 11 respectively.

[4] *Hacılar* II fig. 47:37–38.

[5] James Mellaart, *AnatSt* 11 (1961) 170, fig. 6.

[6] James Mellaart, *AnatSt* 11 (1961) 170, fig. 6:35–39 (for the tubular lugs), 26–27 (for the flaring bowls) and 4, 9–10 (for the inverted jars).

Akçay I Hüyük (pls 76–78)

The Akçay pottery represents a more extended period than Gökpınar, with parallels for **1–35** found throughout the Hacılar sequence. At both sites the pottery is tempered with fine grit, and the pots are coil-built, with handles applied against the wall of the pot. A red burnished slip is the most common surface treatment, but unslipped burnished wares do occur in the Akçay collection. At Hacılar unslipped burnished wares are found mostly in the lower levels (IX–VIII).[7]

Parallels with the LN levels at Hacılar are numerous. Inverted rim jars and bowls like Akçay **1** and **2** occur throughout Hacılar IX–VI,[8] as do deep bowls with everted rims like **9–12.**[9] Deep straight-sided bowls (**17–24**) and flaring bowls (**28–30**) also have a long life there.[10] However, some Akçay shapes, for example the hole-mouth pots (**4–5**), the small vertical neck (**13**) and the flat rimmed bowl (**25**), are found at Hacılar only in the earlier LN levels.[11] Their presence at Akçay is balanced by the occurrence of high, wide vertical necks and the small tubular lug of Hacılar VII–VI type.[12]

The EC period in Anatolia is usually equated with a period of red on cream painted pottery styles[13] and, despite the basic continuity of the pottery tradition throughout the Hacılar sequence, the levels from V to I, where painted pottery styles are increasingly popular, were termed EC.[14] The suitability of this terminology for southwestern Anatolia in general may, however, be questioned, for the practice of painting designs on pottery seems to have been less popular beyond the area of Hacılar. The painted style of Hacılar IV–II has been identified only in that area, at Hacılar itself, at Kuruçay Hüyük and at Dereköy I Hüyük; pottery with linear decoration similar to that of Hacılar I occurs in quantity only in the same area, although it is found as far south as Karain.[15]

Only a few sherds of painted pottery have so far been found in the Elmalı Plain. Mellaart places two Elmalı Plain sites on his distribution map of Hacılar I pottery.[16] The reference is probably to the sherds he published from Akçay (**31**) and Tekke (Koca Hüyük) (**3**).[17] Three painted pottery fragments are now known from Akçay. Two (**31** and **32**) may belong with the LN pottery. The linear nature of the designs, the lack of a cream slip, and the shape of **31** all suggest a Hacılar IX–VI date.[18] However **33,** with light brown painted zig-zags on a cream slip, may be later.[19] It has a fabric similar to that of Tekke **3,** a curved bowl with festoon pattern on the exterior and

[7] *Hacılar* I 102–109.

[8] *Hacılar* II figs. 46:6, 15; 48:9; 51:10; 54:13.

[9] *Hacılar* II figs. 45:32 and 49:4 for **6**; 48:10 and 50:29 for **7**; 53:2 or 50:26 for **11–12.**

[10] *Hacılar* II figs. 45:25, 47:6–7 and 48:13 for the straight-sided bowls, **17–24**; and figs. 47:37–38, 48:29 and 50:12, 18 for the flaring bowls, **28–30.**

[11] *Hacılar* II figs. 48:14, 18 for hole-mouth jars; 47:16 and 50:5 for the vertical neck; 48:30 for the bowl.

[12] *Hacılar* II fig. 52:3 and 4 for the jar and fig. 53:1 for the lug.

[13] James Mellaart in *CAH* I:1, 317.

[14] See *Hacılar* I 109–142.

[15] James Mellaart, *AnatSt* 4 (1954) 181, map 2 and 184, figs. 52–58; *Hacılar* I 146. For the occurrence of Hacılar V–II style at Kuruçay Höyügü see *Kuruçay* I pls. VIII–XII, *Kuruçay* II pls. 5–7 and *Kuruçay* IV pls 4–5.

[16] *Hacılar* I 146 and II fig. 156b.

[17] James Mellaart, *AnatSt* 4 (1954) 181 and 184, figs. 51–59.

[18] For the shape of **31** see *Hacılar* II fig. 45:21 and for the designs figs. 47, 49 and 59. Unslipped painted sherds occur in the collection in the British Institute of Archaeology in Ankara, e.g. sherd 1071 from level VII.

[19] Compare e.g. *Hacılar* II figs. 115 and 145 for the use of zig-zag patterns in level I and also *Kuruçay* I pl. XI:80. In August 1980 another cream slipped and red painted body sherd was found at Akçay. It has a broad vertical painted band.

cross-hatching on the interior. This fragment is close to Hacılar I in style, although cross-hatching is more common on Hacılar VI pottery.[20] The fabric of these two sherds is also similar to some examples from Hacılar I and II. The Akçay incised sherds (**14** and **15**), too, are best paralleled in the EC period; at Hacılar incised decoration belongs mostly to level I, where the festoon pattern is found.[21]

The chipped stone from Akçay also has parallels at Hacılar. Both industries consist predominantly of blades, and flint is the main material used.[22] The absence at Akçay of certain types of tools, notably micro-points and sickle-blades, may be due only to the unrepresentative nature of the Akçay collection.

KIZILBEL AND LOWER BAĞBAŞI

The pottery from Kızılbel and the related fragments from Bağbaşı (the Lower Bağbaşı pottery) have different shapes, but the fabrics are similar and they are made in the same tradition. Although similar pottery is rare in southwestern Anatolia, the grit tempering, thin walls and flat application of handles connect them to the LN/EC pottery tradition.

Kızılbel (pls 74–75)

On the mainland some parallels for the Kızılbel pottery can be found in the LN Hacılar assemblage. The hole-mouth pot series (**3–7**), the flaring dark burnished bowl with flat rim (**1**), and the various jar necks (**8–10**) can all be compared with Hacılar shapes.[23] However, most of the Hacılar shapes are not found at Kızılbel, the characteristic Kızılbel knobbed strap handles do not occur at Hacılar, and the slipped and burnished Hacılar fabric is much finer. The EC pottery from Kuruçay Höyük has similar general resemblances and a parallel for Kızılbel **2,** although the Kuruçay handle does not have a knob.[24]

The shapes of some of the sherds from Moralı, Akhisar also resemble the Kızılbel pottery, although the fiber-tempered Moralı fabric is not like that of the Kızılbel pottery.[25] Parallels exist for the burnished flat rimmed bowl (**1**), the hole-mouth jar series (**4–7**) and the neck rim (**10**).[26] A neck rim from Hamidiye, Nazilli is very like Kızılbel **8.**[27] Again, however, the most characteristic Kızılbel features are missing.

The earliest excavated levels at Emporio on Chios (levels X–VIII) produced parallels for the Kızılbel hole-mouth and incurved shapes (**3–7**), the rising handle (**2**), the pans with high sides and row of perforations below the rim (**14**), the pot with internal lug (**16**), the strap handles decorated with knobs and placed either on bowl rims or on the sides of jars (**2** and **11**), and for the infrequent use of simple incised decoration (especially dashes) without white filling (**18–20**). Many of these features, such as the pans and knobbed handles, have a long life at Emporio, continuing even to

[20] Compare *Hacılar* II figs. 124:8 and 59.

[21] *Hacılar* II fig. 109:9. One sherd from level IX (*Hacılar* I 103 and II fig. 47:28) has incised decoration but cannot be compared to the Akçay sherds.

[22] *Hacılar* I 153–57.

[23] *Hacılar* II figs. 46; 48:29; 53:17, 53:14, 49:13.

[24] *Kuruçay* IV pl. 4:11.

[25] D.H. French, *BIAL* 5 (1965) 18–19.

[26] D.H. French, *BIAL* 5 (1965) 22–23, figs. 4:12–13; 3:21–23; 4:18.

[27] D.H. French, *BIAL* 5 (1965) 22, fig. 3:4.

levels VII and VI, but it is in the earliest levels, before the widespread use of pattern burnish and incision in level VIII, that the assemblage as a whole is comparable to that from Kızılbel.[28]

Similar shapes are also found in the repertoire at Tigani on Samos where incurved bowls, hole-mouth jars, knobbed strap handles and pans with a row of perforations below the rim were all found.[29] They belong to the coarse unburnished wares, either undecorated or decorated with incision (class A). A bowl with high strap handle occurs, but it is rare.[30] These features occur in an assemblage that includes a wide range of material extending into the LC period. Similar assemblages were found at several sites from Leros to Rhodes.[31]

The Kızılbel pottery is apparently more closely related to that of the eastern Aegean than to the known assemblages from the mainland. Unfortunately the dating, both relative and absolute, of much of the Aegean material is far from clear. The Tigani material was not well stratified and the date of some classes is open to question.[32] The bulk of the pottery is certainly LC in date, but class A does not include definite LC features, and it is possible that it belongs to an earlier period.[33] The evidence from Chios is rather clearer. The Ayio Gala Lower Cave produced pottery related to the Hacılar VI tradition, and Emporio levels VIII–VI produced pottery related to the mainland LC. In the apparent absence of gaps or breaks in the Emporio sequence, levels X–IX should fall between these occurrences. In western Anatolian terms this suggests a date for Emporio X–IX in the EC or MC periods.[34]

Lower Bağbaşı (pls 63–65)

The Lower Bağbaşı pottery has fewer parallels at other sites. The closest connection appears to be with group B pottery from Kuruçay Höyük level 7.[35] This level is close to Hacılar I, but the presence of the group B pottery—a dark, burnished ware, tempered with grit and fiber—suggests it may be slightly later. The Lower Bağbaşı straight-sided and inverted shapes (**1, 2, 6, 7**) have parallels there, and the characteristic strap handle with pinched up ridge (**9** and **15**) has a parallel in the contemporary painted pottery.[36] The straight-sided pot (**1**), jar (**2**), curved bowls (**4** and **5**) and hole-mouth vessels (**6** and **7**) all have parallels at Hacılar too,[37] but in the grit tempered EC ware, and the strap handle with ridge is not found there.

The strap handle with pinched up ridge on top, as distinct from the horned handles that have a wide distribution in Anatolia and the Aegean in the Chalcolithic period, is not a common form. It is also found at Tigani on Samos and at Saliagos.[38] The coarse wares of the latter site can also provide parallels for **1**, for the hemispherical bowl, and the ledge-lug. However, the fine wares from Saliagos are not similar to the Lower Bağbaşı pottery, and the few red painted sherds there

[28] *Emporio* 240–300, pots 179–181, 162, 17, 20 and 24, 184, 401–3.

[29] *Tigani* figs. F6–10; F31 and 33; pls. 43:6 and 48:3; pl. 34:6 respectively.

[30] *Tigani* 140–41, figs. F19 and 20.

[31] Audrey Furness, "Some early pottery of Samos, Kalimnos and Chios," *ProcPS* 22 (1956) 189, fig. 10 and pl. XVIII; Adamantios Sampson, "The Neolithic of the Dodecanese and Aegean Neolithic," *BSA* 79 (1984) 239–249.

[32] *Tigani* 123; Audrey Furness, *ProcPS* 22 (1956) 174.

[33] As suggested by Audrey Furness, *ProcPS* 22 (1956) 209 and fig. 16; *Beycesultan* I 107–108 (but F31 and F33 of class A are not really close to the Beycesultan shape quoted); Colin Renfrew, *The Emergence of Civilisation* (London 1972) 72.

[34] See Christine Eslick, *AJA* 84 (1980) 5–14. M.S.F. Hood dates these levels to the EN period.

[35] *Kuruçay* II 20.

[36] *Kuruçay* II pl. 8:1, 11–12 and for the handles pl. 6:16.

[37] *Hacılar* II figs. 46:5, 8; 48:27, 30; and fig. 46 respectively.

[38] *Tigani* 150, fig. F58; *Saliagos* fig. 45:6.

were probably imported.[39] The straight-sided and inverted shapes (**1–2, 4–7**) and the lug (**8**) have parallels in levels X–VIII at Emporio.[40]

BOZTEPE, KARABURUN AND BAĞBAŞI

The material from these three sites can be compared with LC assemblages from many sites in western Anatolia, from as far north as Kumtepe and west to Samos.[41] However, connections with other sites in the southwest are naturally the closest, and the two sites with the most useful material are Beycesultan and Aphrodisias.[42] The pottery from these sites is made in the same tradition as that of Boztepe, Karaburun and Bağbaşı, in respect of both fabric and manufacturing tradition. Therefore, the shape sequences of the various sites have been assumed to run essentially parallel.

Boztepe (pls 67–69)

The Boztepe bowls with flat everted rims (**2–4**) are paralleled in Beycesultan LC 1.[43] **1,** a more extreme form of the shape, is not found there, but is clearly related to them. Folded-over rims, as on **10** and **16,** also occur, as do flat rimmed jars like **12–14** and **19,** and flaring bowls like **10.**[44] However, no trace of the white painting found so frequently in these levels at Beycesultan occurred at Boztepe, and at Beycesultan the bowls with rolled rim, such as Boztepe **5–8,** do not apparently occur before level XIX.[45]

Aphrodisias levels VIIIB–VII produced bowl types comparable to both the main Boztepe rim types—those with flat everted rims and those with rolled rims.[46] At this site the latter form seems to be most popular in levels VIIIB–A. The flaring bowl (**10**) and the jar rims (**14, 16–19**) also have parallels,[47] and the pierced and smoothed fragment from level VIIB may perhaps be compared with the pan with perforated base (**21**).[48] White painting occurs on the burnished pottery from this site also.

The use of applied pellet decoration like that on Boztepe **20** is found over a wide area, and seems to have little chronological or cultural significance.[49] In the Elmalı Plain it does, however, appear to be restricted to the beginning of the LC period, as it occurs only here and at Karaburun.

Karaburun (pls 70–73)

Most of the pottery from the Karaburun ridge can be compared to that from the beginning of the Beycesultan sequence, from levels XL–XXXIX. Both the bowls with everted rim (**1–2**), and

[39] **1** could be from a "deep bowl" such as *Saliagos* fig. 40:4; for the other shapes see fig. 40:1 and fig. 46:8, 17; *Saliagos* 42.

[40] *Emporio* pots 260 (if **1** is from a jar), 178, 117, 94, 194, 179, 54.

[41] See e.g. Jerome W. Sperling, *Hesperia* 45 (1976) 305–64 and *Tigani* 125 ff.

[42] *Beycesultan* I 75 ff.; *Aphrodisias.*

[43] *Beycesultan* I fig. P1:2 and P2:14–15.

[44] *Beycesultan* I figs. P5:16–19; P1:40–41 and P2:34; and P2:35.

[45] *Beycesultan* I figs. P14:2, 4–6 and P15:18.

[46] *Aphrodisias* I fig. 35:13 (type CX8, a rare shape in level VIIIB, for **3**), fig. 33:3 (type XC29, a rare shape in level VIIA, for **9**); *Aphrodisias* II fig. 377:6 and fig. 399:3 and 6 (types CX4, XC23 and XC25 for **8, 5** and **1**).

[47] *Aphrodisias* II fig. 377:17 (type CJ2), fig. 384:74 (type CJ5), fig. 389:13 (type CC20), fig. 392:44 (type CX79) and fig. 405:5 and 38 (types CP34 and CJ11).

[48] *Aphrodisias* II fig. 389:3.

[49] E.g. *Saliagos* fig. 43:14 and pl. XXVIII:b; H. Koşay and M. Akok, *Büyük Güllücek Kazısı* (Ankara 1957) pl. XVIII:1.

those with rounded rims (**3–6**) find parallels there, as do the large jars with vertical neck such as **9.**[50]

Aphrodisias VIIIB–VII produced parallels for both types of bowl and for some of the necks, with most parallels in levels VIID–B. The pan with a row of perforations below the rim (**26**) also finds a counterpart there.[51] This pan shape is also found at Karain, and in the Aegean.[52] The flaring bowls (**5–6**), the pan with row of perforations and the lug handles are found at Miletos.[53] The horizontal tubular handle (**24**) also occurs in the Aegean, at Tigani on Samos and at Kalymnos,[54] and it is one of the few features of these assemblages paralleled in the LC of the Konya Plain.[55]

Kuruçay has produced parallels for the flat everted rims (**1, 2**) and the concave-sided bowls (**3–5**) in its earlier LC group B, characteristic of level 6A.[56] Sherd **23** with vertical handle from the rim may be from a tankard similar to the Kuruçay LC examples and the lug handles are also paralleled there.[57]

Two of the Karaburun bowls (**7** and **8**) suggest that there was also later occupation on the ridge in the EB I period.[58]

Bağbaşı

Pottery (pls 16–56)

The main Bağbaşı assemblage has extensive parallels with the pottery from the middle part of the Beycesultan LC sequence.[59] At Bağbaşı bowls with everted rim (**1–3**) are uncommon; at Beycesultan they are characteristic of LC 1, although some versions continue later.[60] Characteristic of Bağbaşı are flaring bowls with simple flattened rim (**15–21**). They begin at Beycesultan in LC 1, but are characteristic of LC 2.[61] They sometimes have two holes pierced below the rim, as **9** and **225** apparently had.[62] These flaring bowls have walls that are usually only slightly concave, but at both sites the tendency can be emphasized.[63] Concave bowls continue to be found at Beycesultan until LC 4. Shallow bowls like Bağbaşı **6** can be compared to Beycesultan bowls of

[50] *Beycesultan* I figs. P1:6, P2:12; P1:29, 32, 44; and P1:47 respectively.

[51] For the bowls see *Aphrodisias* II fig. 399:6 (type XC25) for **1–2**; fig. 392:3 (type CX71) for **3**; fig. 384:12 (type CX37) for **5** and fig. 389:30 (type CH68) for **6.** For **8** see fig. 399:5 (type X81), and for **10, 17** and **19, 20** see fig. 399:38, fig. 384:71 and fig. 399:33 (types CJ15, CJ4 and CJ 13). For the pans see fig. 389:9 (type CX86 of level VII) and fig. 377:48 (level VIIIB).

[52] For Karain see sherds in Antalya Museum; for the Aegean sites Audrey Furness, *ProcPS* 22 (1956) pls. XVIII:2 and XXII:15; *Tigani* pl. 34:6; Adamantios Sampson, *BSA* 79 (1984) 242–243.

[53] Walter Voigtländer, "Funde aus der Insula westlich des Buleuterion in Milet," *Ist Mitt* 32 (1982) figs. 1–2 for the bowls and pans and fig. 5:23 for the lug.

[54] *Tigani* 152, fig. F61–63; Audrey Furness, *ProcPS* 22 (1956) pl. XVIII: 10–12.

[55] At Can Hasan. James Mellaart, *AnatSt* 13 (1963) 204, fig. 3:1.

[56] *Kuruçay* IV 44–5, pls 24–5.

[57] *Kuruçay* II pl. 19:2 or 6 and pl. 21:1–6.

[58] Compare *Beycesultan* I figs. P15:24 and 25.

[59] *Beycesultan* I 79–103.

[60] E.g. *Beycesultan* I figs. P2:15 (for **1**) and P9:9 (for **2**).

[61] E.g. *Beycesultan* I figs. P2:1 and P6:9.

[62] E.g. *Beycesultan* I 87 and fig. P5:7.

[63] **11** and **12** and *Beycesultan* I fig. P8:21–23.

LC 3 and 4,[64] and some of the rarer Bağbaşı bowl shapes (**28–31, 50**) and the basin (**48**) also find parallels there.[65]

Although none of the painted juglets of Beycesultan type occurs at Bağbaşı, most of the Bağbaşı jugs can be paralleled at Beycesultan among the unpainted juglets,[66] and the squat bodied jug (**91**) is similar in shape to a larger Beycesultan pot.[67] The use of a ridge at the base of a jug neck, such as that on **92,** is known at Beycesultan from the beginning of the LC sequence.[68]

Among the jar shapes there are also parallels, although they are not as numerous. The jar with flaring neck (**123**) can be compared with pots of LC 3 and 4, as can the large pots with everted rim (**125–127**).[69] Some of the rarer Bağbaşı jug/jar shapes were found at Beycesultan only in LC 4: **100** with sharply everted rim; **144,** a hole-mouth shape with everted rim; **145,** a pot with inverted neck.[70]

Coarse rim fragments from open pots occur throughout the Beycesultan sequence, and some appear to be of the Bağbaşı open pot type, although many are from inverted shapes.[71] Lugs, usually vertically perforated, appear on jars with necks but not apparently on open pots.[72]

The miniature shapes (**223–224**) have parallels in Beycesultan LC 3 and 4,[73] and the Bağbaşı pans are the equivalent of the Beycesultan baking platters found in LC 2 and afterwards.[74] Knobs on the body of jugs and knobs on handles also occur at both sites,[75] and the pattern burnished sherd (**148**) has parallels in Beycesultan XXXII and XXXI.[76]

The Bağbaşı finds also suggest that some of the subsidiary features attributable only to the EBA at Beycesultan begin earlier at other southwestern sites, for example, the solid pedestal (**230**)[77]; the feet (**233–237**)[78]; and the multiple vessel (**228**).[79]

In many ways the Bağbaşı assemblage parallels that of Beycesultan, especially at the end of LC 2 and LC 3. However, there are also notable differences. The Bağbaşı open pots with disk bases and lug handles do not occur at Beycesultan, nor do the Beycesultan carinated bowls, white painted juglets and pots with small lug handles on the rim occur at Bağbaşı.

At Aphrodisias there are extensive parallels for the Bağbaşı pottery. Everted rim bowls like **1** are found in levels VIIIB and VII, and plain flat rimmed bowls like **4–7** and **13–21** also occur in both levels.[80] Concave bowls comparable to **11** and **12** occur in levels VIIIA–VIIC, and bowls

[64] *Beycesultan* I figs. P9:14 and P10:10.

[65] *Beycesultan* I figs. P6:26, P4:14, P5:1, P1:11, P10:9.

[66] For **88, 92** and **93,** compare *Beycesultan* I figs. P13:2, P9:1, P3:6 respectively, and in general **99** seems to belong with these jugs too.

[67] *Beycesultan* I fig. P2:8.

[68] E.g. *Beycesultan* I fig. P1:21.

[69] *Beycesultan* I figs. P12:43 and P9:2.

[70] Compare *Beycesultan* I figs. P12:12, P12:28, P12:8 respectively.

[71] E.g. *Beycesultan* I figs. P1:40–41 and P7:14–15.

[72] E.g. *Beycesultan* I fig. P6:3.

[73] Compare *Beycesultan* I fig. P12:7 and 30 respectively.

[74] *Beycesultan* I 90.

[75] E.g. *Beycesultan* I figs. P9:1, 23 and P5:24.

[76] *Beycesultan* I 91 and fig. P6:6, 10.

[77] Possibly from a lid, as *Beycesultan* I fig. P20:5–7 (EB shape 24).

[78] Compare *Beycesultan* I fig. P16:16.

[79] *Beycesultan* I 127 and figs. P14:32 and P20:3.

[80] *Aphrodisias* I fig. 35:13 (type CX8, rare in level VIIIB); *Aphrodisias* II fig. 384:12 (type CX37) and fig. 399:22.

similar to **31** in VIID–VII.[81] Necks of flaring shape or with everted rim are common,[82] and a range of deep vessels with everted rim or inverted neck resemble Bağbaşı **142–146.**[83] From levels VIIB–VI came rim sherds possibly from open pot shapes, and a few bases approach disk bases in type.[84] Lug handles, however, are absent at Aphrodisias. A bowl with a series of holes extending around the rim and onto the loop handle also occurs,[85] but it is from level VI and can be compared to Bağbaşı **101** in general terms only. Flat pans of **238–240** type occur from level VIIIA on, although at Aphrodisias they are burnished on the upper surface,[86] and feet of the same types as **231–234** occur from levels VIIIB–VI.[87] Although in this period of gradually changing shapes it is often difficult to make precise correlations, Bağbaşı does share many features with Aphrodisias levels VIIB–A.

Beycesultan and Aphrodisias have produced the most useful LC sequences so far, but the closest parallels for the Bağbaşı assemblage are from sites south of Burdur. The pottery from Kuruçay Höyük levels 6A-4 belongs to the southwest Anatolian LC tradition.[88] Parallels can be found there for the Bağbaşı open pots, for lug handles (including ones with a thumb impression), for the combined use of lug and strap handles as Bağbaşı **116, 128** and **147,** for pierced holes at the junction of the handle and rim like **51–53,** and for the use of knob decoration on handles like **156.** Baking pans are found, and some of the smaller Bağbaşı basins, for example **38** and **39,** can be compared with the Kuruçay one-handled cups. Flaring bowls, including an example with flat everted rim, occur at Kuruçay, although they are not as common as they are at most southwestern sites and they are not burnished.[89] Nevertheless these levels appear to be comparable to the Bağbaşı assemblage.

Karain, on the edge of the Antalya Plain, produced dark burnished flaring bowls of the shapes normal at Bağbaşı, a combination strap/lug handle and painted pottery of Bağbaşı type.[90] Similar pottery was also found at Çarkini nearby.[91]

Other Artifacts (pls 57–59, 62, 109)

The other artifacts from Bağbaşı are not unlike those from other LC sites of western Anatolia. The simple and utilitarian forms of the objects would allow for widespread comparisons, but the assemblage as a whole is best paralleled in nearby areas. At none of the western Anatolian sites is the collection large.

The various artifacts from the LC levels at Beycesultan are of the same types as the Bağbaşı ones. Fired clay objects from that site include parallels for the scoop (**255**), loomweights

[81] *Aphrodisias* I fig. 35:7 (type CX41); *Aphrodisias* II fig. 392:56.

[82] For **96** compare *Aphrodisias* II fig. 399:12 (type CJ14), for **99–100** fig. 399:33 (type CJ13), for **106** fig. 377:2 (type CJ2), for **112** fig. 405:11 (type CC17) and for **125** fig. 402:6 (type CC15).

[83] *Aphrodisias* I fig. 31:9, 11 and 15 (types CX51, CX42 and XC10).

[84] For small examples comparable to **58** and **60** see *Aphrodisias* II fig. 389:29 and 30 (types CH66 and CH61); for larger varieties see fig. 393:44, 47 and 48 (types B94, CB5 and CB6), and fig. 399:32 (type CC28).

[85] *Aphrodisias* II fig. 405:40 (type CH47).

[86] *Aphrodisias* II fig. 385:10–12, 27 and 36–53, and fig. 392:59 (types BT1–BT11).

[87] *Aphrodisias* II fig. 393:38 and 46, and fig. 402:31 (types B90, B91 and CB4).

[88] *Kuruçay* II figs. 17–26.

[89] *Kuruçay* II 32 and fig. 26.

[90] Sherds in Karain and Antalya Museums, and see İ. Kılıç Kökten, *Belleten* 19 (1955) pl. III:top center.

[91] Öküzini, a third cave in the area, may also have similar pottery. For both see İ. Kılıç Kökten, "Tarsus-Antalya Arası Sahil Şeriti Üzerinde ve Antalya Bölgesinde Yapılan Tarihöncesi Araştırmaları Hakkında", *TürkArkDerg* 8:2 (1958) 13 and pl. 15, fig. 6.

(**256–258**) and spindle whorls (especially **259–260** and **265**). Rather stumpy animal figurines not unlike **275** and **276** also occur. The ground stone axe (**313**), the whetstone (**314**), bone point (**325**) and deer antlers (e.g. **328**) can also be paralleled there.[92] The metal objects are comparable, although because of the hoard found in level XXXIV, there is more variety at Beycesultan. As well as copper needles with loop heads and awls like **323–324,** there was a large chisel, a fragment of a dagger or knife, and a silver ring. Like the Bağbaşı objects most of these seem to have been formed by hammering.[93] The chipped stone industry of Beycesultan is not recorded in detail, but is again apparently comparable, consisting mostly of blade-sections of flint and obsidian, with an occasional side scraper.[94]

The artifacts from Aphrodisias levels VIIIB–VII are not numerous, but again they are in many ways similar to those from Bağbaşı. There are undecorated spindle whorls of the type of **265** in levels VIIIA and VIID, biconical examples similar to **262** and **263** from level VIIB on; a loomweight of the same shape as **256–258** was found in VIIA; an incised clay bead, similar to **270** also in VIIA. Bone spatulas of the type of **326** were found in VIIIA, and fragments of a copper needle and awl comparable to **323–324** in VIIIA and VIIB. The ground stone included axes and whetstones similar to **313** and **314.** There were grinding stones of the two types found at Bağbaşı. The chipped stone consisted mainly of flint with six percent obsidian. The largest category consisted of blades with silica sheen, and there were also other blade fragments, scrapers and several points. Four shells and a fragment of polished antler complete the parallels to Bağbaşı.[95]

Kuruçay Höyük has produced the first LC parallels for the Bağbaşı spit supports (**250–253**). Both round and rectangular based ones were found there. Also from Kuruçay were ground stone axes, an antler hammer similar to **328,** bone needles and copper objects.[96]

One type of object common elsewhere, but not present at Bağbaşı, is the pierced or unpierced stone or clay disk.[97] Bone awls are also missing from the Bağbaşı collection, but this may be due to the chances of preservation.

Two types of objects not previously identified in the western Anatolian LC period were found at Bağbaşı—the stamp seal (**273**) and the counter (**274**). "Stamp seals" of clay with a design on one face have a long history in Anatolia. They were found at Çatal Hüyük and Hacılar, and are common in the EBA.[98] Whether the Bağbaşı example is evidence of continuity between the two groups is doubtful, for it is unlikely that the earlier ones were, in fact, used as seals. The shape of **273** is closer to that of the EB examples. Objects of similar shape to the counter have been found in level I at Hacılar, but are not otherwise known in the Chalcolithic.[99]

92 *Beycesultan* I fig. F2.

93 *Beycesultan* I 280–83, 291. Ten of the copper objects were analyzed; eight were of unalloyed copper and two of low arsenical copper (Prentiss S. de Jesus, *The Development of Prehistoric Mining and Metallurgy in Anatolia* (British Archaeological Reports International Series 74 1980) 129).

94 *Beycesultan* I 273.

95 For whorls see *Aphrodisias* II e.g. fig. 385:29, fig. 389:41–42 and fig. 396:23–24; for loomweights fig. 399:34; for clay bead fig. 399:49; for bone spatulas fig. 385:43; for copper objects fig. 385:49 and fig. 396:21; for ground stone fig. 246 and fig. 251; for chipped stone figs. 253–256.

96 *Kuruçay* II 33, figs. 27–28; *Kuruçay* III pl. 19 and *Kuruçay* IV pl. 28. The metal objects were 99% copper (*Kuruçay* IV 46–7).

97 E.g. *Beycesultan* I fig. F2:3, 15; *Aphrodisias* II figs. 389:45–9, 392:64–6, 399:47, 402:28. They are also common at Karataş-Semayük in the EBA.

98 James Mellaart, "Excavations at Çatal Hüyük," *AnatSt* 12 (1962) pl. VII:c; *Hacılar* I 164 and II fig. 187: 1–4, 7. For EB examples at Karataş-Semayük where they are common see Machteld J. Mellink, *AJA* 69 (1965) pl. 64: fig. 33.

99 *Hacılar* I 164 and II fig. 187:8–10.

Architecture

Bağbaşı is the only site in the Elmalı Plain to have produced architecture of the LC period. Various construction methods were used, all of which combined the use of clay and timber. Most common was apparently the use of mud walling strengthened by vertical timbers, as demonstrated in the house of the upper level of trench 116, but log cabin construction of horizontal timbers coated with mud plaster was also found, in the house in trench 115. The latter has no parallels in prehistoric Anatolia, and the use of mud walling and vertical timbers is also rare. It is found at the nearby EB site of Karataş-Semayük, although at Karataş more attention was paid to the foundations.[100] Most mud and timber construction of the prehistoric periods was wattle-and-daub, which was used only rarely at Bağbaşı.[101]

The combination of mud slabs and horizontal timbers found in the house in trench 105 has few parallels at this period. At the site of Can Hasan in the Konya Plain, layers 2A–5 produced some buildings of mudbrick walls reinforced with timbers. In the well-preserved level 2B, horizontal timbers were placed lengthwise near the edges of the walls and crosswise through them, but vertical timbers were also used at this site.[102]

Elsewhere in western Anatolia in the LC period walls were of mudbrick. At Beycesultan thin, elongated bricks were used. They were bound together with clay mortar and covered with mud plaster.[103] The walls found in level VIID at Aphrodisias are of similar construction; while those at Kuruçay levels 6A and 6 were apparently of mudbrick, sometimes on stone foundations.[104] Although the Bağbaşı mud slabs are exceptionally long (up to 1.18 m), and formed *in situ,* i.e. not truly mudbricks, they are related to the usual mudbrick tradition of Neolithic and Chalcolithic Anatolia.[105]

It is difficult at present to assess the relationship of the plans of the Bağbaşı houses and settlement with contemporary sites, because there is little comparative material. Most of the houses at Kuruçay levels 6A and 6 consisted of a single rectangular room (8–50 square meters), sometimes with a central hearth and an oven in one corner. Several buildings contained more than one room. Although most of these were probably for storage, some may have been houses. The alignment of the buildings was regular.[106] The buildings at Beycesultan were composed of one or more rectangular units, varying from about 10 m^2 to about 20 m^2 in area, and were not, therefore, unlike those of Bağbaşı. At both sites it is possible that units interpreted as multi-roomed buildings were separate houses divided by party walls. In general, however, at Beycesultan as at

[100] Jayne Warner, "The Megaron and Apsidal House in Early Bronze Age Western Anatolia: New Evidence from Karataş," *AJA* 83 (1979) 139.

[101] EBA examples were discussed in Jayne Warner, *AJA* 83 (1979) 139–40, notes 19–20. Neolithic examples were found at Fikirtepe (Kurt Bittel, "Bemerkungen über die prähistorische Ansiedlung auf dem Fikirtepe bei Kadiköy (Istanbul)," *IstMitt* 19/20 (1969/1970) 6–8) and at Hacılar the method was used for partitions and upper storeys (*Hacılar* I 14, 16 and 34).

[102] D.H. French, "Excavations at Can Hasan," *AnatSt* 12 (1962) 30; and *AnatSt* 18 (1968) 45 and 52.

[103] *Beycesultan* I 19–26. Timbers are used in the walls here in the Early Bronze Age, e.g. level XIX (*Beycesultan* I 27).

[104] *Aphrodisias* II 65–67. *Kuruçay* II 23–26 and *Kuruçay* IV 43.

[105] For Hacılar level I (0.63 m) see *Hacılar* I 75; for Çatal Hüyük see James Mellaart, *Çatal Hüyük. A Neolithic Town in Anatolia* (London 1967) 55 (over 0.90 m); for Can Hasan 2B see D.H. French, *AnatSt* 12 (1962) 30 (up to 0.80 m).

[106] *Kuruçay* II fig. 9; *Kuruçay* III pls 12, 16; *Kuruçay* IV pl. 16; *Kuruçay* V pl. III; *Kuruçay* VI fig. 7.

Bağbaşı, buildings seem to have stood independently. This is in contrast to the unified complexes of Hacılar and the sites of central Anatolia.[107]

The Beycesultan buildings contained more built-in features than the Bağbaşı ones—narrow platforms and bins occurred in most houses. The Bağbaşı niche is unparalleled at Beycesultan, but niches and cupboards were common in LN/EC Hacılar, where they were 0.50 to 0.80 m deep and 0.80 to 1.50 m wide.[108] At Beycesultan, Kuruçay and Bağbaşı fixed hearths are usual. At Beycesultan they are circular or, more often, rectangular, and are made of mudbricks. In level XXXI the circular hearth has a screen across part of the edge.[109] At Kuruçay they are placed centrally and a screen across one side is normal.[110]

THE POTTERY SEQUENCE IN THE ELMALI PLAIN

The comparative section has established the general positions within the chronological sequence of the three main groups of archaeological material from the Elmalı Plain. Most of the assemblages consist entirely of pottery and it is, therefore, only the pottery that allows a coherent discussion of its characteristics and development. In this section each of the Elmalı Plain pottery traditions will be defined, and the pottery sequence of the plain, so far as we know it at present, described.

LATE NEOLITHIC AND EARLY CHALCOLITHIC POTTERY

Pottery of LN type has now been found at a number of sites in the Elmalı Plain—at Gökpınar (**1–8**), Akçay (**1–35**) and Tekke (**2**). This pottery is grit tempered. The size of the grits varies from 0.15 to 0.05 cm in diameter, and they are normally about 0.10 cm. The pots appear to have been coil-built, and many were slipped. The color of the slip ranges from brown to crimson, but is usually scarlet. It often looks rather streaky, as though it were applied with a brush or cloth rather than by dipping. The slipped surface is burnished. The fabric is brown to orange in color with a gray or black core, often almost as thick as the sherd. The handles are applied against the wall of the pot.

Shapes are jars with inverted necks, jars and bowls with everted or vertical rims, and some flaring bowls and hole-mouth jars. At Akçay painted decoration was used, though it was not common. This site seems to have been occupied during the whole period of Hacılar IX–VI; Gökpınar has parallels only with the earlier part of the sequence.

The pottery of the EC period in southwestern Anatolia is essentially a continuation of the LN tradition and is distinguished by the increased popularity of painted pottery. Only a few sherds from Akçay (**14, 15** and **33**) and Tekke (**3**) can be attributed to the period. However, it may be that painted pottery was not popular in this area, and that continuity of LN features was strong.

[107] E.g. *Hacılar* II figs. 7 and 20; D.H. French, "Excavations at Can Hasan," *AnatSt* 13 (1963) fig. 1 for MC layer 2B. The LC village at Can Hasan was perhaps less unified in concept—D.H. French, *AnatSt* 14 (1964) figs. 1–4.

[108] *Hacılar* I 14–15.

[109] *Beycesultan* I 19–26. See also e.g. Hetty Goldman, *Excavations at Gözlü Kule, Tarsus* II (Princeton 1956) 5–6, and *Hacılar* I 14 and 34.

[110] *Kuruçay* II figs. 9 and 11:1.

MIDDLE CHALCOLITHIC POTTERY

The pottery assemblages from Kızılbel and Lower Bağbaşı are connected by their fabrics. They are basically grit tempered, unslipped and only lightly burnished. The pots were coil-built, and the walls of the bowls, especially, were quite thin. The ends of the handles and the areas of the pot to which they were attached were deeply scored. The occurrence of hole-mouth jars and the preponderance of strap handles also connect the two assemblages. There are, of course, quite substantial differences between them, both in surface color and in many of the shapes, but both belong to the same tradition. Similar pottery has also been found at Bayındırköy, and possibly at Arapkuyusu and Gökpınar West.

The internal relationship of this pottery to the other traditions in the plain is not clear. The stratigraphic position of the Lower Bağbaşı pottery indicates a date prior to the LC period, and the absence of this tradition from other LC sites in the plain confirms that it is not a LC tradition. Nor has it been identified at the sites with LN/EC occupation.[111] A date for this tradition in either the LN/EC or LC periods would, therefore, entail the co-existence in the plain of villages using two different and independent pottery traditions. While not impossible, this is unlikely.

A number of features connect the Kızılbel and Lower Bağbaşı pottery with the LN/EC tradition (see Chart 2). The grit tempered fabric and elements of the manufacturing tradition, such as the method of handle attachment (although the deep scoring of the areas of attachment is not found in the LN/EC tradition) are the most important. Certain shapes are also common to both traditions, notably curve-sided, flat-rimmed bowls and hole-mouth vessels. However, the stand and pan fragments found at Kızılbel, the use of impressed decoration and knobs, and the occasional use of a plug attachment for a handle, connect rather to the LC tradition. The relationship of the Kızılbel-Lower Bağbaşı tradition with either of the other traditions is not close, but an intermediate position between them would seem to be indicated. A MC date agrees with the evidence from other areas discussed above.

LATE CHALCOLITHIC POTTERY

The pottery from Boztepe, Karaburun, Bağbaşı and the related sites is similar in most respects. It is coarse, poorly fired pottery with grit and fiber inclusions. The pots are coil-built around flat bases, and the handles and lugs are applied with plug attachments. About ten percent of the sherds, from bowls and jugs, are burnished. Dark burnished bowls, a wide range of neck types especially ones with everted rims, large pots with lug handles, and various types of baking pans are typical of the tradition. Comparisons with the LC levels at Beycesultan and Aphrodisias are plentiful.

There are, however, differences between the various Elmalı LC assemblages. Boztepe, Karaburun and the Semayük Bekleme site are distinguished by the occurrence of flat perforated and/or burnished pans, and both Boztepe and Karaburun by certain bowl and handle types—Boztepe by bowls with rolled rim and upturned lugs; Karaburun by bowls with rounded rim and horizontal tubular handles. Horizontal tubular handles are also found at Dinsiz. As none

[111] A few sherds from Kızılbel, including **22,** are close to the LN/EC tradition, but are different in texture and temper.

of these features occurs in the much larger sample from Bağbaşı, they should represent a valid distinction.

Bağbaşı is further distinguished from these sites by the presence of disk bases, impressions on lug handles, pans with raised rim or side, and plain flaring burnished bowls. Less common features restricted to Bağbaşı may be missing from the other assemblages only by chance.

As no functional differences between the sites are perceptible, the differences in the pottery assemblages will be assigned to chronological factors. This can be supported by the comparisons of the various sites with the Beycesultan sequence. The pottery from both Boztepe and Karaburun can be paralleled in Beycesultan LC 1, while the Bağbaşı pottery has many parallels with the later part of the sequence and can probably be equated with LC 2–3.

Other LC sites in the Elmalı Plain are known only from surface finds. Dark burnished bowls with flat everted rims come from Karabayır and Tekke; disk bases of Bağbaşı-type from Buralia, Gökpınar West and Yaka Çiftliği, which also had an upturned lug similar to Boztepe **23.** Maltepe may also have been occupied during this period.

Despite the many parallels with other LC assemblages from southwestern Anatolia, the LC pottery of the Elmalı Plain is distinctive. It lacks the white painting found at most other sites, and the deep-necked "tankards"; and it has such features as lug handles (restricted apparently to the area south of Burdur) and disk bases. Nevertheless, at this period the pottery of the Elmalı Plain was one variant of a tradition widespread in western Anatolia.

COMMENTS

The three groups of pottery discussed obviously do not form a complete sequence. Exploration of the plain has not been exhaustive, and there are undoubtedly other sites, as yet unidentified, with pottery of other Neolithic and Chalcolithic phases.

First, it is possible that villages were established in the plain before the LN period. Similar plains in southwestern Anatolia had permanent settlements by at least the seventh millennium.[112] Although conditions in the Elmalı area may not have been equally propitious,[113] the plain is fertile and settlement may have reached it at an early date.

EN pottery is scarce in southwestern Anatolia, with deposits identified only from the Beldibi and Belbaşı caves.[114] Nothing comparable has been found in the Elmalı area, but there are two fragments, quite unlike the Beldibi pottery, that may be EN in date (Akçay **13** and Hacımusalar **1**). They are sufficiently different from the normal LN pottery to belong to an earlier phase of the Neolithic period, and some sherds of similar fine fabric occur in the earliest levels at Hacılar.[115] The main reason for the scarcity of remains of this early period is probably the heavy overlay that must often cover the sites. The overlay could be cultural deposit, as at Akçay where most of the

[112] *Hacılar* I 189–242.

[113] The early settlements tended to be on the alluvial deposits left by the recession of the lakes in the Pleistocene. The lakes in the Elmalı Plain are subject to underground drainage and were less subject to expansion and contraction during Glacial and post-Glacial periods. See Oğuz Erol, in William C. Brice (ed.), *The Environmental History of the Near and Middle East since the Last Ice Age* (London 1978) 111–39.

[114] Enver Y. Bostancı, "Researches on the Mediterranean Coast of Anatolia," *Anatolia* 4 (1959) 146–47 and pl. IV; and "A New Upper Palaeolithic and Mesolithic Facies at Belbaşı Rock Shelter on the Mediterranean Coast," *Belleten* 26 (1962) 253–54.

[115] E.g. sherds 1287 and 1303 from a pot from level VIII, now in the collection in the British Institute of Archaeology in Ankara.

Neolithic pottery was only found because recent ploughing had cut into the hüyük, or natural deposit such as that covering Gökpınar.

Breaks are apparent in the Elmalı sequence both before and after the Kızılbel-Lower Bağbaşı group. They probably result from gaps in the sequence as we know it. It is possible, but less likely, that the MC and LC pottery traditions both appeared suddenly and fully developed in the plain. Kızılbel and Lower Bağbaşı themselves also seem to be separated by some interval, for there are considerable differences between the shapes at the two sites.

Finally, no deposit clearly assignable to LC 4 has been found. This period may be represented at Akçay where the fabric of **36–38** is similar to the LC pottery from other sites but finer than usual, and **37** may possibly be from a carinated bowl of Beycesultan LC 4 type.[116]

CHRONOLOGY

ABSOLUTE DATES

The establishment of a chronology for the Neolithic and Chalcolithic periods of western Anatolia is difficult. There are few western sites with long stratified sequences, and the local sequences are often imprecise and their correlation disputed. Absolute dates are also few. Direct links with areas of better established chronology, such as Egypt and Mesopotamia, are non-existent, and attempts to correlate the southwestern Late Chalcolithic with Cilicia have not been successful. This period has been variously associated with Tarsus EB I, and with Mersin Middle Chalcolithic.[117]

Radiocarbon dates are, therefore, the only evidence available for establishing a framework of absolute dates. The relevant dates are shown on Chart 3. They are given in radiocarbon years B.C., according to the Libby half-life of 5568 years and, where possible, their calibrated equivalents are also given.[118]

The radiocarbon dates suggest that the Hacılar LN and EC levels belong to the middle and later parts of the sixth millennium (radiocarbon years B.C.), and that the LC period began by at least the middle of the fourth millennium (radiocarbon years B.C.) or by the fifth millennium B.C. It is, therefore, probable that there was a gap of some length between Hacılar EC and the LC of southwest Anatolia, although it is not possible to establish its precise length without knowing the calibration necessary for the Hacılar dates. If we assume the same adjustment factor as that for the LC dates, about 800 to 1000 years, then the gap would be of considerable duration.

The LC period must have ended before the close of the fourth millennium B.C. A precise date cannot be given, as the number of dates for the period is still small, but they are supported by the calibrated dates for the mound at Karataş-Semayük. They place the duration of level II (end of EB I) in the first quarter of the third millennium B.C.

[116] Compare e.g. *Beycesultan* I fig. P12:41. Carinated bowls may have been more common at Beycesultan than elsewhere. At Aphrodisias they were not popular.

[117] Machteld J. Mellink, "Anatolian Chronology," in *Chronologies in Old World Archaeology,* ed. Robert W. Ehrich (Chicago 1965) 114; *Beycesultan* I 111.

[118] H.N. Michael and E.K. Ralph, "University of Pennsylvania Radiocarbon Dates XVI," *Radiocarbon* 16 (1974) 198–218; R.M. Clark, "An objectively derived calibration curve for radiocarbon dates," *Antiquity* 49 (1975) 251–66.

RELATIVE SEQUENCE

At Hacılar, for the first time in the southwest, there is a stratified sequence of levels covering some 500 years from the middle of the sixth millennium (radiocarbon years). This is the earliest period for which there is extensive evidence over the southwest, and the earliest pottery from Elmalı belongs to it.

The site of Hacılar was abandoned while the Hacılar culture was apparently still flourishing.[119] The LC culture of the area is completely different and does not develop from that at Hacılar, but no excavated site has yet produced a sequence in which the changeover has been clearly demonstrated. At Aphrodisias pottery similar to Hacılar VII–VI was found in the lowest excavated level VIIIC together with LC pottery, but as the material came from a deep sounding without architectural remains, some telescoping of the deposits is possible.[120]

The precise relationship between the two cultures has been disputed. Mellink proposed a long hiatus between them; Mellaart the sudden introduction of the LC culture into the area, almost directly after the end of level I at Hacılar.[121] As the end of the LC period can be fixed towards the end of the fourth millennium B.C., the length of the period varies considerably in the two assessments.

The identification of MC remains in the Elmalı Plain suggests that at least there the LC culture did not follow the local EC directly. The lack of radiocarbon dates for the LC before the mid fifth millennium B.C. is, therefore, probably significant. The late sixth and early fifth millennia B.C. is the period in which the MC pottery can be placed, thus making it approximately contemporary with the Middle Neolithic in the Aegean, with Saliagos and the lowest levels at Emporio.[122]

ELMALI: INDEPENDENT BUT CONNECTED

The earliest villages so far discovered in the Elmalı Plain belong to the LN period.[123] They have not been excavated but the pottery is similar to that of Hacılar IX–VI. The pottery of this tradition is grit tempered and coil built, with the handles applied flat against the wall of the pot. Black cores are usual. It is characterized by the extensive use of red slips and tubular lugs. The hole-mouth shapes have straight rather than curved upper walls. Similar pottery has been found over a wide area from the Elmalı Plain and Karain in the south, throughout the Tefenni, Burdur and Dinar areas, to Aphrodisias and as far north as Mercimek Tepe near Afyon.[124] To the west it occurs in the area of Miletus and on Chios[125] but further north, in the Aydın and Akhisar areas, there is a variant of this pottery with similar shapes and surface finish but fiber temper.[126] To the east the pottery of the upper levels at Erbaba, although showing similarities to the Hacılar ware, has a

[119] As indicated most obviously by the continuing increase in the popularity of the EC painted pottery—*Hacılar* I 132–33.

[120] *Aphrodisias* I fig. 30:16, 22, 29 (types CX21, CX48, CX22) for Hacılar types and figs. 35:14, 18 and 39:4,6 (types CX18, CX23, P23, P8) for the LC types; *Aphrodisias* II 521–522.

[121] Machteld J. Mellink, in *Chronologies in Old World Archaeology,* ed. Robert W. Ehrich (Chicago 1965) 127 (chart); James Mellaart, "Anatolia and the Balkans," *Antiquity* 34 (1960) 278 and in *CAH* I:2, 403–405.

[122] Colin Renfrew, *The Emergence of Civilisation* (London 1972) 72–76.

[123] A few possible EN sherds have been found (see above) but their identification is not certain.

[124] *Hacılar* I, 146 and II, fig. 156a; J. Mellaart, *AnatSt* 4 (1954) 182, figs. 27–30; *Aphrodisias* I, 577.

[125] W. Voigtländer, "Frühe Funde von Killiktepe bei Milet," *IstMitt* 33 (1983) 5–39; *Emporio* 14–24.

[126] D. French, *BIAL* 5 (1965) 18–19. This pottery is included on the distribution map of Hacılar pottery, *Hacılar* II, fig. 156a.

different fabric.[127] If these variants are indeed contemporary, the distribution area of the Hacılar LN pottery is well defined.

Many of the Hacılar-tradition sites are known only from surface sherds but there is little evidence as yet for local variation and the tradition of the whole area seems to have been homogeneous. This suggests that each locality in the southwest, including Elmalı, would have been closely related to its neighbors and that a common origin and sustained contact are likely. Repeated exchanges from village to village are a possible form of contact, a form already suggested for this period in connection with the distribution of obsidian.[128]

During the EC period the homogeneity of the pottery tradition weakens. Continuity from LN is everywhere clear but local features increase. At Hacılar, from level V on, painted pottery increases in proportion to the monochrome and has a distinctive design repertoire. In level I a new style of painting is found, still based on the same tradition but with more linear designs. The pottery from the Dinar region has designs similar to those from Hacılar, but a high proportion of the pots was unslipped.[129] The sherds from Çaykenarı II in the Korkuteli Plain were made in the same tradition, but with shapes and designs that cannot be exactly paralleled at Hacılar. [130] The Elmalı Plain sherds have been discussed above. They are again similar to some Hacılar examples but display an individual and less complex style.

The precise chronological correlations of these various painted pottery styles is not yet clear, although many may belong only to the latter part of the period. In the Tefenni and Bucak areas monochrome pottery of Hacılar IV–II type has been found, but none of the corresponding painted pottery.[131] However, pottery that is close to that of Hacılar I in style does occur in this area and further south at Karain.[132] It is possible that the southern painted pottery styles belong only to the later part of the EC period and that monochrome wares continued unchallenged in the south for much of the EC.[133]

The more widespread use and increasing popularity of painted decoration on the pottery must have been a factor in the breakdown in homogeneity in the Hacılar pottery tradition. It would have made it easier for the potters of a village or area to develop their own style than it had been when to do so would have meant varying the shapes (determined to a large extent by the functions of the pots) or the fabric.[134] The decrease in homogeneity may not, therefore, necessarily reflect a change in the frequency or type of contacts between local areas; it may reflect, rather, increased opportunity to express local identity within the established tradition.

[127] J. Bordaz, *TürkArkDerg* 18–2 (1969) 61 and 23–2 (1976) 41–42.

[128] C. Renfrew, J. Dixon and J. Cann, "Obsidian and Early Cultural Contact in the Near East," *ProcPS* 32 (1966) 30–72 and "Further Analysis of Near Eastern Obsidians," *ProcPS* 34 (1968) 326–330. Elmalı was part of this system as is shown by the obsidian from Akçay (**39–40**).

[129] J. Mellaart, *AnatSt* 4 (1954) 184, figs. 52–54.

[130] J. Mellaart, *AnatSt* 4 (1954) 184, figs. 57–58.

[131] *Hacılar* I, 146–147 and II, fig. 156c.

[132] K. Kökten, *Anatolia* 7 (1963) 86, fig. 9b.

[133] In this respect the map, *Hacılar* II, fig. 156b, is correct, although it does not make allowances for the local nature of the styles.

[134] Helene Balfet, "Ethnological Observations in North Africa and Archaeological Interpretation," in *Ceramics and Man,* ed. F.R. Matson (Chicago 1965) 164–168. In view of the style differences between areas the hypothesis of J. Mellaart, *Hacılar* I, 146–147, that Hacılar I pottery may have been a luxury ware exported over a wide area is unlikely. There was, moreover, apparently no effective transportation available to effect such a distribution—we have no evidence of pack animals and the distribution is not riverine. See George M. Foster, "The Sociology of Pottery," in *Ceramics and Man,* ed. F.R. Matson (Chicago 1965) 56 and Keith Nicklin, "Stability and Innovation in Pottery Manufacture," *World Archaeology* 3 (1971) 14–16.

The following period is not well known. It is probable that there had been disruptions of some kind at the end of EC, for the well-established LN/EC sites were abandoned. Mellaart attributed these abandonments to an invasion of people bringing LC culture into the southwest, but the earliest dates we have for LC remains are in the mid-fifth millennium B.C., possibly as much as 1000 years after the end of the EC settlements. It is possible that the agriculture on which the LN/EC economy was based was disrupted by drought, pests or plant diseases, so that the people were forced to leave their villages and find alternative sources of food. The paucity of sites datable to this intermediate, MC, period suggests a drop in the population of the area.[135] The previous social structure must have been seriously disturbed.

In Elmalı the two sites of this MC period have produced no architecture or finds apart from some pottery. The pottery appears to have developed from the LN/EC tradition but contains other elements connected to the traditions of the east Aegean. With so little material available, we cannot tell whether contacts with the east Aegean were sustained or what form they took. However, the new features—the pan with row of piercings below the rim and the strap handles—are technological innovations, the one presumably a new method of handling some form of food[136] and the other a feature that increases the ease of carrying and tipping pots. Taken with the changed distribution pattern of sites, which are now on the high ground on the edge of the plain instead of out in it, we may speculate that there had been a change in the subsistence activities of the area, perhaps under the stimulus of contact with the west.

In the LC period settlements were numerous throughout western Anatolia and, as far as we know, they were all small villages. The period was long and the cultural sequence, which developed directly into that of the EBA, was uninterrupted. During this period the same pottery tradition was used all over western Anatolia. The pottery is handmade and tempered with both grits and fiber. It is coil built, and at the Elmalı sites and at Aphrodisias it has been observed that the upper coil was regularly smoothed down on the outside of the lower one. The pots were poorly fired and have black cores and dark, mottled surfaces. The firing atmosphere was uneven for, even apart from the dark mottling, the surface color varies from red, orange and brown to gray and black. Handles are often applied with plug attachments. In the Elmalı Plain this method is almost universal, and it has also been recognized at Pazaryeri I, Beycesultan and Aphrodisias, although at the last site some handles were applied flat against the pot wall.[137] Bowls and jugs are usually burnished; large pots are simply smoothed. At some sites, including Beycesultan and Aphrodisias, some of the pottery was covered with a slip.

The most characteristic shapes are dark burnished bowls. They have simple flat bases and are low and wide, with flaring or curved sides and a variety of rim forms. Open pots, small one-handled jugs or tankards and necked jars also occur in a variety of forms, but these shapes are less standardized and they are less thoroughly documented for most sites. The usual forms of

[135] James Mellaart, "Anatolia and the Balkans," *Antiquity* 34 (1960) 278; *Beycesultan* 106 and 112; *Cambridge Ancient History* I:1, 326 and I:2, 403–405. Refik Duru (*Kuruçay* II, 70) dates Kuruçay levels 6–4 to the period between Hacılar I and Beycesultan XL, but level 4 has since been shown to belong to the very end of LC (*Kuruçay* VI, 605) and there are no gaps in the sequence of levels 6–4.

[136] In the Aegean the shape is called a "cheese pot," see John S. Belmont and Colin Renfrew, "Two Prehistoric Sites on Mykonos," *AJA* 68 (1964) 398–399 and A. Sampson, *BSA* 79 (1984) 242–243.

[137] D. French, *AnatSt* 17 (1967) 79, fig. 16:14 (sherd seen in British Institute of Archaeology in Ankara collection); *Beycesultan* fig. P5:13–14 etc.; *Aphrodisias* I, fig. 42 etc.

decoration are white painting and pattern burnishing, but they are not universal. Impressed, incised and applied decoration are used less frequently. The variations in decoration do not, however, obscure the basic uniformity of this pot-making tradition.

A different pottery tradition was used in central Anatolia, where the fabric is fiber and pebble tempered and the handles are applied flat against the pot wall. Poor firing and burnished surfaces are characteristic of this pottery, too. However, the shape repertoire, with its shallow, flaring bowls on high pedestals and its deep jars with constricted mouth and everted rim, is different. Some white painted decoration occurs, but incised and impressed decoration, often with white filling, is more common.[138] This tradition extends at least as far west as Yazır in the Sivrihisar district, and some elements may also extend into the Eskişehir area, as indicated by the possible pedestalled bowls from Pazaryeri I.[139] In general, however, the Eskişehir and Afyon regions contain more elements related to the western Anatolian tradition. The Konya Plain, despite the resemblances of some of its coarse wares to that of western Anatolia, should also be regarded as a separate pottery area. Its predominantly red slipped, incurved bowls are unrelated to those of the west.[140]

The relationships between the LC settlements within western Anatolia have been discussed several times. Mellaart, in 1962, presented the view that western Anatolia in the LC period consisted of two pottery provinces, the northwest and the southwest.[141] This hypothesis was formulated when good sequences were available only for Kumtepe and Beycesultan and they were regarded as type sites for their respective areas. French refined this hypothesis to explain overlaps in the distributions of characteristic bowl types.[142] He suggested that in the earlier LC western Anatolia had a homogeneous pottery tradition with a divergence between north and south occurring in the LC 3 period, when Kumtepe IB rolled rim bowls with tubular handle occurred in the northwest, but not in the southwest.[143] In fact, more recent finds have shown that the distribution of each type is different and that the distributions overlap without forming subprovinces within western Anatolia. The results from the long sequence at Aphrodisias, in particular, have shown that the types were also often used for longer periods than had been thought.

The LC dark burnished bowls take various forms and only the most distinctive—the bowl with flat, everted rim, that with concave sides, that with carinated sides and that with rolled rim—will be examined here. Flaring bowls with flat everted rim have a wide distribution, extending from the İznik area in the north to the Elmalı Plain in the south and as far east as the Afyon area. They also occur at Tigani on Samos. At Beycesultan they are found only in levels XXXIX–XXXVI (LC 1), but the Bağbaşı evidence suggests that in some areas they continued later in the LC period.[144]

Slightly concave-sided bowls with thinned rim, such as those characteristic of Kumtepe IA, are

[138] For example, H. Koşay and M. Akok, *Büyük Güllücek Kazısı* (Ankara 1957) 32–37 and pls. XVII–XXII; H. Koşay and M. Akok, *Alaca Hüyük Kazısı 1940–1948* (Ankara 1966) pls. 150–151.

[139] D. French, *AnatSt* 17 (1967) 58.

[140] For example, D. French, "Excavations at Can Hasan," *AnatSt* 15 (1965) 93–94, fig. 4–5.

[141] *Beycesultan* 103–110.

[142] D. French, *AnatSt* 11 (1961) 103.

[143] D. French, *AnatSt* 11 (1961) 113 and "Prehistoric Sites in Northwest Anatolia II," *AnatSt* 19 (1969) 75.

[144] D. French, *AnatSt* 17 (1967) 57–58; *Beycesultan* fig. P1:4 and P2:13; *Aphrodisias* I fig. 35:13 (type CX8, level VIIIB) and *Aphrodisias* II fig. 399:6 (type XC25, level VIIA); *Kuruçay* IV, pl. 25:3.

mostly found in the Troad, but similar shapes also occur at Emporio on Chios from level VIII on and at Bağbaşı.[145] Bowls with flaring, sometimes concave, sides and simple flat rims have a wide distribution from the Balıkesir Plain in the north and Emporio and Miletus in the west to the Antalya area and the Elmalı Plain in the south. At Beycesultan they occur in the LC 1–3 periods.[146]

Carinated bowls are not common, but they occur in the İznik area, at Emporio from level IX, Beycesultan LC 3–4, Aphrodisias and in the Dinar and Burdur areas.[147] Bowls with rolled rim and horizontal, tubular lug of Kumtepe IB type occur over an area from the Troad south to Emporio and the Gediz River and inland to the Akhisar, Manisa and Balıkesir plains. Rolled rim bowls without the tubular lug also occur at Aphrodisias VIII–VII, Beycesultan XIX–XVII and Boztepe.[148]

As most of these types were in use for long periods (flaring rims LC 1–3, concave sides LC 1–3, rolled rims LC 1–EB) the overlapping distribution areas cannot have been caused by boundaries between distribution areas changing over time. Moreover, the decorative features of the LC pottery have, on the whole, distributions different from the bowl types. Within western Anatolia impressed decoration has been found only in the south. Impressions on lug handles seem to be restricted to the area south of Burdur and other impressed decoration has been noted only at Bağbaşı.

White painting is found over most of western and central Anatolia. Although it does not occur in the Elmalı Plain, it is found in the south in the Antalya, Korkuteli and Burdur areas.[149] At Beycesultan it is found in all LC phases, but it is most common in LC 1.[150] The designs are all linear and they can be complex, including cross-hatched, chequerboard and intersecting parallel line patterns. Bowl rims and jug bodies are the areas usually painted. Two white painted jugs from Kusura period A bear designs close to those on Beycesultan LC 3–4 jugs.[151] At Aphrodisias white painted pottery closely comparable to Beycesultan was found in all levels, but especially in VIIIA.[152]

In northwestern Anatolia white painting occurs throughout the LC period, but again there are areas where it has not yet been found.[153] At Kayışlar cross-hatched triangles, hatched triangles and parallel vertical lines were used on the inside rims of bowls[154] and at Kumtepe three white

[145] J. Sperling, *Hesperia* 45 (1976) 316 and 318; Winifred Lamb, "Schliemann's Prehistoric Sites in the Troad," *PrähZ* 23 (1932) fig. 14. D. French, "Late Chalcolithic Pottery in North-West Turkey and the Aegean," *AnatSt* 14 (1964) 137 shows that they occur on the north side of the Bosphorus too. They also occur at *Emporio* e.g. fig. 123:156, and possibly at *Tigani,* pl. 42.

[146] D. French, *AnatSt* 11 (1961) 101; *Emporio* e.g. fig. 142:450; W. Voigtländer, *IstMitt* 32 (1982) fig. 2:5–6; examples from Karain in the Antalya and Karain museums; *Beycesultan* fig. P2:1 and P6:19; *Aphrodisias* I 978 and II fig. 384:11 and 12 (types CX36 and CX37, levels VIIIA–VII); *Kuruçay* IV, pl. 25:4.

[147] D. French, *AnatSt* 17 (1967) 57–58; *Emporio* fig. 123:150 and 154; *Beycesultan* 104 and fig. P10:1–8; *Aphrodisias* I 994 and II e.g. fig. 396:7 (type XC1, levels VIIB-A); J. Mellaart, *AnatSt* 4 (1954) 182, fig. 35.

[148] J. Sperling, *Hesperia* 45 (1976) 357–358 and fig. 13; D. French, *AnatSt* 11 (1961) 103–104, 112 and fig. 2; *Emporio* fig. 148; *Aphrodisias* I 994, 1000 and 1006, II fig. 377:4 and fig. 399:3 (types XC23, CX4 and CX67); *Beycesultan* fig. P14:2, 4–6 and fig. P15:18.

[149] *Beycesultan* 104; Kuruçay Höyük has produced a few examples of white painted and white filled incised decoration on the outside of closed vessels and rectangular pots (*Kuruçay* III, 30–31 and pl. 19; *Kuruçay* IV, pl. 20; *Kuruçay* V, pl. 10).

[150] *Beycesultan* 81–83.

[151] Winifred Lamb, "Excavations at Kusura near Afyon Karahisar," *Archaeologia* 86 (1937) 18, fig. 6:12–13.

[152] *Aphrodisias* II 310–311.

[153] For example, the Marmara area—D. French, *AnatSt* 17 (1967) 58.

[154] D. French, *AnatSt* 11 (1961) 113 and 124, figs. 5:1–2 and 9–12.

painted jug sherds were found in levels 1A2 and 1B4.[155] None of these northern designs resembled those from Beycesultan.

White painted wares also occurred in the eastern Aegean islands at Poliochni (Black) on Lemnos, Emporio and Ayio Gala on Chios, Tigani on Samos and Vathy on Kalymnos.[156] The examples are all similar, with simple, linear designs on bowls and jugs. The painted sherds from Kumtepe belong with them. This group is separated from Beycesultan by the use of different designs and the fact that the jugs are painted on the necks and handles.

The other main decorative form of the period is pattern burnishing. It occurs at a number of sites in western Anatolia and the eastern Aegean, although it is common only at Tigani on Samos and Beşiktepe in the Troad.[157] The pattern burnishing from these two sites, with that from Kumtepe 1A1, Akbaş (on the northern side of the Bosphorus), Gümüşova I-Çandarlı and perhaps Ovaköy I-Balıkesir, forms a group characterized by panelled decoration, often on the inside of bowls.[158] The group is restricted to the northwest coastal area of Anatolia, with Tigani as a southern outlier. The Kumtepe 1A2–1B examples show less uniformity than the earlier examples but are probably survivals of this group. The distribution of these sites does not coincide with that of any of the burnished bowl types. In fact, in the Troad pattern burnishing occurs on bowls with thinned rim and curved sides and at Tigani it occurs on various shapes, including the bowl with flat everted rim that does not occur in the Troad.

The other examples of pattern burnishing show little similarity to this group or to each other. They include the occurrence on a closed shape from Kennez II-Akhisar.[159] The examples from Emporio and Ayio Gala on Chios,[160] Beycesultan[161] and Aphrodisias[162] are probably local developments under the influence of the local painted pottery, and the Bağbaşı example, **148,** is probably also an independent occurrence.

The features discussed above, chosen because they are the most fully documented, give an idea of the variety of distribution areas for LC pottery features. They show that individual features had definable distributions within the broad tradition of western Anatolian LC pottery but that the distributions of features overlapped so that the area cannot be subdivided. The whole area did not produce pottery of exactly the same types but can be regarded as a continuum, each site differing slightly from its neighbors.

Each LC site should, then, be expected to have its own particular pottery assemblage, although it will share many features with its neighbors. In the southwest this is clearly demonstrated by

155 J. Sperling, *Hesperia* 45 (1976) 324 note 12 and pl. 73:216, 222a and pl. 77:622.

156 L. Bernabo-Brea, *Poliochni* I (Rome 1964) 539 and pl. 1:d–g; *Emporio* 59, 326, 347; *Tigani* pls. 39–40; A. Furness, *ProcPS* 22 (1956) 185, 190 and pls. XIX:11–14 and XX:10.

157 A. Furness, *ProcPS* 22 (1956) 187; *Tigani* pls. 41–43; H. Schliemann, *Ilios* (New York 1880) 667; W. Lamb, *PrähZ* 23 (1932) figs. 13–14; A. Furness, *ProcPS* 22 (1956) 206, fig. 15.

158 J. Sperling, *Hesperia* 45 (1976) pl. 72: 101, 112, 113a–b and pl. 73:223 and 306; D. French, *AnatSt* 14 (1964) 37 and fig. 3; J. Driehaus, "Prähistorische Siedlungsfunde in der unteren Kaikosebene und an dem Golfe von Çandarlı," *IstMitt* 7 (1957) 78, 81 and fig. 1:11–12; D. French, *AnatSt* 11 (1961) 102 and fig. 5:50. For comments on this pattern burnishing group see C. Renfrew, *The Emergence of Civilisation* (London 1972) 77; J. Sperling, *Hesperia* 45 (1976) 316 note 7; F. Fischer, "Agäische Politurmusterware," *IstMitt* 17 (1967) 22–23; D. French, *AnatSt* 11 (1961) 114 and *AnatSt* 19 (1969) 59–60.

159 D. French, *AnatSt* 11 (1961) 124, fig. 5:52. The example from Pamukçu South (fig. 5:51) is too badly worn to be certainly pattern burnished. It is a roughly made bowl and could simply be poorly burnished.

160 *Emporio* 59, 294.

161 *Beycesultan* fig. P6:10 and 6.

162 *Aphrodisias* II 313. Fifty-eight examples were identified but many may have been white painted sherds that had lost their paint.

Bağbaşı, Kuruçay Höyük 6A–4 and Beycesultan XL–XX. The three assemblages have many features in common to demonstrate their contemporaneity but each also has (and maintains over some time) a local repertoire of features not paralleled at other sites.[163]

The other objects and the architecture from Bağbaşı show the same combination of connections and independent features. Most of the small finds can be paralleled at other LC sites in western Anatolia. Each site yielded only a relatively small number of objects but at each site the types of objects and the technologies used were much the same. Baked clay and ground and chipped stone are the most common materials, with worked bone and antler and metal, usually copper, also represented. Clay loomweights, beads/whorls, scoops and animal figurines; ground stone axes, whetstones and grinding stones; chipped stone sickle blades, scrapers and points; bone points and spatulas; antler hammers; and copper needles and awls were all found at Bağbaşı and one or more of Aphrodisias, Beycesultan and Kuruçay Höyük.[164] There are, however, indications that some types of object had restricted distributions, although evidence from more sites is needed before this could be definitely established. Clay spit supports were not found at Aphrodisias or Beycesultan but they do occur at Kuruçay Höyük and Bağbaşı, suggesting that these objects had a distribution restricted to the far south. Stamp seals or counters, found so far only at Bağbaşı, apparently had an even more restricted distribution.

The limited range of finds and especially the lack of metal other than very small objects could be evidence that Bağbaşı was a relatively poor settlement. However, the presence of the stamp seal suggests otherwise. If, as seems likely, the stamp seal is a forerunner of the EB seals, its presence shows that the economic organization at Bağbaşı was sufficiently complex to require identification methods—and that the inhabitants were sufficiently innovative to develop this method or adopt it from elsewhere.[165] The few objects other than pots found in the houses at Bağbaşı may simply reflect the careful housekeeping of the inhabitants and the circumstances of the site's abandonment (premeditated?).

The plans of the rectangular, free-standing houses suggest that Bağbaşı had a social organization similar to that of Kuruçay Höyük and thus possibly of other western Anatolian sites, although no other sites are sufficiently widely excavated to allow comparison. Architectural features such as the fixed hearths also belong in the common domain of the area. However, the people of Bağbaşı did not adopt the ovens used elsewhere and the construction methods they used show an unparalleled variety, as well as methods, such as the "log cabin" technique, so far not found at any other site. The variety of construction techniques used is hard to explain, especially as we do not know how long each had been used in the area (none of the earlier LC and MC sites has produced architectural remains).

LC Bağbaşı was apparently a small village with an economy dependent on herding a variety of animals and, probably, growing crops. Life was presumably fairly peaceful, at least there is no evidence of organized warfare—no fortifications or obvious weapons. In these respects it resembled other LC villages in western Anatolia, but it does differ in one respect from those other

[163] Attempts to explain the differences between these sites in chronological terms are not convincing in view of the many parallels that can be drawn (see above note 135).

[164] See above, notes 92–96.

[165] Evidence of the use of these objects as seals was found at Karataş-Semayük in the EB deposits—Machteld J. Mellink, *AJA* 68 (1964) 275 and pl. 82: fig. 26; *AJA* 76 (1972) pl. 55: fig. 5.

sites: Bağbaşı, and the other LC sites in Elmalı, were short-lived. The depth of deposit at Bağbaşı was nowhere more than 1 meter and was often no more than 0.20 meter. In comparison, the LC deposits at Beycesultan were at least 11 meters deep and those at Aphrodisias were over 6 meters deep.[166] The Bağbaşı area is a good place for settlement, as later occupations in the EB, MB and Iron Ages attest, but the LC people clearly lived there for only a short time. There is nothing in the archaeological record to suggest why the Elmalı sites differed from contemporary ones in this respect, but some feature of life—economic, religious or social—must have been different. One possibility is that the people of Elmalı practised swidden agriculture, moving often so that the land could lie fallow.[167] Another is that at different times areas of the plain were marshy and unsuitable for agriculture. Before the introduction of modern drainage systems the southern part of the plain contained two lakes, the levels of which fluctuated considerably, and marshy areas, and even the northern part of the plain could be marshy in places.[168]

The pattern of interaction for the LC people of the Elmalı Plain suggests sustained contacts with neighboring areas but an underlying strong local culture. This pattern is what would be expected from a series of essentially self-sufficient villages that nevertheless maintained some contact, possibly even on a regular basis, with surrounding areas.[169] The area of LC interaction, covering all of western Anatolia, is much wider than had been that of the earlier southwest Anatolian traditions surveyed. The disregard of earlier boundaries to cultural contact and the maintenance of a common direction of development suggest an increased mobility of the population or part of it. This may be connected to an increase in trade in this period—certainly the number of obviously traded goods increases. Given the limited sources of copper ores in the southwest, the growing use of metal in this period would have been important in this exchange.[170] It would have led to a gradual reduction in the degree of self-sufficiency of the area's villages, whether by increased trading contacts to obtain the ore and disseminate the technology, or by visits from travelling smiths.[171] Copper was not, however, the only material being exchanged. On the evidence of Bağbaşı alone we can add obsidian, greenstone, shells and probably pottery, and there was no doubt also trade in perishable goods.

Just as Bağbaşı was connected to contemporary villages in nearby areas, it was also connected to later occupation in the Elmalı area—as can be seen at the EB settlement at Karataş, 700 meters to the east. The material culture at Karataş was clearly the result of direct development from that of the LC period, although some time must have elapsed between the latest known LC site (Bağbaşı) and the earliest (EB I) Karataş deposits. The pottery of Karataş EB I (from the pits in the area of the later cemetery and from levels I and II of the mound) belonged to the same

[166] *Beycesultan* I, opposite p. 18; *Aphrodisias* I 955, fig. 12.

[167] A. Sherratt in *Models in Archaeology,* ed. D. Clarke (London 1972) 494–499; D. Harris in *Man, Settlement and Urbanism,* ed. P. Ucko, R. Tringham and G. Dimbleby (London 1970) 245–249.

[168] C. Fellows, *An Account of Discoveries in Lycia* (London 1841) 227–230; Great Britain, Naval Intelligence Division, *Turkey* (B.R. 507 Geographical Handbook Series 1942) 146–147; G. Bean, *Sonderabdruck aus dem Anzeiger der phil. hist. Klasse der Österreichischen Akademie der Wissenschaften* 8 (1968) 160; A. Woodward and H. Ormerod, *BSA* 16 (1909/1910) 93.

[169] H. Balfet, in *Ceramics and Man,* ed. F.R. Matson (Chicago 1965) 168.

[170] For ores in western Anatolia see P.S. de Jesus, "Metal Resources in Ancient Anatolia," *AnatSt* 28 (1978) 97 and *The Development of Prehistoric Mining and Metallurgy in Anatolia* (BAR International Series 74 1980) map 8. For the importance of metallurgy in the shift to less self-sufficiency see C. Renfrew, *The Emergence of Civilisation* (London 1972) 303–313.

[171] W. Englebrecht, "The Iroquois," *World Archaeology* 6 (1974) 52–65 found an increase in homogeneity between the pottery of various American Indian groups paralleled an increase in trade. Women made the pottery and took part in the trading.

tradition as that of the LC sites in the plain.[172] It was manufactured in the same way. All the pots contain grit and fiber temper and were handmade using overlapping flattened coils. Handles were often applied with plugs but were sometimes simply pressed against the wall of the pot. Larger pots are often irregular in shape. Firing was largely uncontrolled and black cores and mottled surfaces are still common. However, burnished surfaces were more common on EB I pots and there are a number of new features in the assemblage. Most obvious are the use of a red burnished slip and new types of decoration, such as applied strips to form medallions, curved patterns and animals, and white filled incision. Many shapes are similar to those from Bağbaşı but the variety is greater and again new features, such as oblique or rising spouts and ring bases, appear.

The other finds from Karataş show the same relationship. For example, the stamp seals found in some numbers at Karataş are in form and design clearly developed from the LC example, although that was less regular in shape and lacked the suspension hole usual in the EB examples.[173] The incised bead found at Bağbaşı may also be regarded as the forerunner of the Karataş beads.[174] In this case the connection is less obvious as the designs on the beads at the two sites are not similar but the idea of decorated clay beads was already present at LC Bağbaşı and the more elaborate EB patterns can be related to those on the seals or the EB pottery. The earliest preserved buildings at Karataş, the large central house and fence houses of levels I–II, also show construction methods similar to those of Bağbaşı, with the central house of mud slabs and the fence houses of timber and mud.[175]

[172] For example, M.J. Mellink, *AJA* 69 (1965) 244–245, pl. 62: figs. 19–24, pl. 64: figs. 29–32 and pl. 66: figs. 42–44; *AJA* 70 (1966) 247–250, pl. 60: figs. 21, 23, 26.

[173] M.J. Mellink, *AJA* 69 (1965) pl. 64: fig. 33 and pl. 65: fig. 37.

[174] M.J. Mellink, *AJA* 70 (1966) pl. 62: figs. 34–36.

[175] M.J. Mellink, *AJA* 70 (1966) 247–250; *AJA* 78 (1974) 351–353.

APPENDICES

1. DESCRIPTION OF POTTERY COLORS

In the catalogues in Chapters 1 and 3 the pottery colors are described only in general color terms. Precise definition using a color chart was found to be impractical, for the color of any sherd varied with mottling and smudging, and there was no consistency over even small areas.

A general guide to the terminology used can, however, be gained from the following list. Readings were taken on the surface of dry sherds, in the shade, and using the *Munsell Soil Color Chart* (Baltimore, 1975).

brown	7.5YR 6/2–5/4
light brown	7.5YR 7/4
pale brown	10YR 7/3–7.5 YR 7/3
dark brown	5YR 5/3
chocolate brown	7.5YR 4/2
gray	5Y 6/1
dark gray	5Y 5/1
gray-brown	10YR 5/2
orange	7.5YR–5YR 6/6
yellow	10YR 7/3
red	2.5YR 6/6–6/8
pink	5YR 7/4–6/4
cream	10YR 8/3
green	5GY 7/1
green-gray	2.5Y 7/2
Paint Colors:	
bright orange (**147**)	5YR 6/6
crimson (**153**)	7.5R 3/6
pinky-red (**154**)	7.5R 5/6

2. STUDY OF POTTERY THIN SECTIONS (by Maria Luisa Crawford and Christine Eslick)

Thin sections were made from twenty of the Elmalı Plain Neolithic and Chalcolithic sherds. Ten LC sherds from Bağbaşı were chosen to demonstrate the fabric range in that assemblage. They included two burnished sherds, no. 7 from a jug and no. 20 from a bowl. Examples of more unusual appearance were no. 6, which had large white inclusions in a well-baked yellow body, similar to that of **31,** and no. 5, taken from **27,** which has a platey stone temper. The other sherds, all typical of their respective assemblages, were taken two from the Lower Bağbaşı group, four from Kızılbel and four from the LN assemblage from Akçay I Hüyük.

MICROSCOPE STUDY

The thin sections were first examined with a petrographic microscope, fitted with a Swift Automatic Point Counter with increments of ⅓ mm. One thousand readings were taken for each thin section and the percentage of each type of identifiable grain was calculated. The results are shown in Chart 6. The size of individual grains was then measured with the results shown on plates 82 and 113.

The size range of the particles in the Bağbaşı LC pottery was wide, with some particles up to 35 mm in length, although most were less than 5 mm in maximum diameter. Most of the samples contained rounded calcium carbonate lumps and chert with smaller amounts of quartz; in no. 20 the amounts of carbonate and chert were almost equal. In none of the samples was the fabric dense and each contained many holes—2.8–23.9 percent of the body. Only sample no. 5 yielded different results. It was denser than the other Bağbaşı samples (only 1.6 percent holes) and contained large inclusions, up to 30 mm in diameter, that comprised a high proportion of the sample (27 percent). These inclusions were carbonate which differed from that of the other samples as it contained fossil radiolaria.

Both the Lower Bağbaşı samples also contained more chert than quartz but the proportion of holes in each varied. Sample no. 17 had 13.8 percent holes; no. 16 only 5.8 percent. No. 17 was taken from **16** which was apparently refired, and at least some of the holes in this sample may be from the resulting cracking of the pot.

The Kızılbel samples had a more homogeneous composition. Each contained 6.4–9.4 percent quartz, including a small amount of quartzite, 1.7–2.2 percent chert and, in two samples, a little calcium carbonate. The grains were 0.5–4.5 mm in diameter, with a few in no. 19 measuring up to 6.0 mm and a few in no. 14 up to 6.5 mm. There were few holes. The fineness of the fabric is also indicated by the high count for the undifferentiated matrix—80.9–86.9 percent.

The samples from Akçay had a rather different composition. Although the proportion of each type of grain varies from sample to sample, each sample contained quartz, some chert and serpentine and large quantities of carbonate. The carbonate grains, unlike those in the samples from the other sites, were often angular in shape.

CHEMICAL ANALYSES

In the second part of the study, electron beam area scans were made of six of the samples, to identify the various elements that had been observed in the microscope study. An ARL-EMX electron probe microanalyzer with beam energy of 20 KV and sample current of 0.05 microamperes was used. The radiation was detected by an energy dispersive detector. The electron beam of approximately 1 micron radius was scanned over an area of 100 × 75 microns (except for sample no. 17 when the area was 25 × 20 microns). The distribution of Kα radiation of each element analyzed was displayed on an oscilloscope screen and photographed.

The major element concentrations in all samples were of silicon (Si) and calcium (Ca), with considerable aluminum (Al). Iron (Fe), potassium (K) and magnesium (Mg) were also present in significant quantities.

Of the Bağbaşı LC samples examined two, nos. 8 and 21, consisted primarily of silicon, although calcium and aluminum also occurred in the matrix of each. Some of the grains in no. 21 were a form of carbonate. In no. 5 the matrix and some of the grains were again of silicon; there was also some aluminum in the matrix of this sample. Most of the large grains, and the fossils in them, were calcium carbonate.

The Lower Bağbaşı sample, no. 17, was primarily of silicon with some calcium and minor aluminum in the background. The Kızılbel sample, no. 15, in addition to the usual silicon, contained some calcium carbonate grains and there was some calcium and a lot of aluminum in the matrix. No. 9 from Akçay was again principally composed of silicon but with some grains of calcium and minor aluminum, potassium and iron.

Therefore in almost all the samples the matrix, consisting of those grains too small to be individually identified, consisted of the same material as the larger grains in that particular sample. Only in no. 5 were the lumps predominantly calcium and the background silicon.

X-RAY DIFFRACTION ANALYSIS

Fragments of two sherds were ground and run on an X-ray diffractometer to determine the clay content. Unexpectedly this technique failed to identify significant quantities of clay minerals in the samples. This failure suggests that these minerals are present only in minor amounts, if at all. Small grains of feldspar were identified optically and chemically in a few samples; the high aluminum content in the matrix of sample no. 15 may represent finely crushed feldspar rather than clay. The apparent lack of clay and the presence of fresh grains of feldspar and pyroxene in some samples suggests that the pots were made from earth containing a low proportion of weathered rock.

INTERPRETATION

The Elmalı Plain potters used locally available material for their pots, even though it was not good pot-making clay. This must have placed limitations on the quality of the finished product and on the possible methods of production. There seems to have been little variation in production within each assemblage.

The Bağbaşı LC pottery was made from material that had little preparation so that the large grains were not removed. All are of types that could have occurred naturally in the clay. The fiber, which burnt out during firing and left holes in the body, would, however, have been added by the potter. One sample, no. 5 from **27,** is from a pot that may have been imported. It differs from the other Bağbaşı LC samples in the small proportion of holes, that is, it had no added fiber temper but fragments of fossil-bearing rock were added.

The interpretation of the Lower Bağbaşı samples is more difficult and further samples would have to be examined before any results could be obtained. The percentages of the different types of grains are similar to those in the LC Bağbaşı pottery and apparently reflect the local "clay" composition. The fineness of no. 16 suggests a care in preparation not otherwise found at Bağbaşı and similar to that of the Kızılbel samples. However, no. 17 does not seem to have been as well prepared.

The Kızılbel pottery contained no large grains, and either material without them had been selected for the pots, or they had been deliberately removed by the potter. All the inclusions in the Kızılbel samples could have occurred naturally in the clay. The LN pottery from Akçay was again made from a relatively fine material. The angular shape of many of the carbonate grains in these samples suggests that they were derived from freshly crushed rock and that they did not occur naturally in the clay, but were added by the potter.

3. CONCORDANCE OF CATALOGUE NUMBERS

All except KA 953, 967, 970, 972 are in the Archaeology Museum, Antalya.

KARATAŞ CATALOGUE	BAĞBAŞI (this volume)
KA 582	**273**
KA 620	**93**
KA 621	**42**
KA 685	**88**
KA 690	**228**
KA 709	**95**
KA 710	**94**
KA 711	**229**
KA 712	**92**
KA 714	**91**
KA 717	**313**
KA 722	**275**
KA 727	**328**
KA 733	**274**
KA 737	**276**
KA 746	**225**
KA 767	**43**
KA 953	**71**
KA 967	**135**
KA 970	**68**
KA 972	**65**
B 32	**322**
B 119	**324**
B 120	**323**

CHART 1: BAGBAŞI POTTERY

Type	102-5	105	107	109	110	112	115	116 I	116 II	116 III	116 Total	117	118	119	Total	Catalogued Examples
bowl-everted rim	1	1	1	1	—	4	1	4	—	1	5	1	—	—	15	1–3
bowl-flaring	4	10	2	1	7	—	1	11	10	10	31	1	1	4	62	4–22
bowl-flat rim	—	2	—	—	—	—	—	—	—	—	—	—	—	—	2	23, 31
bowl-deep	—	—	—	—	—	—	—	—	—	3	3	—	—	—	3	24–25
bowl-curved	—	2	—	—	—	—	—	—	1	3	4	1	—	—	7	26–28
bowl-wide	—	4	—	—	—	—	—	—	—	—	—	—	—	—	4	29–30
bowl-spouted	1	1	—	1	5	—	—	—	1	1	2	—	—	—	10	32–33
pot-spouted	—	1	—	—	1	—	—	—	—	—	—	—	—	—	2	34–35
tankard	—	1	—	—	—	—	—	—	1	—	1	—	—	—	2	36–37
basin-small	1	1	—	—	1	—	—	—	1	—	1	—	—	—	4	38–40
basin-normal	4	3	—	—	—	—	—	—	—	1	1	—	—	—	8	41–47
basin-flaring rim	—	2	—	—	—	—	—	—	—	—	—	—	—	—	2	48
open pot-rim handle	2	2	—	—	1	—	—	—	5	2	7	—	—	—	12	51–59
open pot	13	50	2	10	13	—	6	22	117	68	207	4	1	6	312	60–86
open pot-rect.	—	1	—	—	—	—	—	—	—	—	—	—	—	—	1	87
neck-vertical	3	16	—	—	4	1	2	3	4	4	11	2	—	2	41	105,113,116–8, 120,130,133,135–6
neck-everted rim	2	4	—	—	2	—	1	—	4	4	8	1	—	—	18	88,92–3,104
neck-outcurved	—	7	—	—	—	—	1	1	2	—	3	1	1	1	14	89–91,95–8,106–7, 119,123
neck-everted	—	13	1	1	2	—	1	1	5	4	10	1	—	—	29	99–100,108–112, 114,121–2,124–9, 134,137
other jars	—	4	—	1	1	—	—	—	—	—	—	1	—	1	8	140–146
handles	11	23	1	6	3	—	3	14	45	30	89	2	1	1	140	e.g. 155–6
handles-combination	2	4	—	—	—	—	—	2	1	—	3	—	—	—	9	116,128,147
lugs-ledge	20	25	5	10	19	3	4	7	24	18	49	3	—	2	140	e.g. 160–171
lugs-pierced	1	1	—	—	1	—	—	1	—	—	1	—	—	—	4	114,157–8
base-disk	17	78	1	7	25	1	1	13	53	34	100	8	1	1	240	eg. 202–221
base-other	3	40	1	1	8	—	3	8	32	11	51	1	—	—	108	e.g. 177–201
beaker	—	—	—	—	1	—	—	—	—	—	—	—	—	—	1	221
miniature bowls	—	2	—	—	—	1	—	1	1	1	3	—	—	—	6	222–7
double pot	—	—	—	—	1	—	—	—	—	—	—	—	—	—	1	228
small pedestal	—	—	—	—	—	—	—	—	—	—	—	—	—	1	1	230
pedestal base	—	3	—	—	—	—	—	1	2	1	4	1	—	—	8	231–2
foot-circular	—	3	—	—	—	—	2	—	1	1	2	—	—	—	7	233–4,236–7
foot-semi-circ.	—	—	—	—	1	—	—	—	—	—	—	—	—	—	1	235
pan-flat	1	3	1	—	3	—	—	1	—	3	4	—	—	—	12	238–241
pan-with rim	1	2	—	—	—	—	—	1	—	1	2	—	—	—	5	242–5
pan-with sides	2	2	—	—	1	—	—	1	3	1	5	—	—	—	10	246–9
pan-flat, burnished	—	—	—	—	—	—	—	1	—	1	2	—	—	—	2	—

jugs	1	10	—	1	1	—	1	1	2	1	4	1	—	—	19	88–95
jars-small	—	4	—	1	1	—	—	1	1	—	2	1	—	1	10	112–5
jars-medium	—	1	—	—	—	—	—	2	—	1	3	—	—	—	4	123–4
jars-large	—	1	—	—	1	—	—	1	1	1	3	1	—	—	6	131–6
necks-indeterminate	4	28	1	—	6	1	4	—	11	9	20	3	1	3	71	
knob-body	—	3	—	—	1	—	—	1	2	2	5	—	—	—	9	90,92,150
knob-handle	—	1	—	—	—	—	—	—	—	—	—	—	—	—	1	156
ribbed handle	—	1	—	—	—	—	1	—	—	1	1	—	—	—	3	62,130,136
holes in handle	—	—	—	—	1	—	1	—	2	2	4	—	—	—	6	51–3,101
ridge at neck	1	2	—	—	2	—	—	—	1	2	3	—	—	—	8	92,113,125,131,138,147
moulding	—	—	—	—	—	—	—	—	1	1	2	—	—	—	2	112,139
impressed dec.	—	—	—	—	1	—	1	—	—	—	—	—	—	—	2	228–9
painted dec.	2	2	—	—	—	—	—	1	1	1	3	—	—	—	7	58,128,147,153–4
incised dec.	—	—	—	—	1	—	—	—	—	—	—	—	—	—	1	152
pattern burnish	—	—	—	—	—	—	—	1	—	—	1	—	—	—	1	148
lug, impression	—	2	1	—	3	1	—	2	3	2	7	2	—	—	16	71,76
lug, impression on end	—	—	1	—	—	—	—	—	—	1	1	—	—	—	2	176
lug, impression × 3	—	—	—	—	1	—	—	—	—	—	—	—	—	—	1	169
sherds with features	73	287	14	39	96	10	20	88	300	165		25	3	18	1138	N.B. some frr. have several features
body sherds	—	48	4	16	16	—	—	916	1316	496		—	—	—	2812	
Total sherds	73	335	18	55	112	10	20	1004	1616	661		25	3	18	3950	

CHART 2: ELMALI PLAIN POTTERY

Type	Bağbaşı	Boztepe	Semayük Bekleme	Karaburun	Dinsiz	Kızılbel	Lower Bağbaşı	Akçay	Gökpınar
bowl-inverted neck	—	—	—	—	—	—	—	1	2
bowl-everted neck	—	—	—	—	—	—	—	4	—
bowl-vertical neck	—	—	—	—	—	—	—	1	—
bowl-flat rim, curved	—	—	—	—	—	—	2	3	—
bowl-deep	3	—	—	—	—	—	—	8	1
bowl-flaring	62	—	—	—	2	—	—	4	1
bowl flat rim, flared	1	—	—	—	—	1	—	—	—
bowl-incurved	1	—	—	—	—	1	—	—	—
bowl-folded rim	—	1	—	—	—	—	—	—	—
bowl-rolled rim	—	7	—	—	—	—	—	—	—
bowl-rounded rim	—	—	—	5	—	—	—	—	—
bowl-flat, evert. rim	15	5	1?	4	—	—	—	—	—
bowl-curved	5	1	—	—	—	—	—	—	—
bowl-flaring rim	2	—	—	—	—	—	—	—	—
bowl-wide	4	—	—	—	—	—	—	—	—
open pot	312	1	1?	—	1	—	—	—	—
pot-constricted	—	—	—	4	—	—	—	1	—
hole-mouth jar	—	—	—	—	—	6	4	2	—
hole-mouth-ev. rim	3	—	—	—	—	—	—	—	—
jar-short vert. neck	2	7	—	6	—	1	1	1	—
neck-vertical	41	4	—	1	—	—	1	1	1
neck-everted	29	4	—	1	—	1	—	3	—
neck-everted rim	18	8	—	5	—	—	—	—	—
neck-outcurved	14	3	1	3	—	—	—	—	—
neck-inverted	2	—	—	3	—	—	—	—	—
handles-loop	140	8	—	6	—	12	3	1	—
handles-vert. tubular	—	—	—	—	—	—	—	1	2
handles-high strap	—	—	—	—	—	1	—	—	—
handles with ridge	—	—	—	—	—	—	2	—	—
handles-horiz. tubular	—	—	—	2	1	—	—	—	—
lug-small ledge	1	—	—	—	—	—	1	—	—
lug-small upturned	—	—	—	—	—	1	—	—	—
lug-upturned	—	2	—	—	—	—	—	—	—
lug-pierced	4	—	—	—	—	—	—	—	—
lug-ledge	140	3	1	8	2	—	—	—	—
base-flat	108	2	1	—	—	1	2	2	—
base-disc	240	—	—	—	—	—	—	—	—

stand	5	—	—	—	—	1	—	—	—
pan-pierced sides	—	—	—	—	—	5	—	—	—
pan-pierced, flat	—	3	1	2	—	—	—	—	—
pan-burnished flat	2	—	—	—	—	—	—	—	—
pan-flat	12	—	—	—	—	—	—	—	—
pan-raised rim	5	—	—	—	—	—	—	—	—
pan-sides	10	—	—	—	—	—	—	—	—
incised decoration	1	—	—	—	—	—	—	1	—
painted decoration	7	—	—	—	—	—	1	3	—
impressed decoration	2	—	—	—	—	1	—	—	—
knob on body	9	—	1	—	—	—	1	—	—
knob on handle	1	—	—	—	—	2	—	—	—
knob-row of	—	1	—	1	—	—	—	—	—
moulding	2	—	—	1	—	—	—	—	—
impression-lug	16	—	—	—	—	—	—	—	—

CHART 3: RADIOCARBON DATES

Site	*Sample*	*Material*	*Radiocarbon Date B.C.**	*Calibrated Date B.C.***
Hacılar				
IX	P.314A	charcoal	5487 ± 115	
VII	BM-125	charcoal	5820 ± 180	
VI	BM-48	charcoal	5590 ± 180	
	P.313A	charcoal	5399 ± 79	
II	P.316A	charcoal	5219 ± 131	
Ia	P.315A	charcoal	4976 ± 90	
Kuruçay 7			5264 ± 38	
Saliagos	P-1311	soil	4222 ± 74	5100**
	P-1396	shell	4124 ± 79	5125**
	P-1368	shell	3959 ± 87	4850**
	P-1333	shell	3825 ± 84	4660**
	P-1393	shell	3766 ± 85	4600**
Aphrodisias				
VIII	P-2029	charcoal	3500 ± 80	4380 ± 90
	P-2031	ash and charcoal	3330 ± 70	4100, 4180 ± 80
	P-2030	charcoal	2910 ± 80	3690 ± 90
Kuruçay 6			3500 ± 52	4400 ± 52
			2845 ± 82	3600 ± 82
Beycesultan				
XXXVI	P-298	charcoal	3014 ± 50	3900**
XXVIII	P-297	charcoal	2740 ± 54	3200**
Karataş II				
pit	P-920	charcoal	2324 ± 62	2902
fill	P-923	charcoal	2278 ± 62	2855
post-hole	P-917	charcoal	2271 ± 61	2848
pit	P-921	charcoal	2188 ± 62	2762
floor	P-918	charcoal	2180 ± 61	2754
beam	P-919	charcoal	2176 ± 60	2750

*5568 year half-life

**Approximate only, after H.N. Michael and E.K. Ralph, *Radiocarbon* 16 (1974) 203–216.

The dates are taken from the following publications: *Hacılar* I 93; *Saliagos* 144; B. Lawn, *Radiocarbon* 17 (1975) 205; *Kuruçay* IV 47; E. Kohler and E. Ralph, *AJA* 65 (1961) 360; G. Wright, *AJA* 77 (1973) 199.

CHART 4: CHRONOLOGICAL CHART

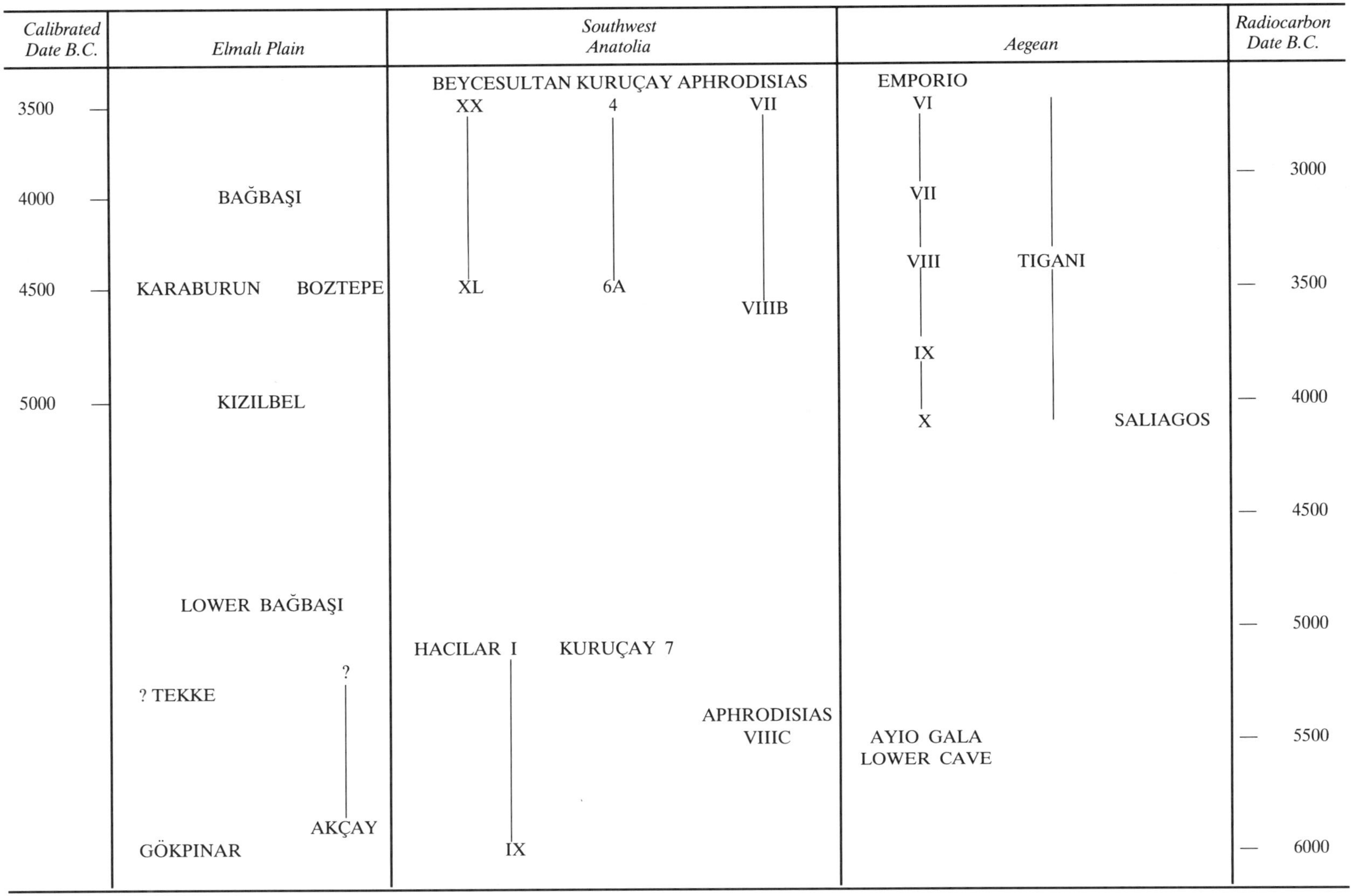

Calibrated Date B.C.	*Elmalı Plain*	*Southwest Anatolia*	*Aegean*	*Radiocarbon Date B.C.*
		BEYCESULTAN KURUÇAY APHRODISIAS	EMPORIO	
3500		XX 4 VII	VI	
				3000
4000	BAĞBAŞI		VII	
			VIII TIGANI	
4500	KARABURUN BOZTEPE	XL 6A		3500
		VIIIB		
			IX	
5000	KIZILBEL			4000
			X SALIAGOS	
				4500
	LOWER BAĞBAŞI			
				5000
		HACILAR I KURUÇAY 7		
	?			
	? TEKKE			
		APHRODISIAS VIIIC	AYIO GALA LOWER CAVE	5500
	AKÇAY			
	GÖKPINAR	IX		6000

CHART 5: BAGBAŞI ARTIFACTS

	105	*116*			*115*	*102*	*107*	*109*	*110*	*112*
		I	*II*	*III*						
loomweight	3	—	—	—	—	—	—	—	—	—
whorl	7	1	1	1	—	—	—	1	2	1
scoop	—	—	—	—	—	—	—	—	1	—
spit support	1	1	2	2	2	—	—	—	3	—
stand	1	—	—	—	—	1	—	1	2	—
copper needle	1	—	—	—	—	—	—	—	—	—
bone pin (?)	1	—	—	—	—	—	—	—	—	—
cutting tool	2	—	2	1	—	1	1	—	—	—
notched tool	—	—	1	1	—	—	—	—	—	—
denticulate tool	—	—	—	—	—	—	—	1	—	—
other stone tools	—	1	2	—	—	—	—	—	—	—
unused blade	—	—	2	3	4	—	—	—	—	—
sickle blade	—	2	2	2	1	—	—	3	—	—
scraper	—	—	—	1	—	—	—	—	1	1
bone spatula	—	—	—	—	—	—	—	1	—	—
worked bone	—	—	1	—	—	—	—	—	—	—
antler	2	—	—	—	—	1	—	1	—	—
copper awl	—	—	—	—	1	1	—	—	—	—
figurine	—	—	—	1	—	—	—	—	—	—
seal/counter	—	—	—	—	1	1	—	—	—	—
shell	—	—	—	—	1	—	—	—	—	—

CHART 6: POTTERY THIN SECTIONS: COMPONENTS

Sample	*No.*	*Quartz*	*Quartzite*	*Chert*	*Silicon Lumps*	*Carbonate Lumps*	*Carbonate Plates*	*Rock with Fossils*	*Serpentine*	*Pyroxene*	*Holes*	*Matrix*
Bağbaşı	1	1.6	—	4.4	—	9.9	—	—	—	—	21.6	62.5
	2	1.1	—	6.3	0.7	9.2	—	—	—	—	2.8	79.9
	4	1.6	—	6.8	—	11.4	—	—	—	—	23.9	56.3
	5	1.2	—	3.6	—	8.9	—	18.1	—	—	1.6	66.6
	6	1.1	—	7.1	—	10.6	—	—	—	—	7.8	73.4
	7	4.8	0.5	2.7	3.3	—	—	—	—	—	11.5	77.2
	8	6.0	0.7	3.0	—	4.0	—	—	—	—	11.3	75.0
	20	2.2	—	11.1	0.3	10.7	—	—	—	—	17.7	58.0
	21	1.4	—	4.2	4.2	3.8	—	—	—	—	14.3	72.1
	22	1.9	—	5.9	—	6.3	—	—	—	—	8.5	77.4
Lower Bağbaşı	16	1.0	—	4.6	—	2.5	—	—	—	—	5.8	86.1
	17	1.7	—	5.8	7.7	—	—	—	—	—	13.8	71.0
Kızılbel	14	5.4	2.0	1.7	—	—	—	—	—	—	7.1	83.8
	15	5.0	1.4	2.1	—	2.0	—	—	—	0.1	4.6	84.8
	18	7.7	1.7	2.2	—	3.5	—	—	—	—	4.1	80.9
	19	5.5	0.9	1.9	—	—	—	—	—	—	4.8	86.9
Akçay	9	5.5	—	0.4	—	1.0	27.2	—	0.2	—	4.6	61.1
	10	5.7	—	4.6	—	12.3		—	0.6	—	7.2	69.6
	11	0.6	—	0.3	—	—	8.2	—	—	—	1.4	89.5
	13	2.7	—	2.1	—	0.5	19.6	—	0.2	—	1.8	73.1

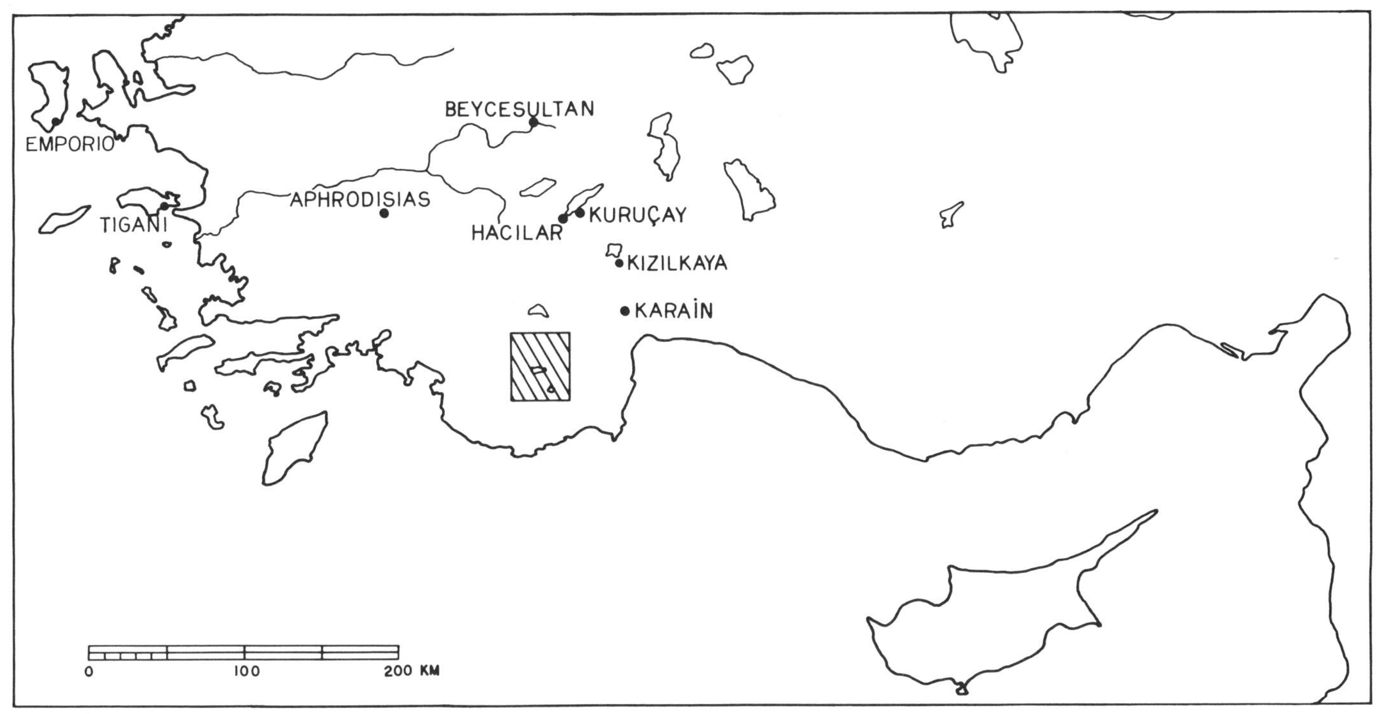

1a. Map of southern Anatolia showing Elmalı area (hatched)

Key:

1. Dinsiz
2. Maltepe
3. Karaburun
4. Boztepe
5. Semayük Bekleme
6. Bağbaşı
7. Bayındırköy
8. Gökpınar
9. Kızılbel
10. Arapkuyusu
11. Hacımusalar
12. Akçay I Hüyük
13. Tekke
14. Buralia
15. Yaka Çiftliği

1b. Map of the Elmalı Plain, showing the area of 1977 survey (sites 1–7) and other sites with Neolithic or Chalcolithic occupation

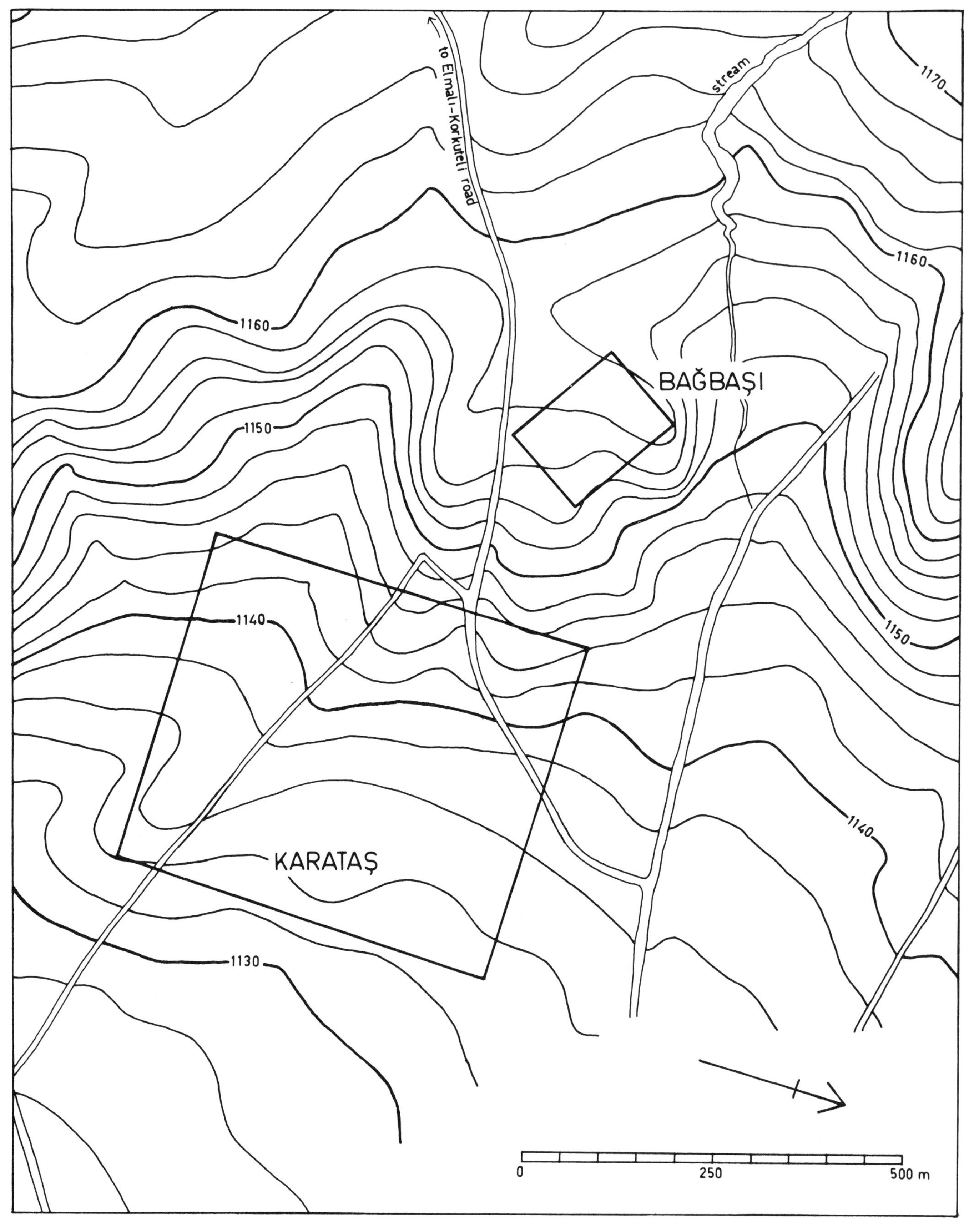

2. Bağbaşı area contour plan with area of excavation outlined

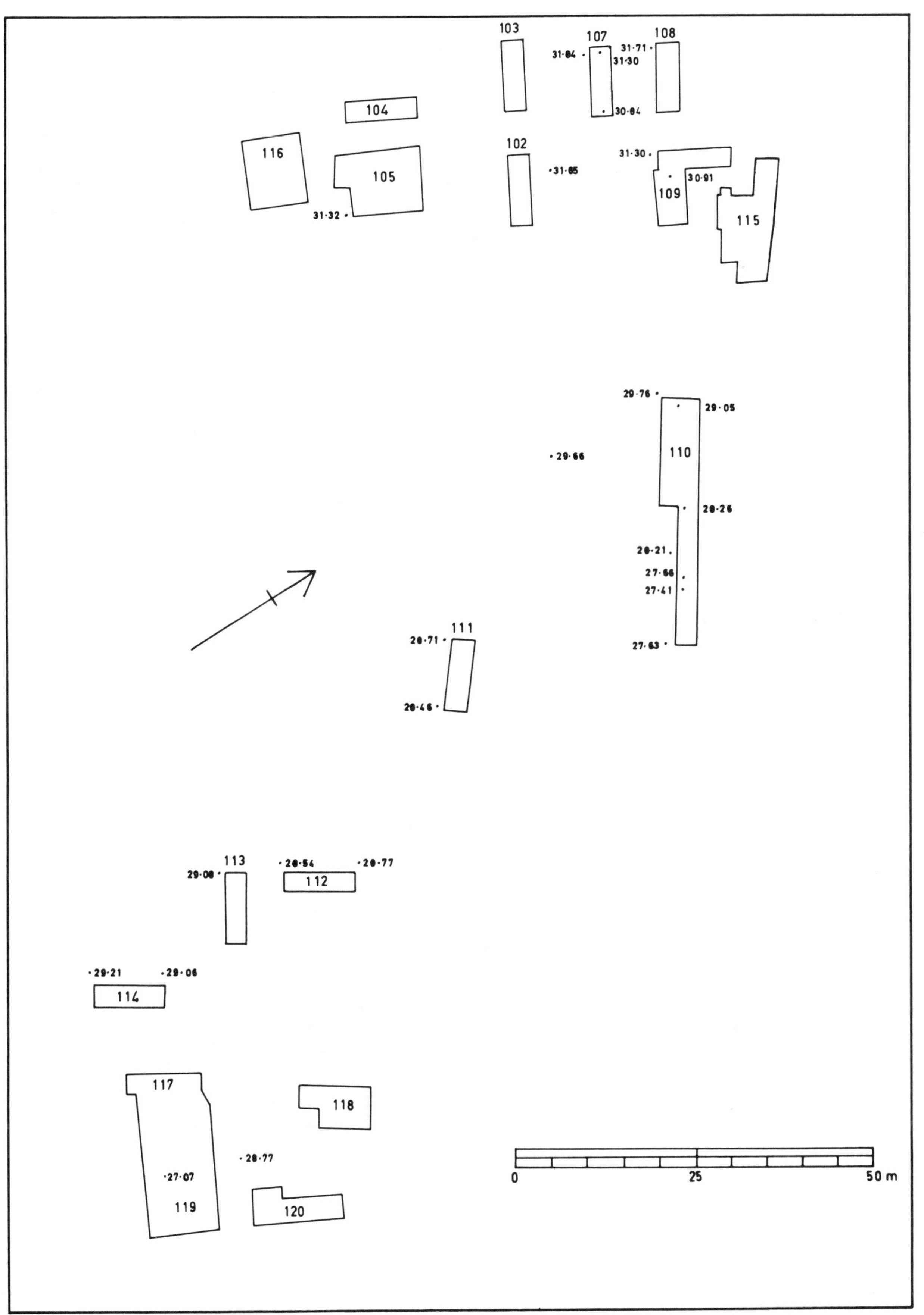

3. Bağbaşı excavation area showing location of trenches

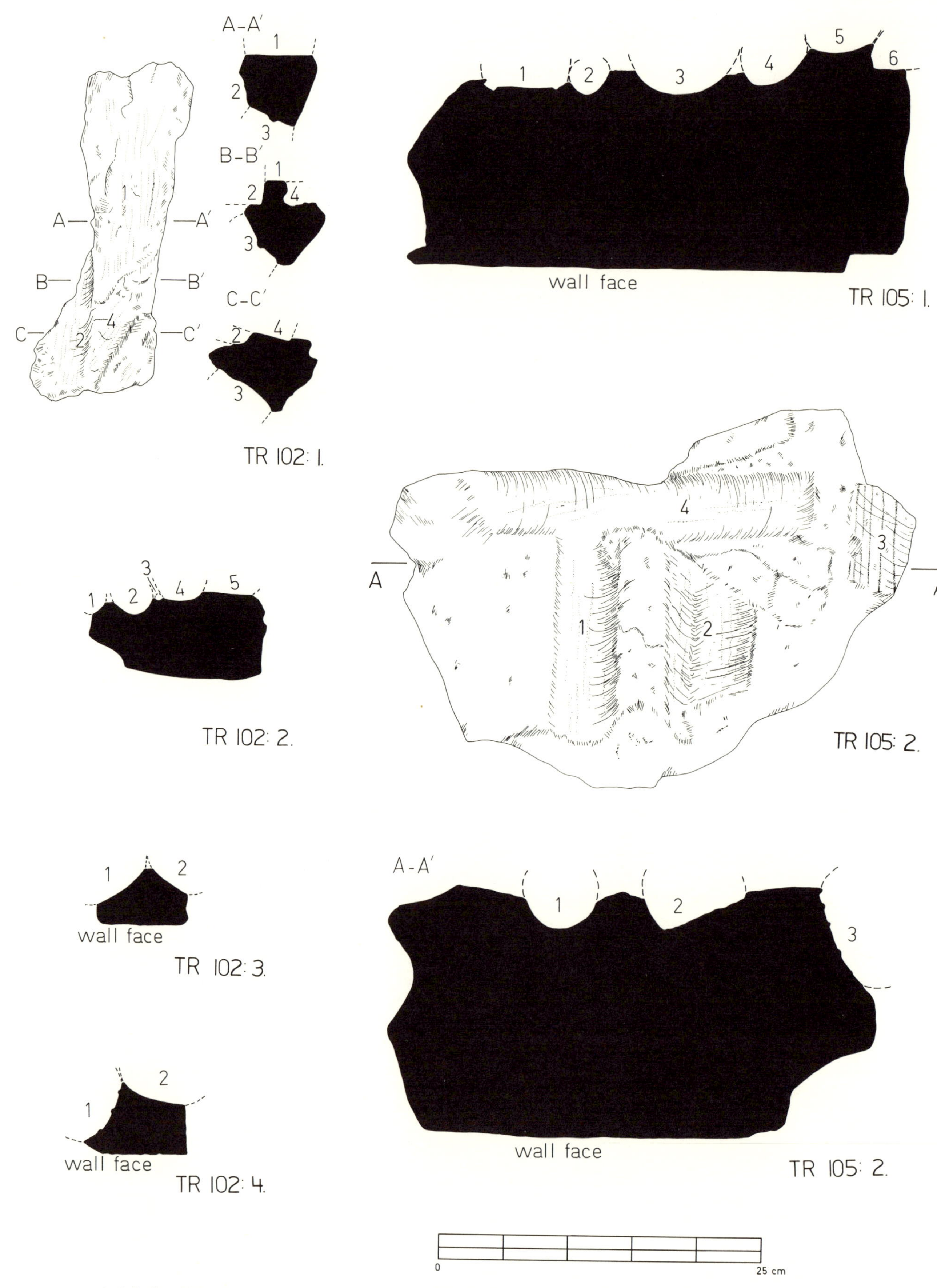

4. Mud walling fragments from trench 102 (left, fragments 1–4) and trench 105 (right, fragments 1–2)

5. Trench 105: plan

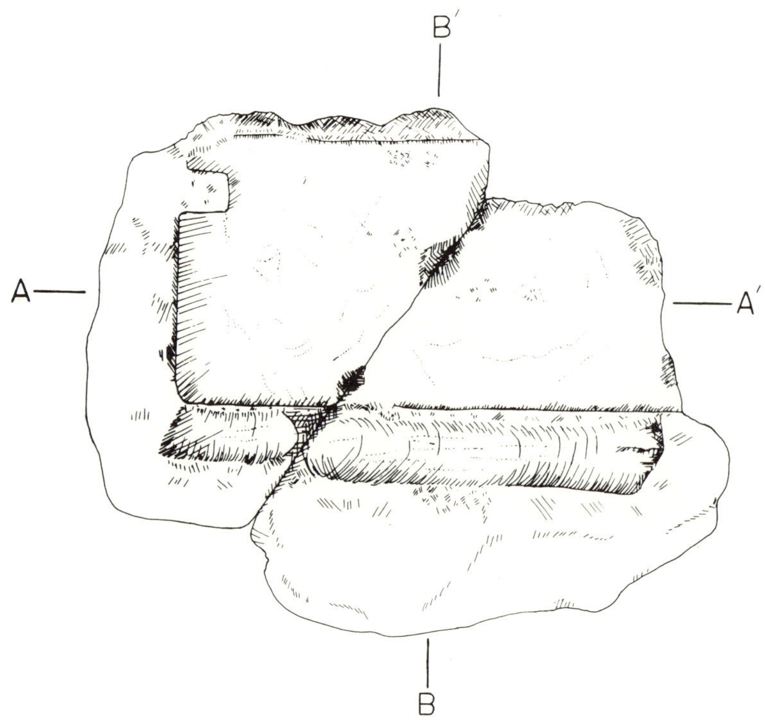

a. FRONTAL VIEW

b. SECTION A-A′

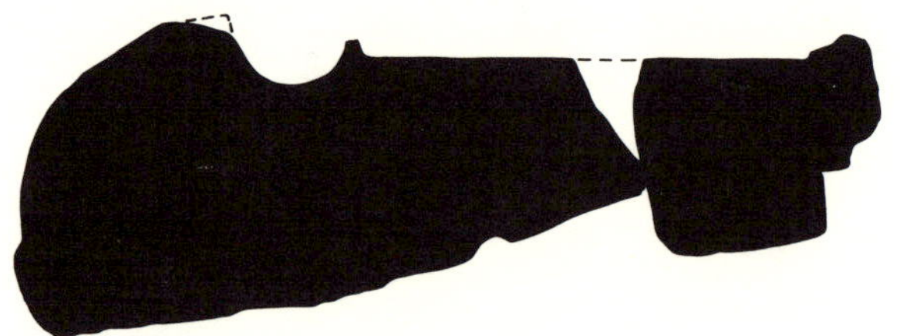

c. SECTION B-B′

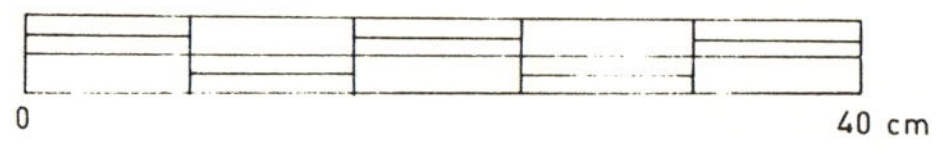

6. Trench 105: niche fragment

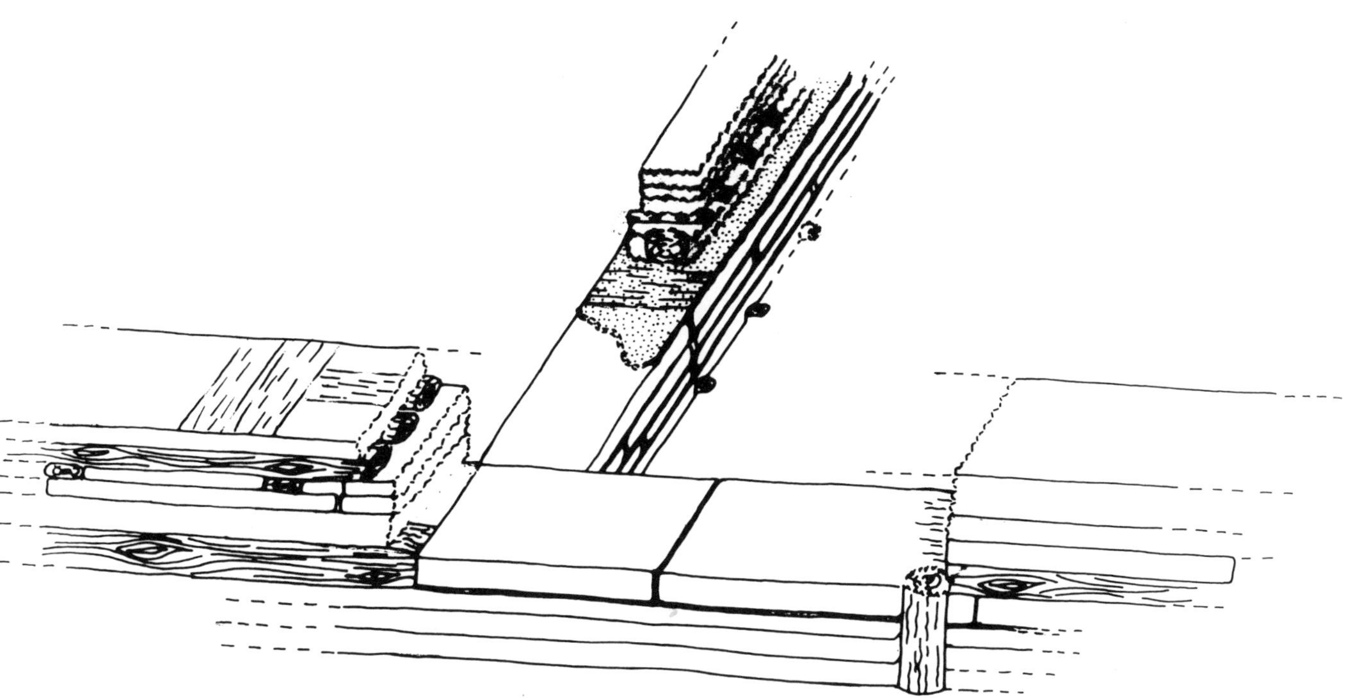

7a. Trench 105: reconstructed view of walls 1 and 2 from northeast

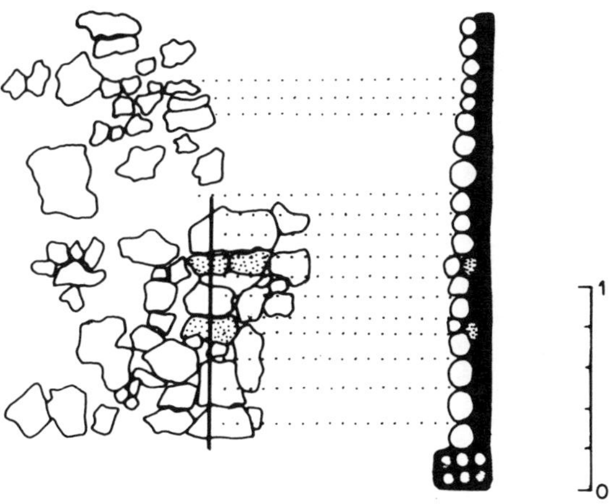

7b. Trench 115: fallen wall plaster turned over and reconstructed section of northwest wall

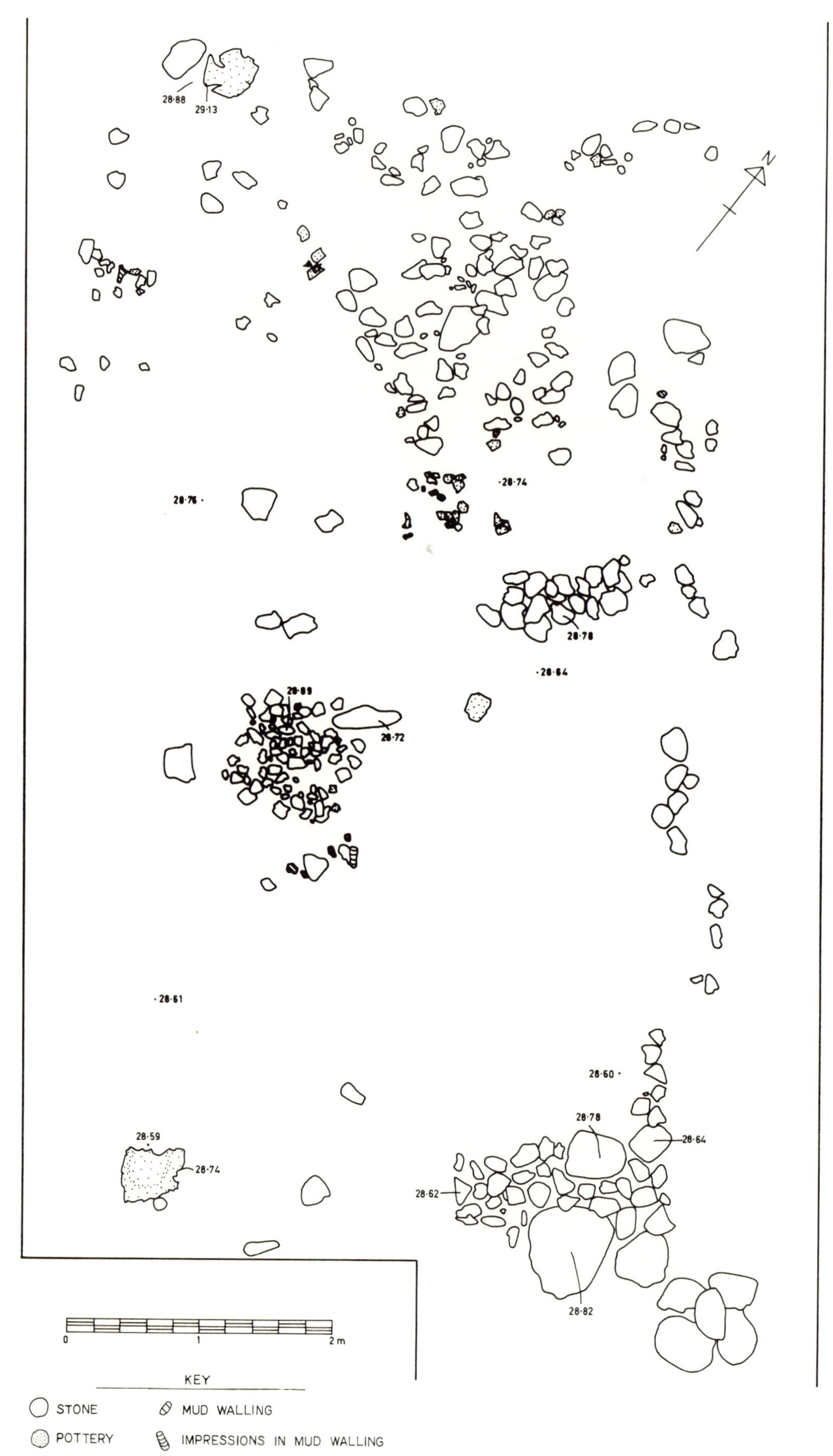

8. Trench 110: plan of central area

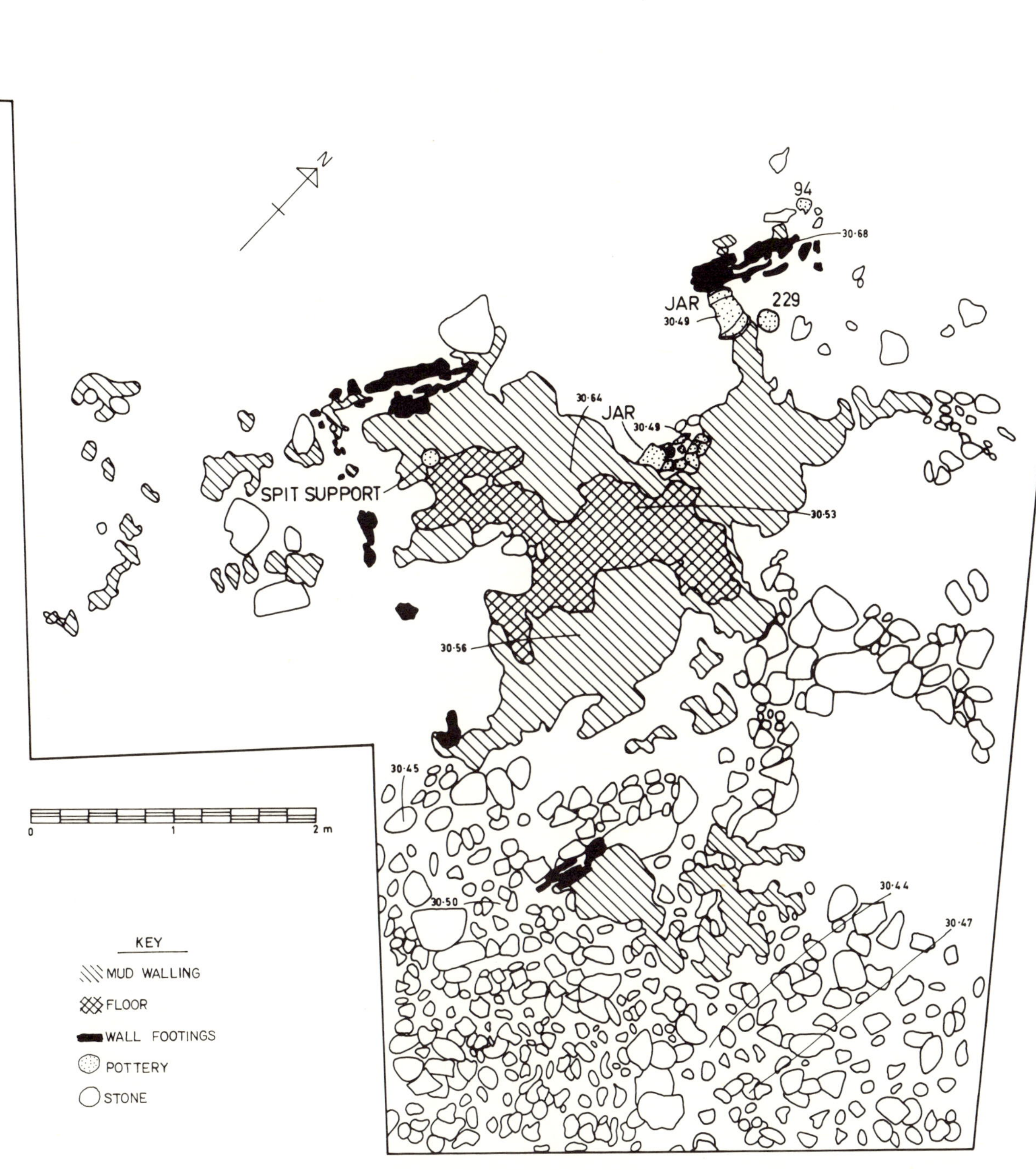

9. Trench 115: plan of southeast area

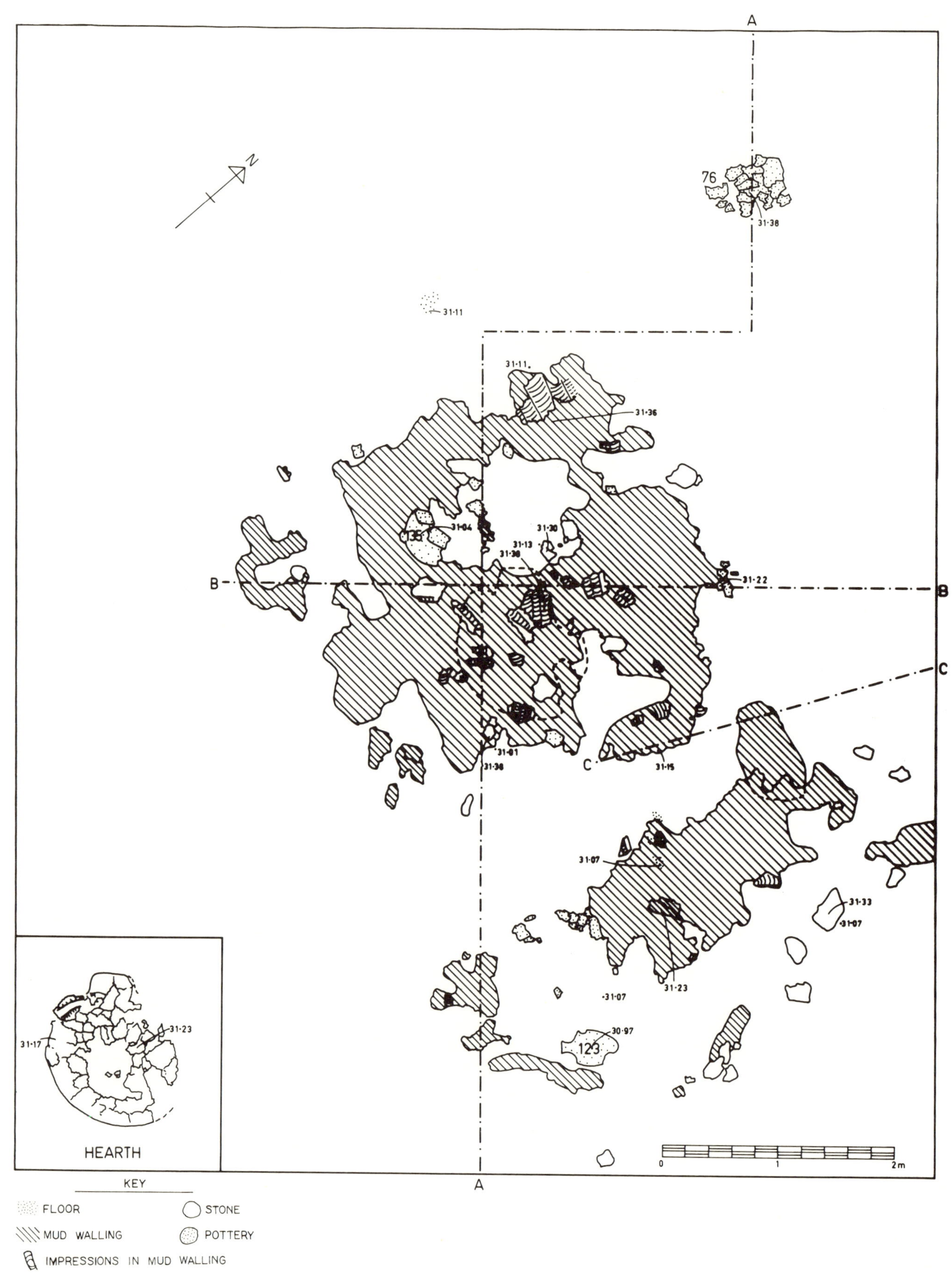

10. Trench 116: plan of level I

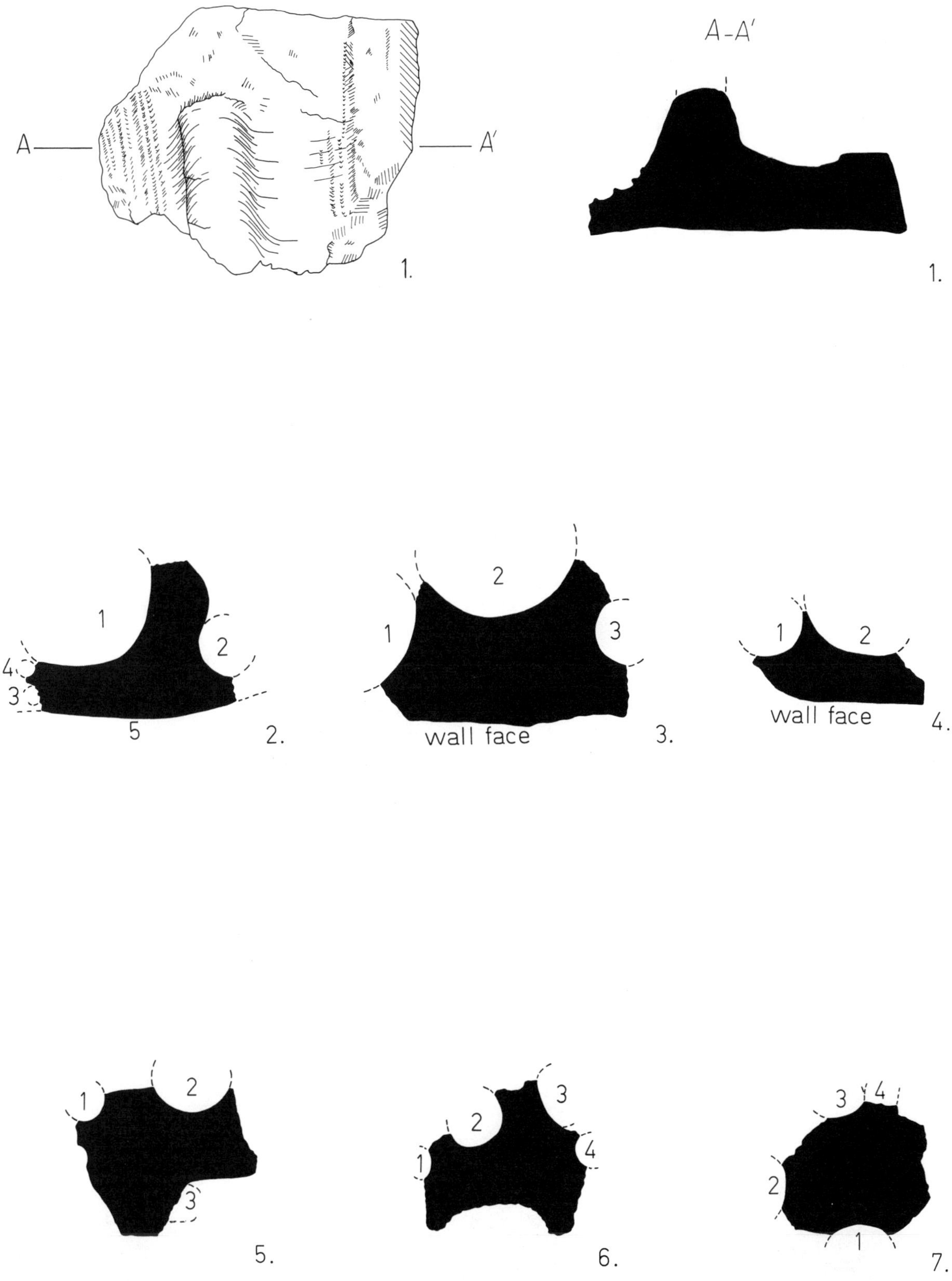

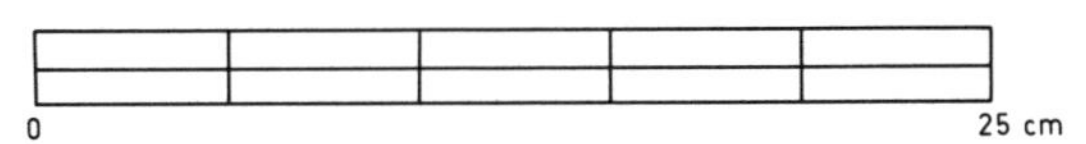

11. Trench 116, level I: mud walling fragments 1–7

PLATE 12

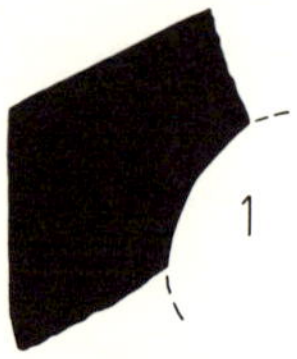

1

8.

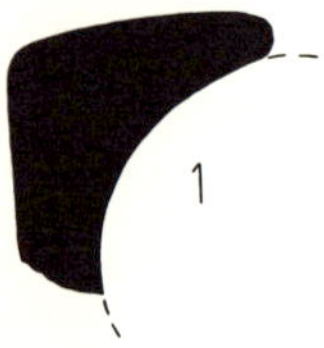

1

9.

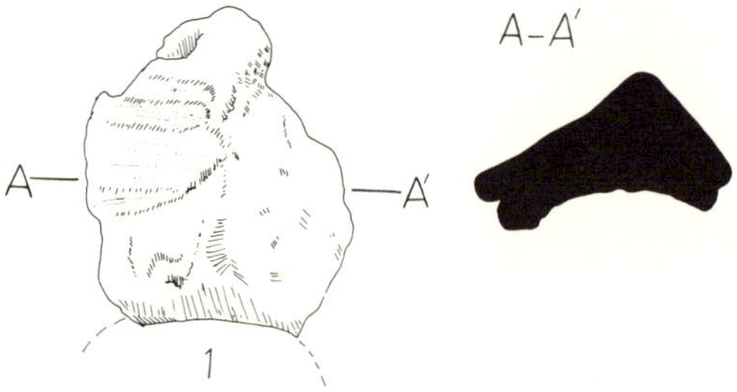

A–A′
A
A′
1

10.

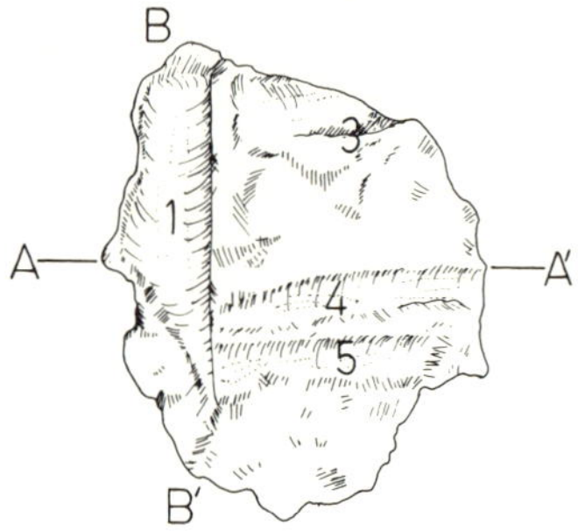

B
3
1
A
A′
4
5
B′

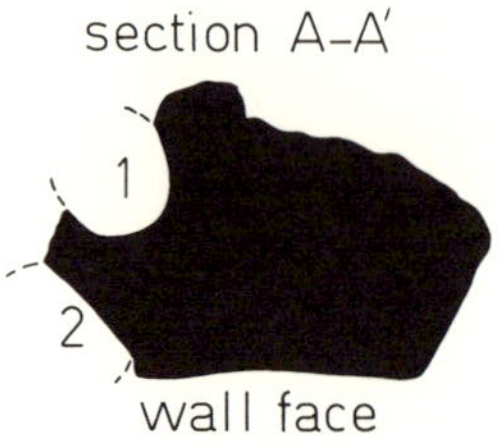

section A–A′
1
2
wall face

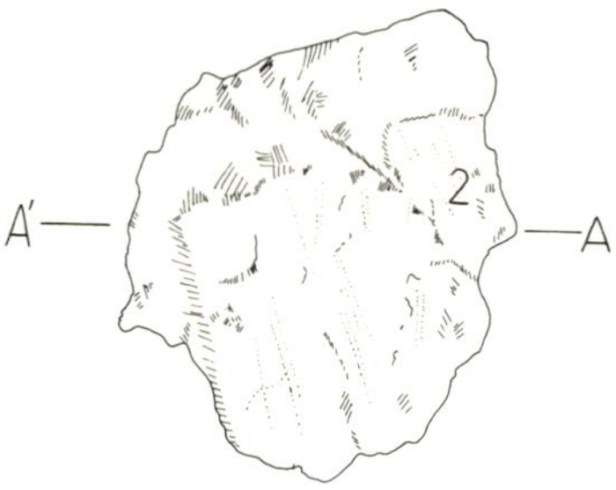

A′
2
A

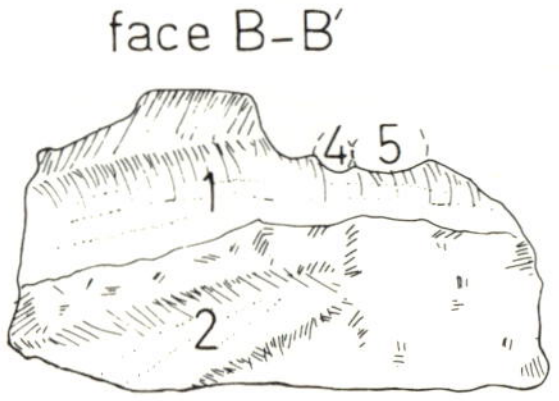

face B–B′
4
5
1
2

11.

wall face
3
2

12.

1
2

13.

2
1
3
4

14.

1
2

15.

0
25 cm

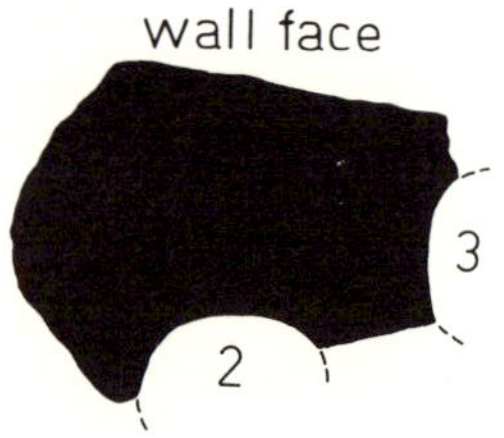

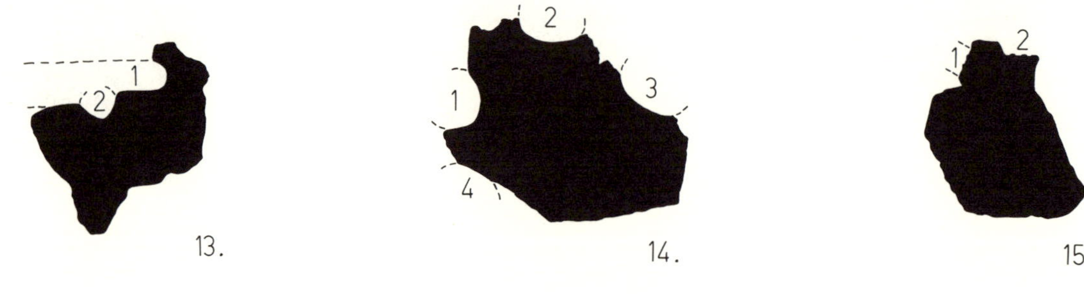

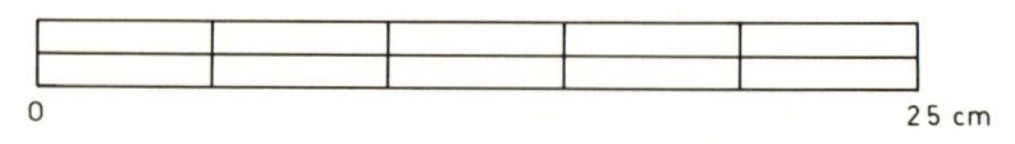

12. Trench 116, level I: mud walling fragments 8–15

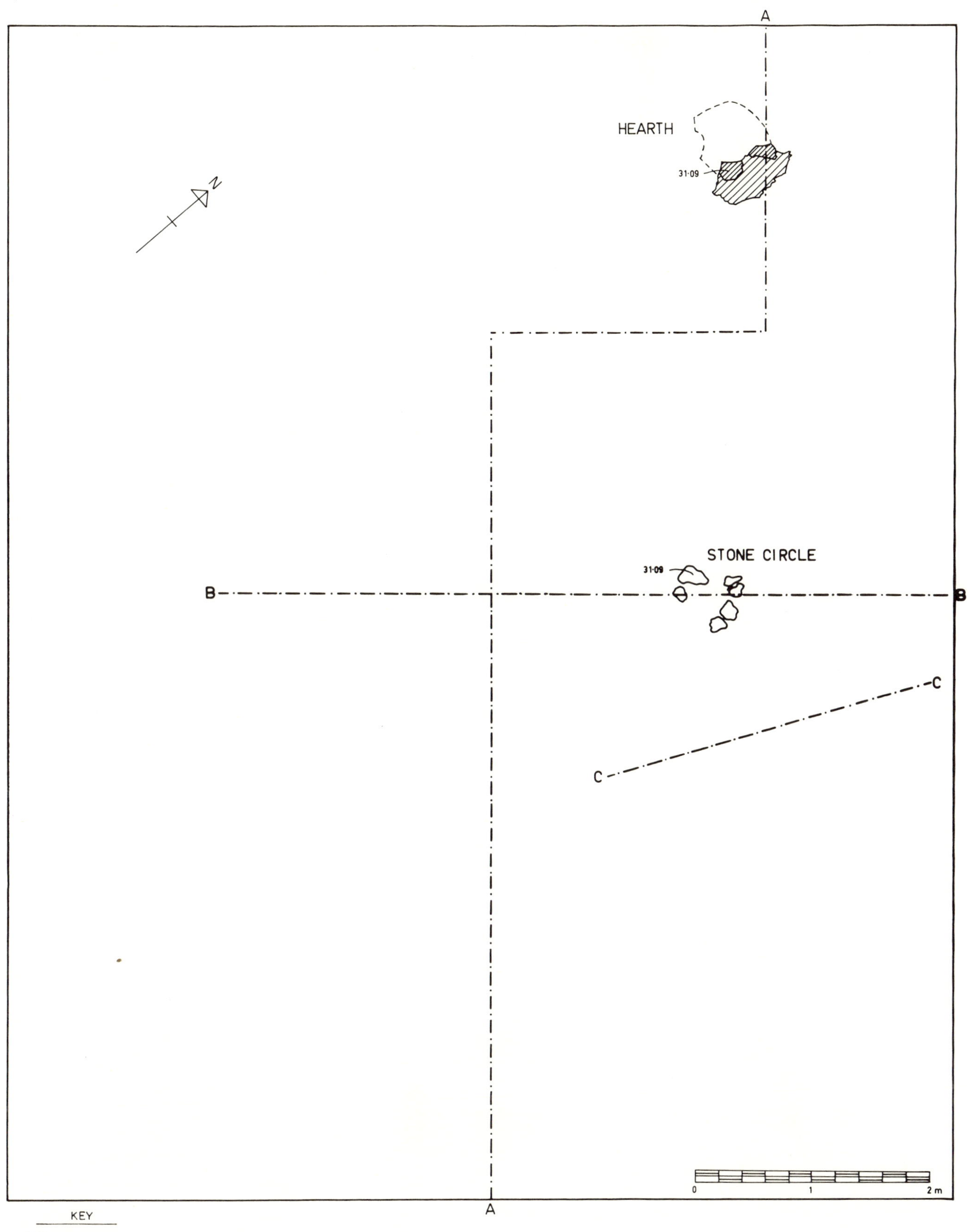

13. Trench 116: plan of level II

PLATE 14

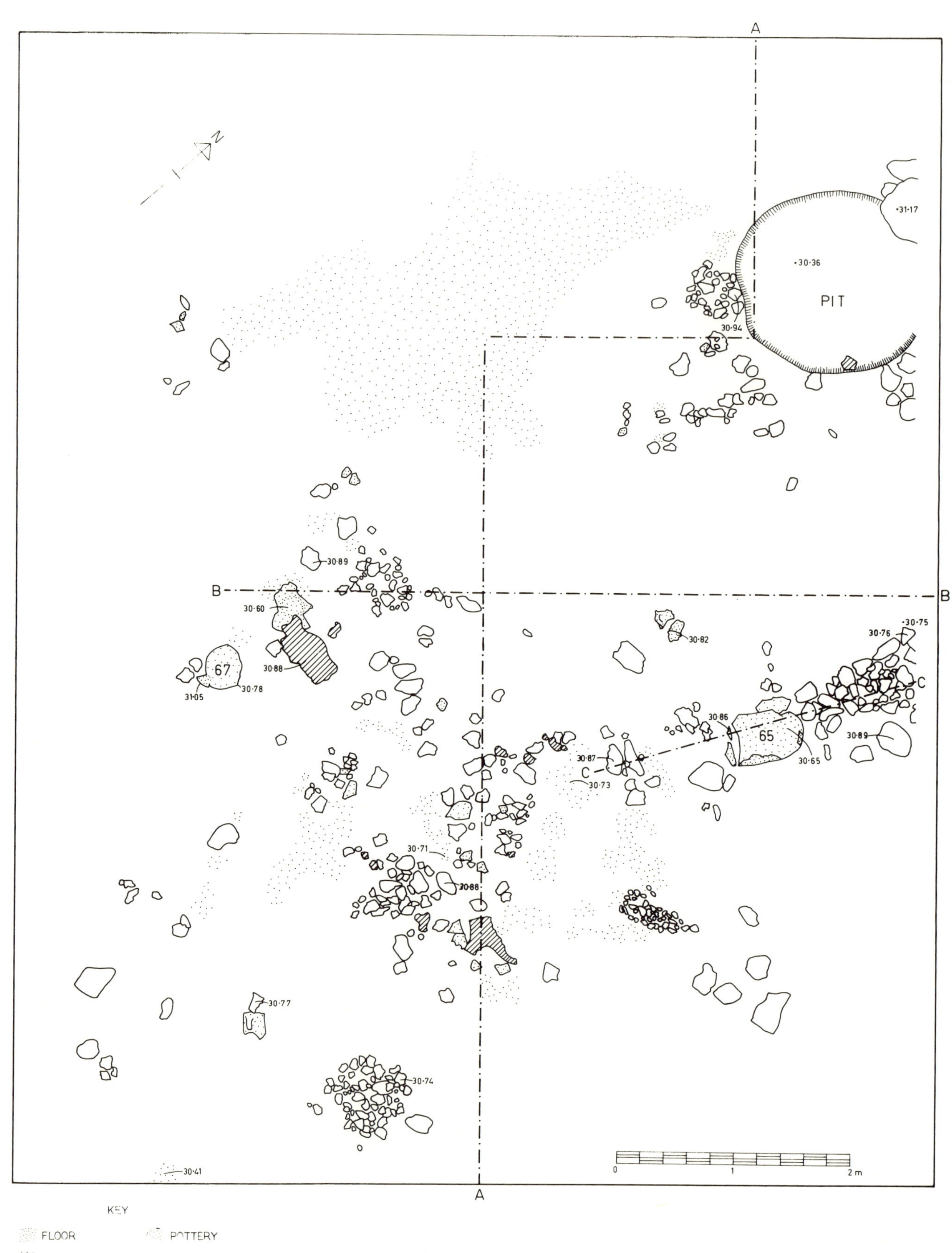

14. Trench 116: plan of level III

PLATE 15

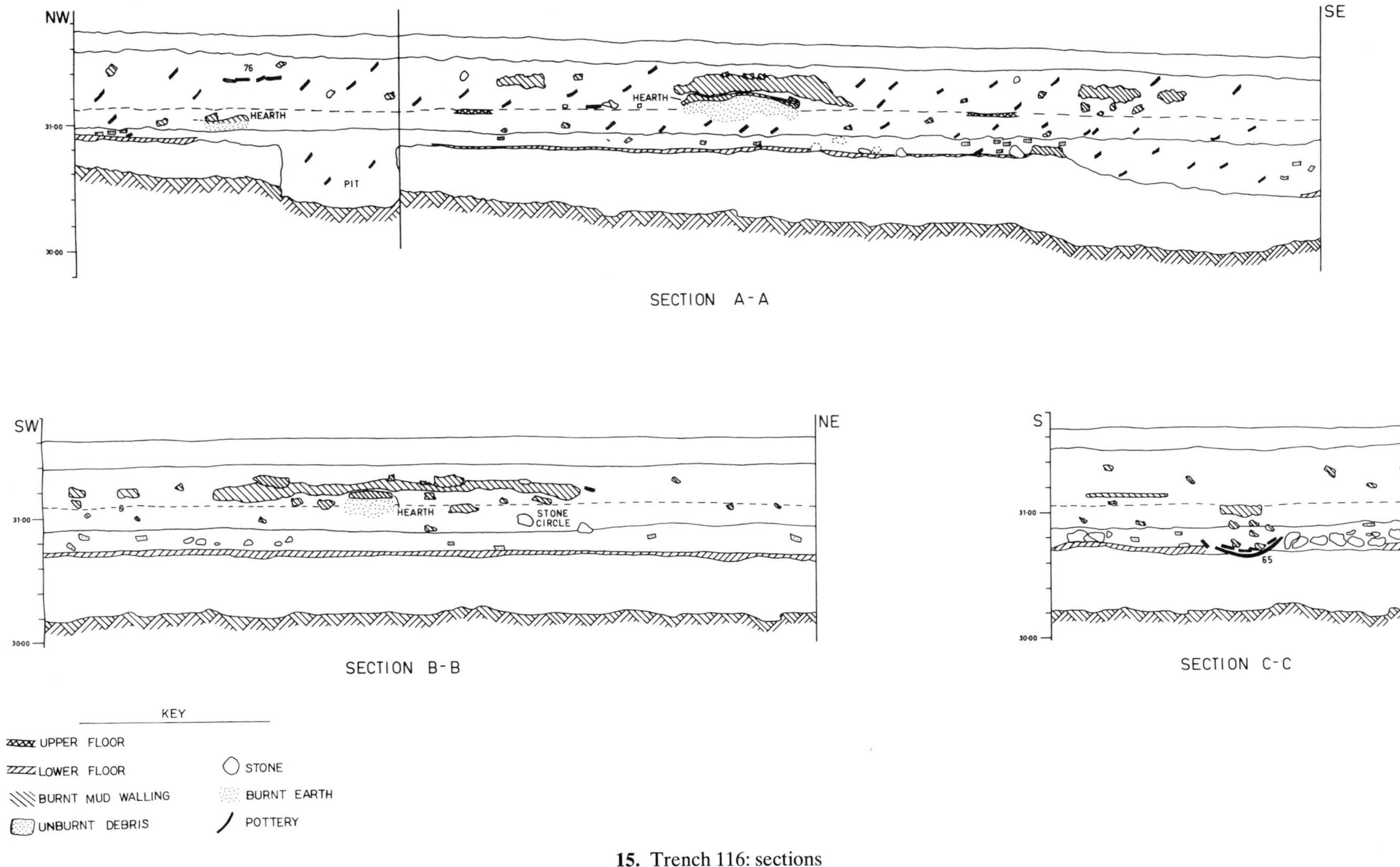

15. Trench 116: sections

16. Bağbaşı pottery **1–7**

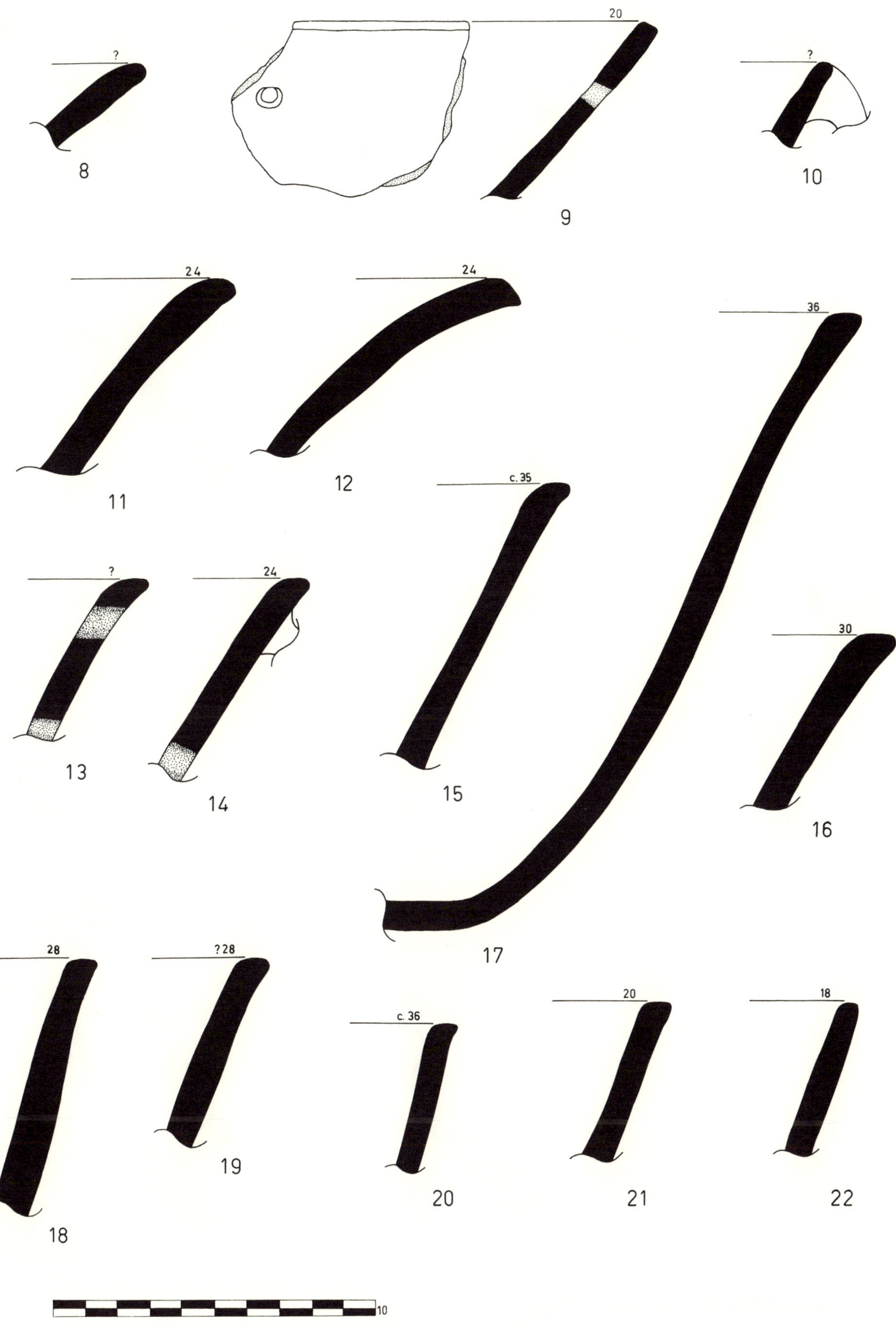

17. Bağbaşı pottery **8–22**

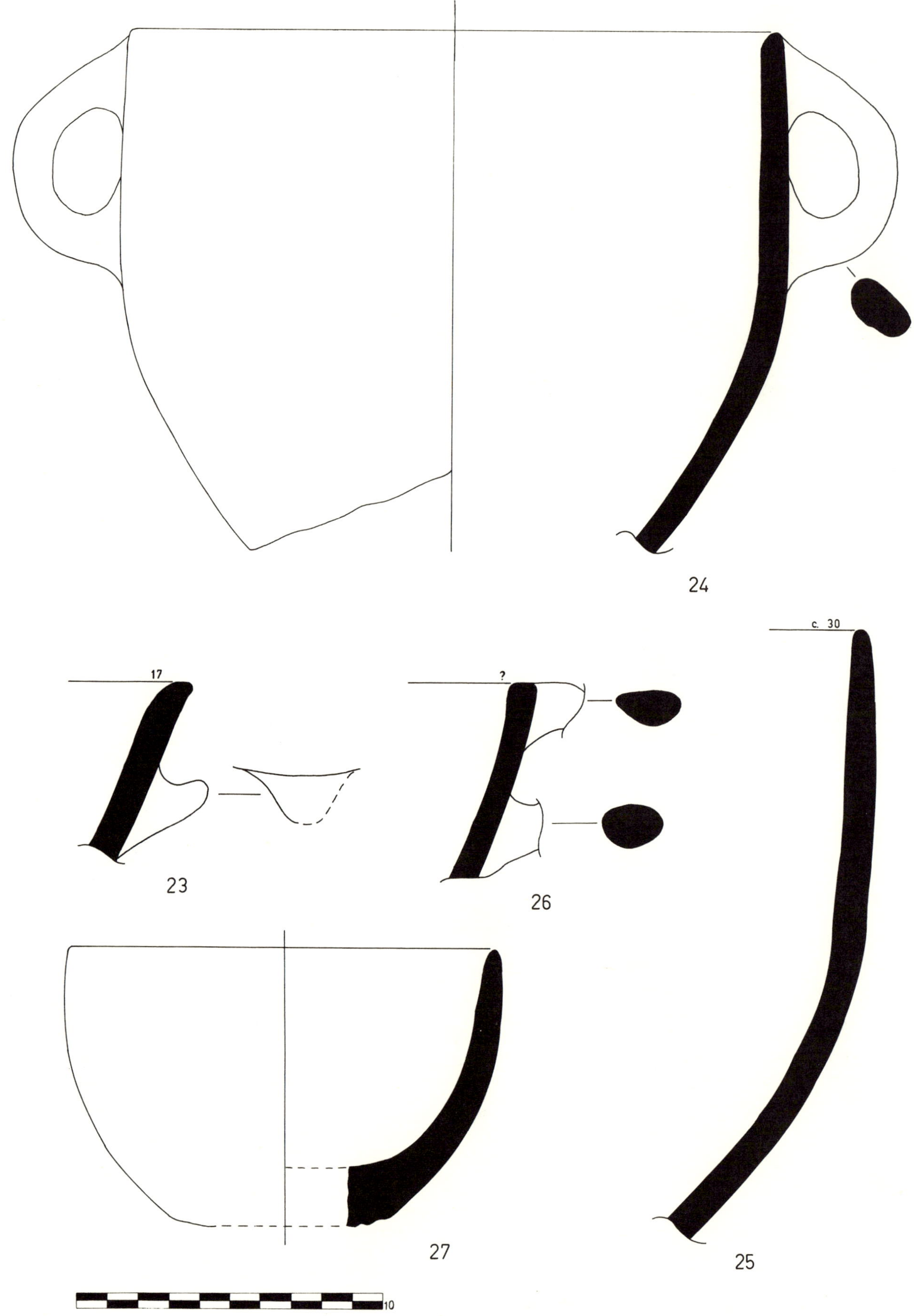

18. Bağbaşı pottery **23–27**

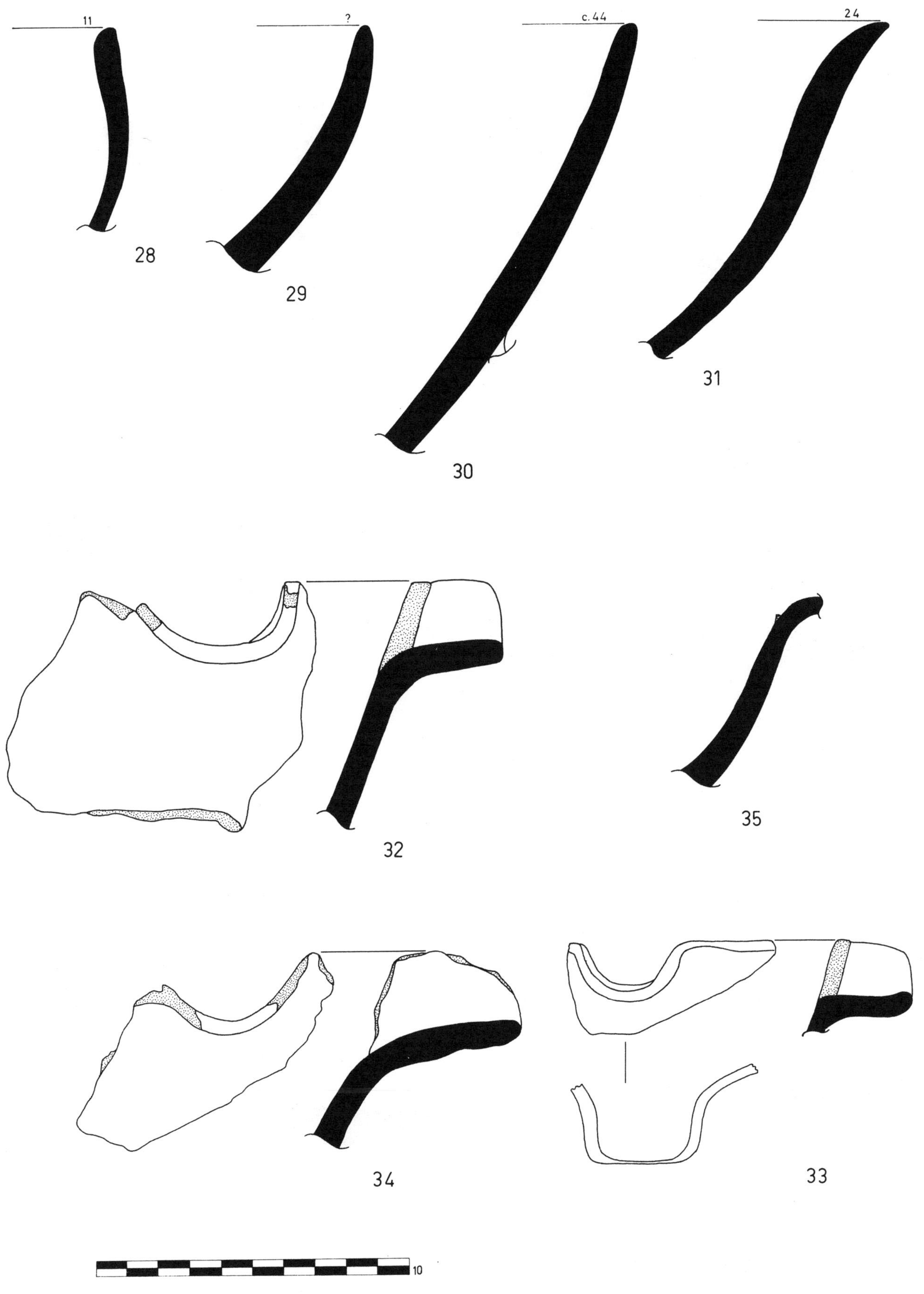

19. Bağbaşı pottery **28–35**

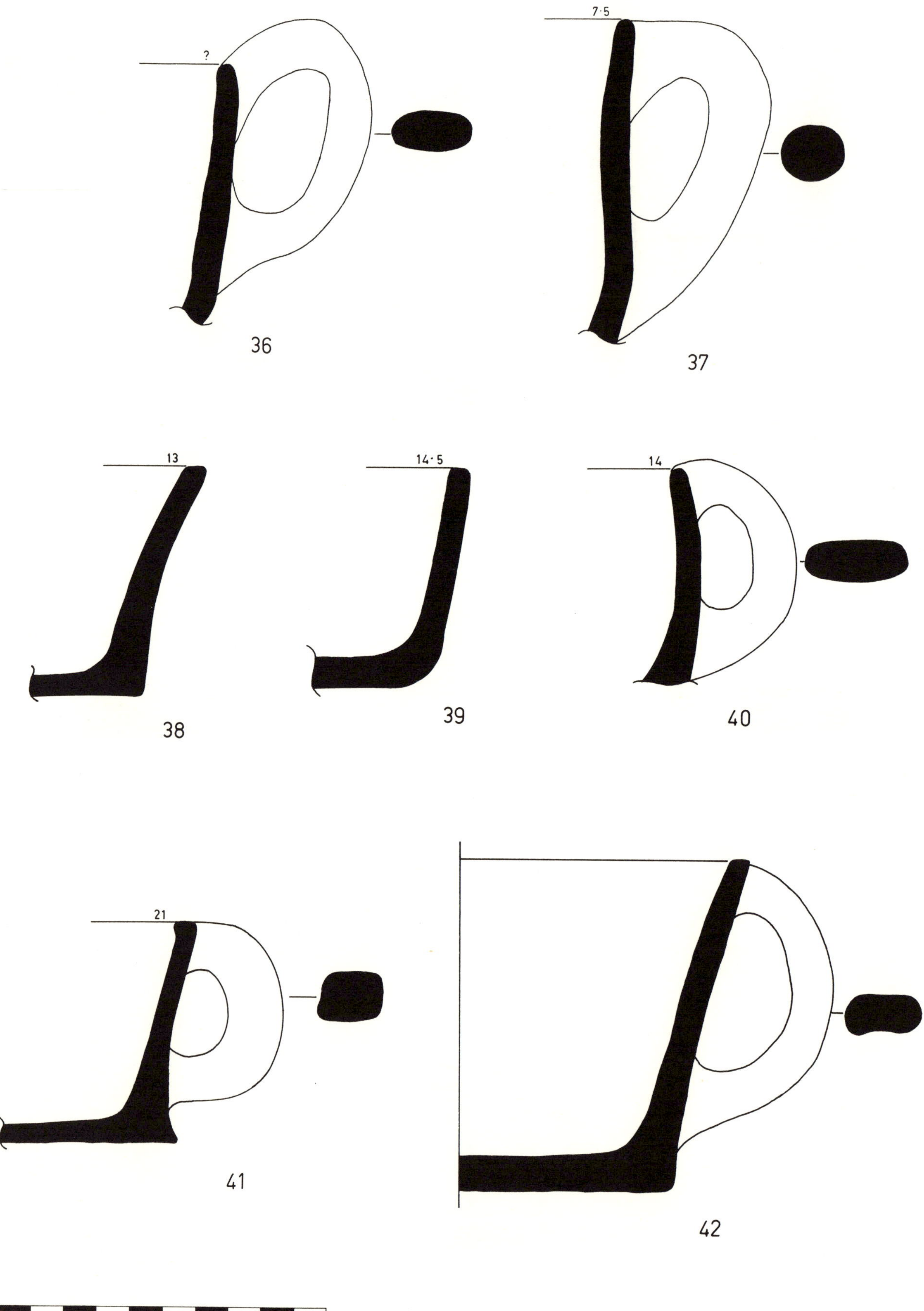

20. Bağbaşı pottery **36–42**

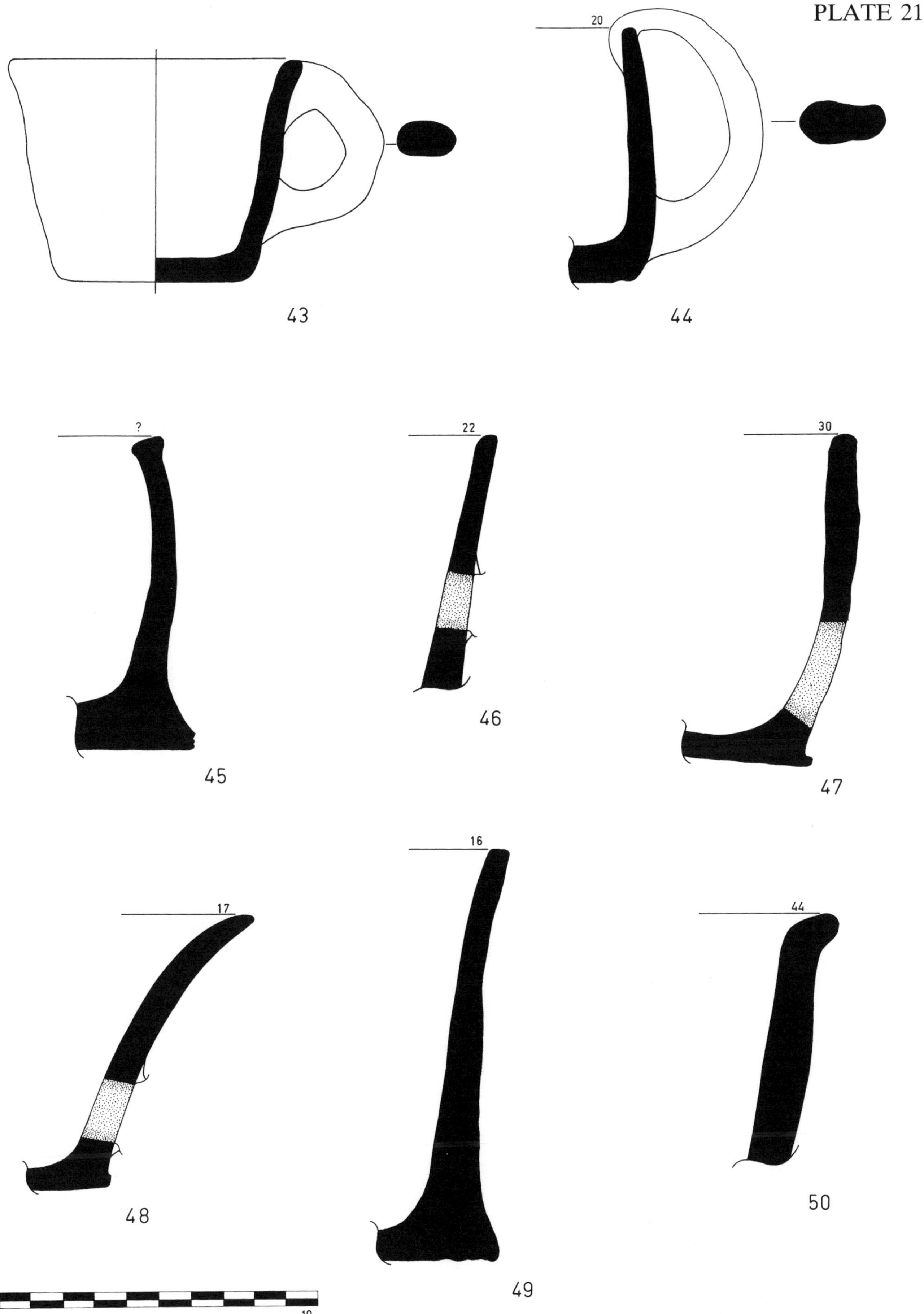

21. Bağbaşı pottery **43–50**

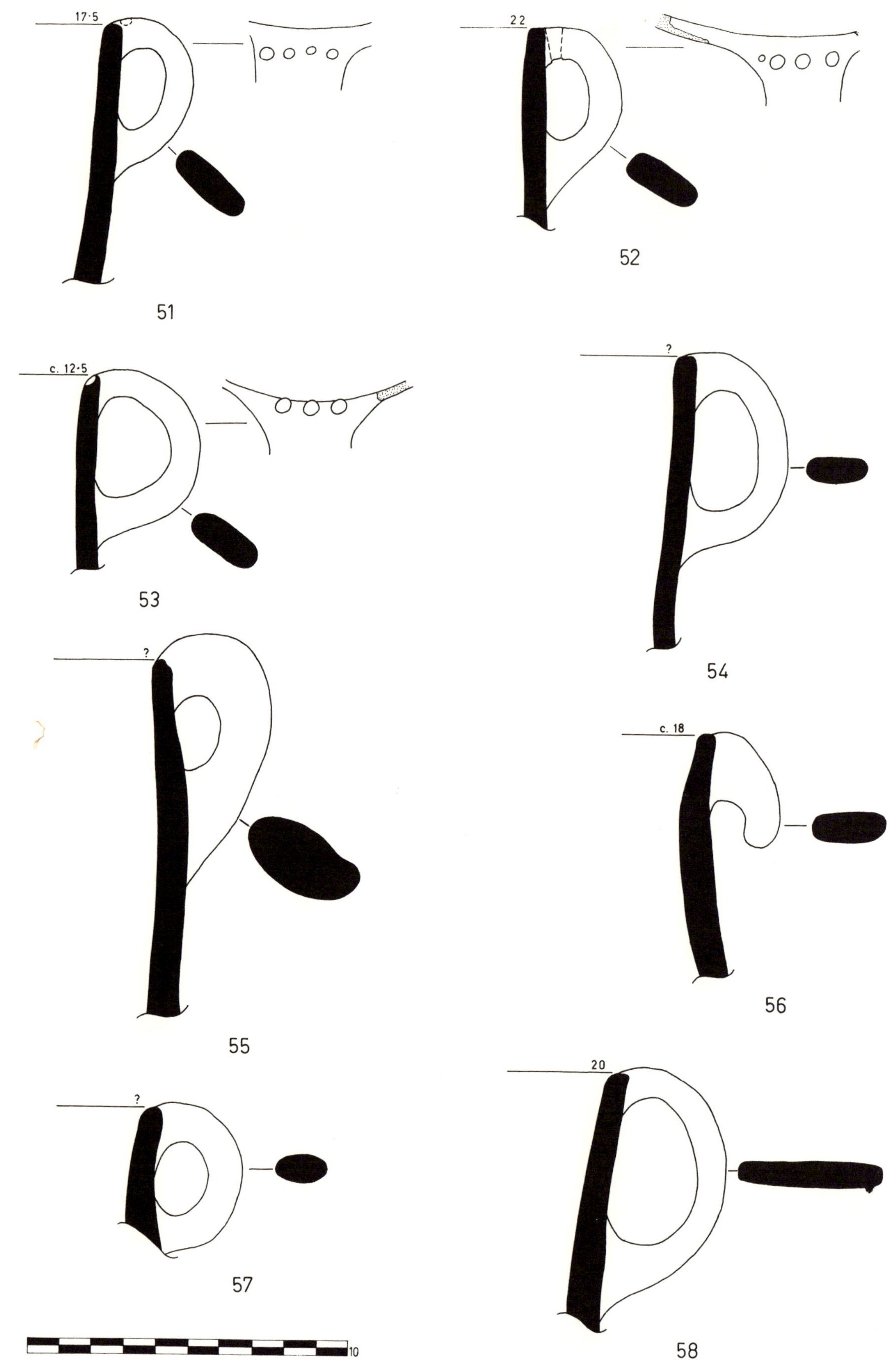

22. Bağbaşı pottery **51–58**

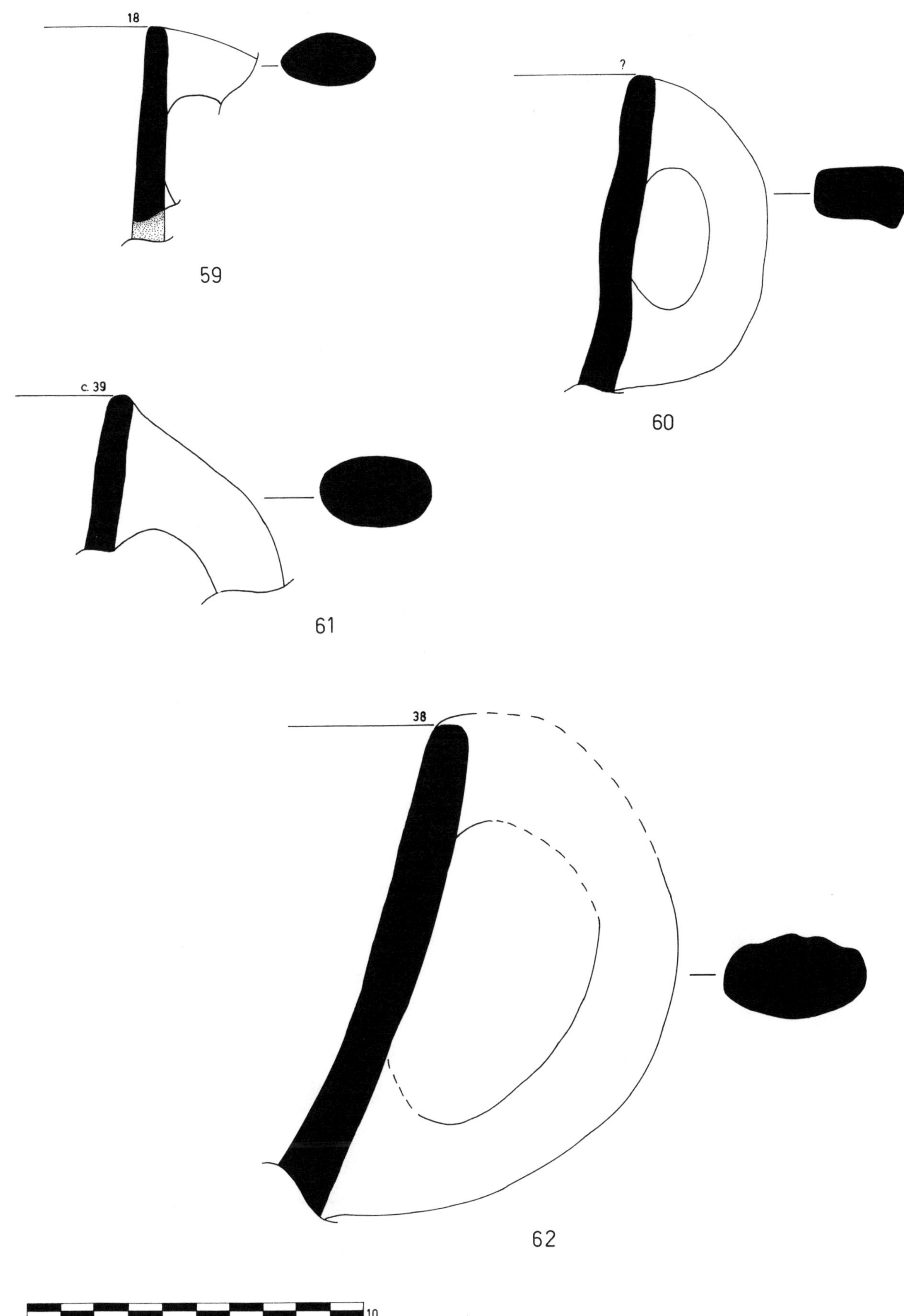

23. Bağbaşı pottery **59–62**

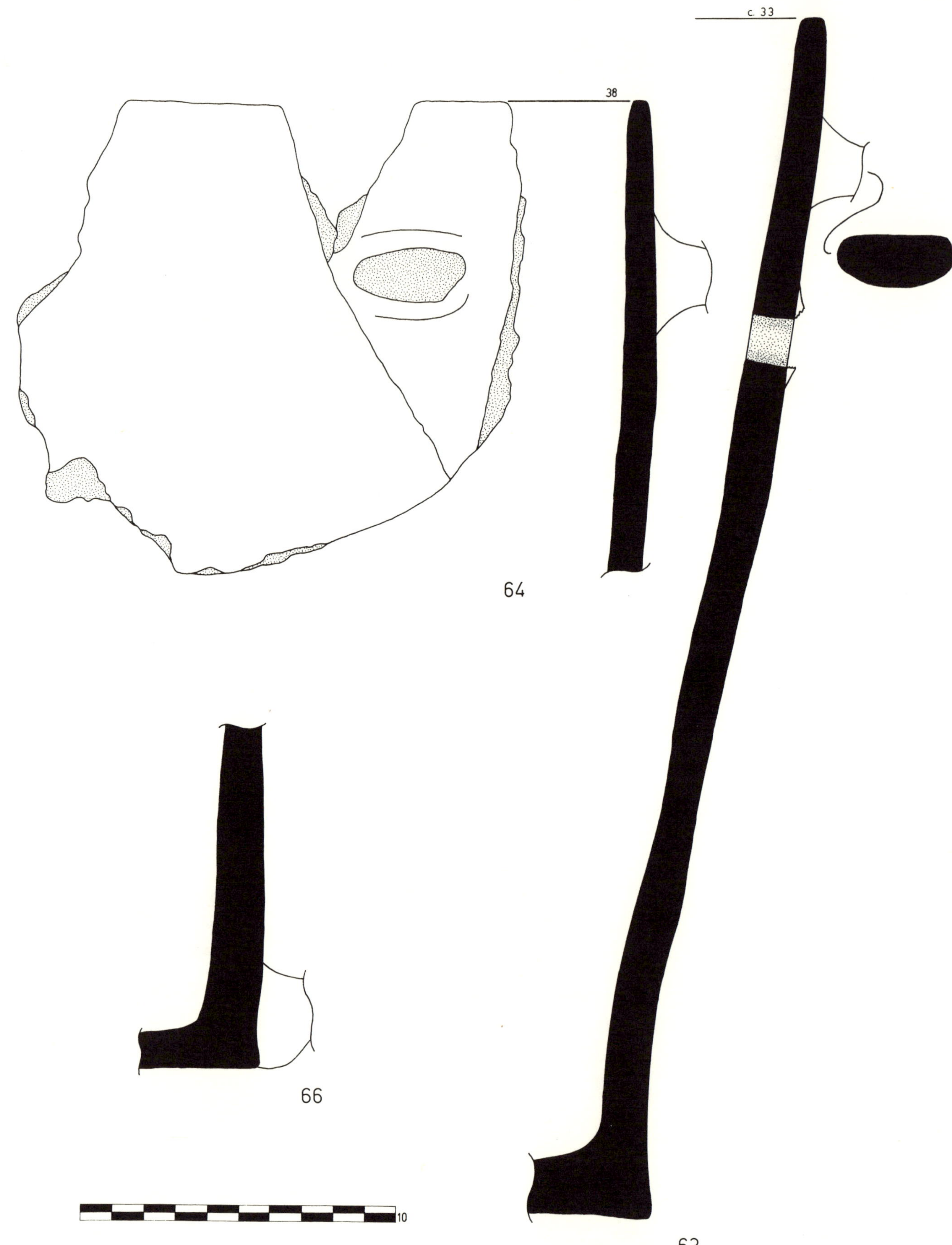

24. Bağbaşı pottery **63–64, 66**

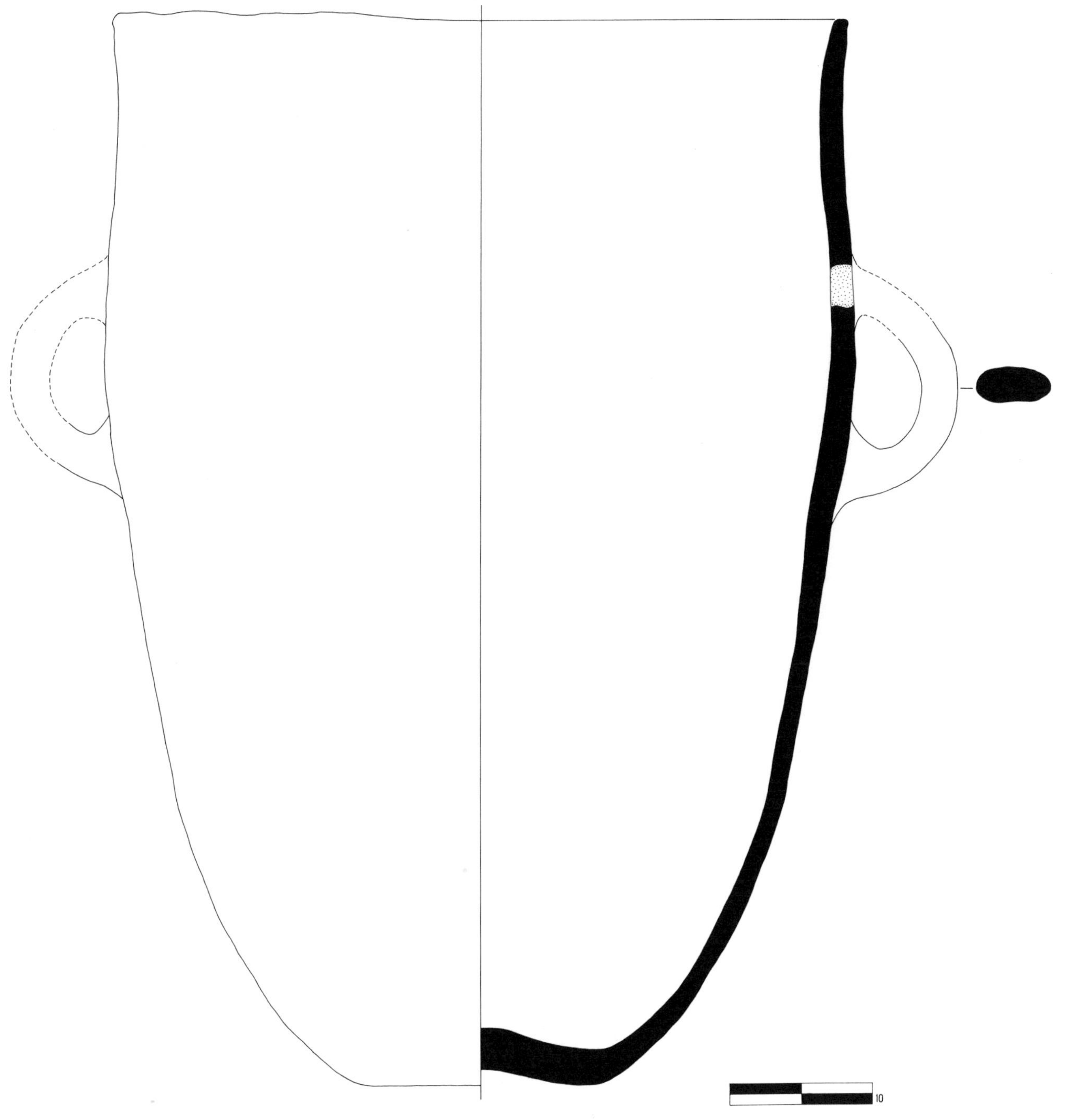

25. Bağbaşı pottery **65**

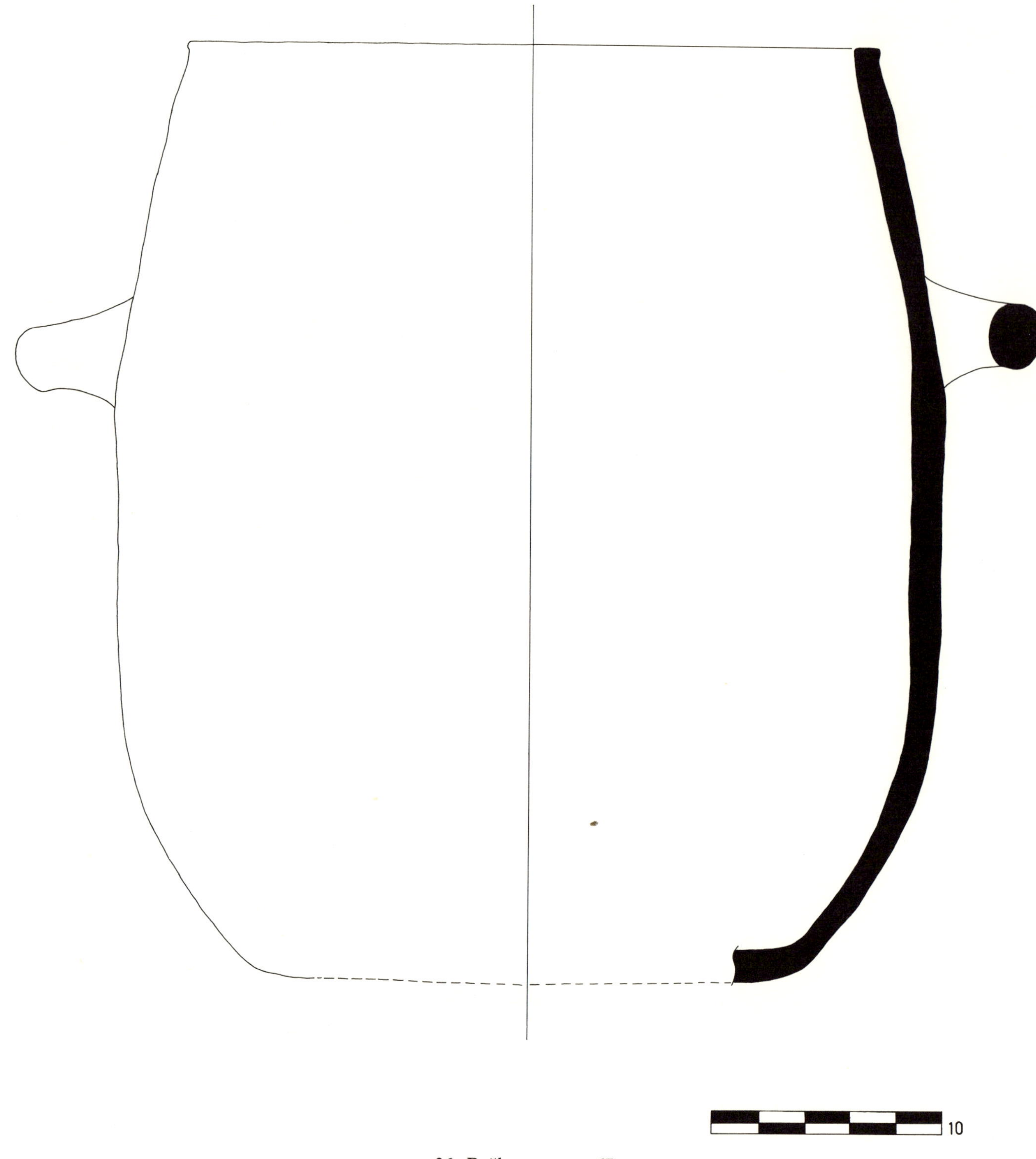

26. Bağbaşı pottery **67**

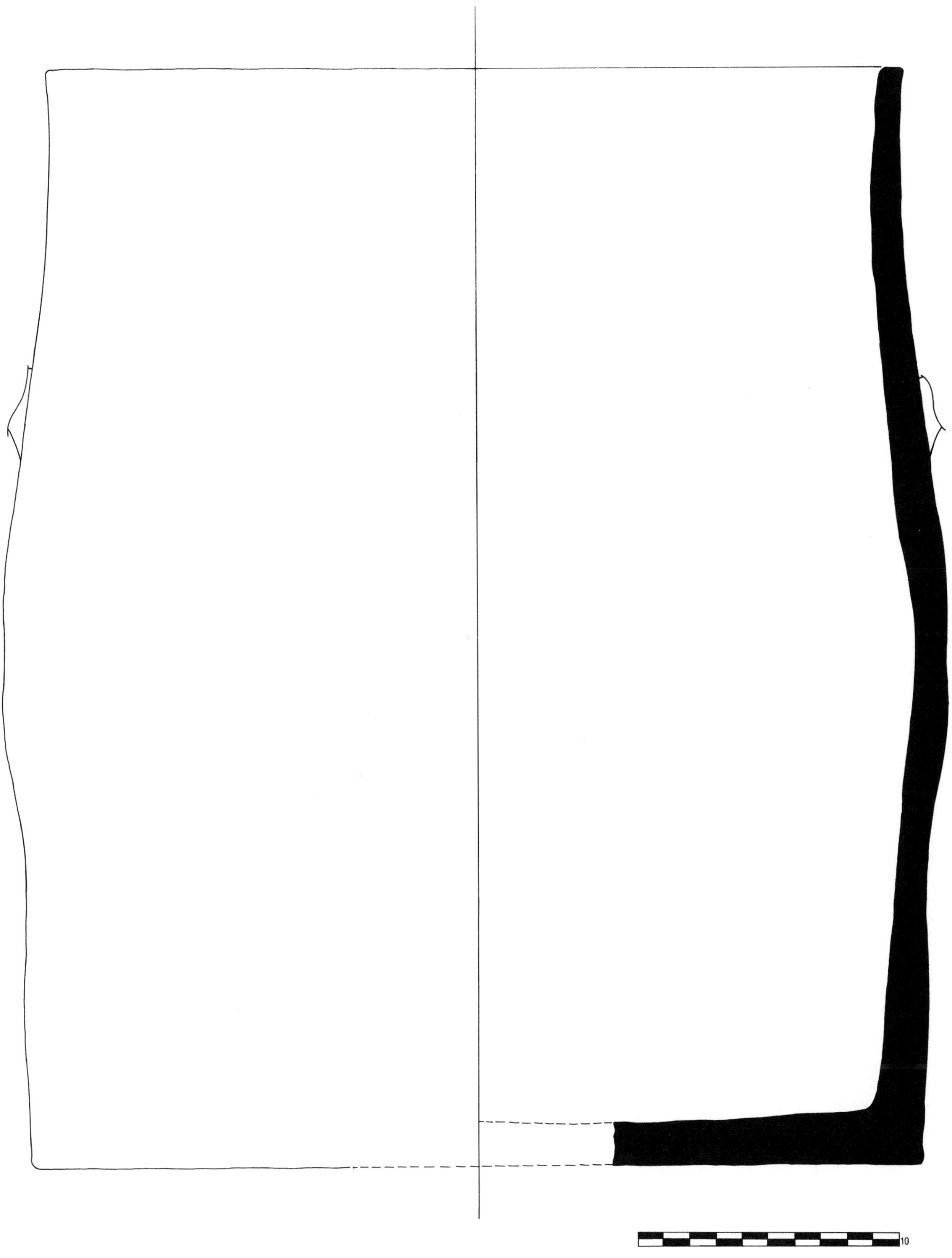

27. Bağbaşı pottery **68**

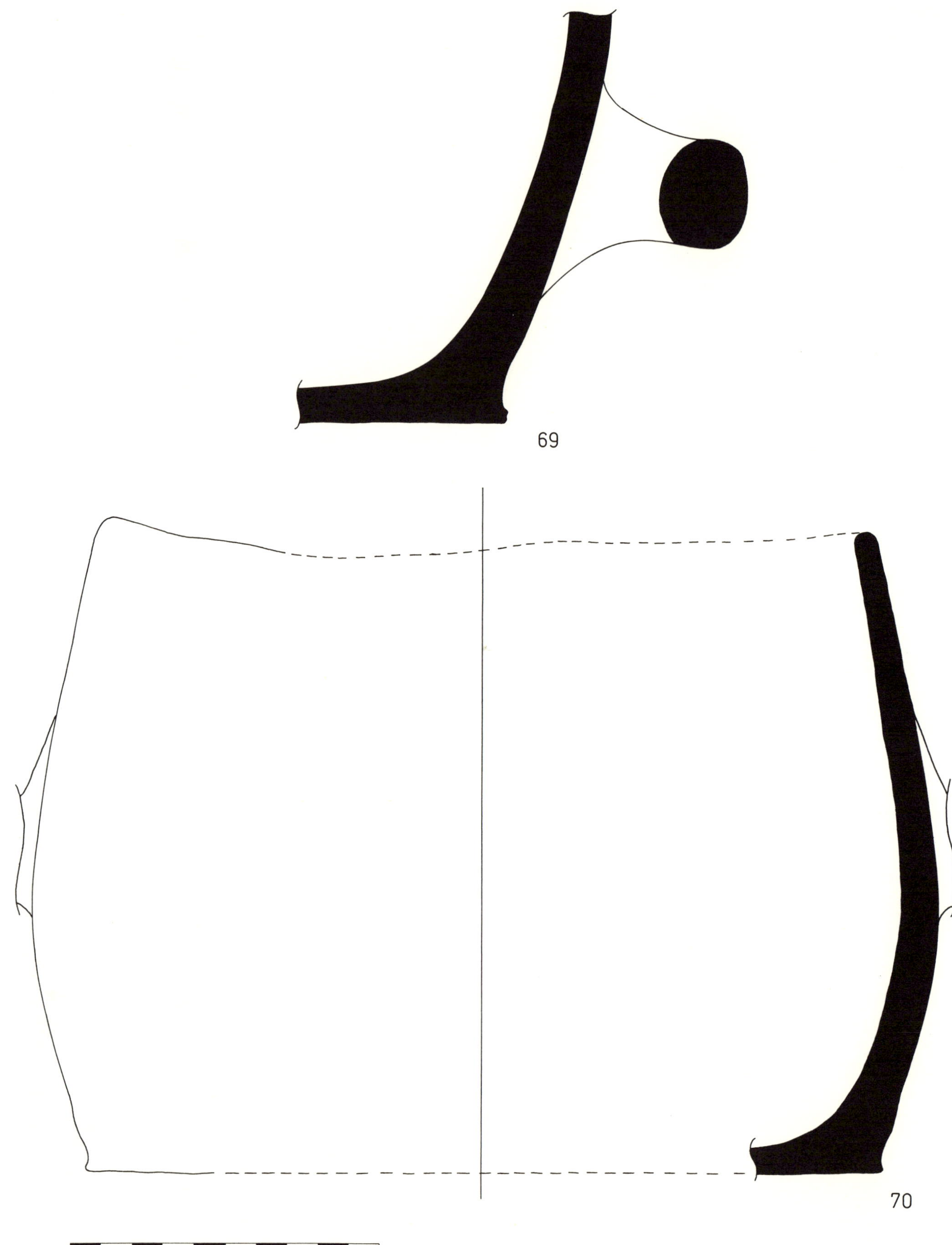

28. Bağbaşı pottery **69–70**

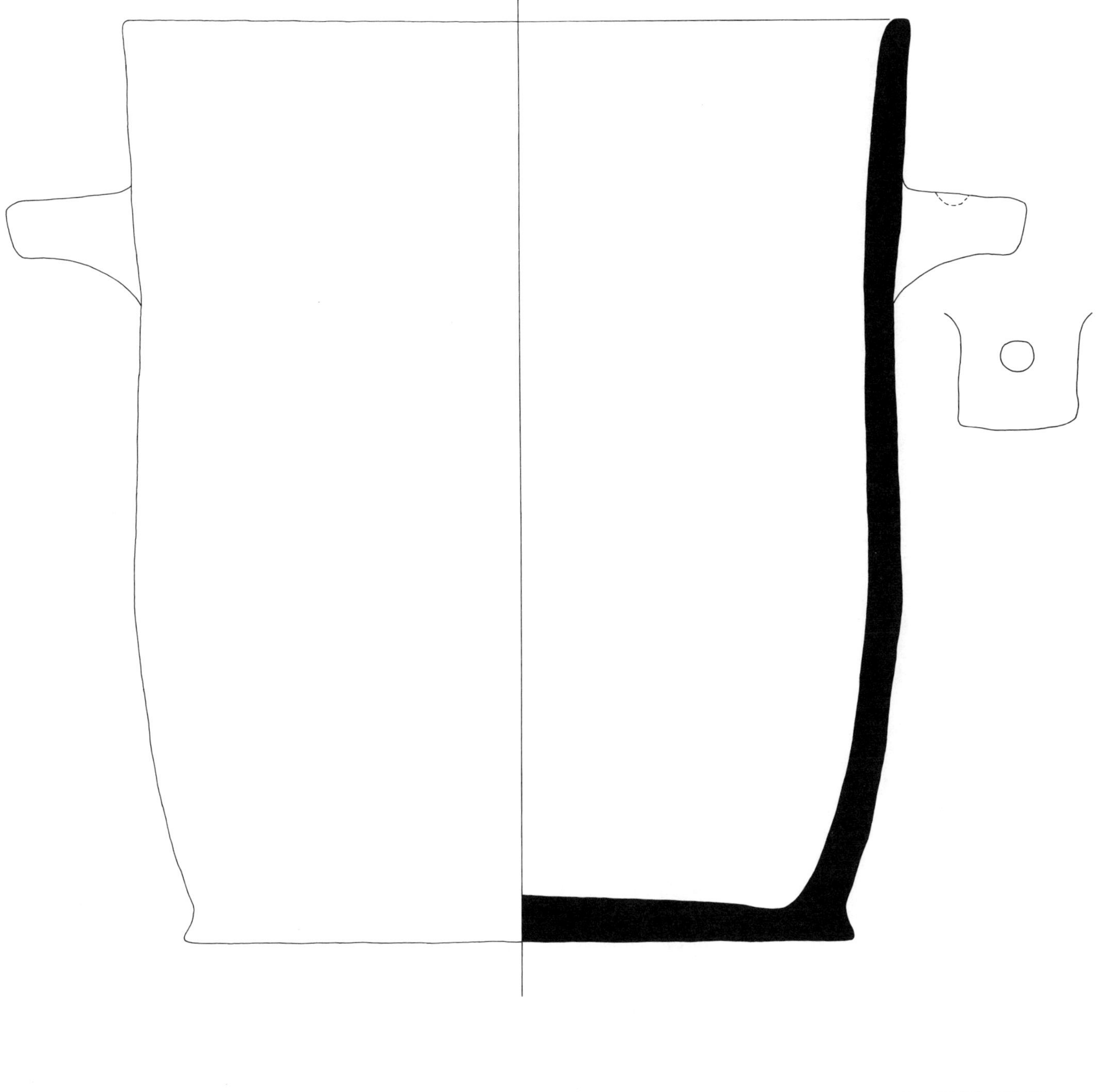

29. Bağbaşı pottery **71**

30. Bağbaşı pottery **72–74**

31. Bağbaşı pottery **75–76**

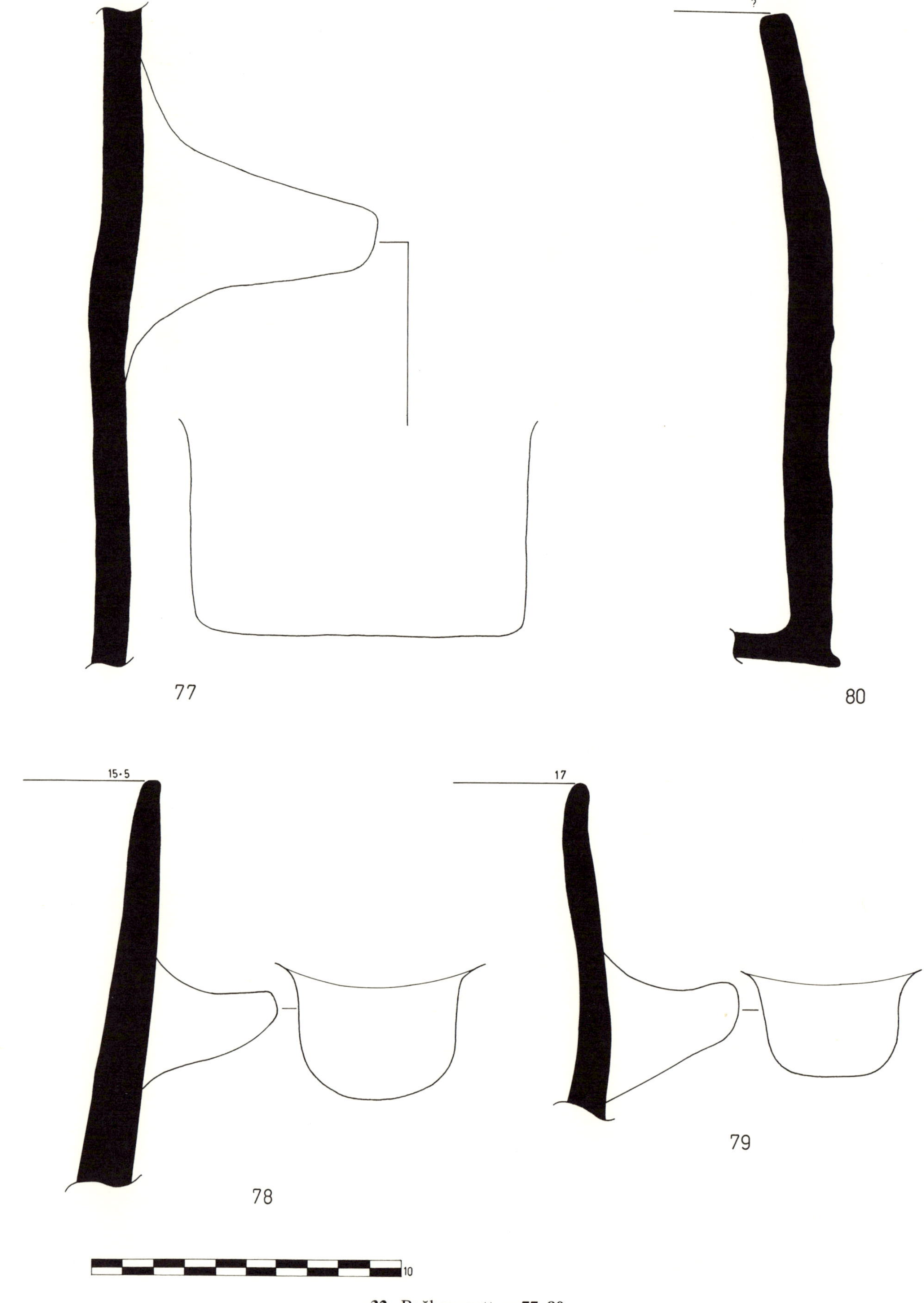

32. Bağbaşı pottery **77–80**

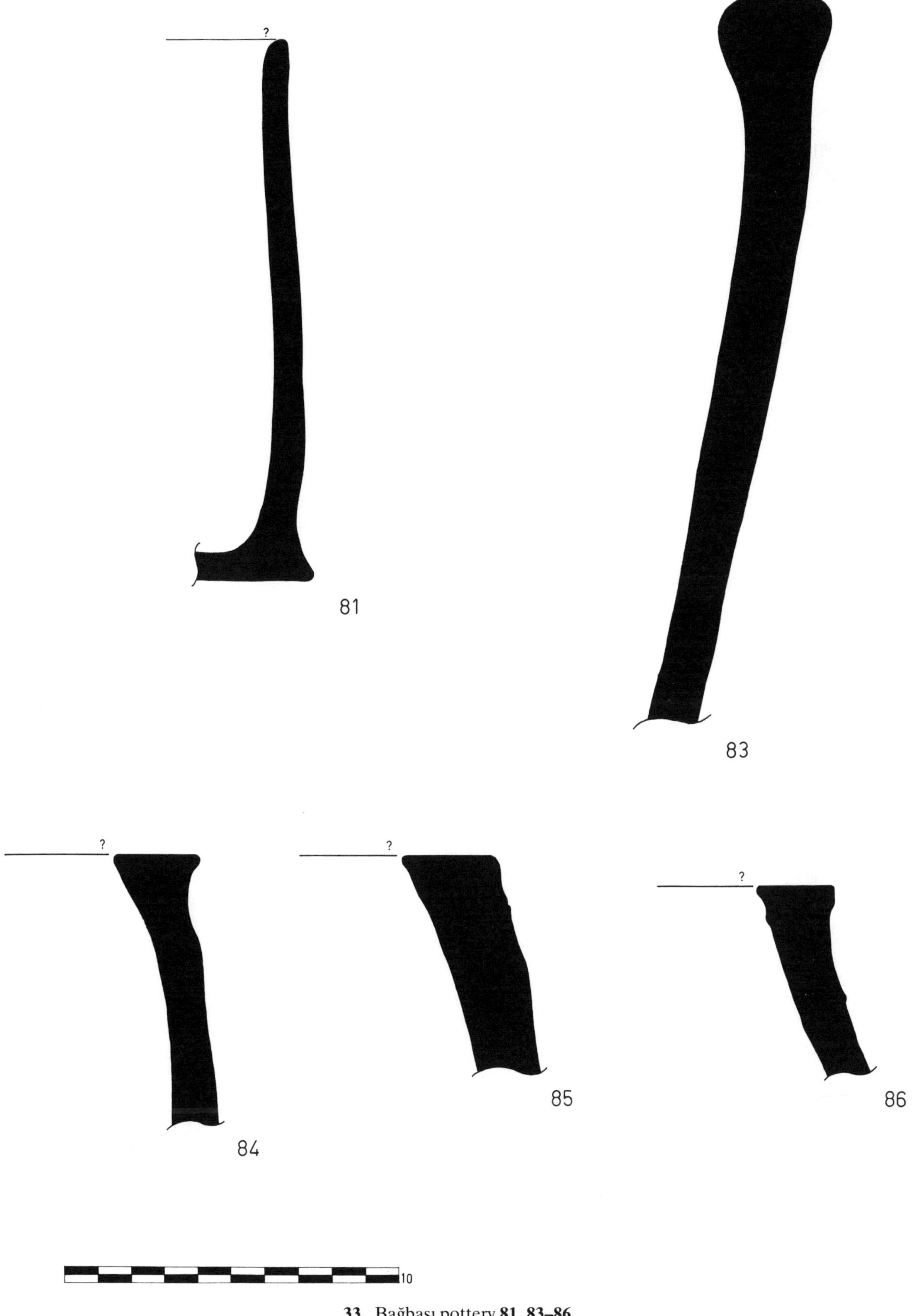

33. Bağbaşı pottery **81, 83–86**

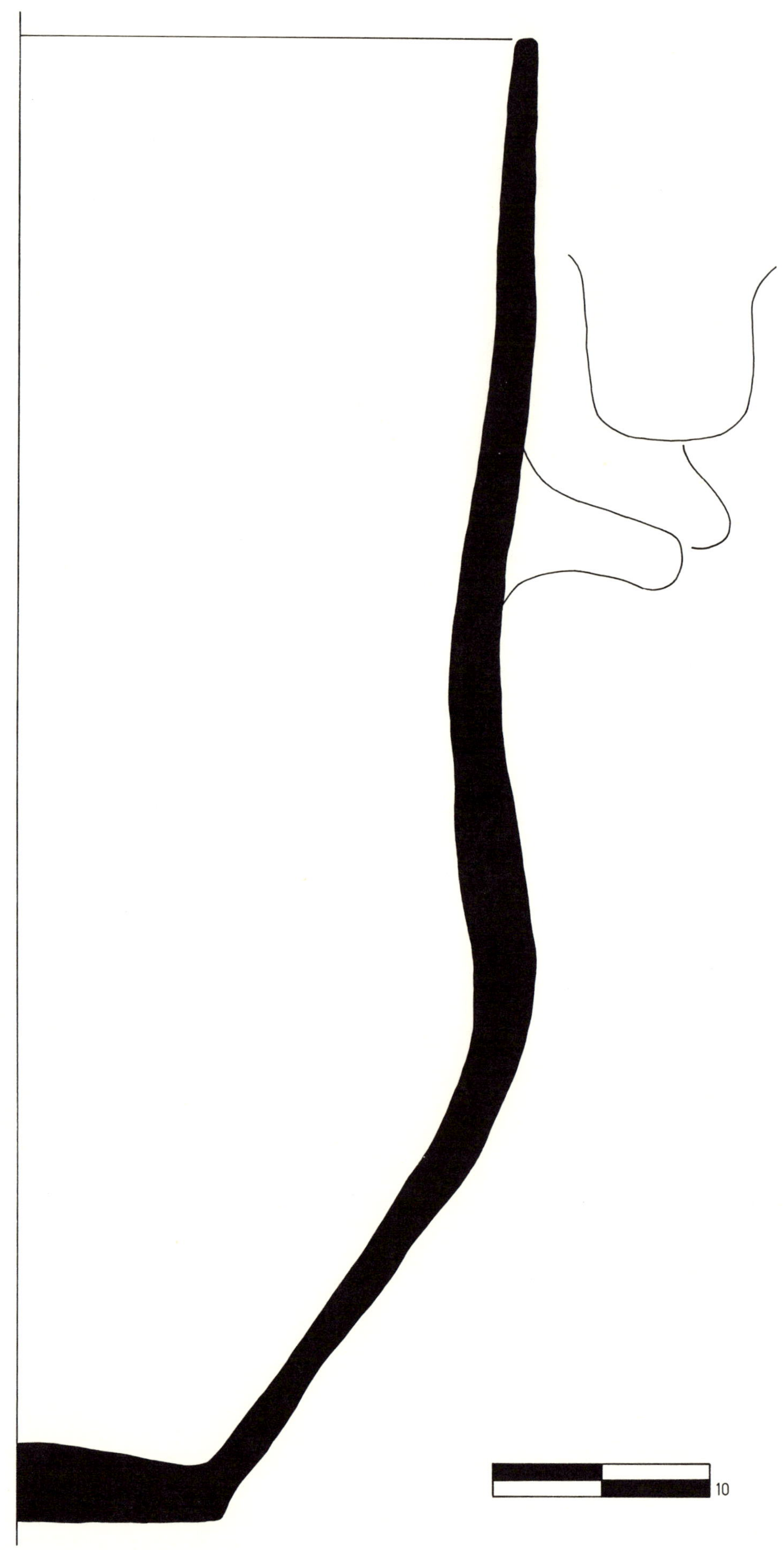

34. Bağbaşı pottery **82**

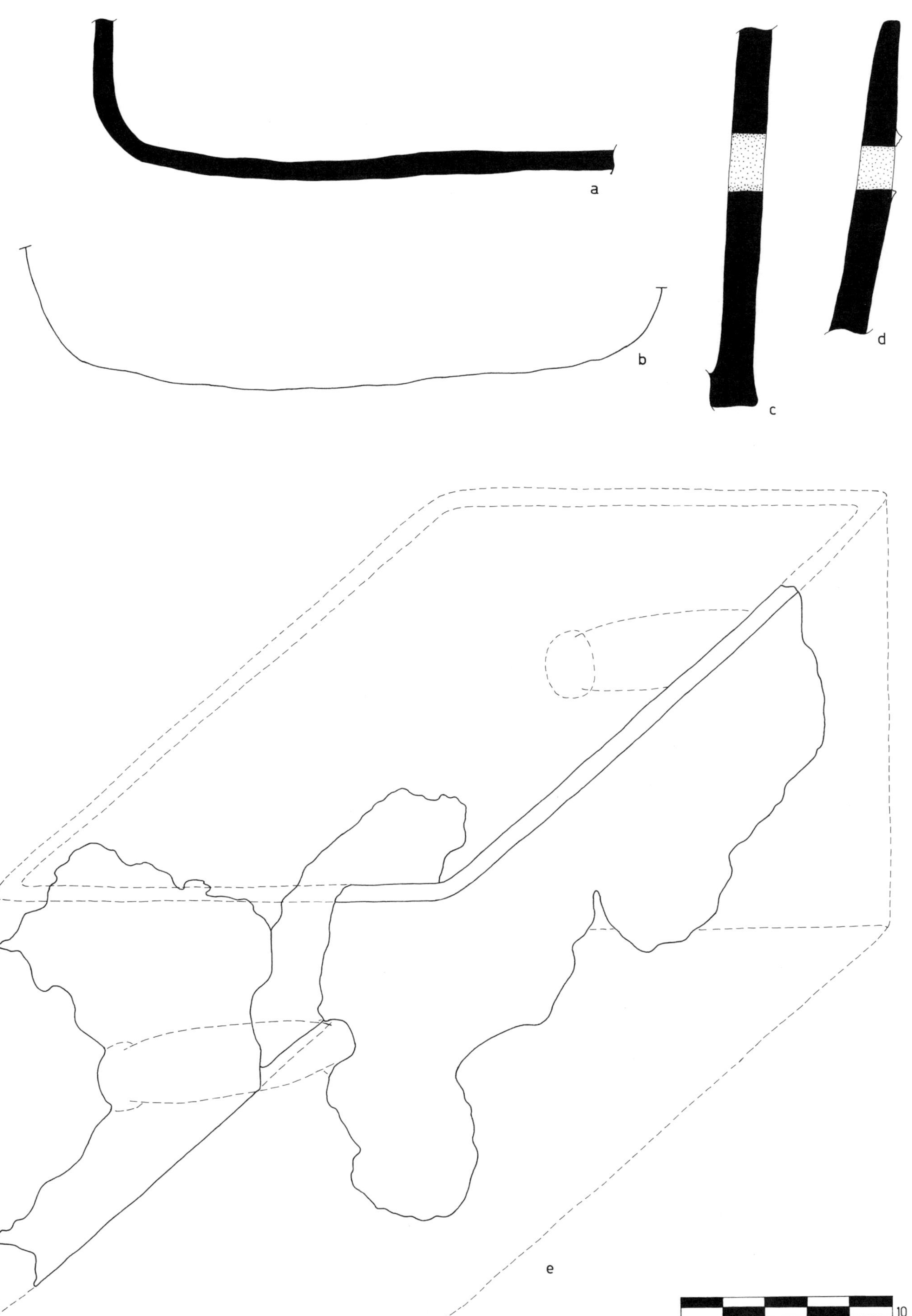

35. Bağbaşı pottery **87,** with a possible reconstruction of the square or rectangular pot

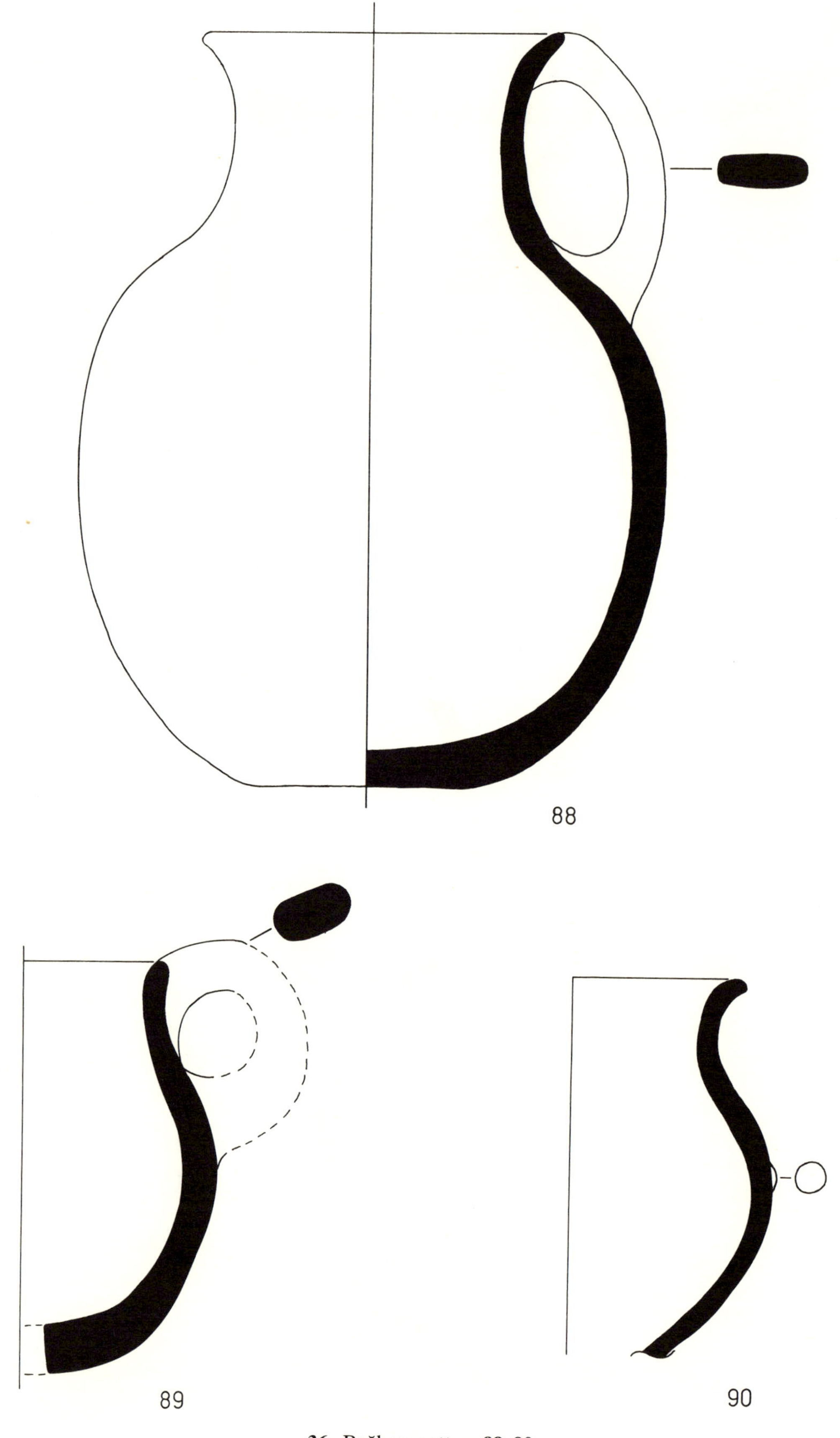

36. Bağbaşı pottery **88–90**

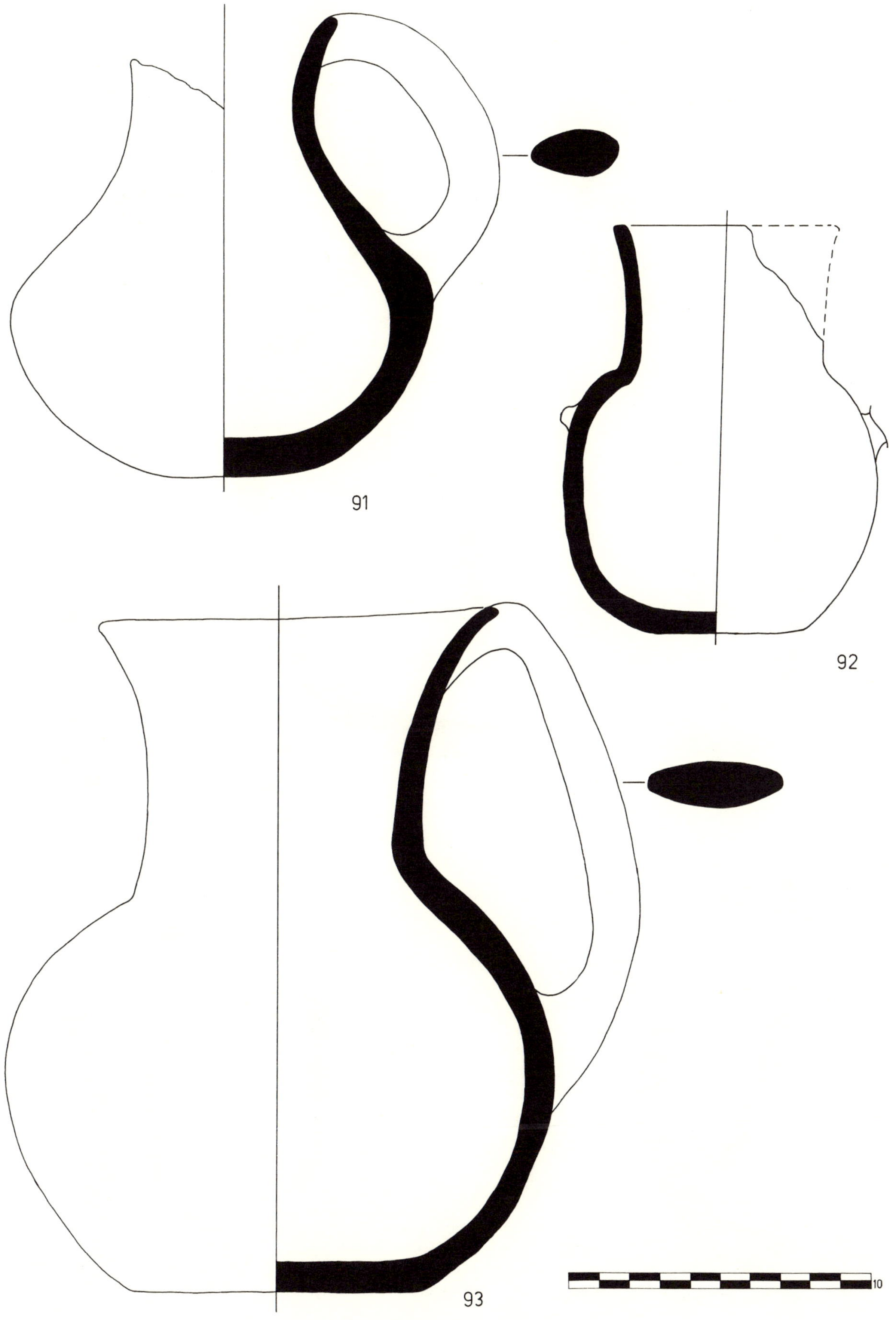

37. Bağbaşı pottery **91–93**

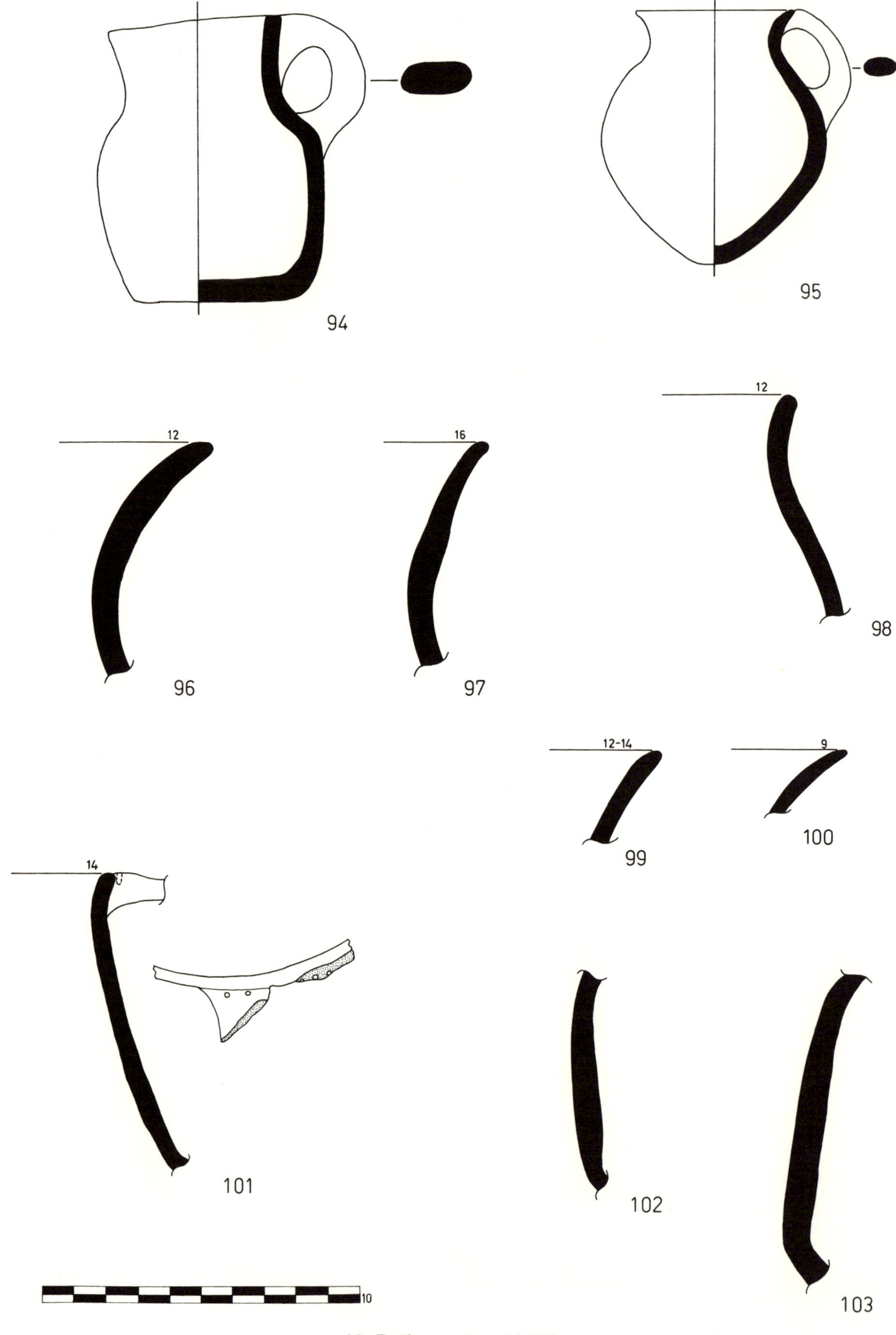

38. Bağbaşı pottery **94–103**

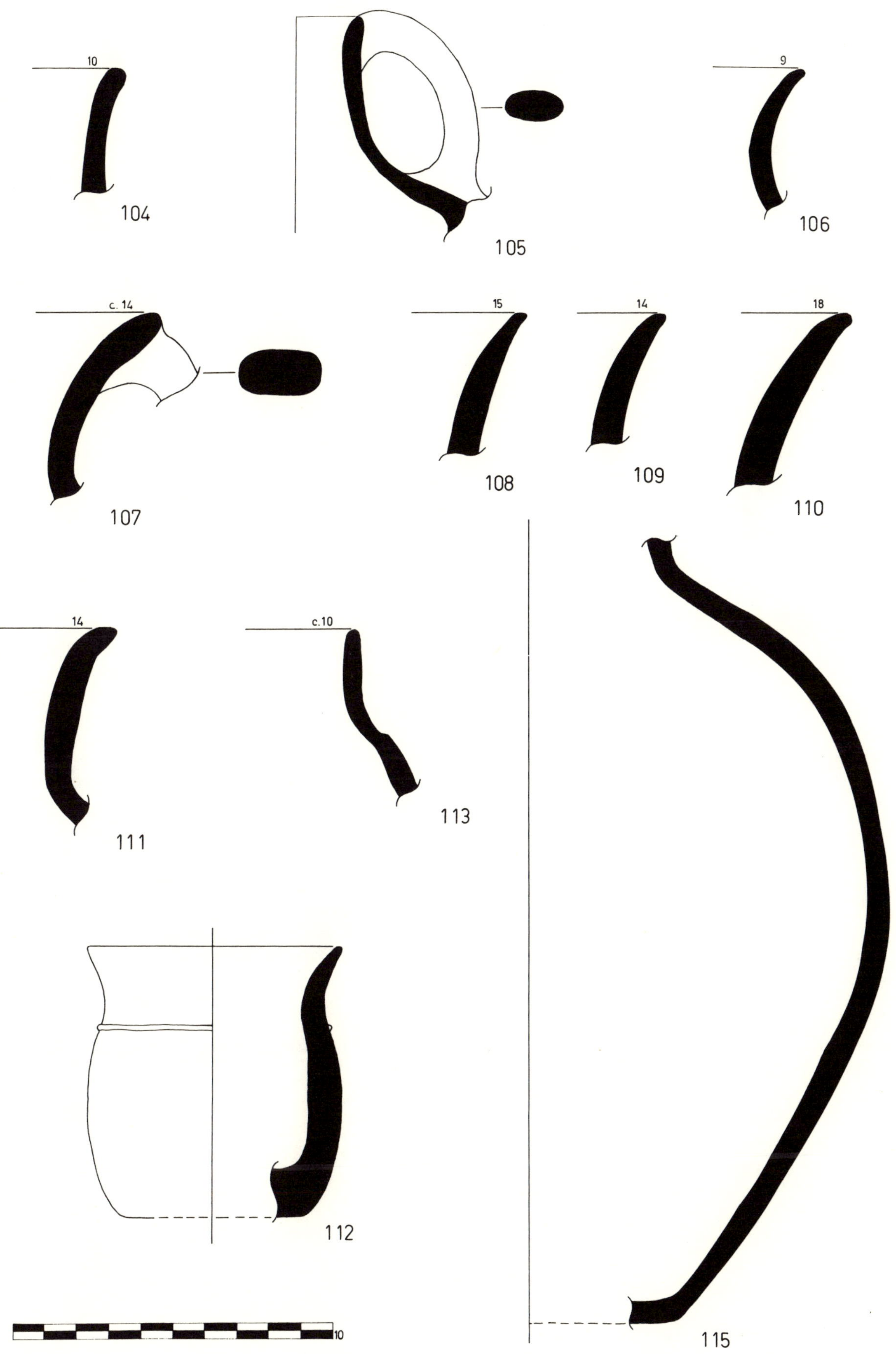

39. Bağbaşı pottery **104–113, 115**

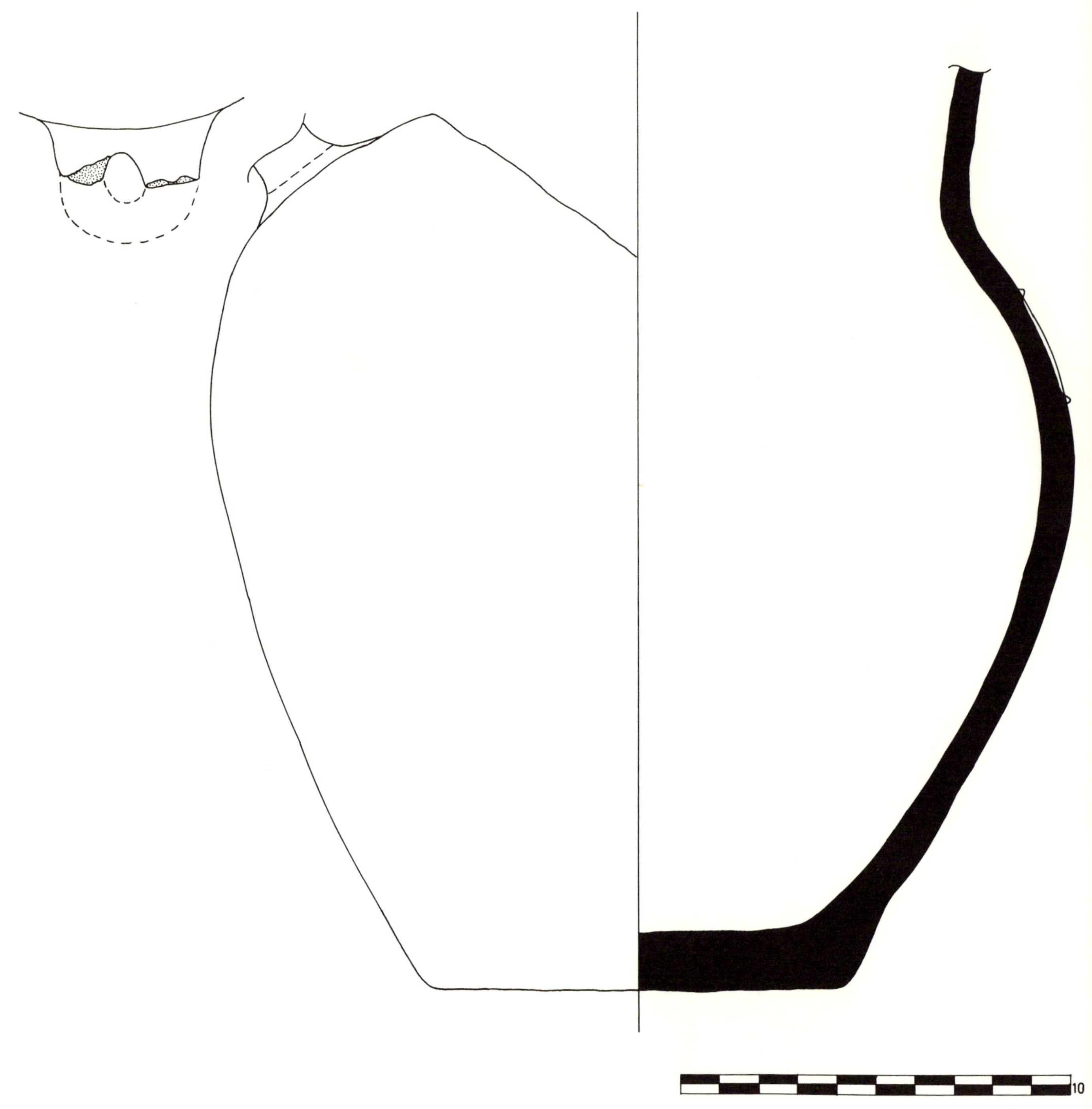

40. Bağbaşı pottery **114**

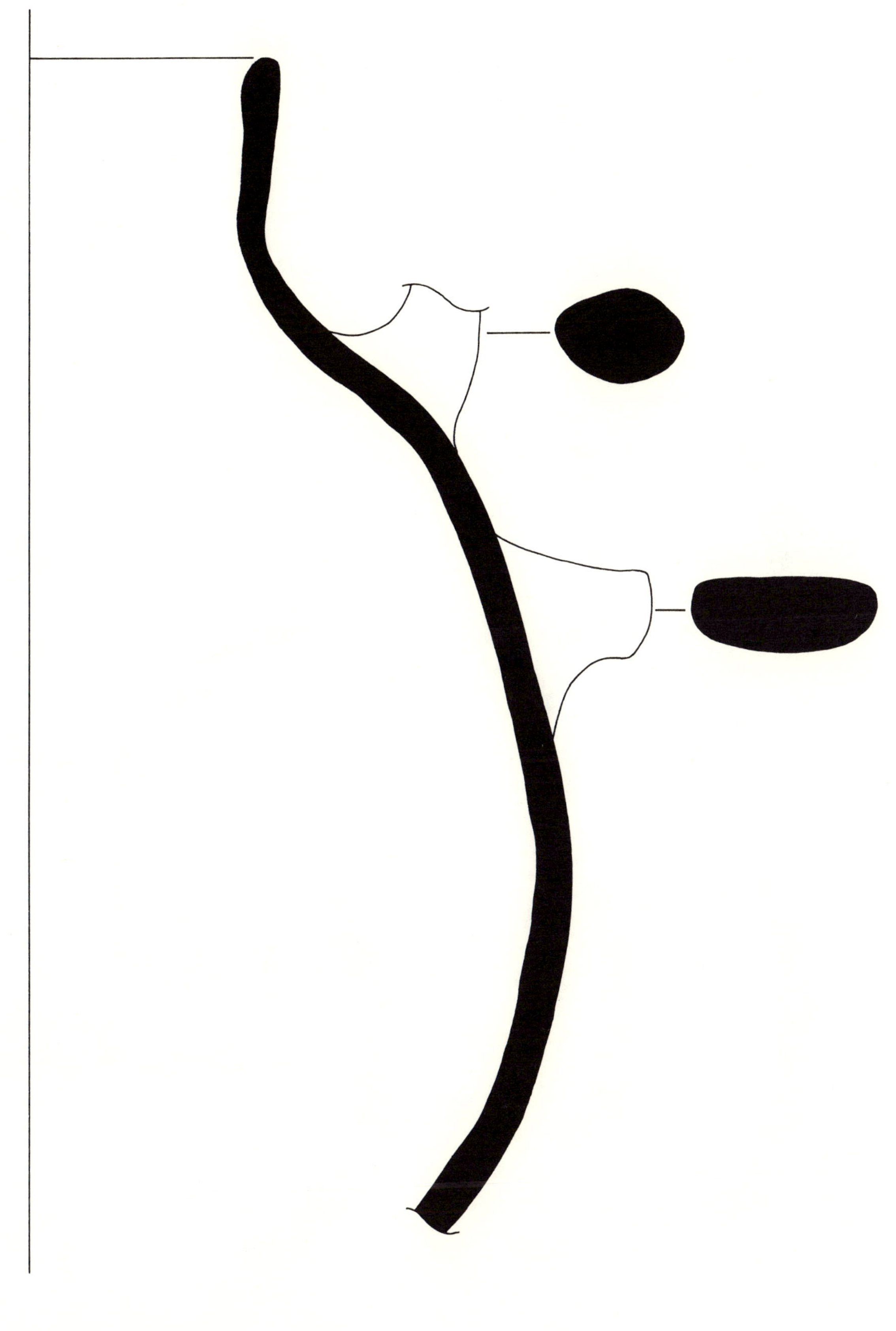

41. Bağbaşı pottery **116**

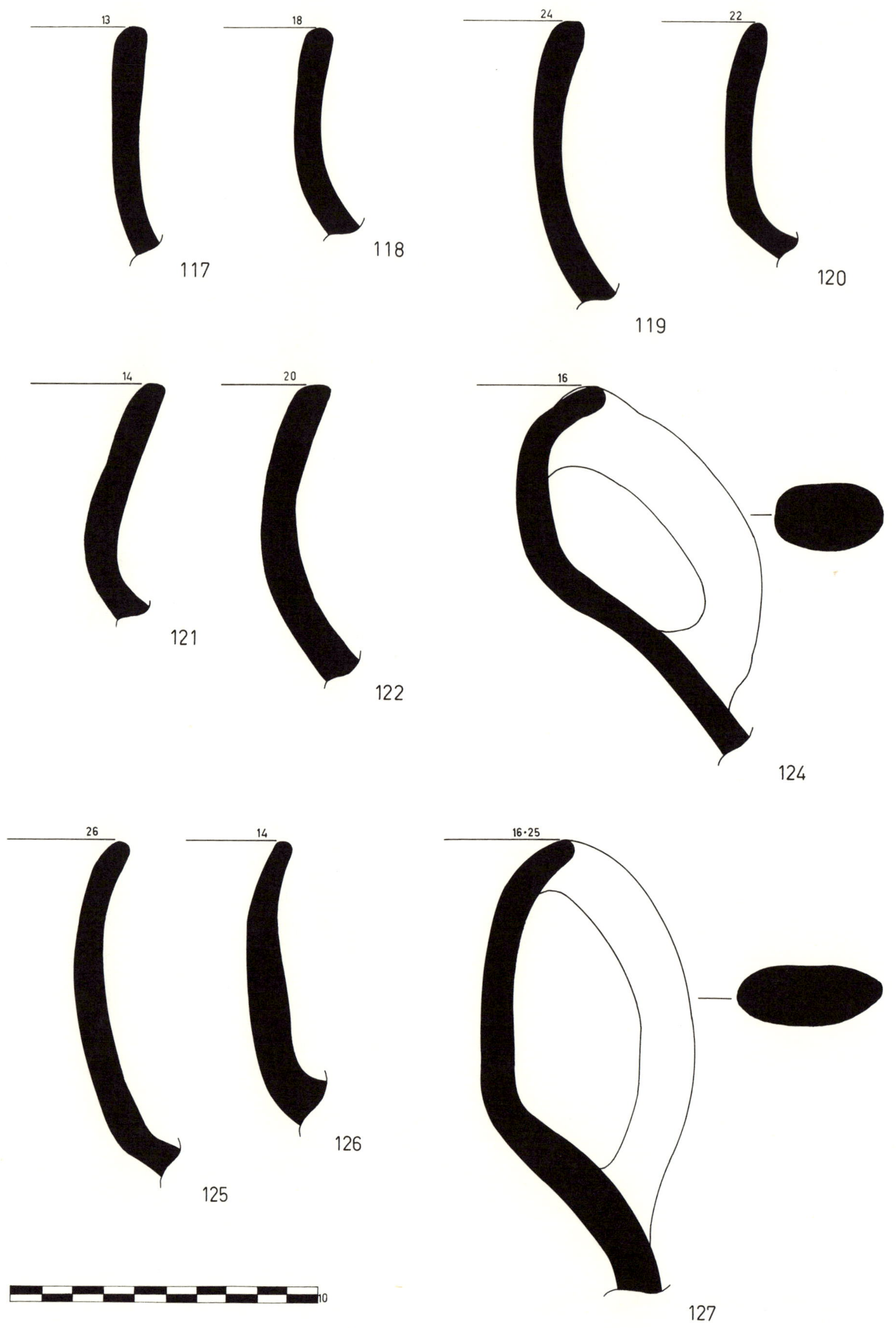

42. Bağbaşı pottery **117–122, 124–127**

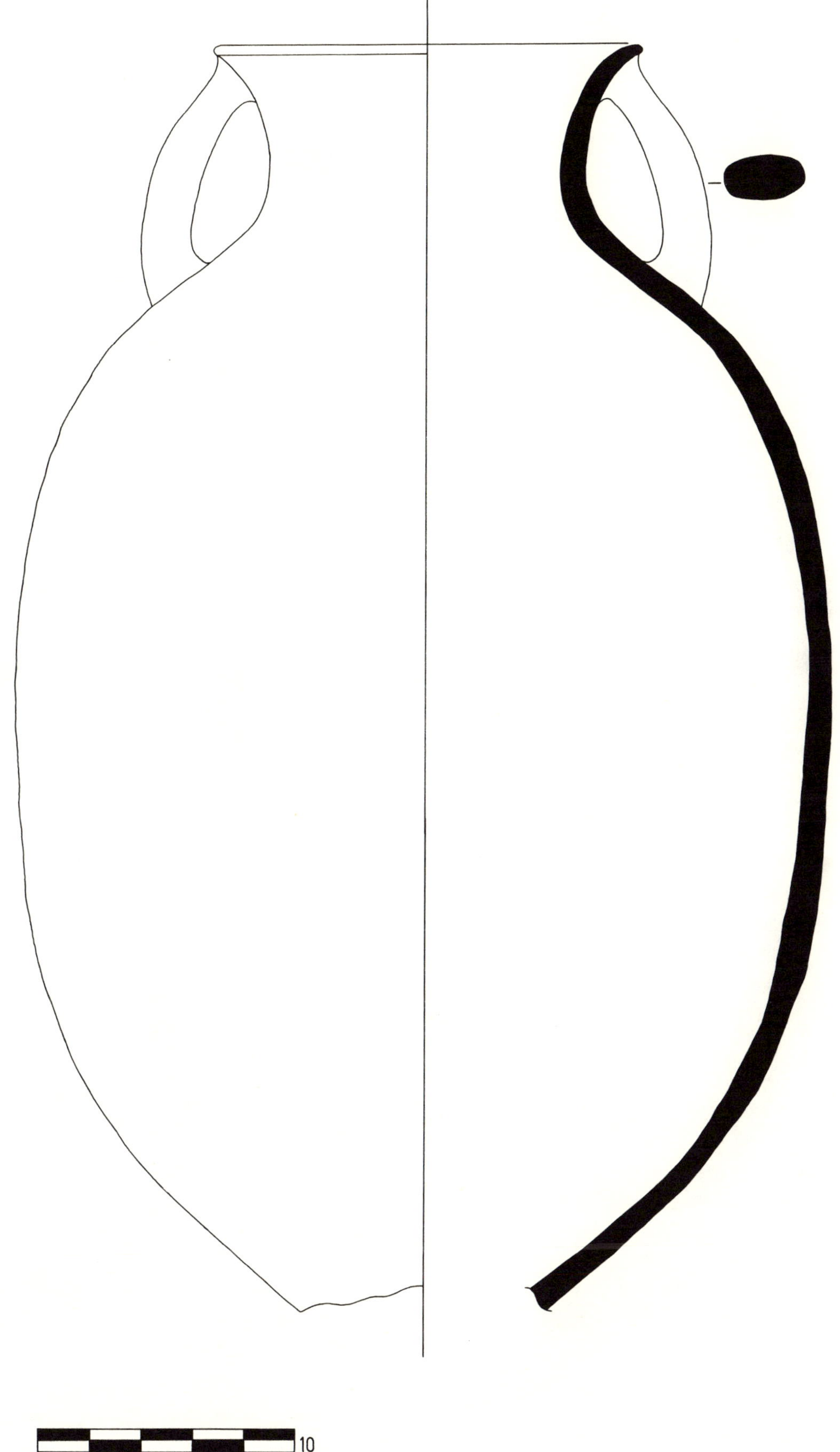

43. Bağbaşı pottery **123**

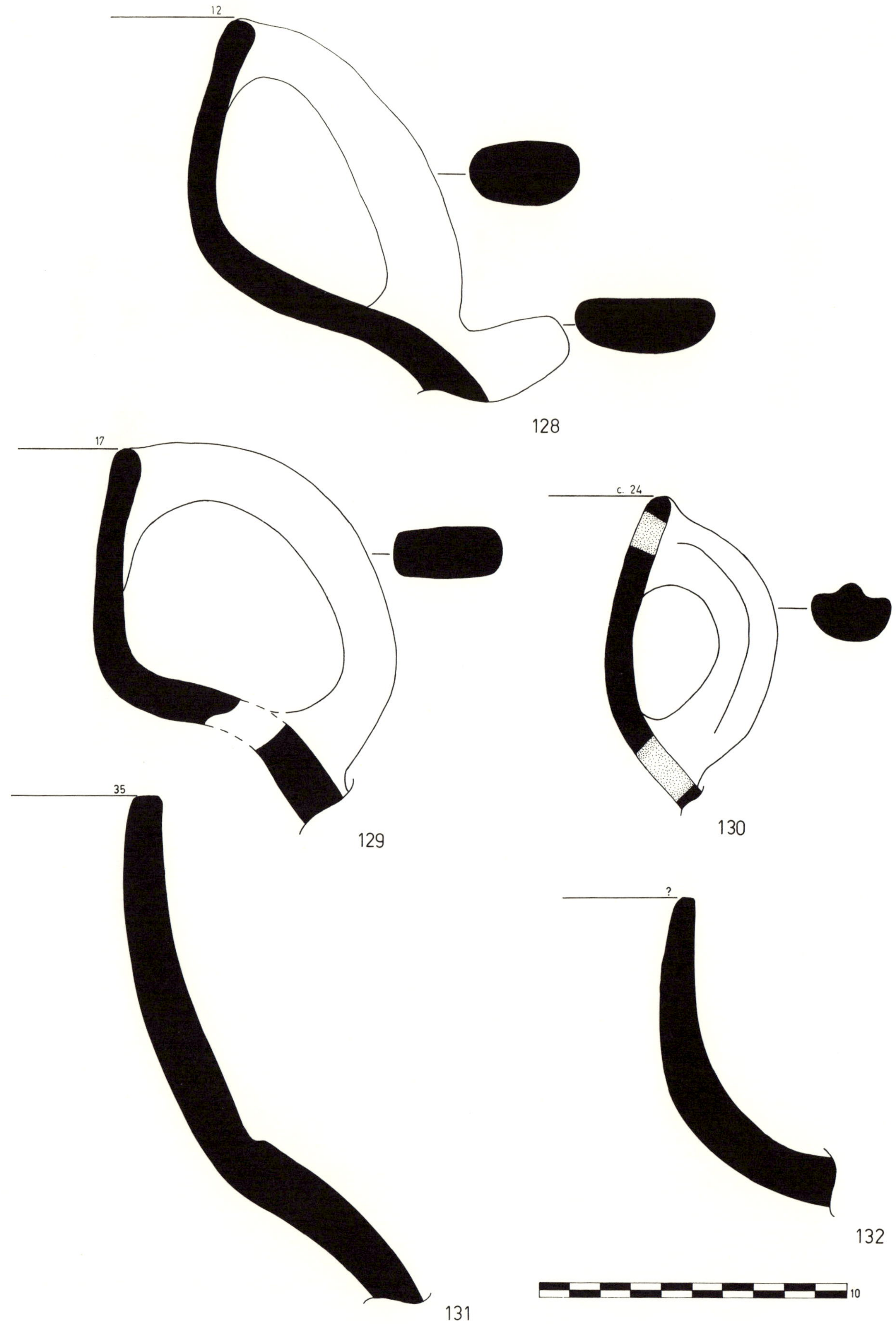

44. Bağbaşı pottery **128–132**

45. Bağbaşı pottery **133–134**

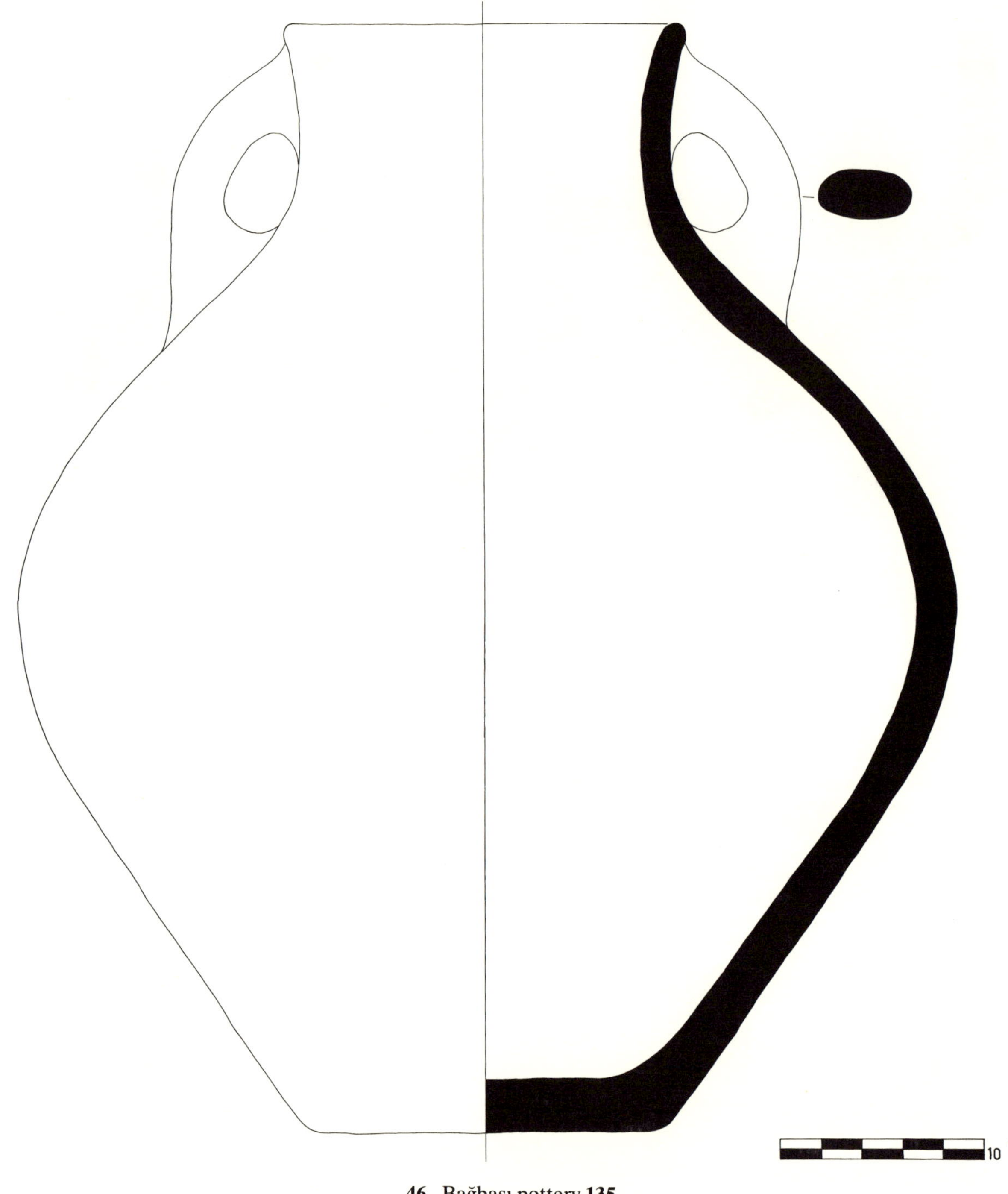

46. Bağbaşı pottery **135**

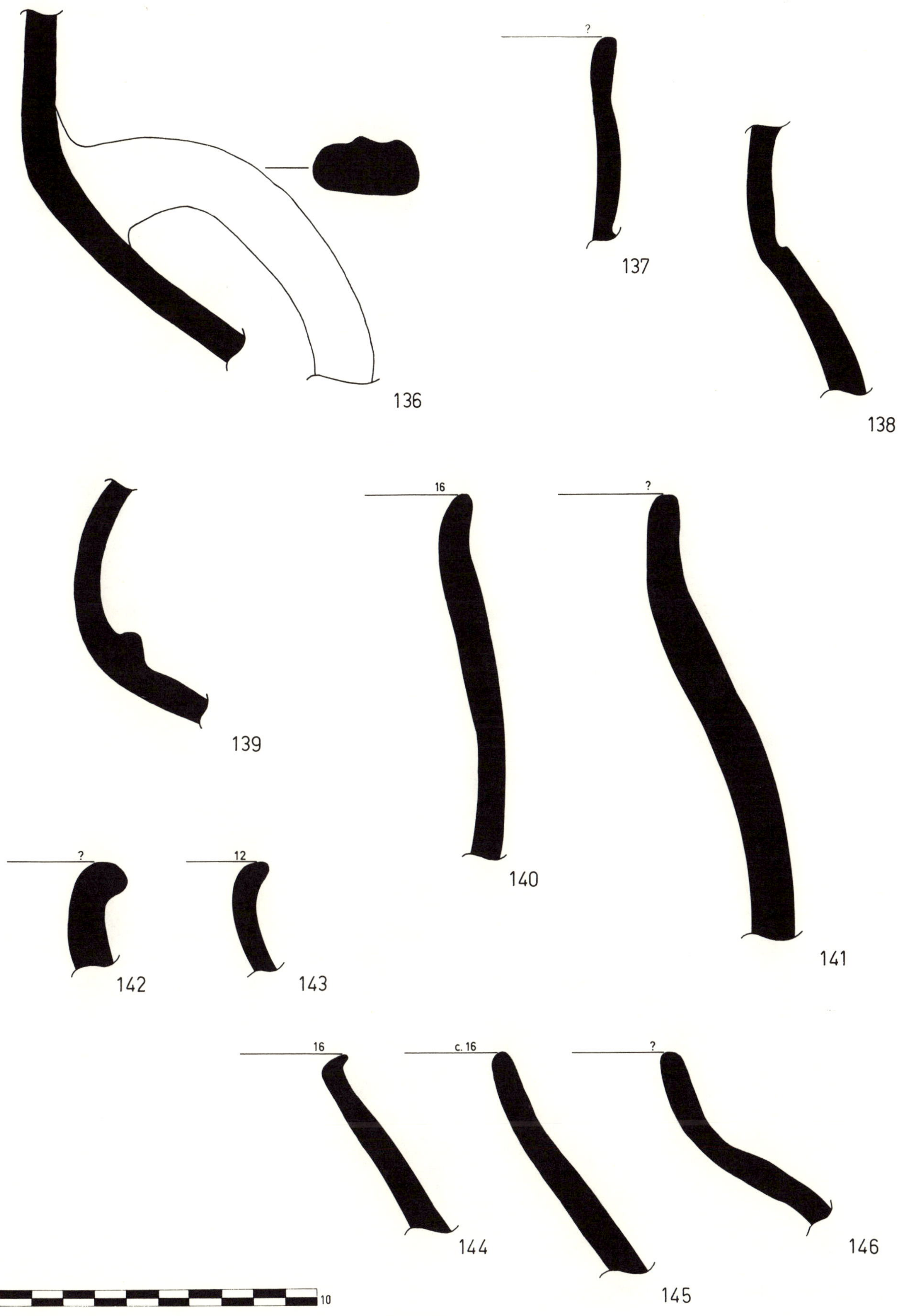

47. Bağbaşı pottery **136–146**

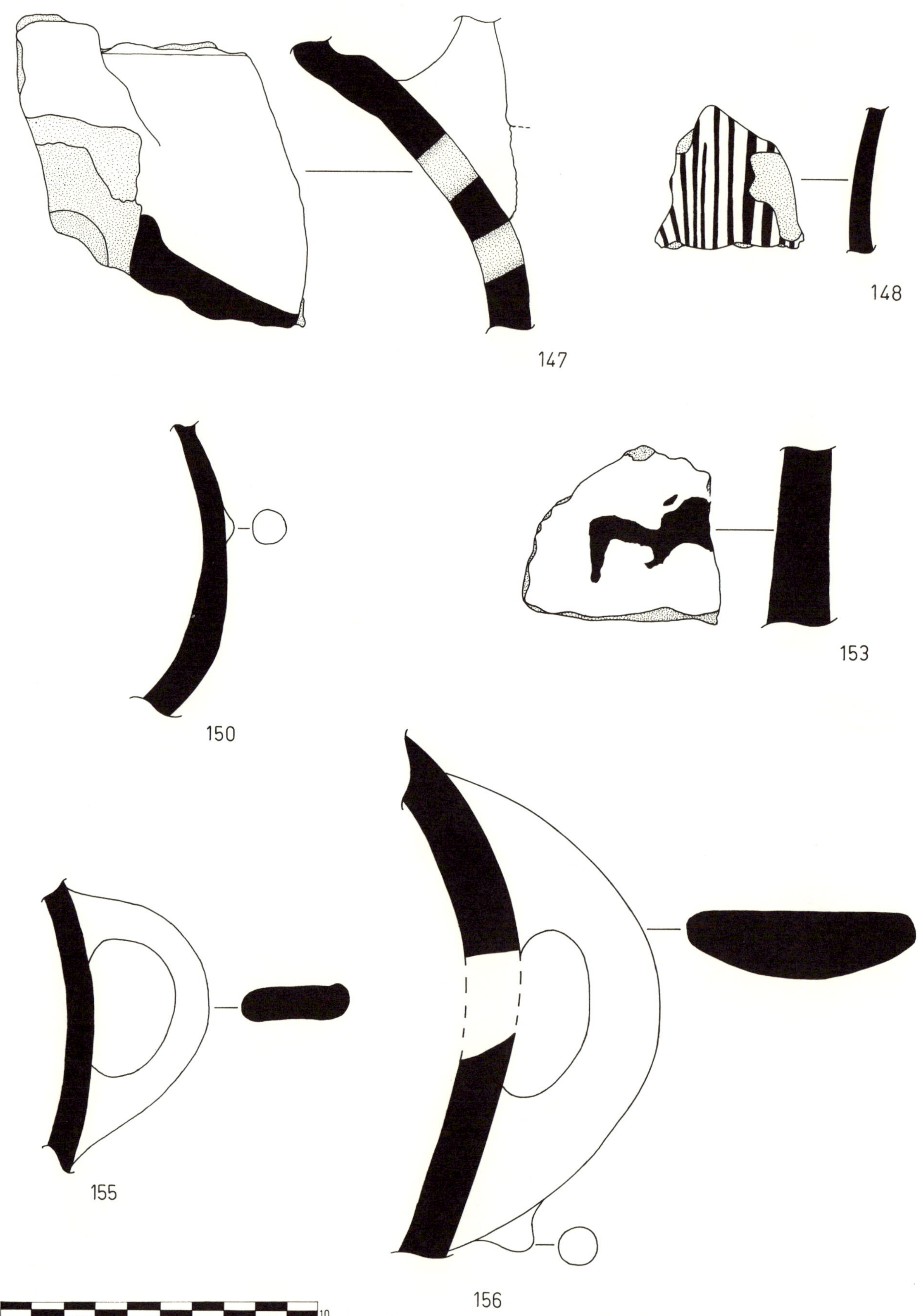

48. Bağbaşı pottery **147–148, 150, 153, 155–156**

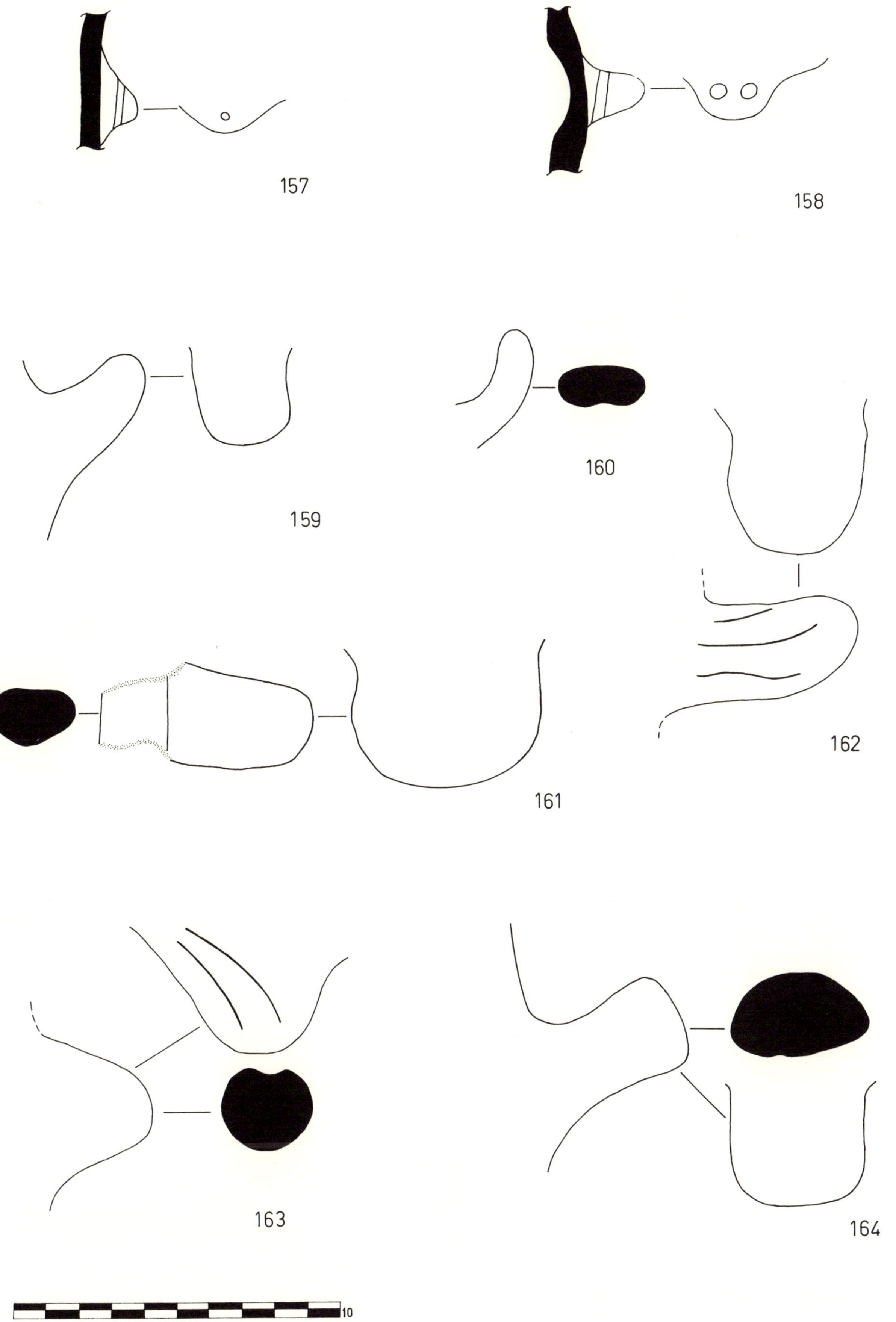

49. Bağbaşı pottery **157–164**

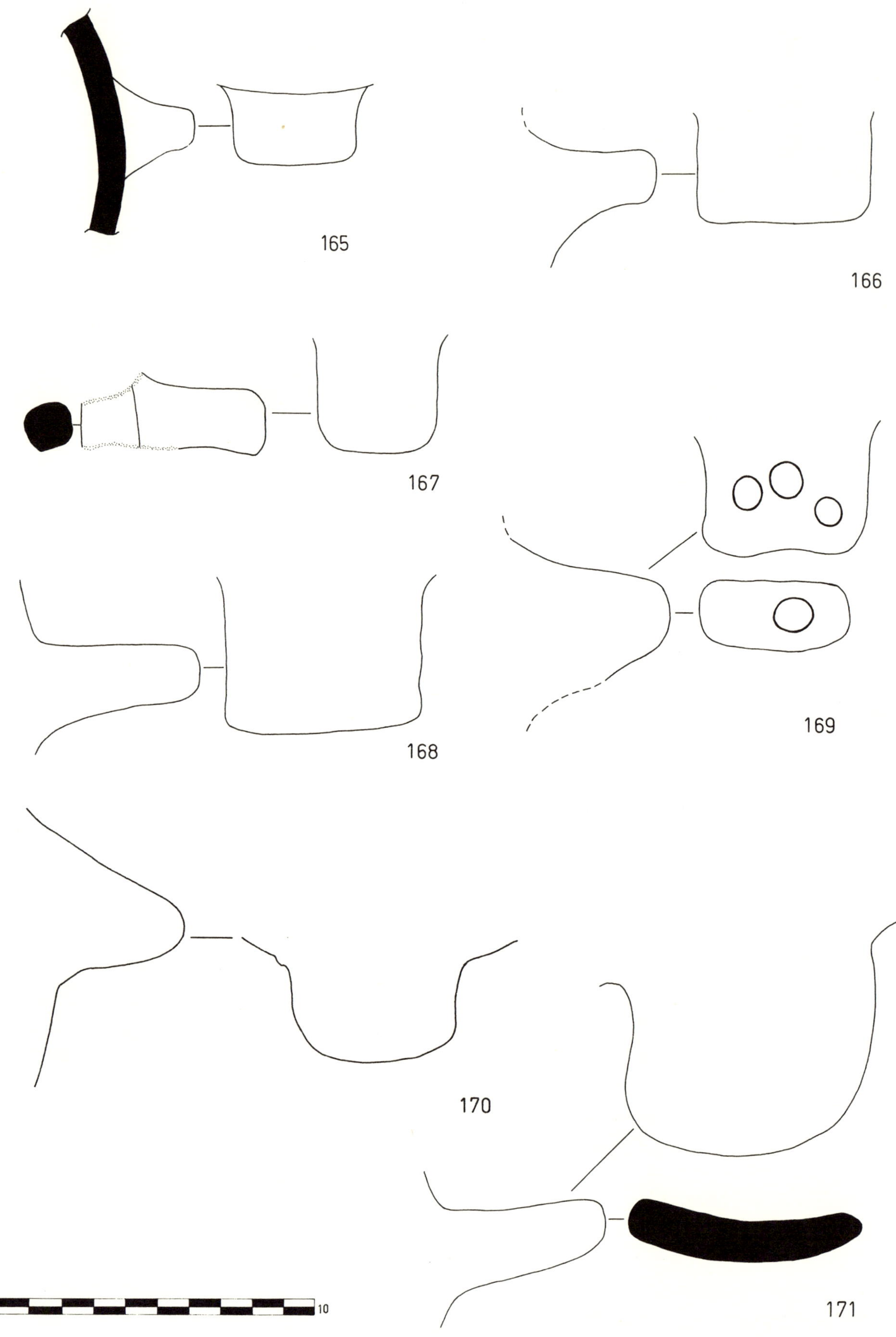

50. Bağbaşı pottery **165–171**

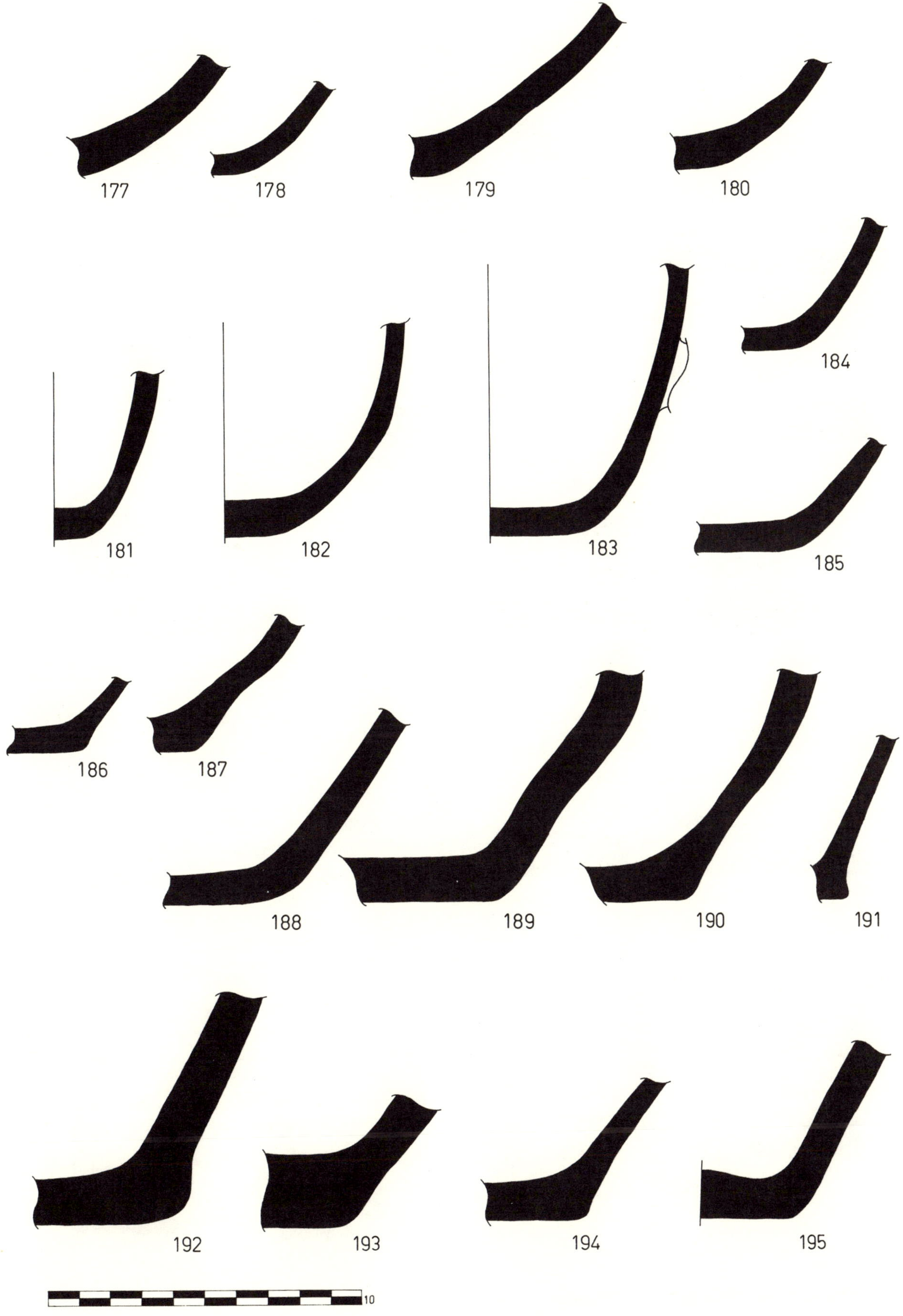

51. Bağbaşı pottery **177–195**

52. Bağbaşı pottery **196–211**

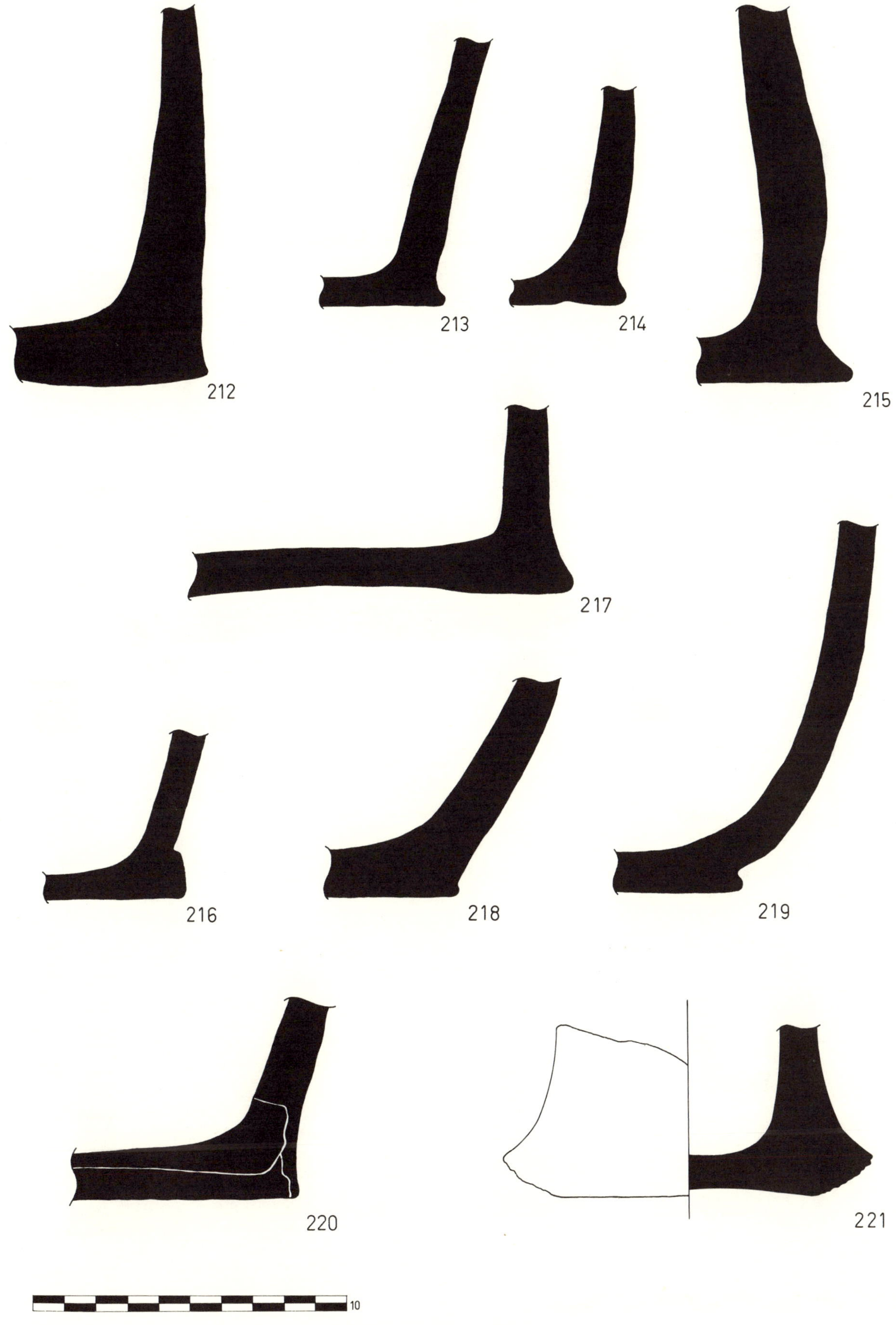

53. Bağbaşı pottery **212–221**

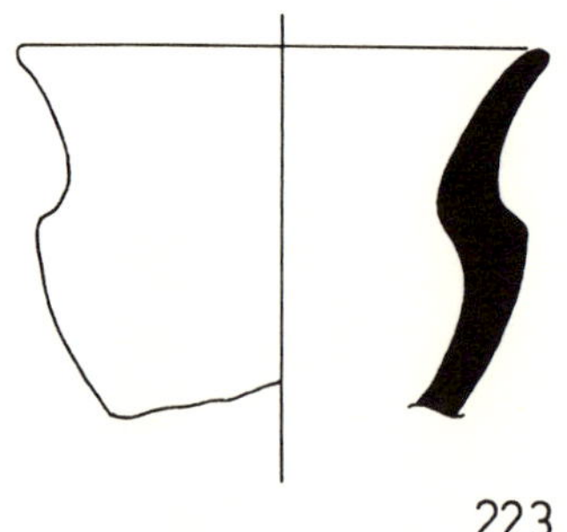

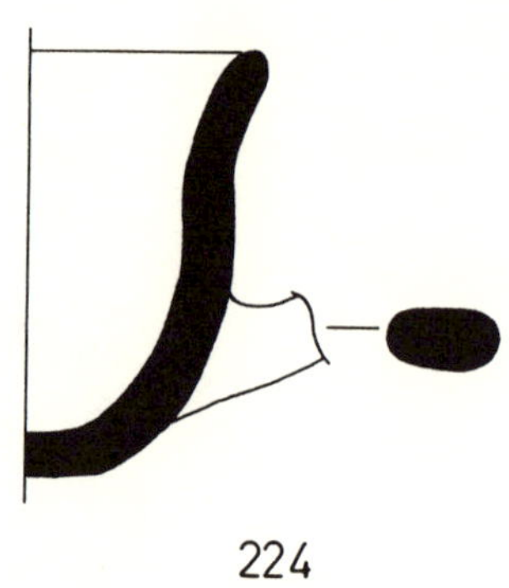

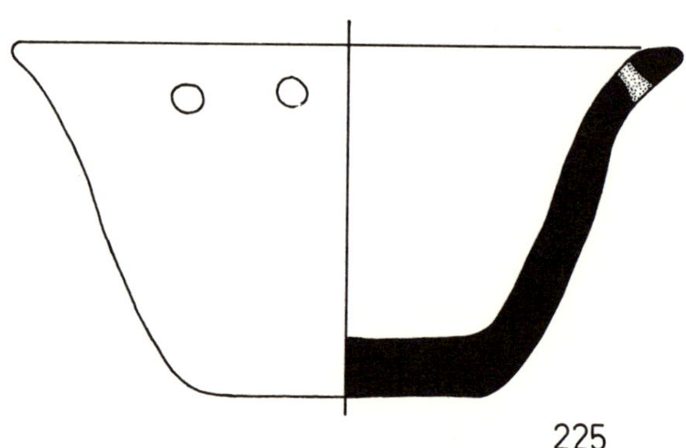

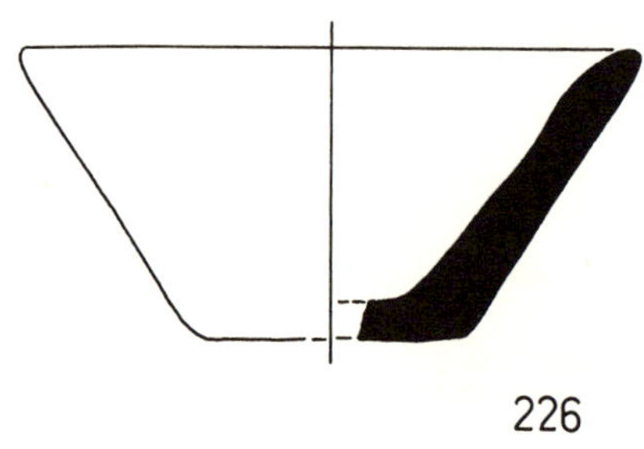

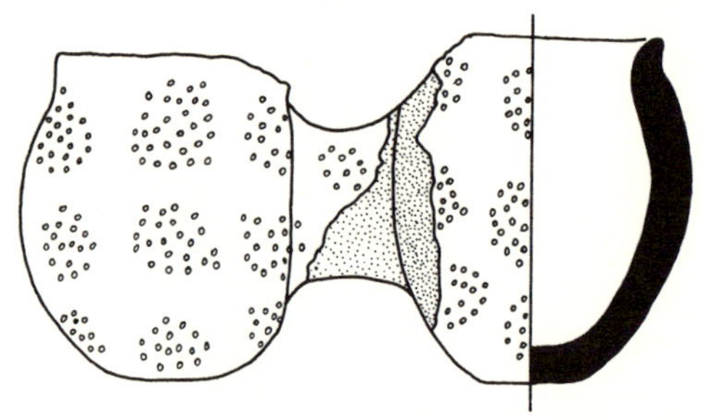

54. Bağbaşı pottery **222–228**

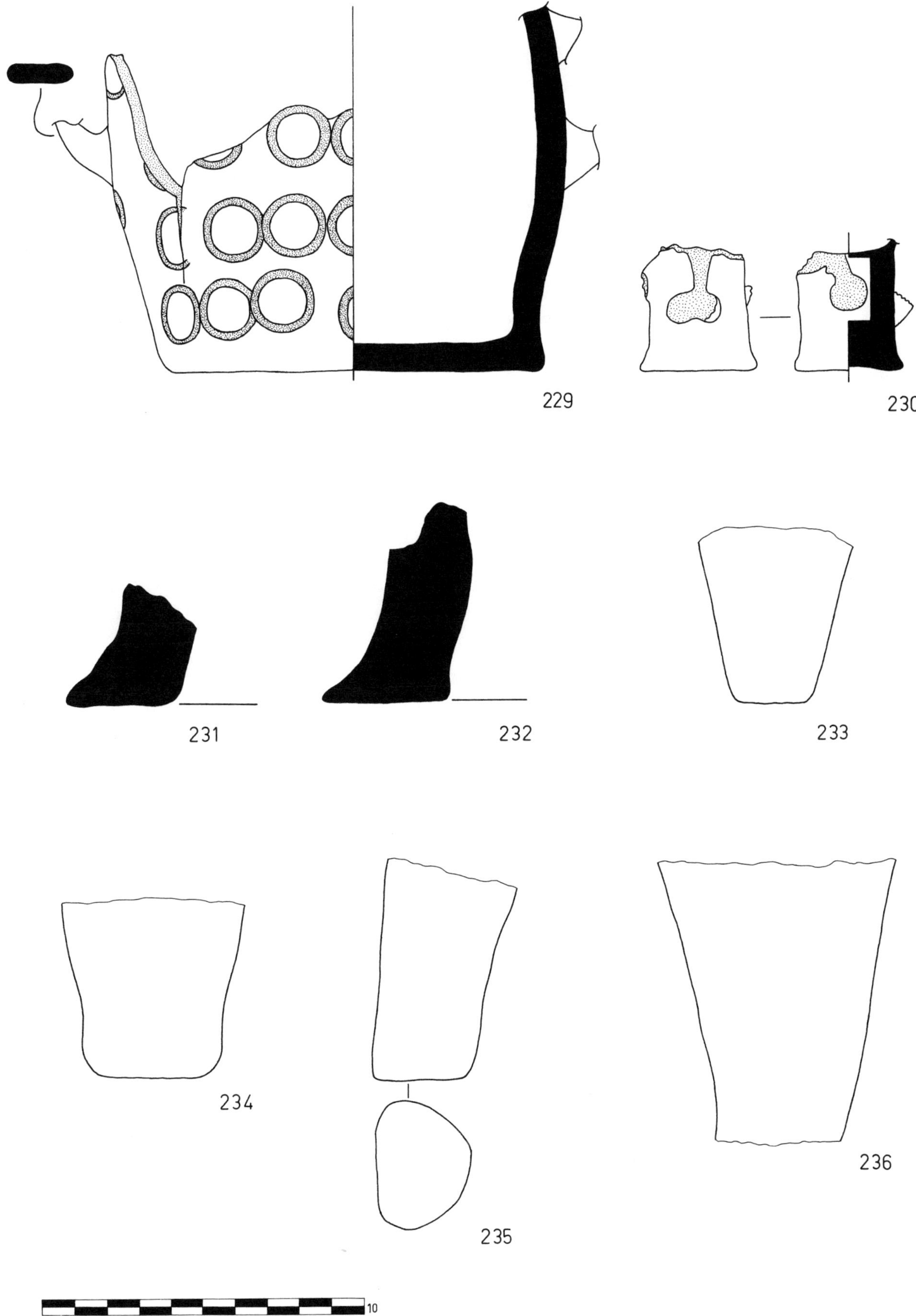

55. Bağbaşı pottery **229–236**

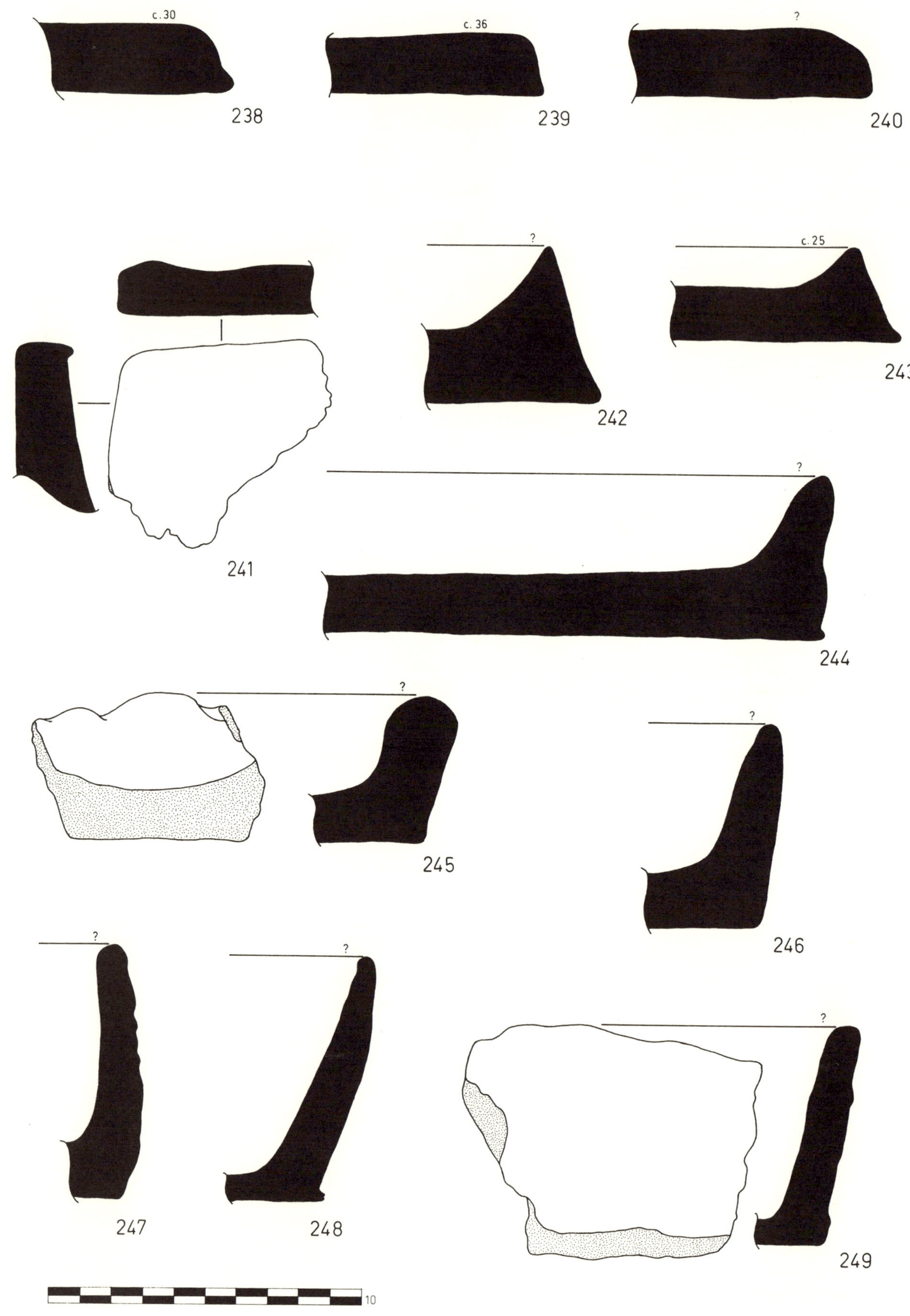

56. Bağbaşı pottery **238–249**

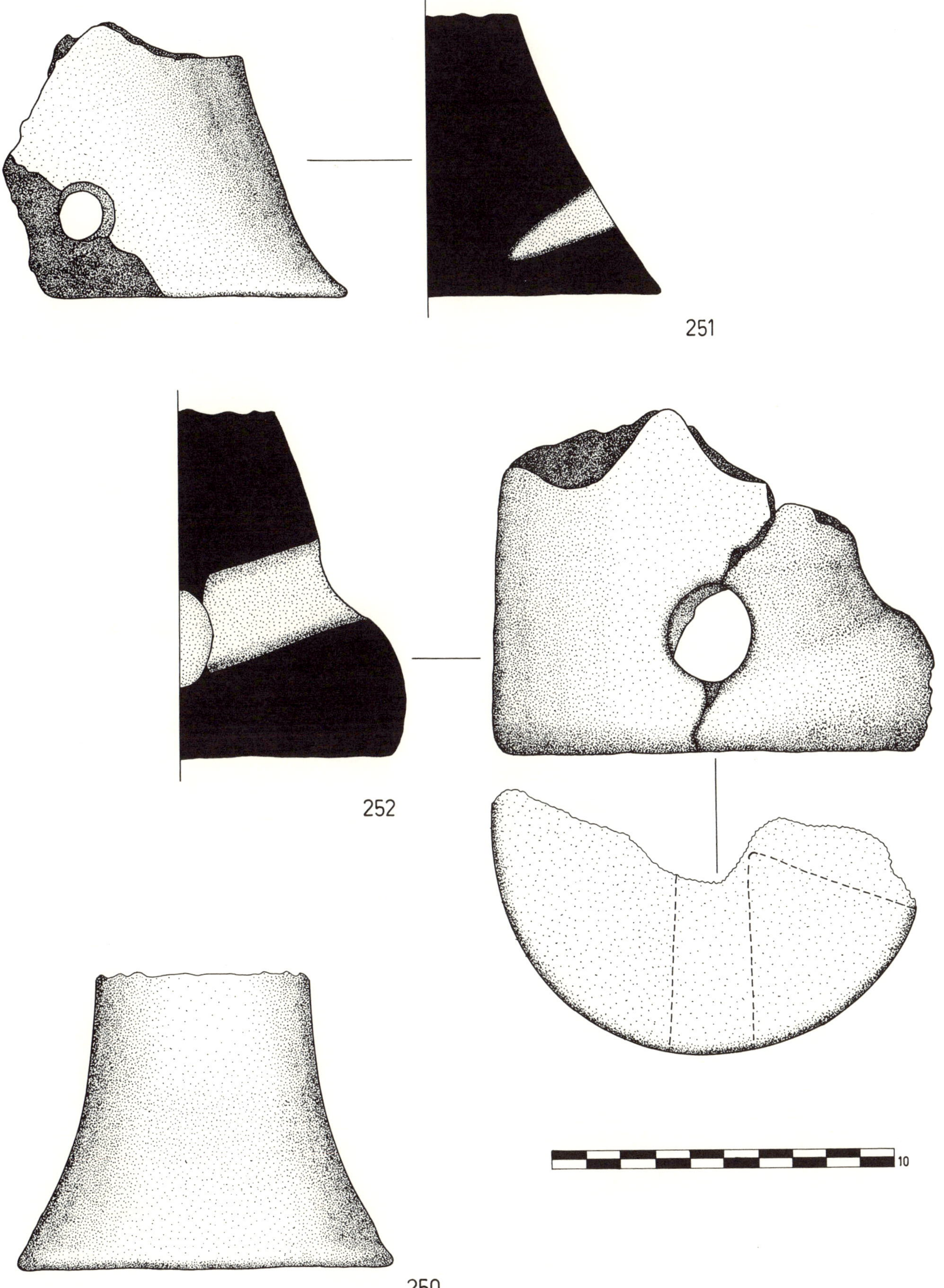

57. Bağbaşı artifacts **250–252**

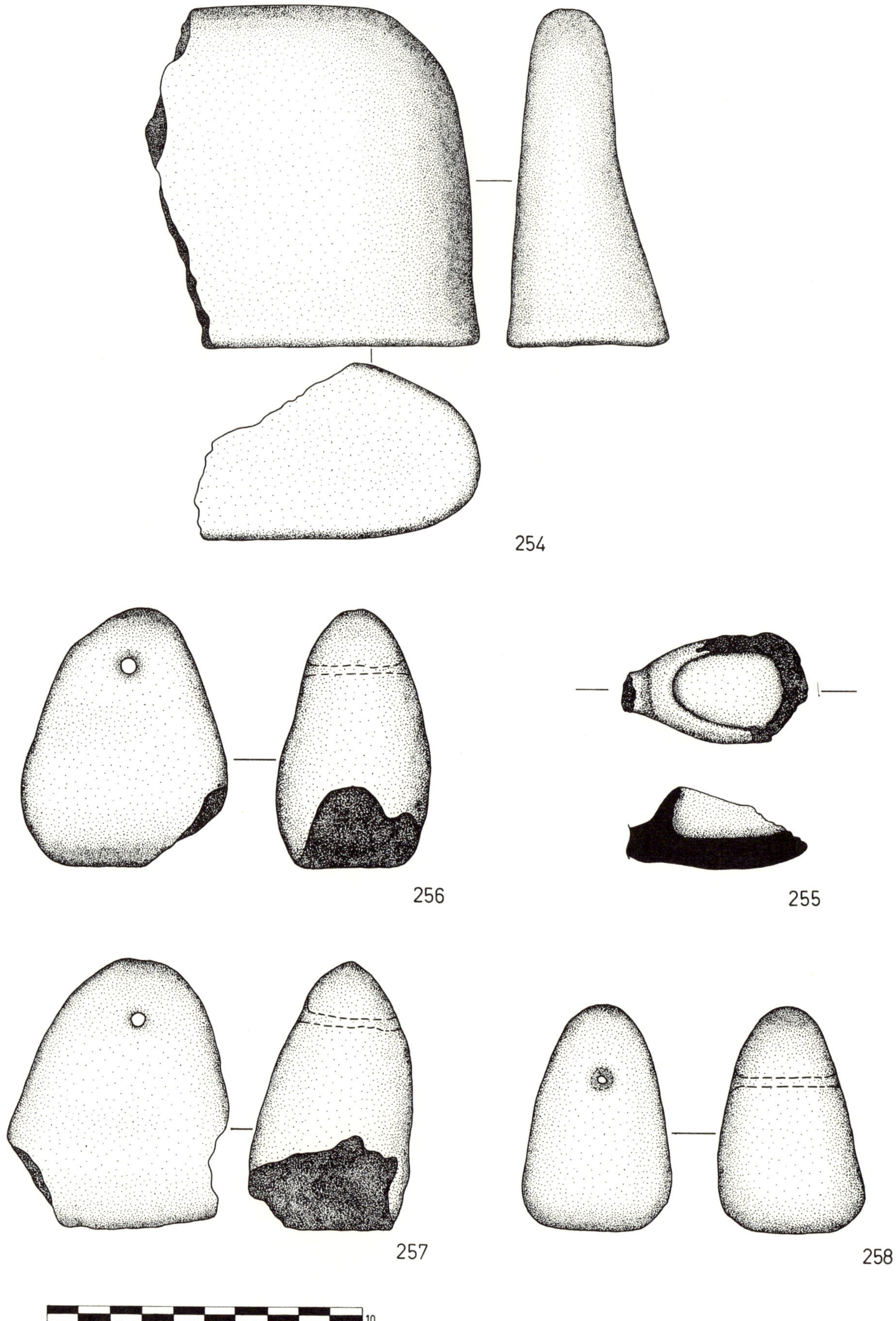

58. Bağbaşı artifacts **254–258**

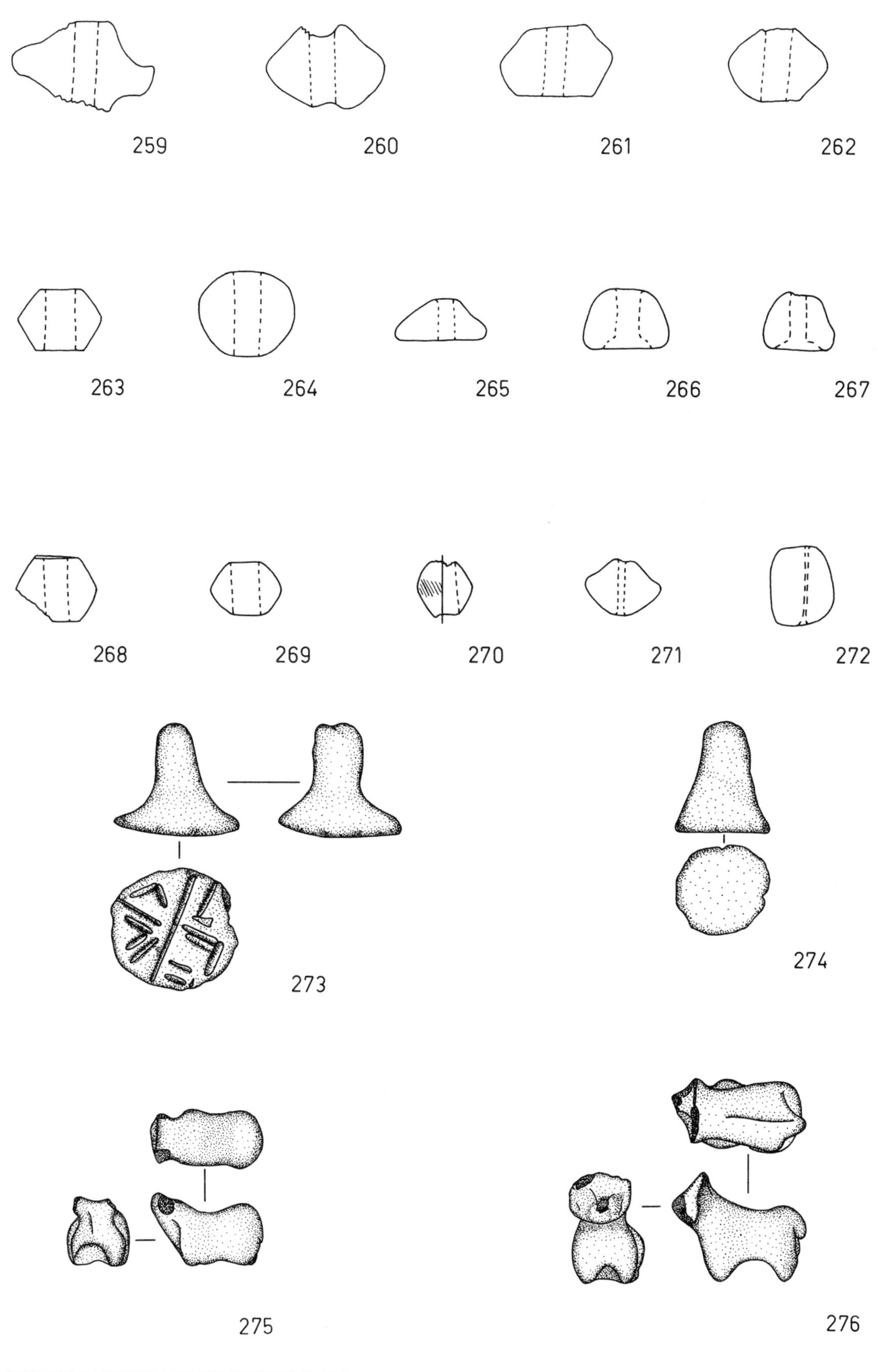

59. Bağbaşı artifacts **259–276**

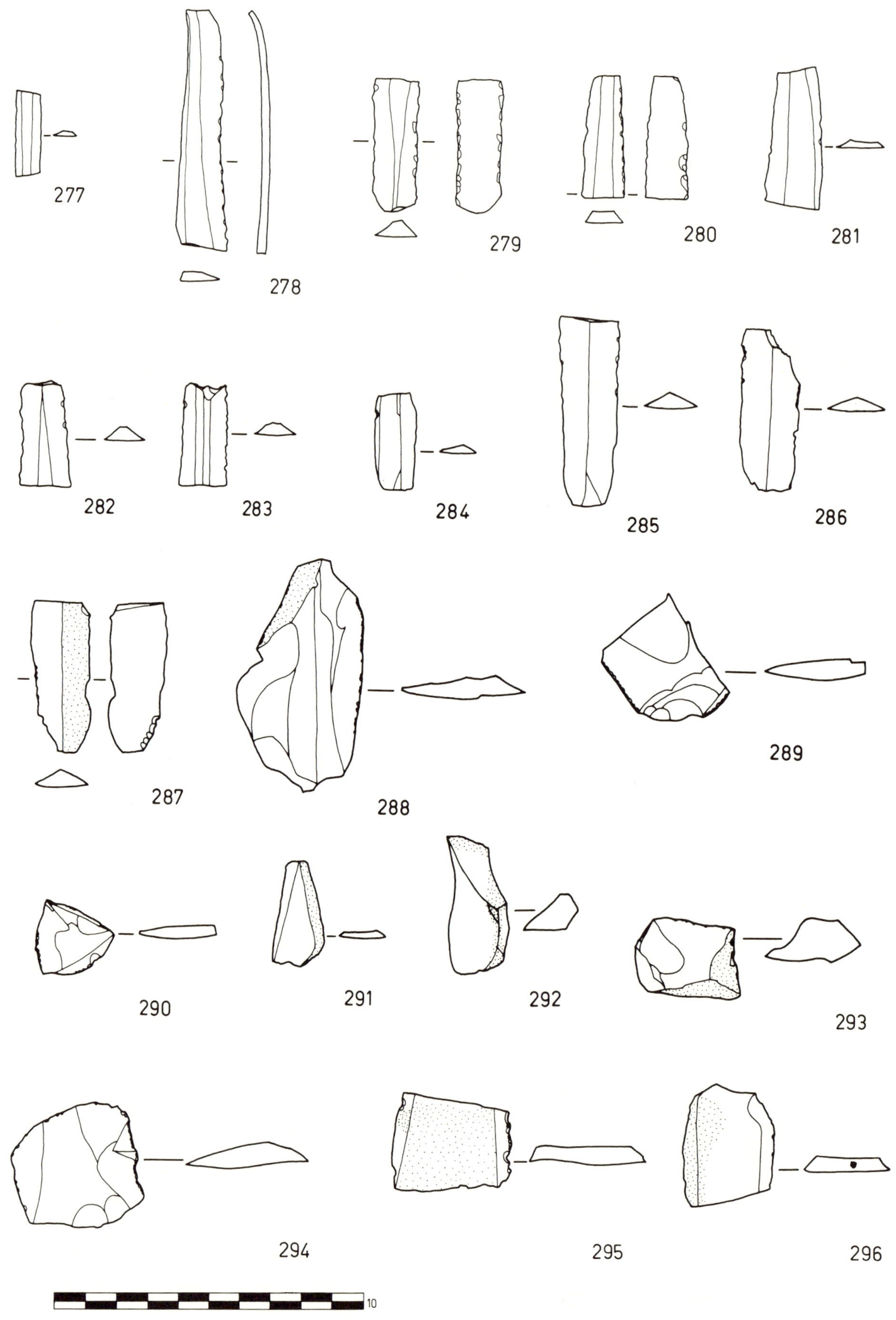

60. Bağbaşı artifacts **277–296**

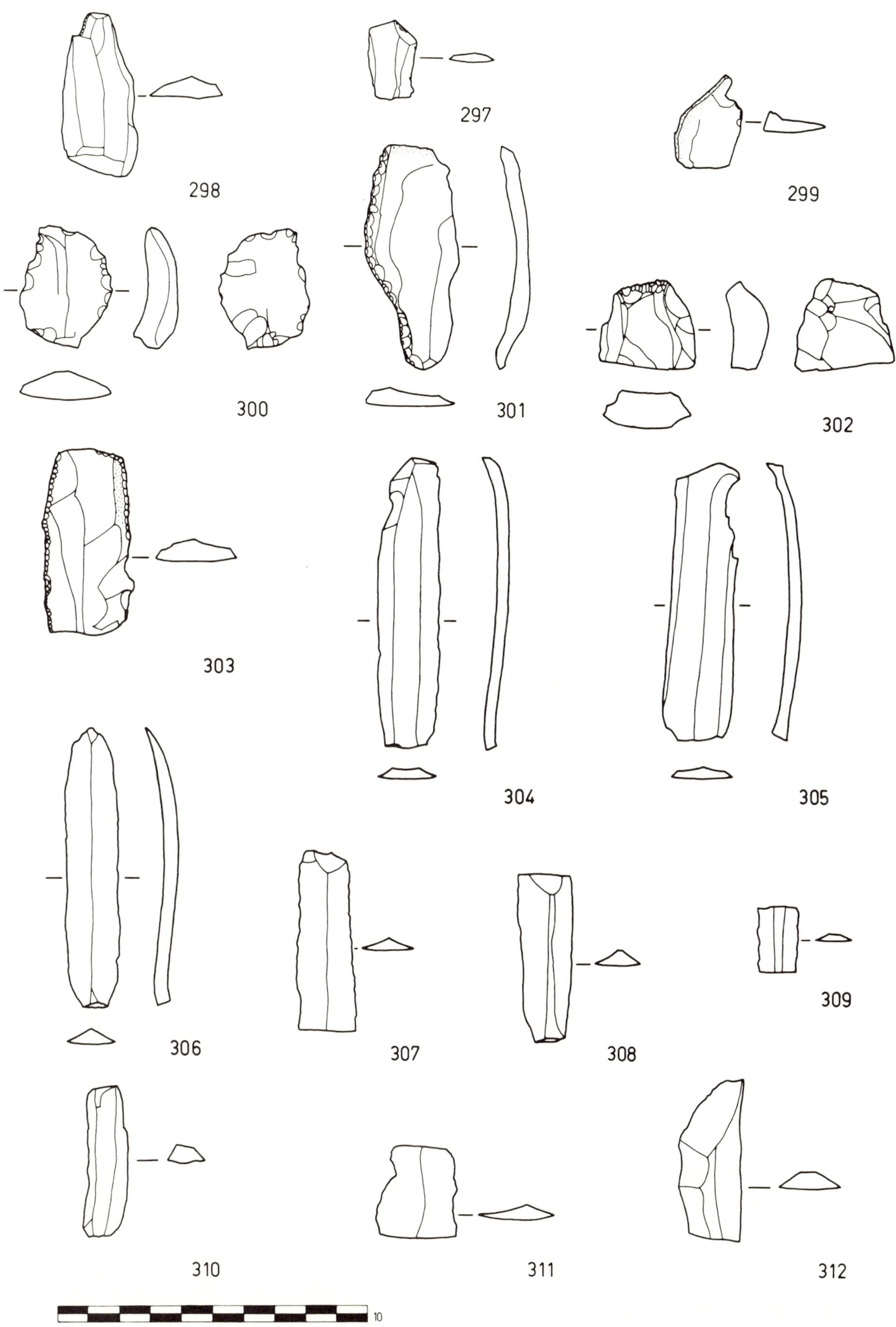

61. Bağbaşı artifacts **297–312**

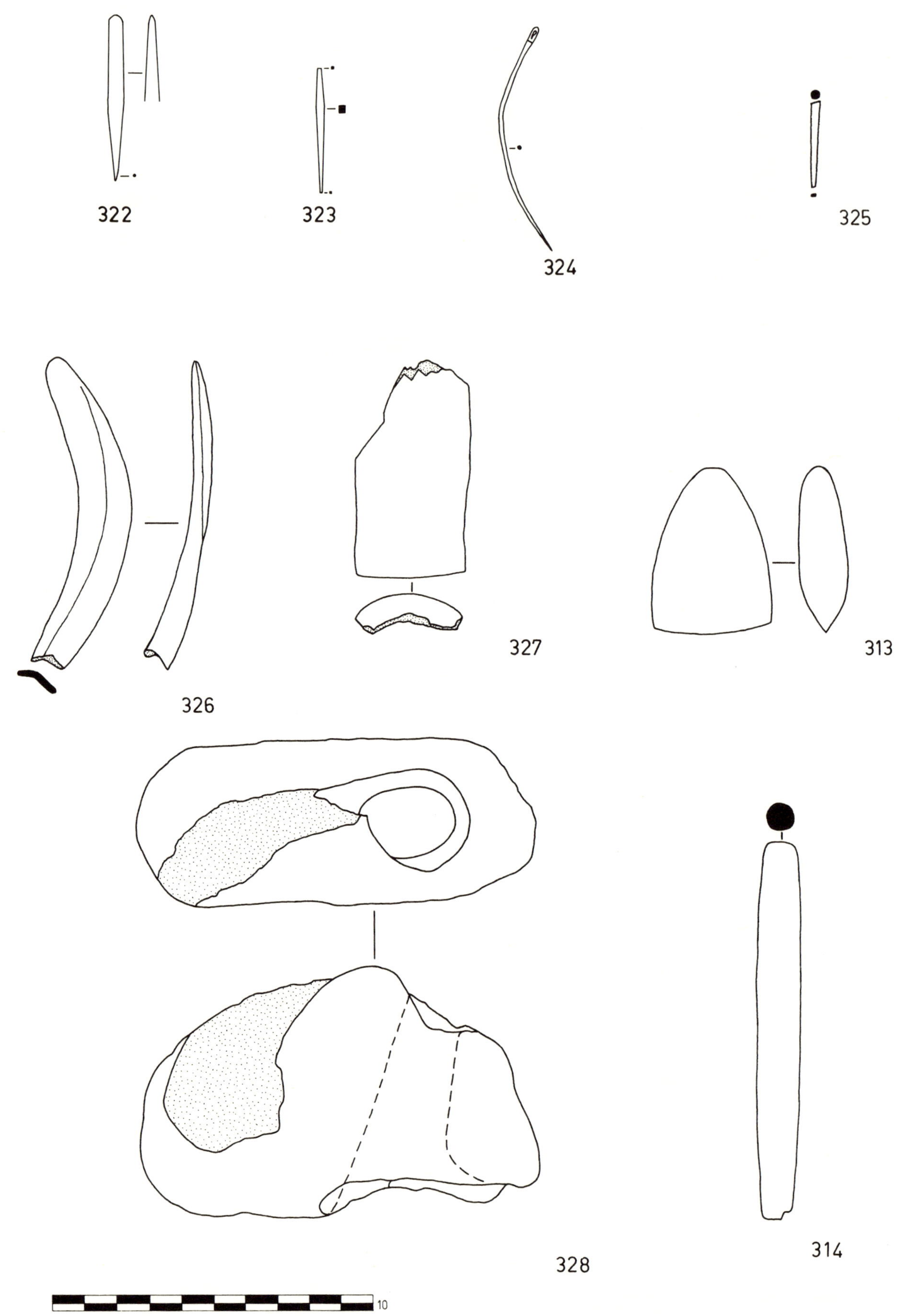

62. Bağbaşı artifacts **313–314, 322–328**

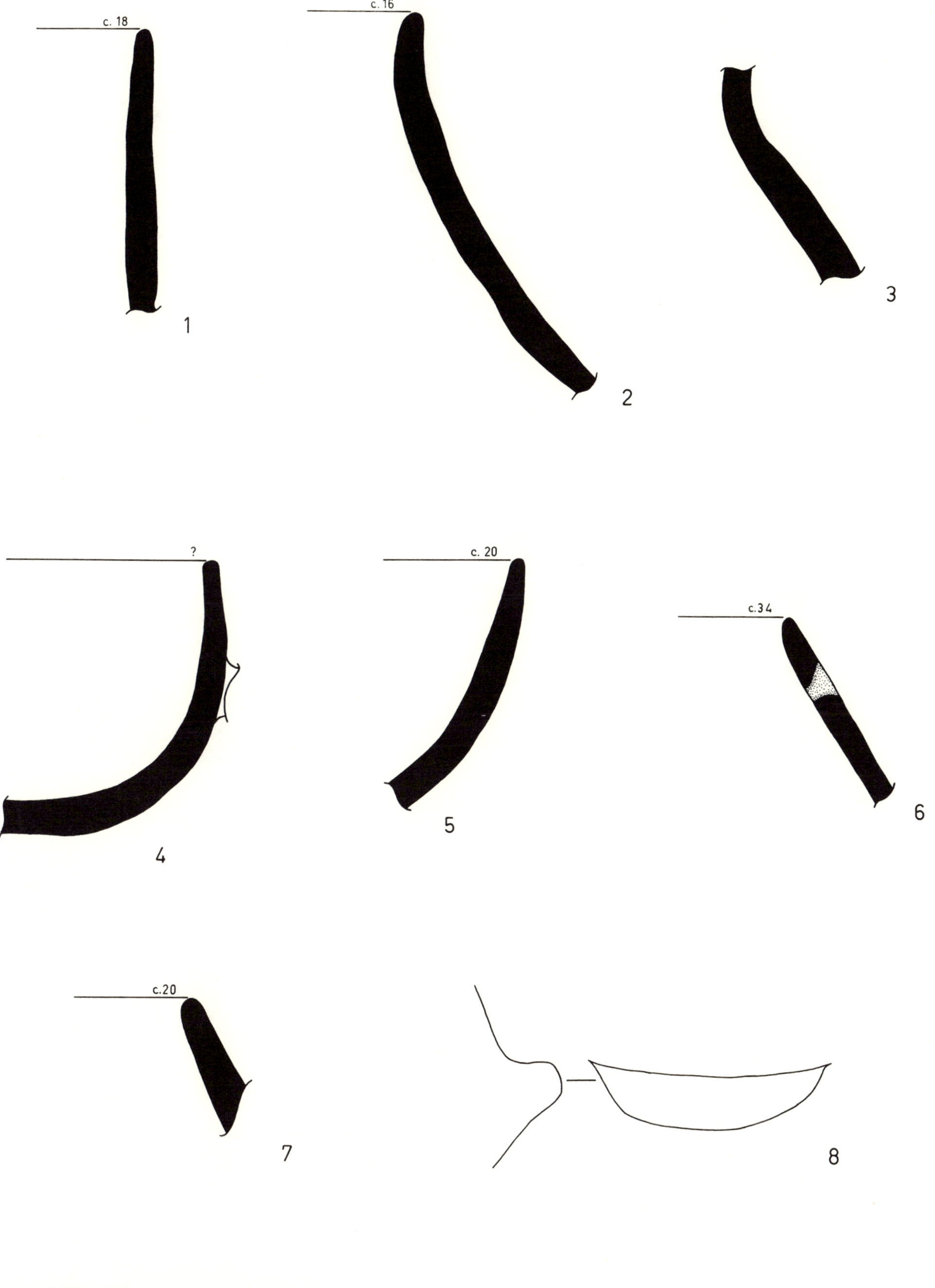

63. Lower Bağbaşı pottery **1–8**

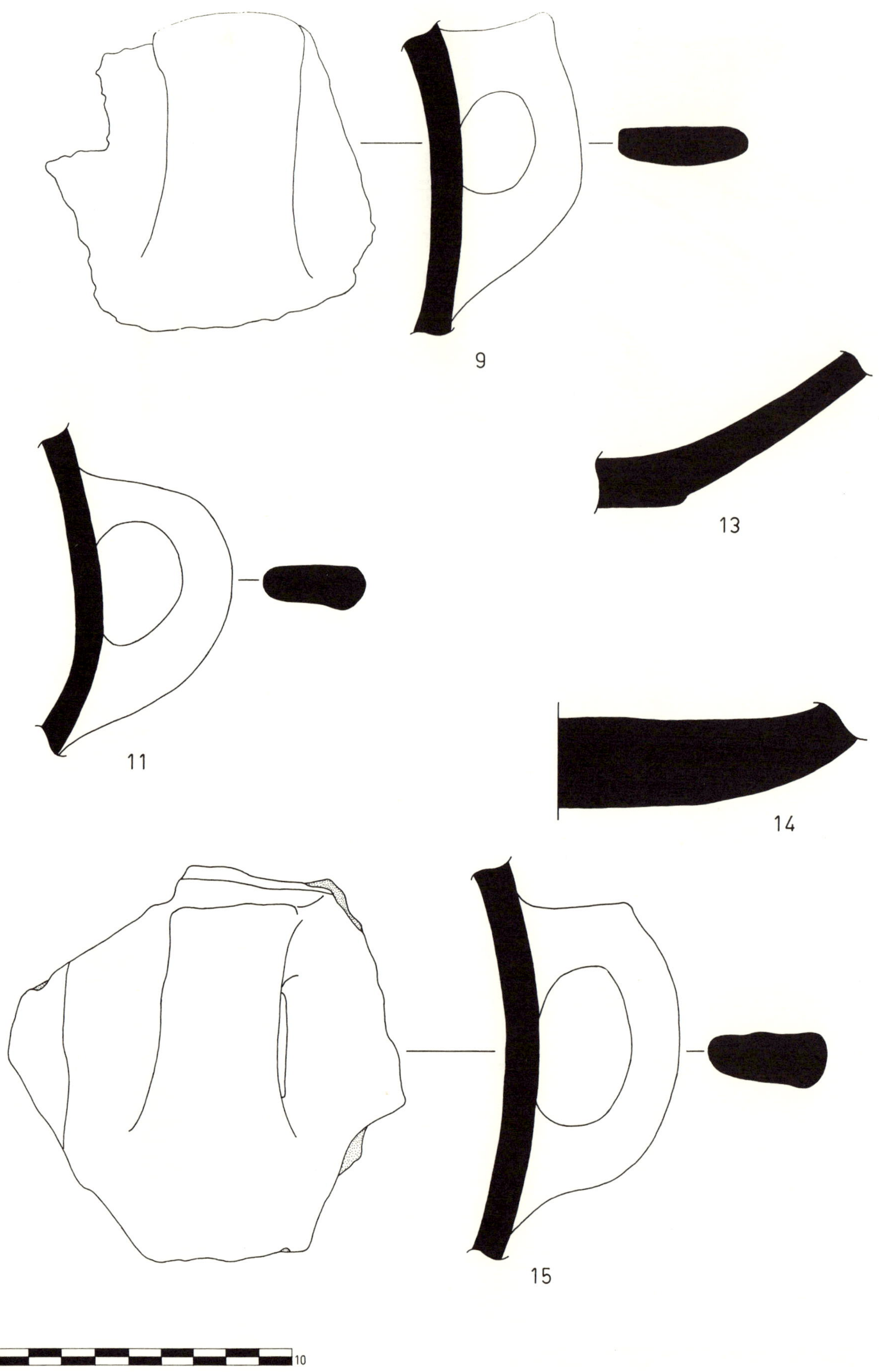

64. Lower Bağbaşı pottery **9, 11, 13–15**

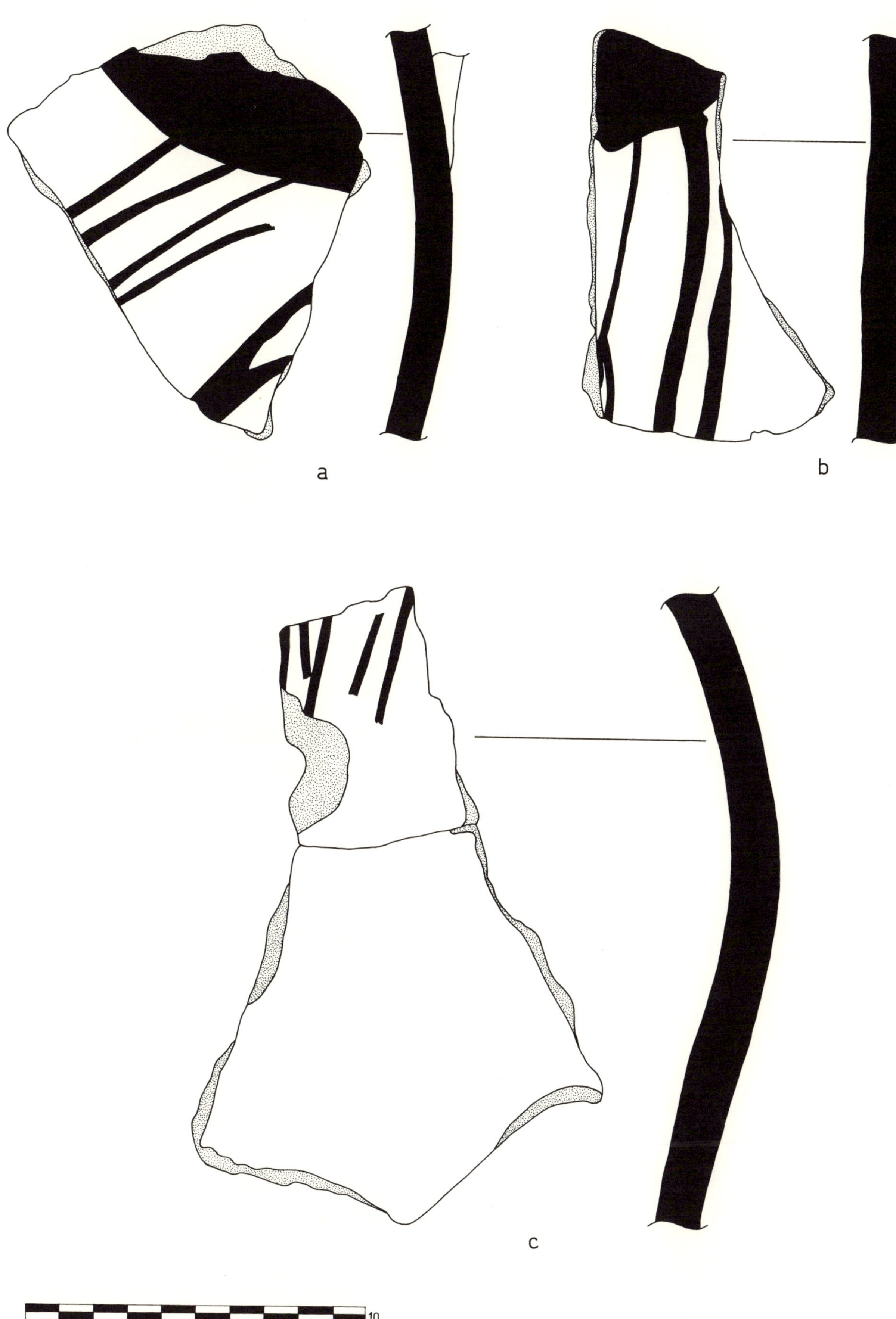

65. Lower Bağbaşı pottery **16**

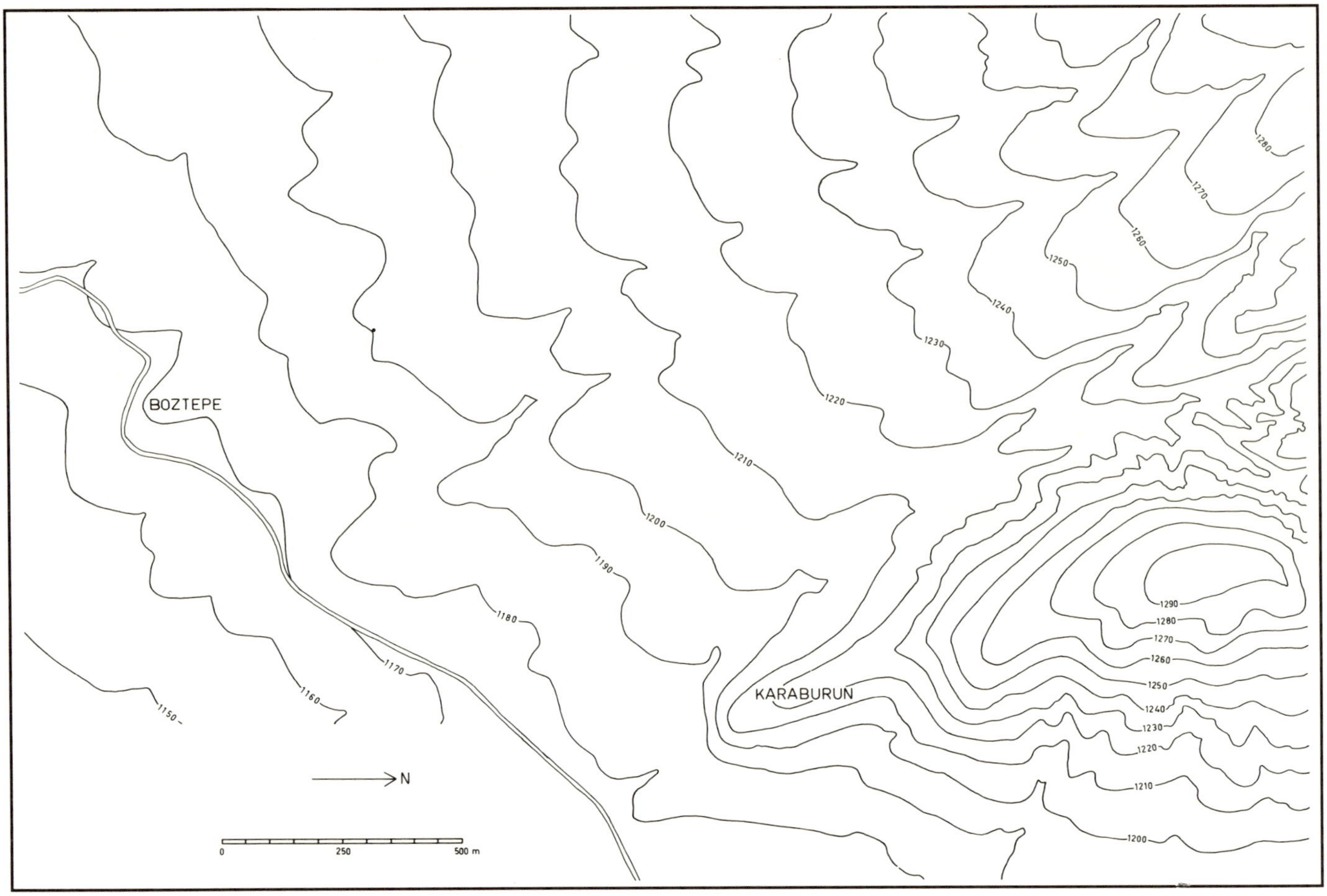

66a. Karaburun and Boztepe: contour plan

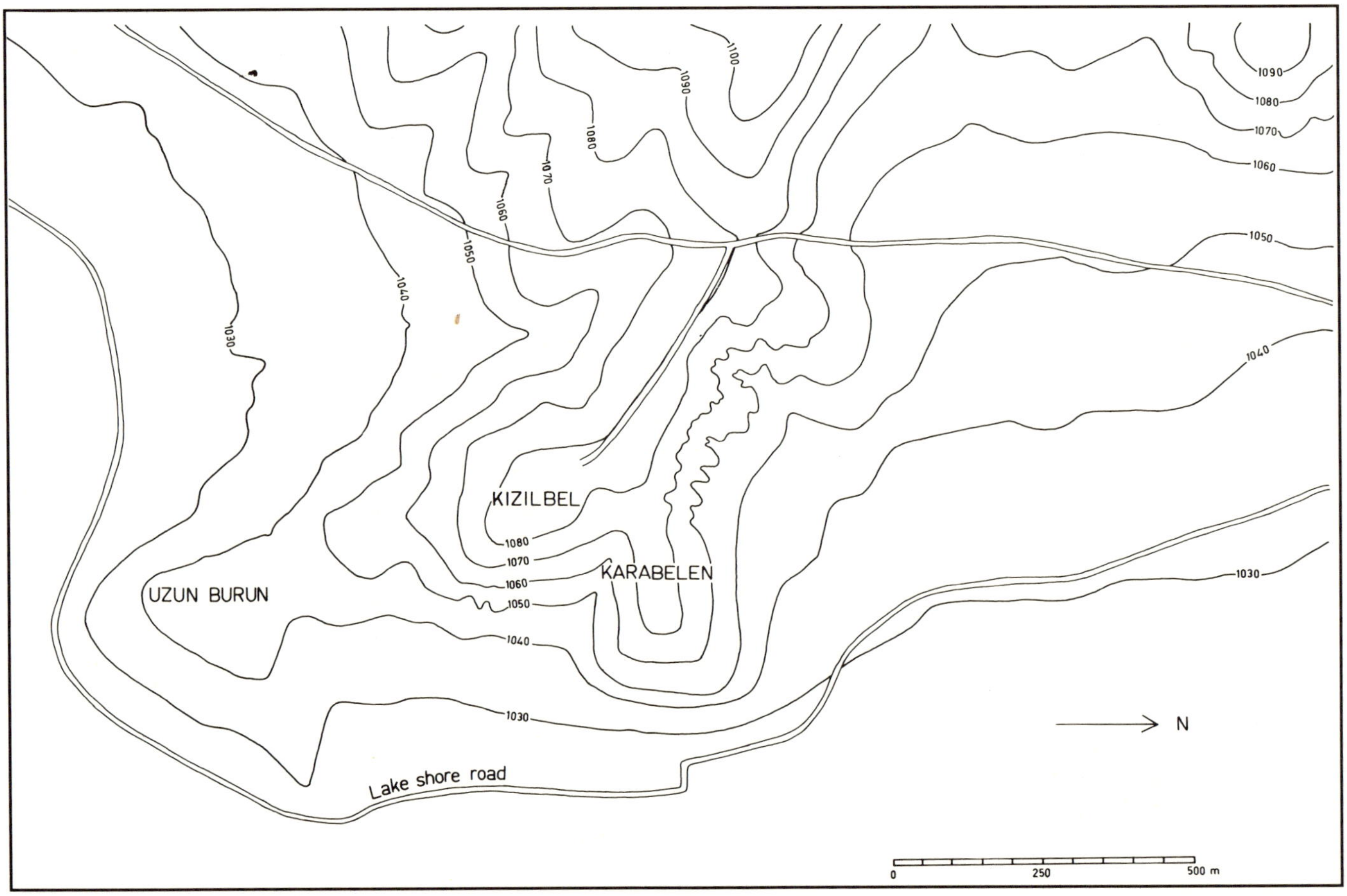

66b. Kızılbel: contour plan

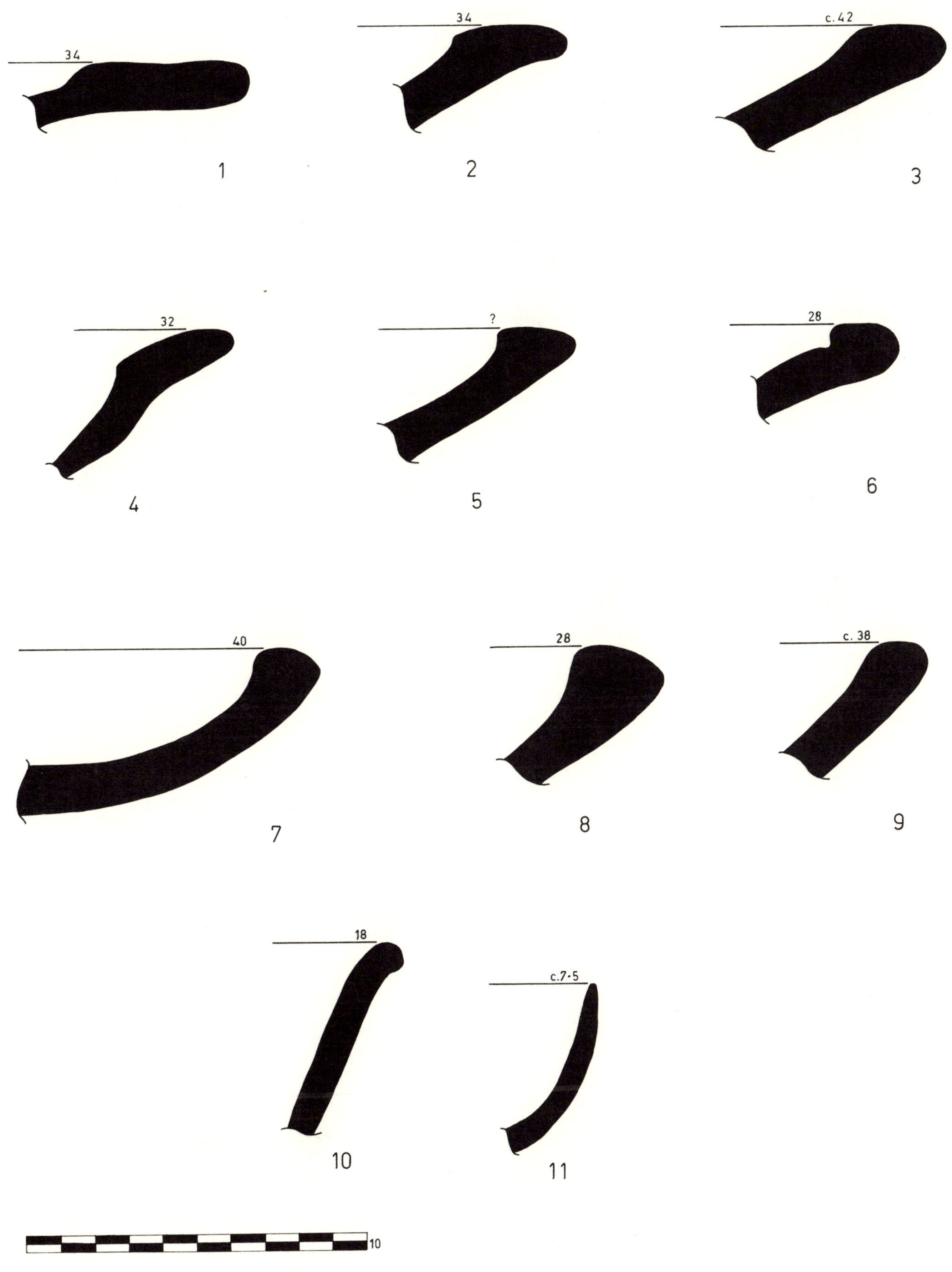

67. Boztepe pottery **1–11**

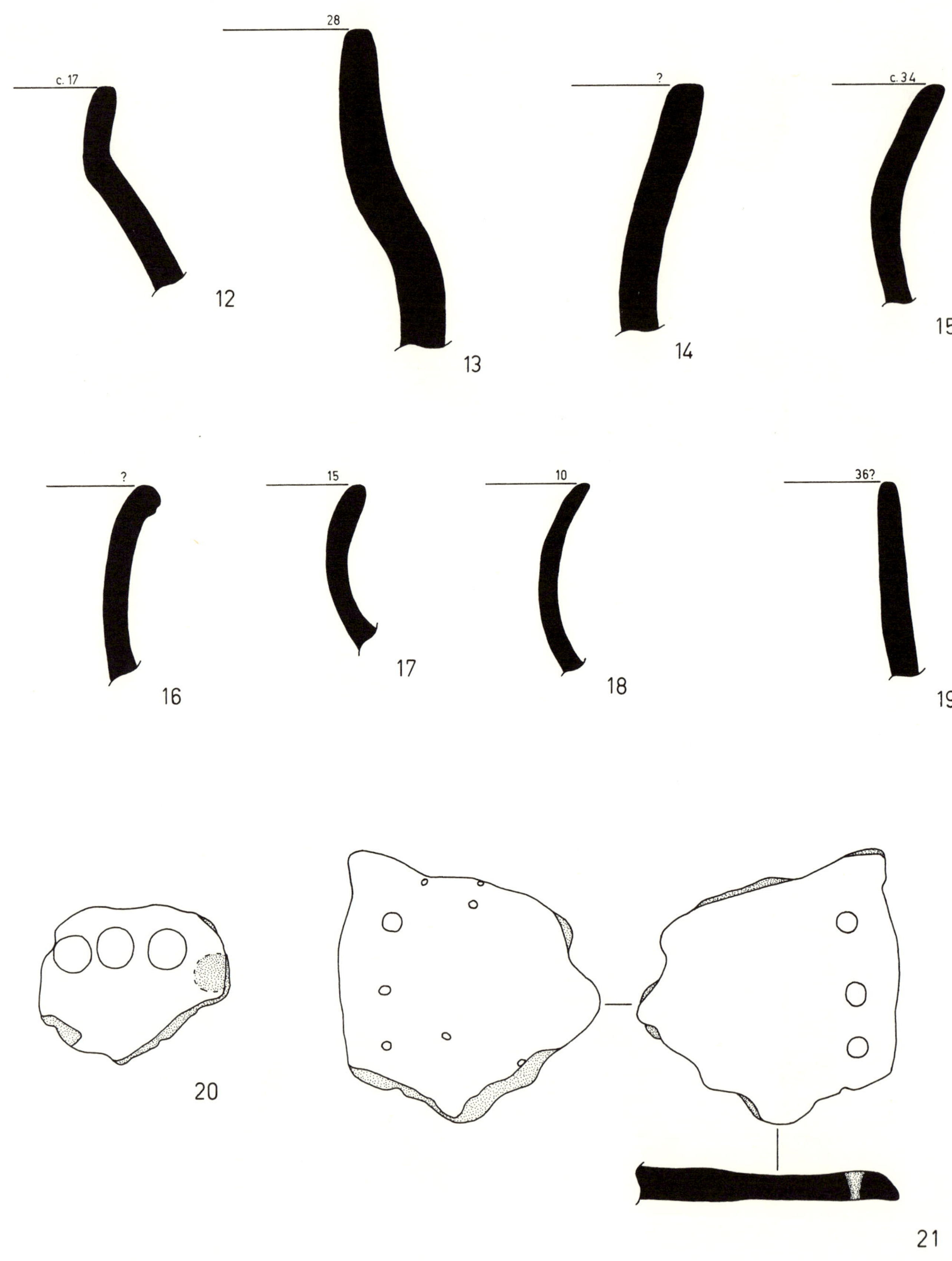

68. Boztepe pottery **12–21**

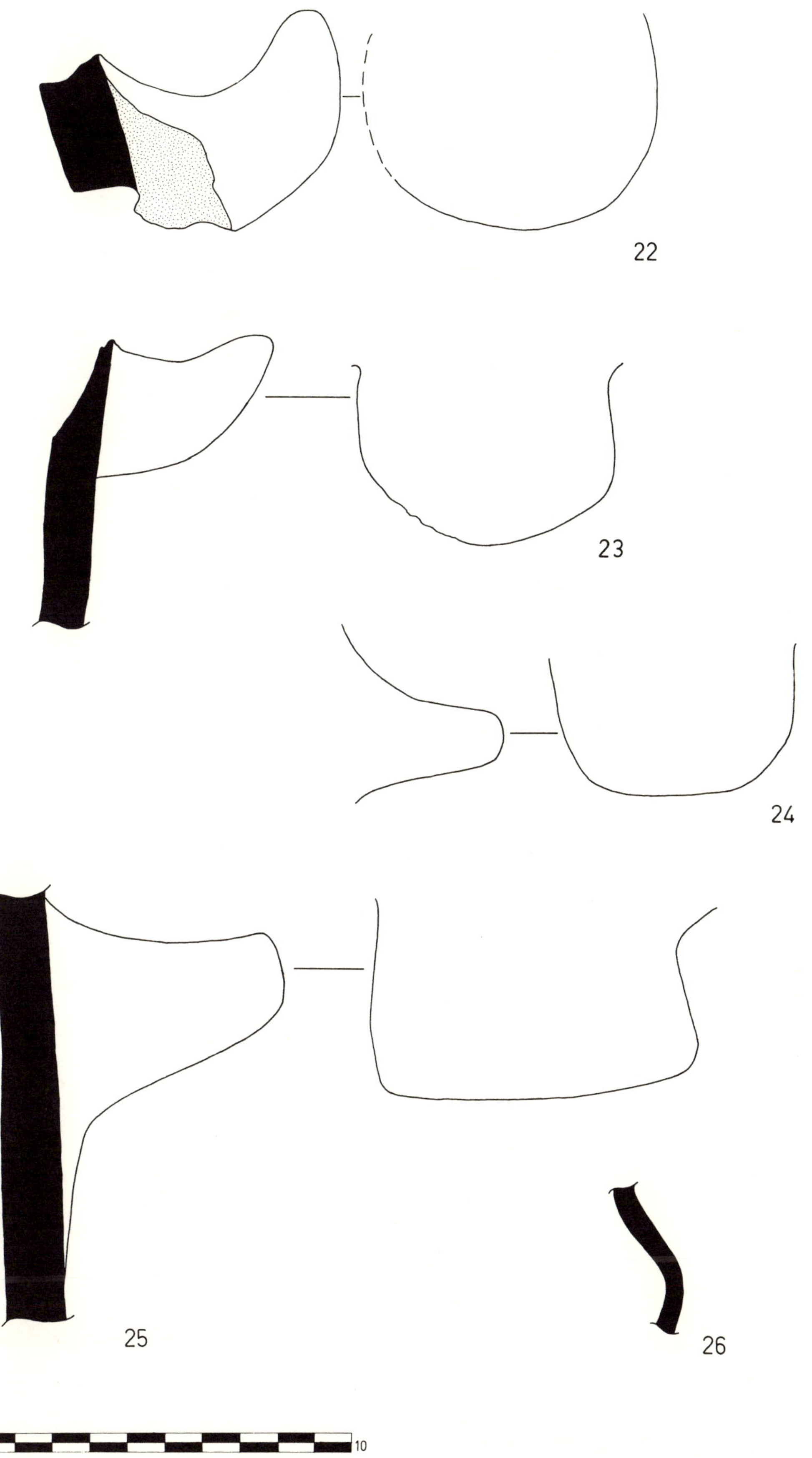

69. Boztepe pottery **22–26**

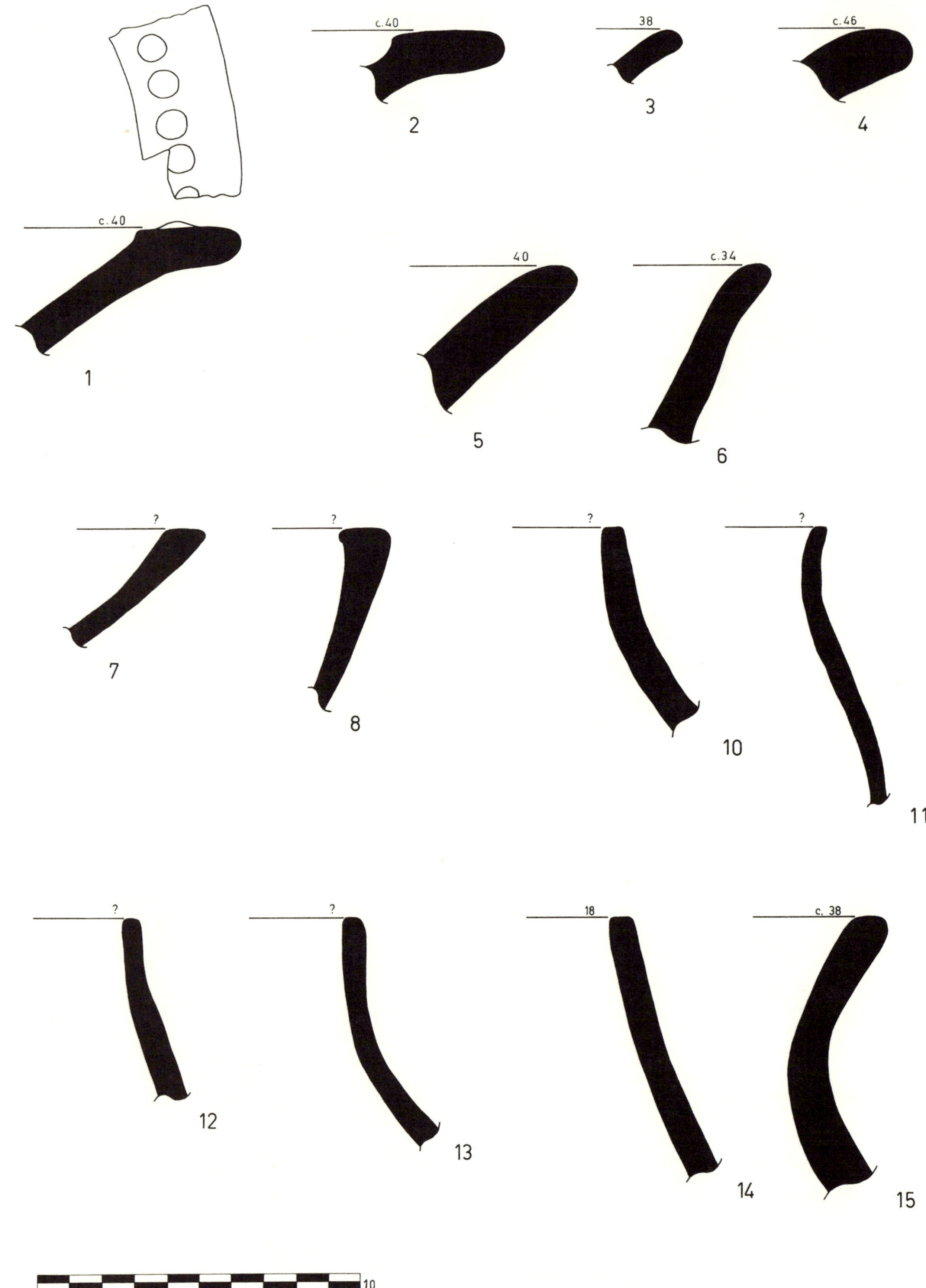

70. Karaburun pottery **1–8, 10–15**

71. Karaburun pottery **9**

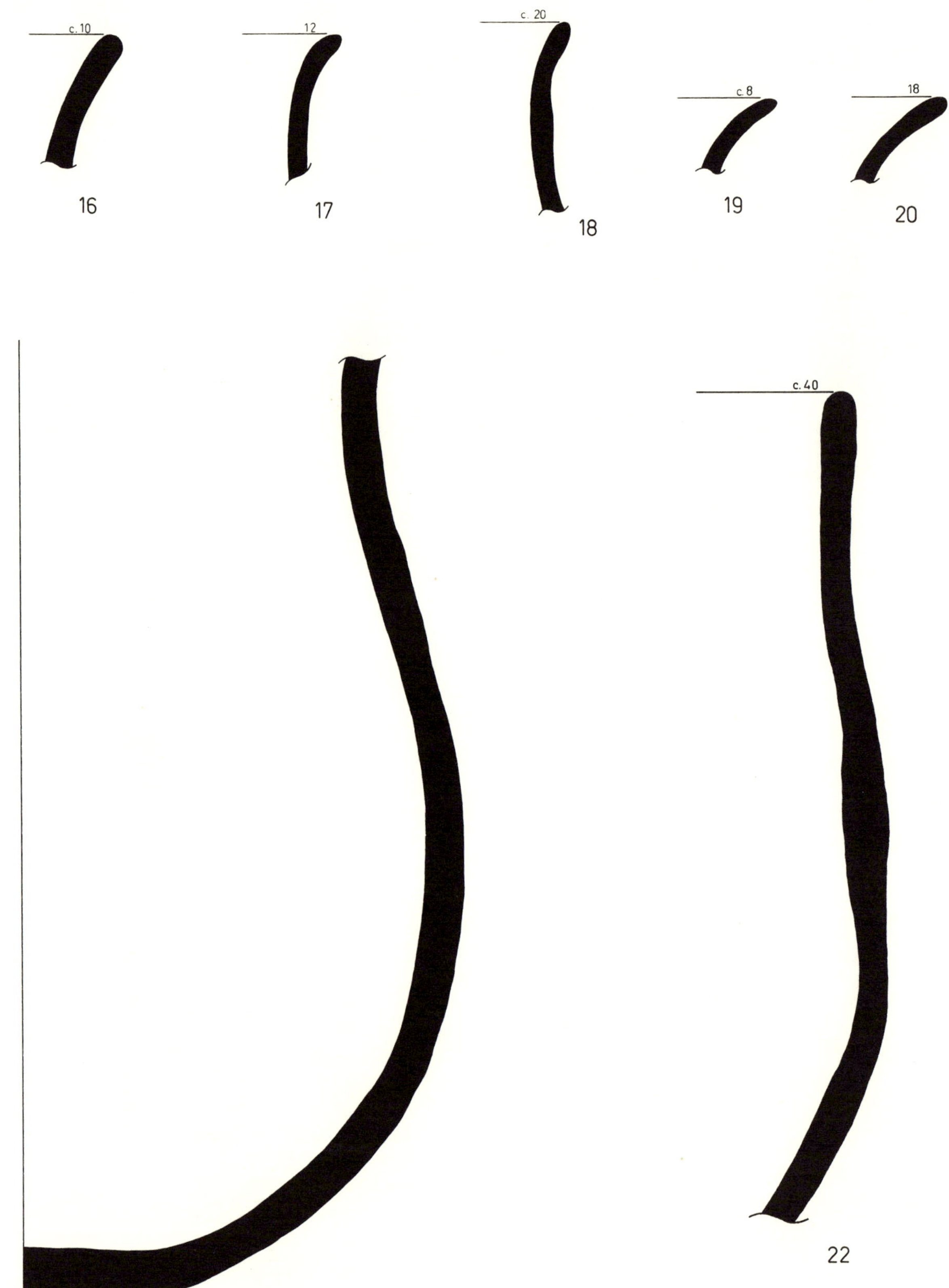

72. Karaburun pottery **16–22**

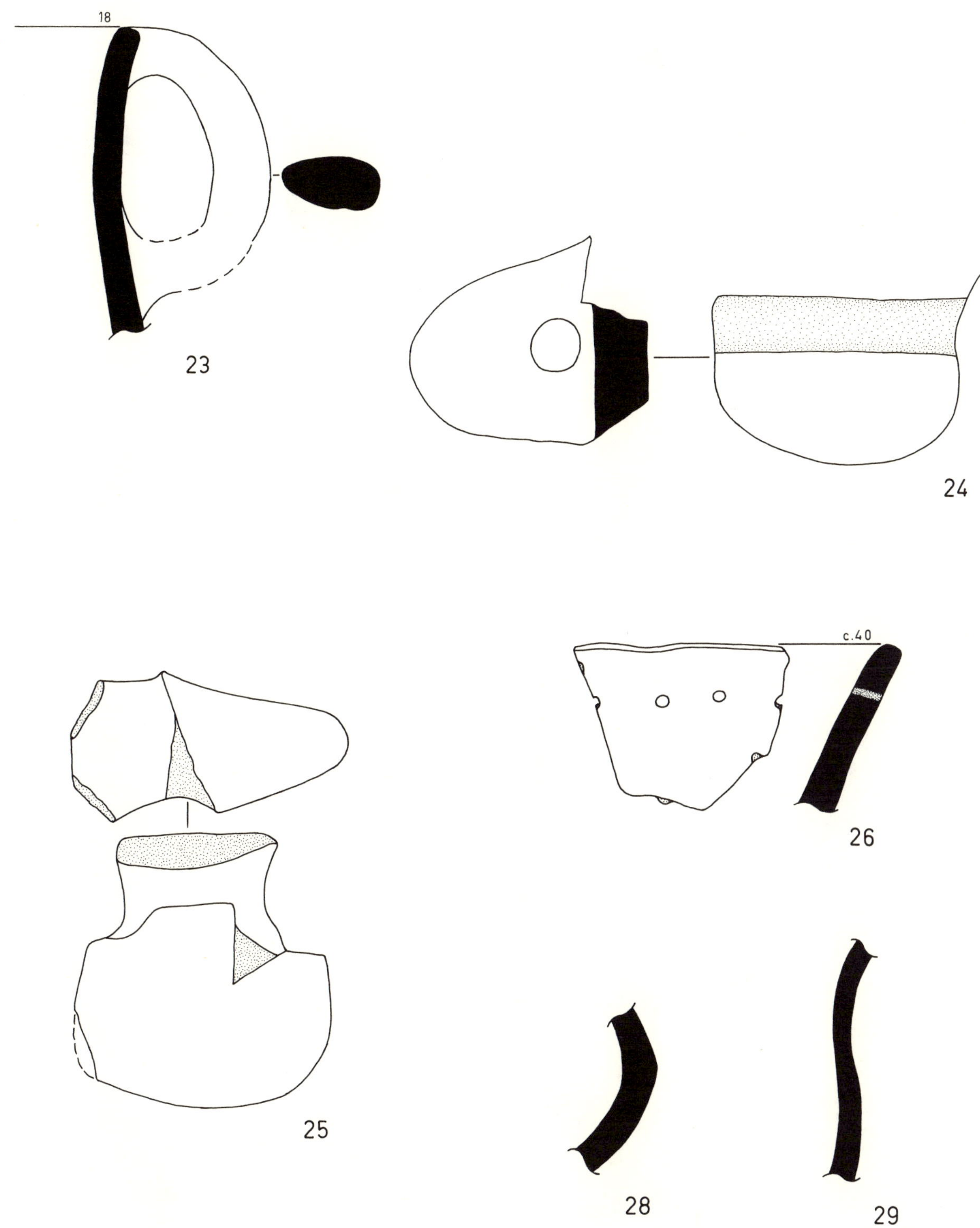

73. Karaburun pottery **23–26, 28–29**

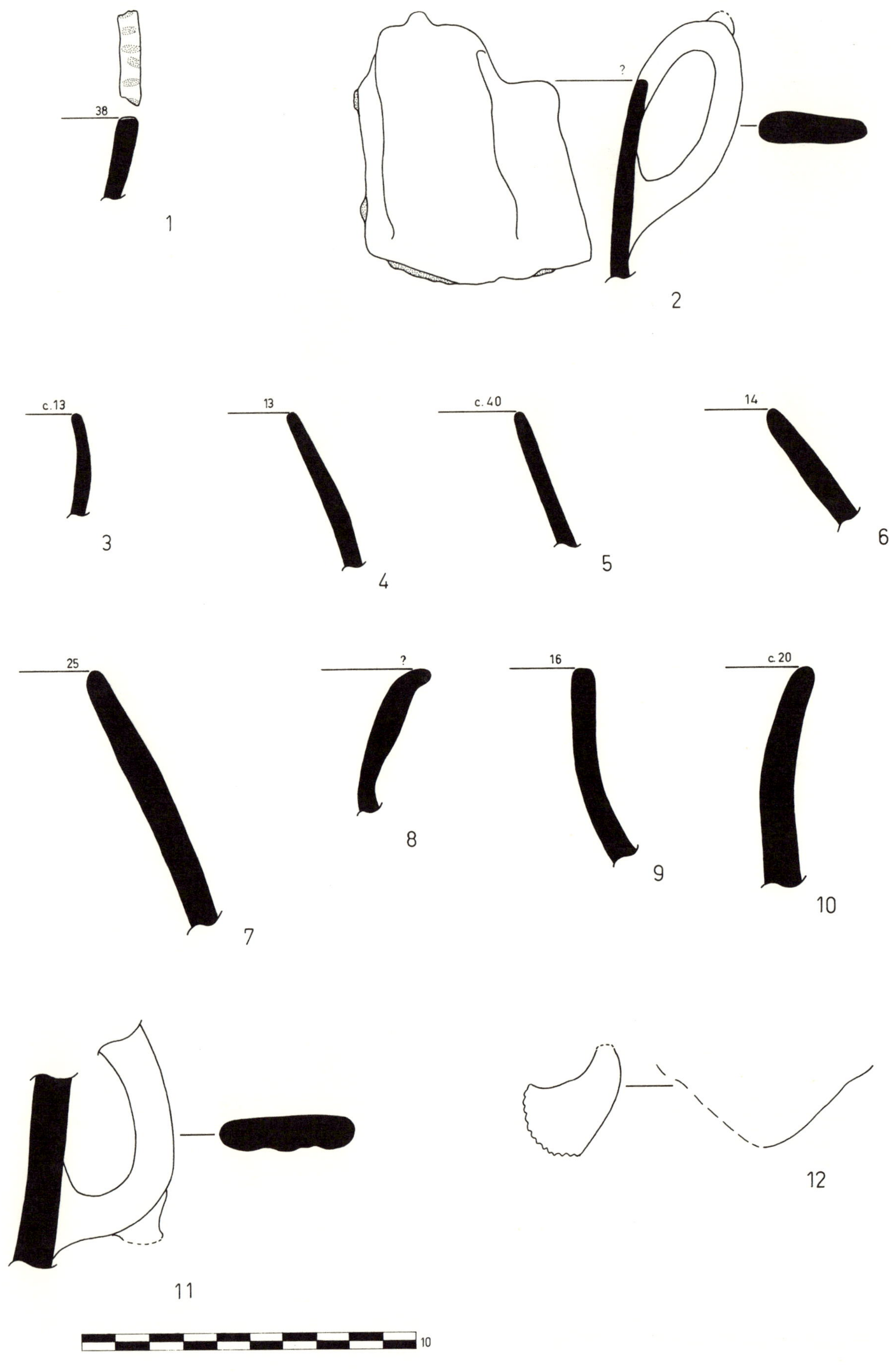

74. Kızılbel pottery **1–12**

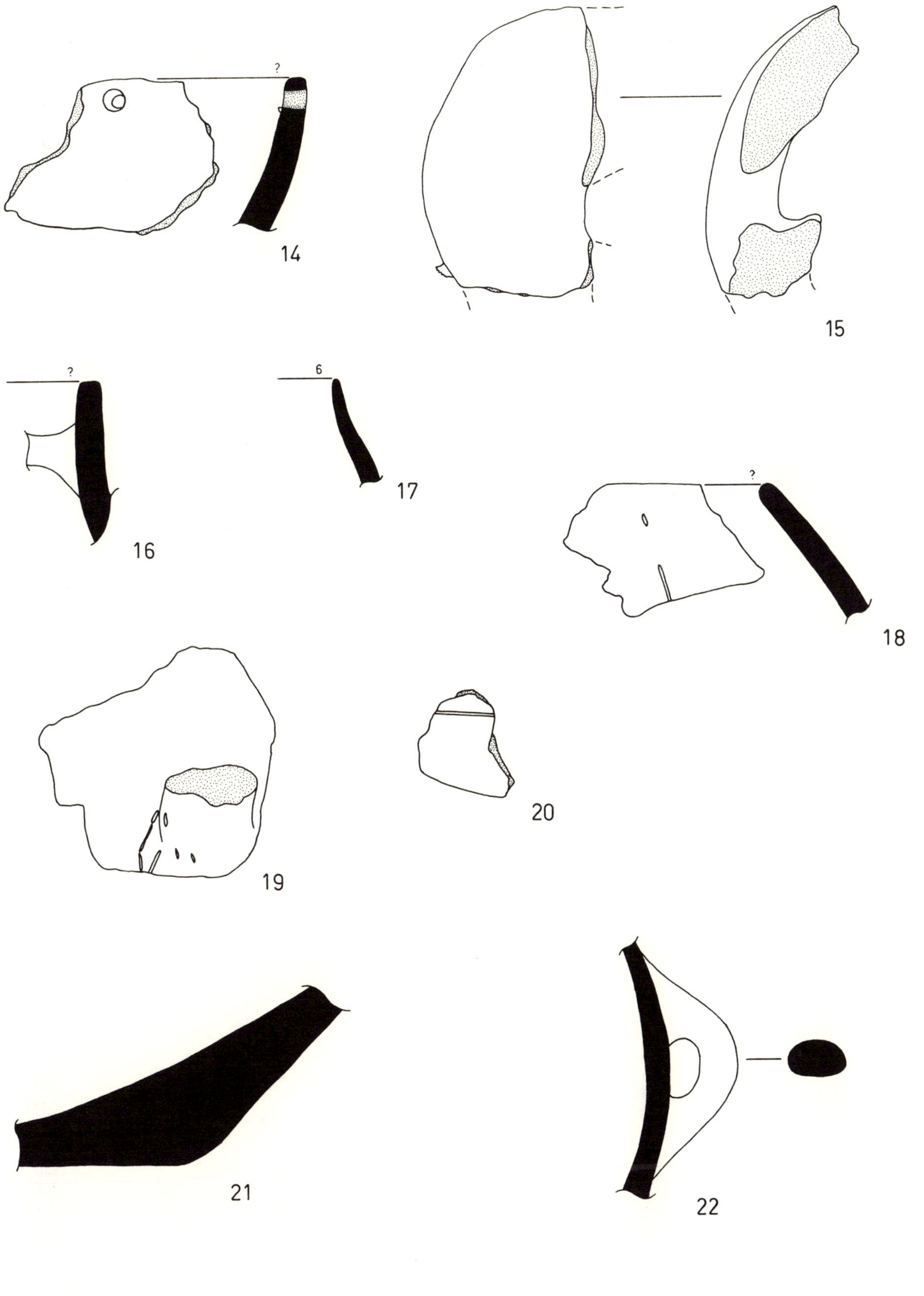

75. Kızılbel pottery **14–22**

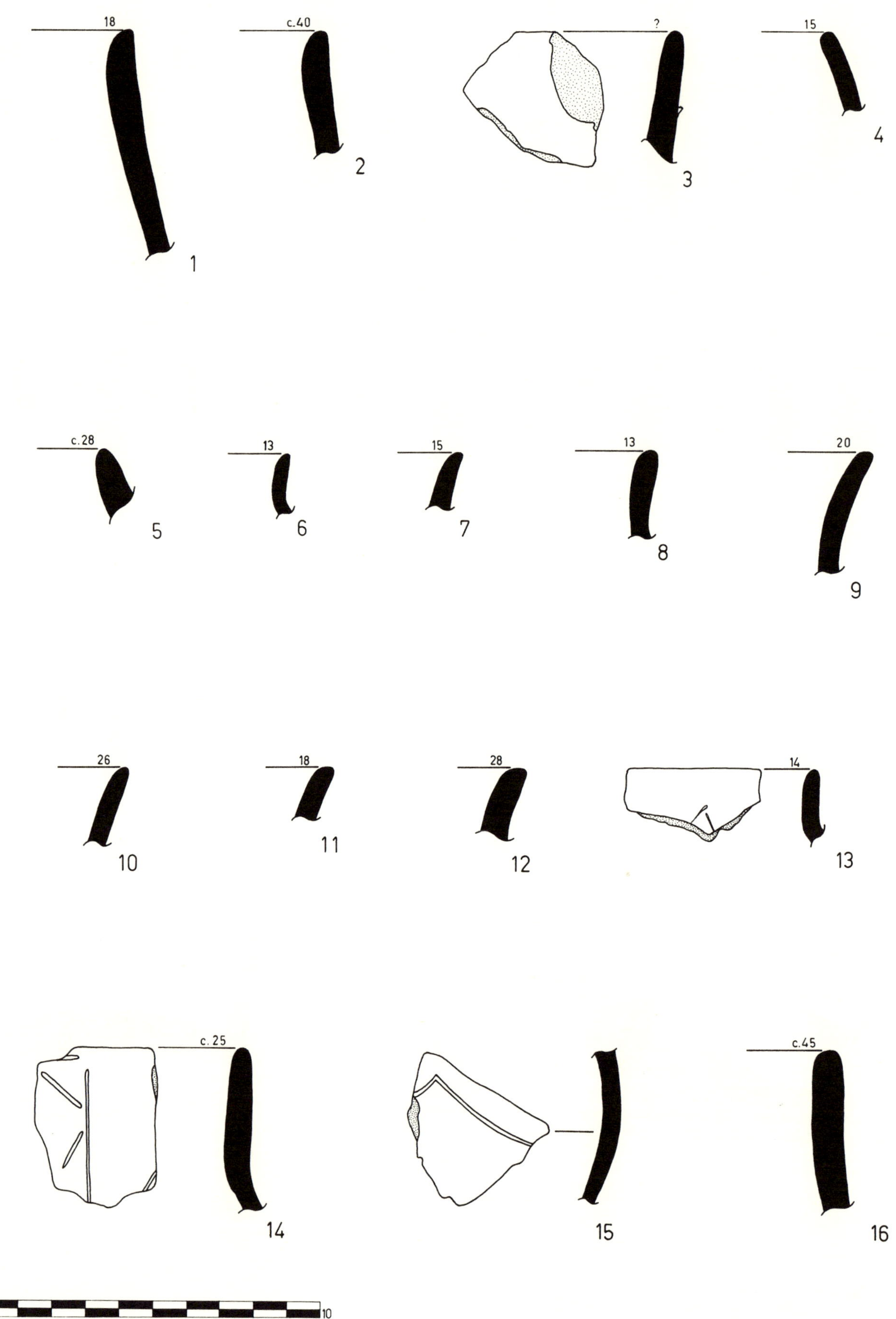

76. Akçay pottery **1–16**

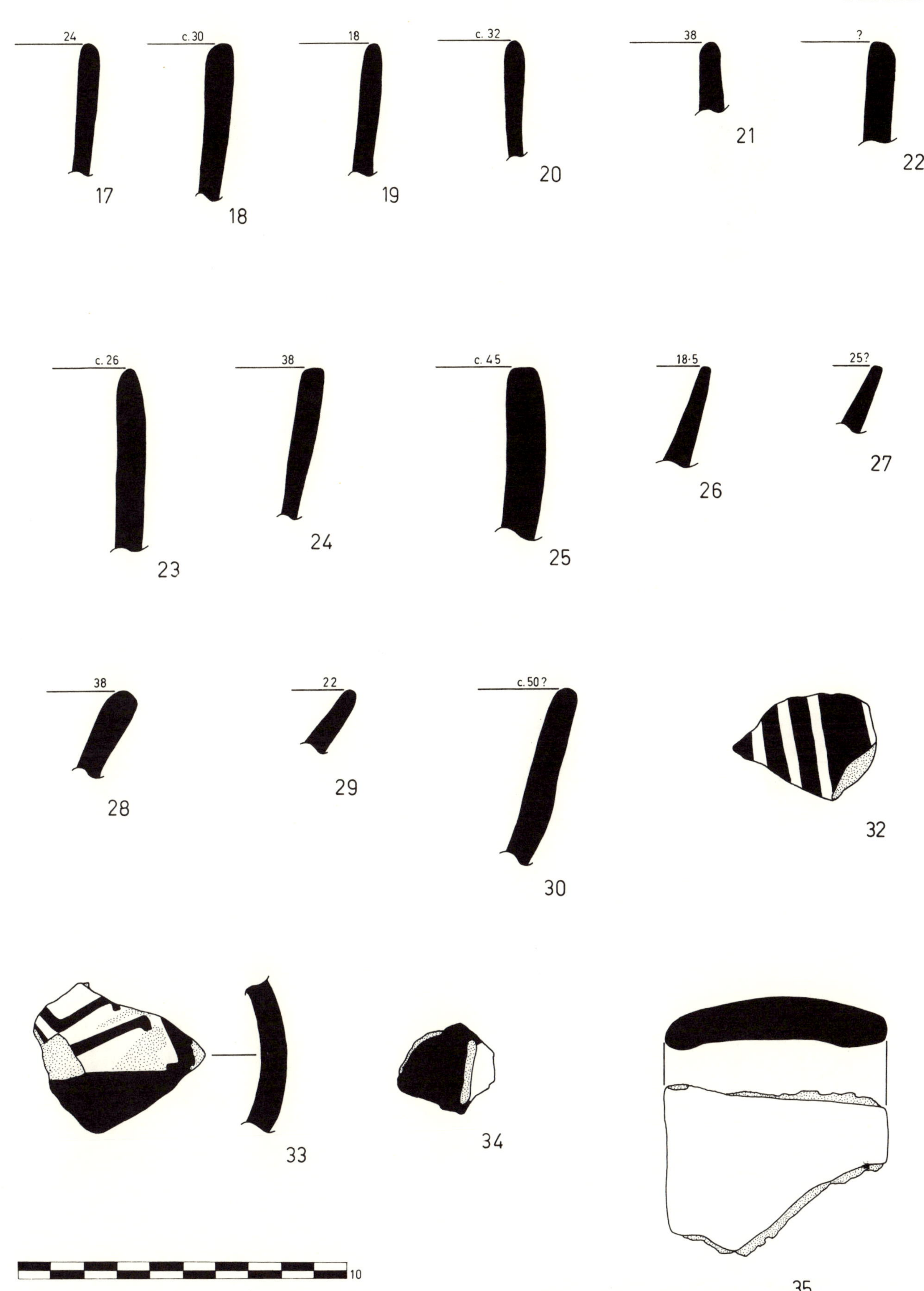

77. Akçay pottery **17–30, 32–35**

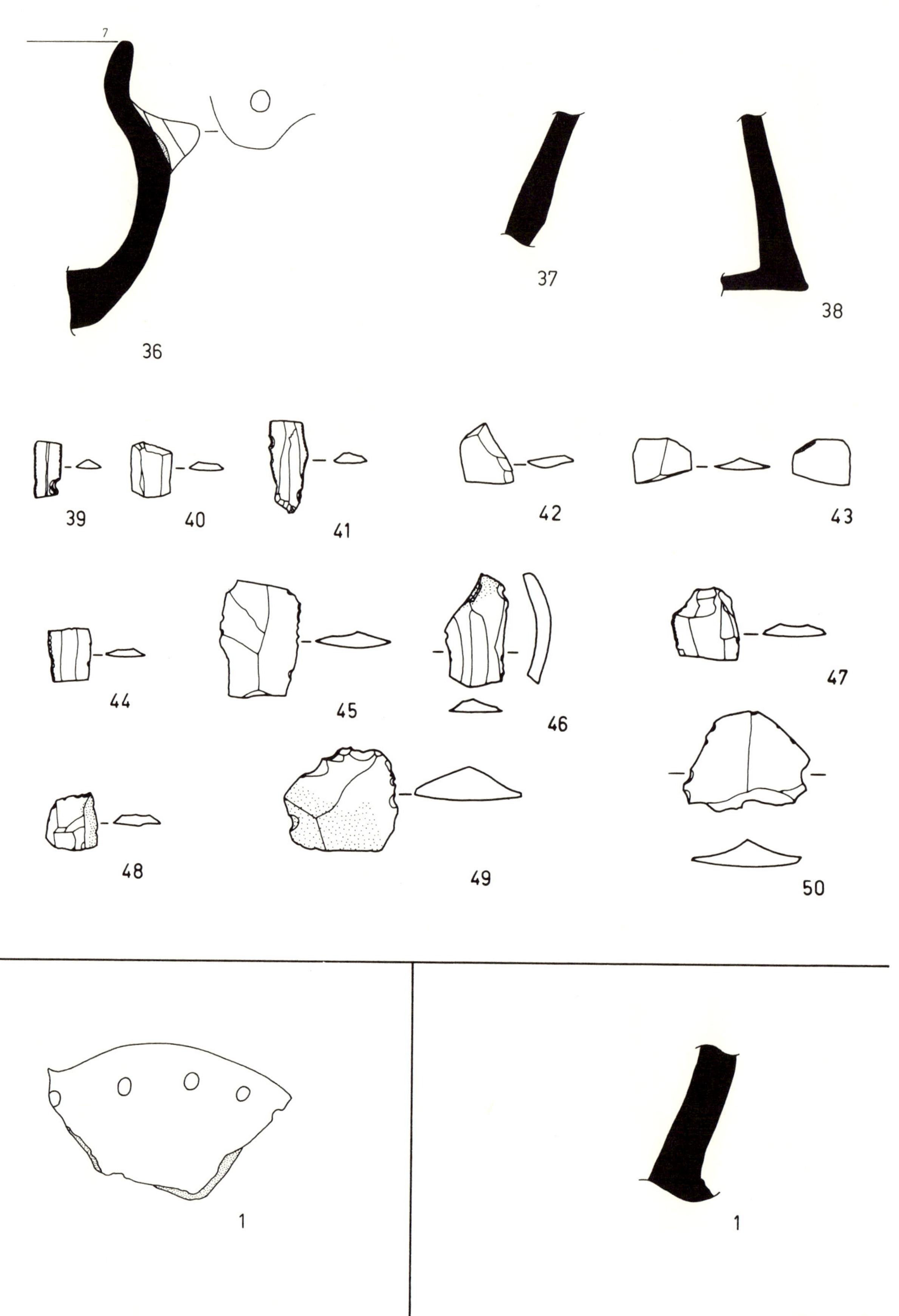

78. Akçay **36–50**; Bayındırköy **1** (bottom left); Buralia **1** (bottom right)

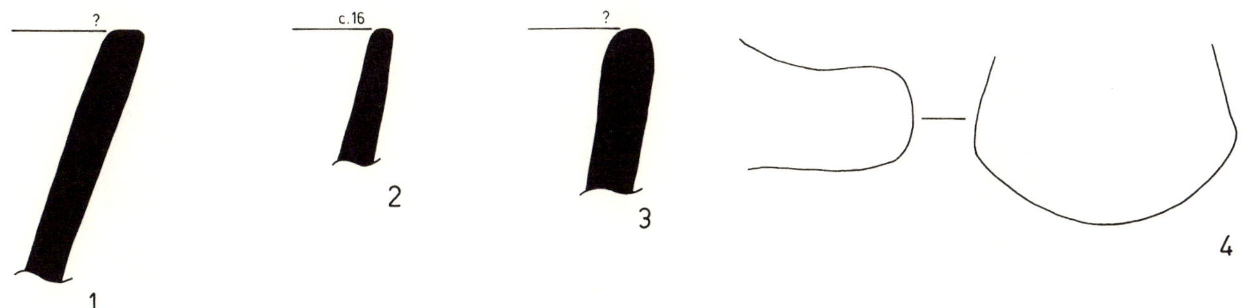

79. Dinsiz pottery **1–4** (top); Gökpınar pottery **1–8** (bottom)

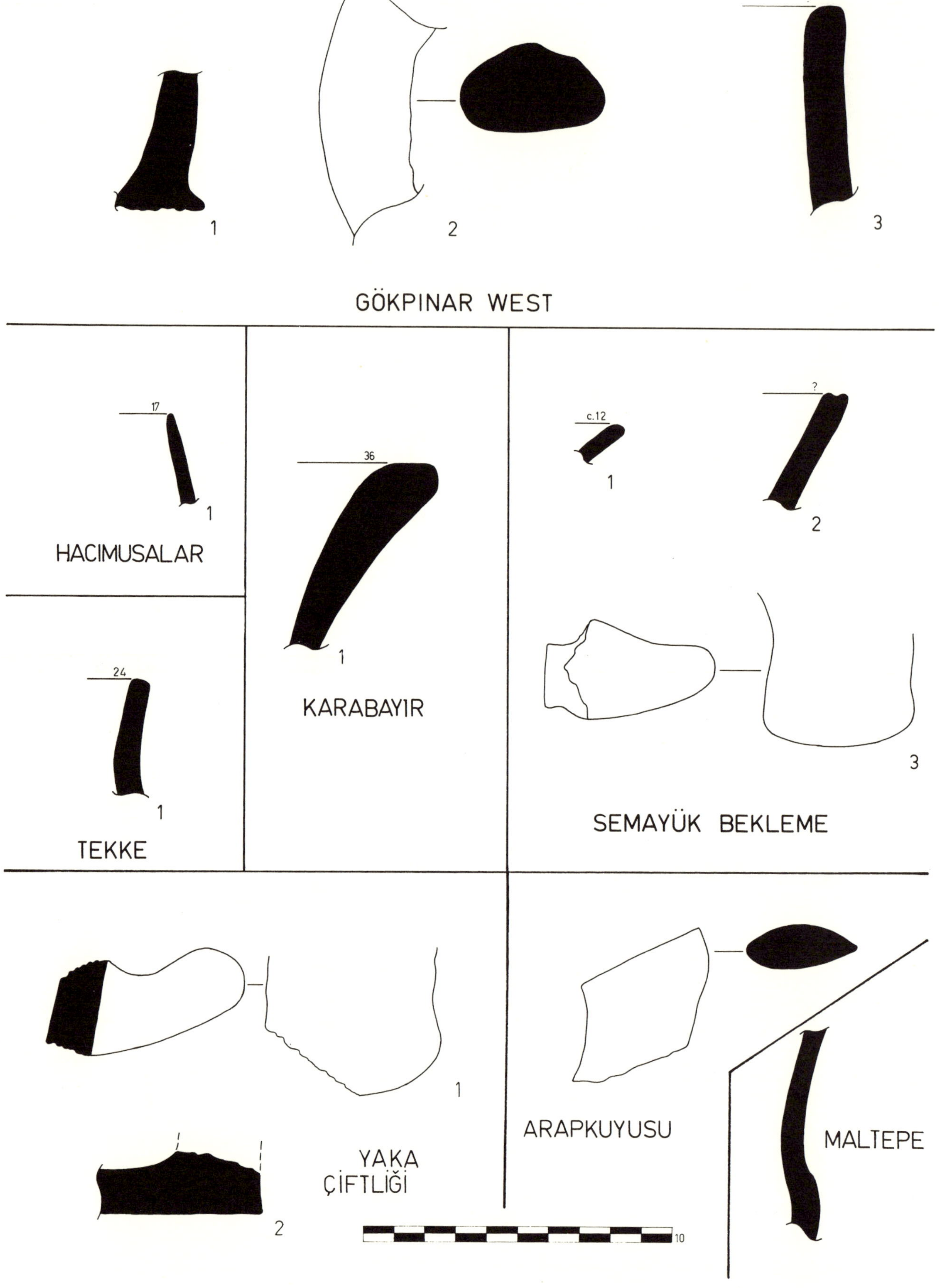

80. Gökpınar West **1–3**; Hacımusalar **1**; Karabayır **1**; Tekke **1**; Semayük Bekleme **1–3**; Yaka Çiftliği **1–2**; Arapkuyusu; Maltepe pottery

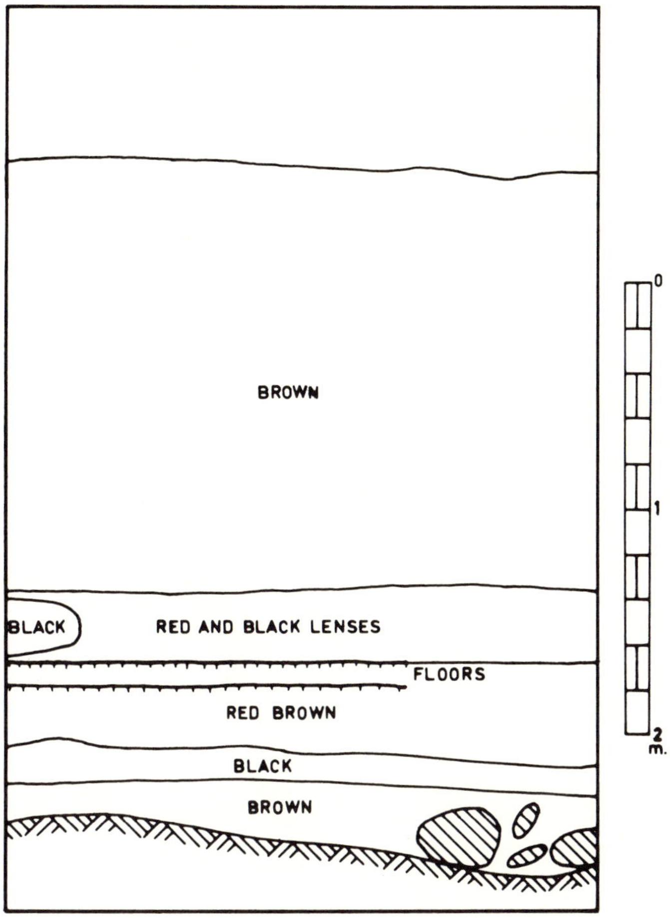

BROWN
BLACK
RED AND BLACK LENSES
FLOORS
RED BROWN
BLACK
BROWN
0
1
2
m.

a. Mehmet's well: south face

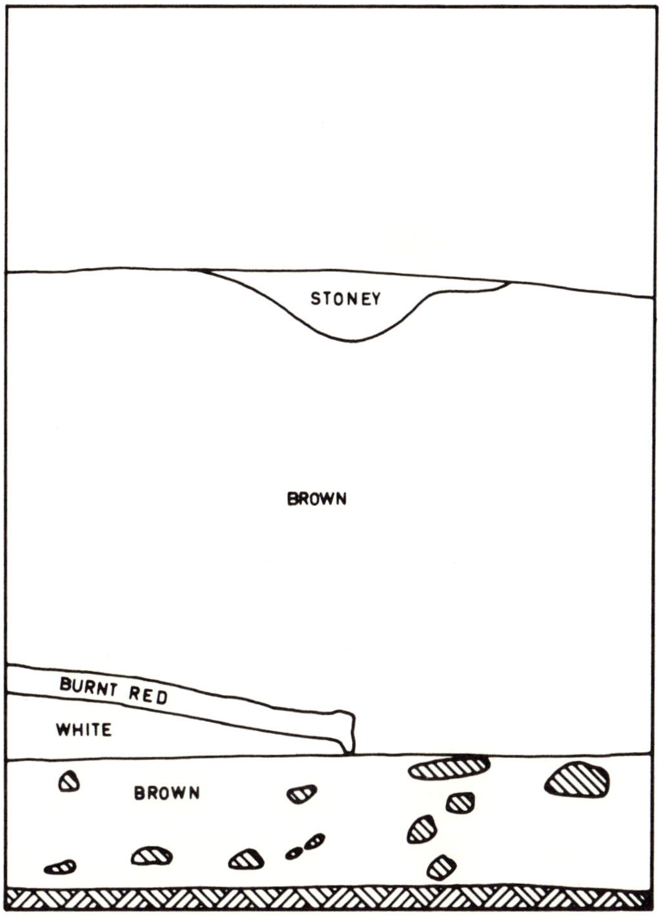

STONEY
BROWN
BURNT RED
WHITE
BROWN

b. north face

ELMALI
N
S
X
X
X
X
W
2
1
W
X
X
W
W
X
X
X
0
100
200
300
m.

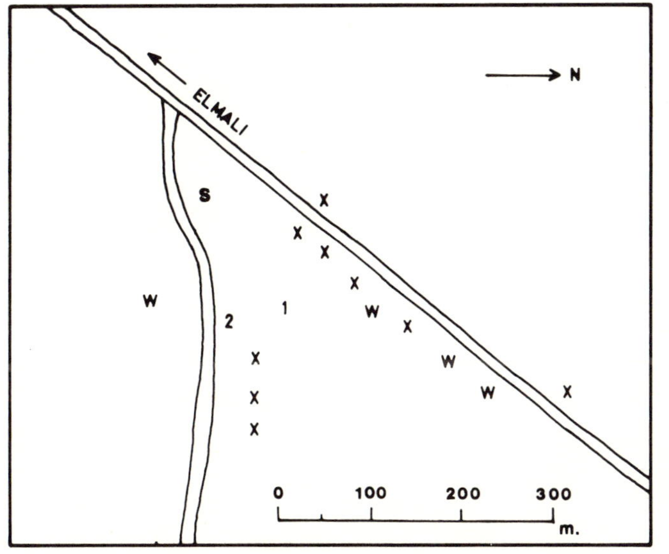

1 Mehmet's well
2 Ali's well
X unwalled well
W walled well
s spring

c. Sketch plan of wells examined 1977

81. Gökpınar: plan and sections

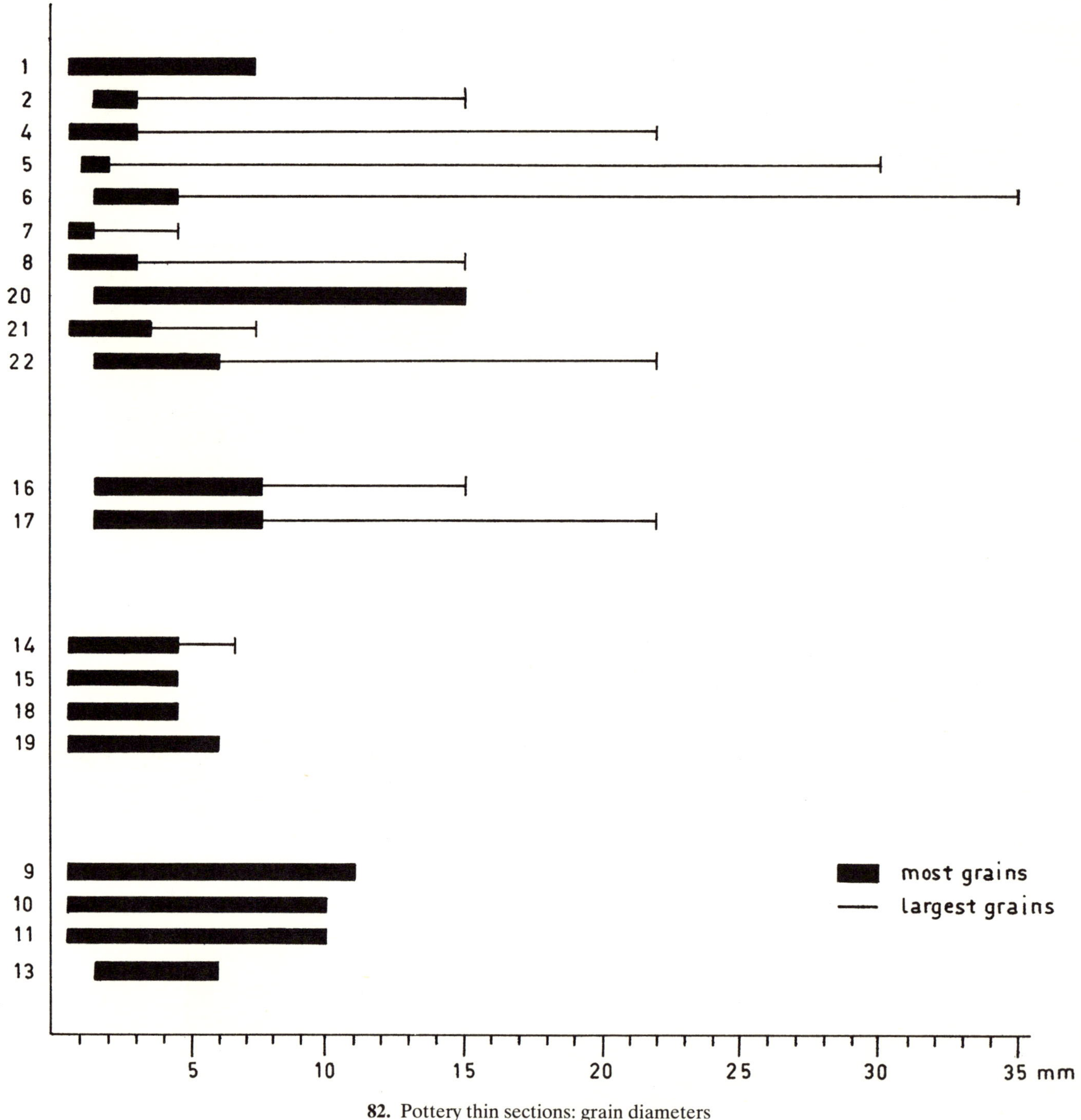

82. Pottery thin sections: grain diameters

a. Trench 105. South face of wall 2, showing timber holes.

b. Trench 105. Wall 2, top of layer 2.

a. Trench 105. Wall 2, top of layer 3.

b. Trench 105. Wall 2, plaster on top of layer 3, showing smoothing marks.

a. Trench 105. Wall 2, layer 5 with impressions of timbers.

b. Trench 105. Walls 1, 2 and partition from southeast.

a. Trench 105. Fallen superstructure and base of partition, with **95** *in situ.* From north.

b. Trench 105. Detail of partition from north, with **95** *in situ.*.

a. Trench 105. Niche fragment.

b. Trench 110. From west.

a. Trench 110. From north, showing stone foundations at east corner of building.

b. Trench 115. From northwest, with Iron Age foundations in foreground.

a. Trench 115. From north, showing wall 1 foundation and fallen mud plaster.

b. Trench 115. From north, showing wall 1 foundation (south end) after removal of fallen mud plaster; spit support *in situ*.

a. Trench 115. From northwest, showing wall 1 foundation (north end) and pots *in situ*.

b. Trench 115. From east, wall 2 foundations.

a. Trench 115. Fragments of wall 1 reversed, showing impressions.

b. Trench 115. Fragments of wall 1 reversed, detail.

a. Trench 116. From north, showing burnt mud walling.

b. Trench 116. From northeast, showing level I, with hearth and **135** *in situ.*

a. Trench 116. From northwest, level I hearth.

b. Trench 116. From east, showing features of three levels.

a. Trench 116. Level I mud walling with log impressions.

b. Trench 116. From northeast, showing level III wall and **65**.

a. Trench 116 at close of excavation. From northwest.

b. Trench 118. Wall and roofing fragments.

a. Fragment 1

b. Fragment 2

c. Fragment 2

d. Fragment 4

e. Fragment 5

f. Fragment 11

Trench 116 level I. Mud walling fragments.

a. Open pot **65**

b. Open pot **65**

c. 65, hole near base

d. Open pot **71**

e. 71, lug handle

f. Basin **42**

Bağbaşı Pottery

a. Rectilinear vessel **87**

b. Rectilinear vessel **87**

c. Open pot **62**, handle

d. Jug 88

e. Jug **93**

f. Jug **93**

Bağbaşı Pottery

a. Jug **92**

b. Jug **94**

c. Juglet **95**

d. Ribbed handle **130**

e. Jar with loop handles **135**

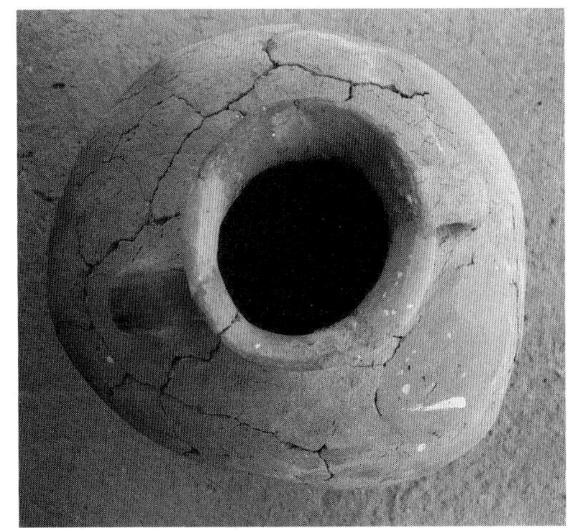

f. Jar with loop handles **135**

Bağbaşı Pottery

a. Jar with loop handles **136**

b. Combination handle **147**

c. Pattern burnished fragment **148**

d. Sherd with ridge **149**

e. Sherd with projection **151**

f. Sherd with incised pattern **152**

Bağbaşı Pottery

a. Painted sherd **154**

b. Lug handle **162**

c. Lug handle **169**

d. Lug handle **172**. Scale 1:2.

e. Lug handle **173**

f. Lug handle **174**. Scale 3:5.

Bağbaşı Pottery

a. Lug handle **175**. Scale 1:2.

b. Lug handle **176**. Scale 2:3.

c. Disk base **220**

d. Miniature bowl **225**

e. Twin vessels **228**

f. Pot with impressions **229**

Bağbaşı Pottery

a. Foot **237**. Scale 2:5.

b. Pan **247**

c. Pan **249**

d. Disk base sherds (uncatalogued)

e. Handle plugs (uncatalogued). Scale 1:3.

f. Lug handle (uncatalogued). Scale 2:3.

Bağbaşı Pottery

a. Lug handle (uncatalogued). Scale 2:3.

b. Deformed bowl rim (uncatalogued). Scale 2:3.

c. Spit support **253**

d. Incised bead **270**

e. Stamp **273**

f. Stamp **273**

Bağbaşı Pottery and Clay Objects

a. Counter **274**

b. Animal figurine **275**

c. Animal figurine **276**

d. Animal figurine **276**

e. Mortar **315**

f. Flat stone **321**

Bağbaşı Clay and Stone Artifacts

a. Mortar **316**

b. Mortar **316**

c. Mortar **317**

d. Grinding stone **318**

e. Grinding stone **319**

f. Grinding stone **320**

Bağbaşı Ground Stone Artifacts

a. Composite copper tool **322**

b. Copper awl **323**

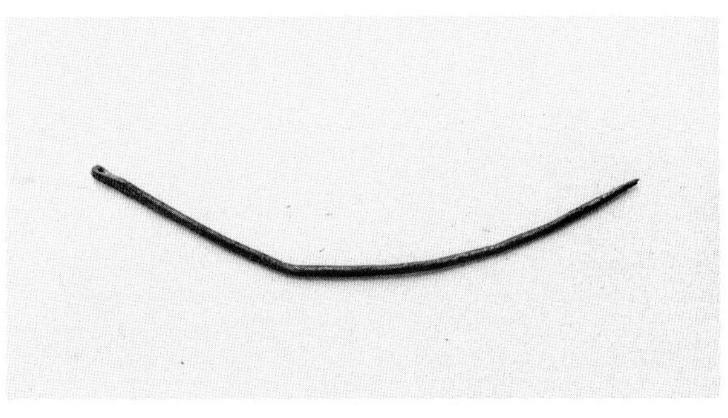

c. Copper needle **324**

d. Shell **329**

e. Antler hammer **328**

f. Antler hammer **328**

Bağbaşı Metal, Shell and Antler Artifacts

a. Lower Bağbaşı handle stump **10**. Scale 1:2.

b. Lower Bağbaşı sherd with knob **12**. Scale 2:3.

c. Lower Bağbaşı painted sherds **16**

d. Boztepe pan fragment (uncatalogued). Scale 1:2.

e. Boztepe pan fragment (reverse)

f. Karaburun **9**, jar neck junction

a. Karaburun sherd with moulding **27**. Scale 3:4.

b. Kızılbel bowl rim **1**

c. Kızılbel bowl with knob on handle **2**

d. Kızılbel pan fragment **13**. Scale 2:3.

e. Akçay incised sherds **14–15**

f. Akçay painted sherd **32**

a. Akçay painted sherd **33**

b. Bayındırköy pan fragment **1**

c. Dinsiz lug handle **5**

d. Dinsiz horizontal tubular handle **6**

e. Semayük Bekleme sherd with knob **4**. Scale 2:3.

f. Semayük Bekleme pan fragment **5**. Scale 1:2.

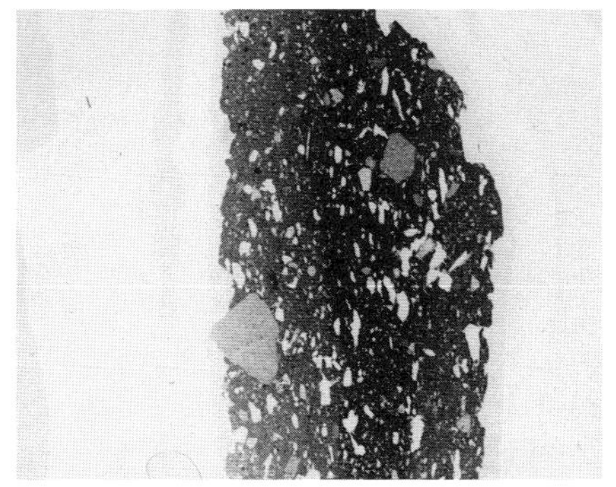

a. Bağbaşı thin section 21

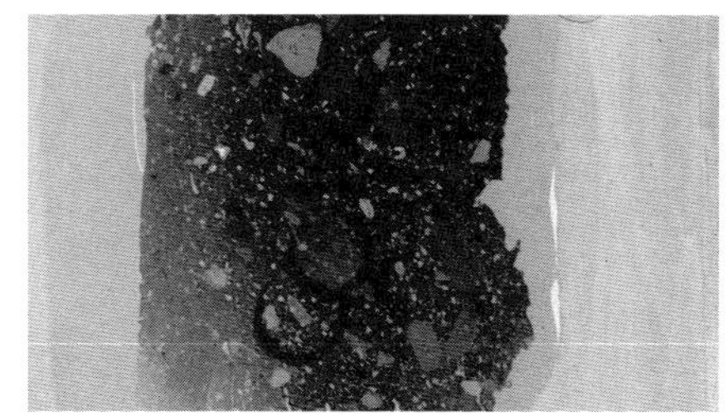

b. Bağbaşı thin section 5

c. Lower Bağbaşı thin section 16

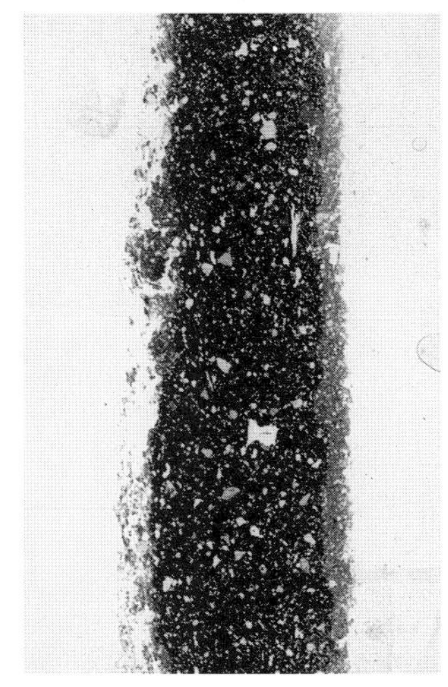

d. Kızılbel thin section 19

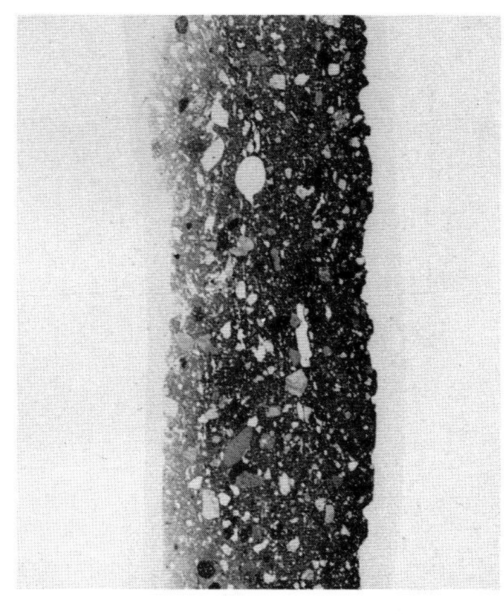

e. Akçay thin section 10

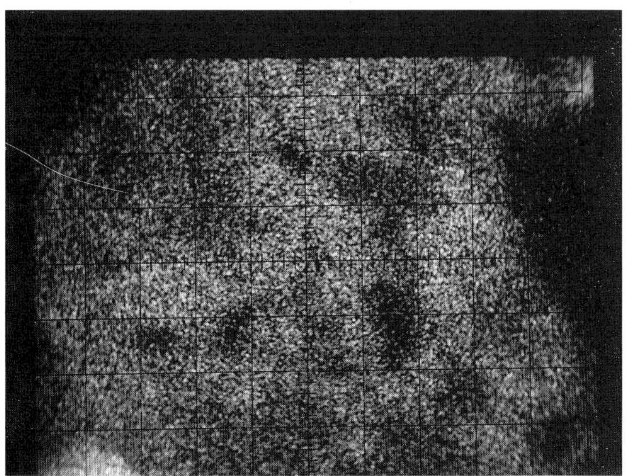

f. Bağbaşı electron beam scan 17 (white areas are Ca)

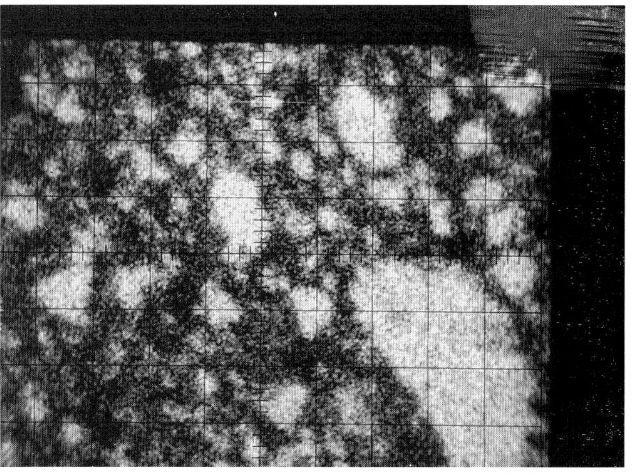

g. Bağbaşı electron beam scan 5 (white areas are Ca)